From Renaissance
to Renaissance

From Renaissance to Renaissance

II

Hebrew Literature in the Land of Israel: 1870-1970

by
EISIG SILBERSCHLAG

KTAV PUBLISHING HOUSE, INC.

NEW YORK

1977

Library of Congress Cataloging in Publication Data

Silberschlag, Eisig, 1903-
From Renaissance to Renaissance.

Includes bibliographical references and indexes.
CONTENTS: v. 1. Hebrew literature from 1492-1970.
—v. 2. Hebrew literature in the land of Israel, 1870-
1970.
1. Hebrew literature, Modern—History and criticism.
I. Title.
PJ5017.S39   892.4'09   72-5817
ISBN 0-87068-184-2 (v. 1)

MANUFACTURED IN THE UNITED STATES OF AMERICA

CONTENTS

Prelude

FOR two thousand years Hebrew literature explored compulsively the twin theme of exile and redemption, uprootedness and hopeful inrootedness. The unique and the not-so-unique disciplines—Halakah and Aggadah, philosophy and mysticism, sacral and secular poetry—indulged in the self-pitying condition, imposed by a harsh diaspora or in the golden dream of a future in the Holy Land which had become an unimaginable paradise on the threshold of "the end of days." For the past one hundred years young Jews forsook their preoccupations with study in the legal academies, the *Yeshivot*, and the universities in many lands to begin a new life in an ancient land. They built the first rural settlements and the cooperatives, they conjured cities with the magic wand of work. And they also created the nucleus of a literature which came home after two thousand years of adaptation to foreign realities. First, it was a romantic embrace of a land and a language which had lived in prayer; then it was the unromantic jolt of unaccustomed manual labor: with the plow and the hoe, the sickle and the hammer and the ubiquitous machine. Roads were built, swamps changed to arable land, deserts turned to settled areas, sand and stone converted into city streets. This feverish activity reverberated in a literature of realism. Finally, the social world yielded to the world of the individual, to his surrealist existence, to his interior monolog. And that's where the literature is at today. But, unlike the literatures of the West, imitated and rejected in turn by the nascent literature in a dangerous corner of the East, it has to live under the shadow of a threatening neighbor, the Arab: a forgotten and forgetting brother of the Jew. If he proffers a friendly hand, both may rise to unexpected accomplishments. If he insists on a mailed fist, both may be annihilated by a new Armageddon. The amicable resolution of their conflict is the hope of mankind.

Homecoming of a literature: this is the theme of the present book. It begins with the early seventies of the former century and it continues into the seventies of this century. Though its future is as unpredictable as the destiny of the people and the land, it can be assumed in the light of past performance that, given the chance, it will evolve a new stance for harassed humanity and it will convert the vision of yesterday into the reality of tomorrow.

1
Hebrew Literature in Its Ancestral Home

Historical Background

IF the trouble with the Jews has been that they have "more than enough history, too little geography,"[1] then the Zionist adventure of redemption can be regarded as a remedial restoration of a balance which begins with the first wave of secular settlers at the end of the nineteenth century. But perceptive observers like David Ben-Gurion realize that modern Israel owes an enormous debt to its religious settlers. In 1699 and in 1700 many disciples of Rabbi Judah Hasid Levi of Podolia—from 1,000 to 1,500—settled in Jerusalem with him. Although some of them returned to their native lands, and some converted to Christianity in the Holy Land when their messianic expectations failed to materialize, the collapsed dream of Rabbi Judah Hasid Levi's visionaries is of such importance that an erudite Israeli historian begins modern Jewish history with the immigration of Podolian Jews.[2] This may be historiography *sub specie Israelitatis*, but it is worthy of note and consideration.

A hundred years later seventy disciples of the Gaon of Vilna arrived in Safed in 1809, and in Jerusalem in 1812. That they suffered cruel humiliations at the hands of the native Arabs and the Turkish government—especially between 1812 and 1840—has been documented time and again.[3] But they were not mere welfare cases, recipients of *Halukkah*—alms collected in the diaspora and distributed in former Palestine; they looked for more dignified sources of income. And they regarded themselves as practical visionaries of Zion—pioneers of a movement sanctioned by their great teacher and named by him *Vision of Zion*.[4] As their numbers increased, they created an institutionalized

1

way of life. In 1854 an organization under the sumptuous name *He-brah Kaddisha Tiferet Yisrael* was established in Jerusalem to pro-mote agricultural work. And it is no coincidence that kibbutz, the word for the characteristic rural settlement in Israel, was originally a designation of an orthodox study group in the diaspora. Paradoxically, toward the end of the nineteenth century, such a kibbutz was led in Vilna, the center of Jewish life, by an opponent of Zionism and a great spiritual authority, Rabbi Hayyim Ozer Grodzinski (1863–1940).

One of the important dates in the history of modern Israel is 1870; in that year the *Alliance Israélite Universelle*, at the suggestion of one of its leaders, Charles Netter, founded an agricultural school near Jaffa and called it Mikveh Yisrael, "The Hope of Israel." It was an appropri-ate designation for a seminal event. Ben-Gurion dates the establish-ment of the State of Israel in that year.[5]

New urban settlements began to dot the land at the same time. On August 4, 1869 Joseph Rivlin (1837–1896) moved to his home in Naha-lat Shivah,[6] outside the walls of Jerusalem—the nucleus of the new city.[7] In 1874 he began to organize Meah She'arim,[8] the present stronghold of orthodoxy in Jerusalem, as well as other sections west and south of the walls of the ancient city. These settlements were based on a sound economic principle: work instead of welfare. Their pi-ous inhabitants founded an organization of artisans by the name of *Po'ale Zedek*, "Righteous Workers," and later a society, *Torah 'Im Me-lakah*, "Torah and Work."

Pogroms in 1881 and 1882 brought a new wave of immigration to Palestine from the ranks of Bilu[9] which was founded in the spring of 1882 in Kharkov in response to the antisemitic excesses in Russia. The organization consisted of students who not only preached but imple-mented immigration to Palestine. Over the years, their settlements have developed into cooperatives, kibbutzim, which are admired and imitated in emerging countries. From their meager communitarian be-ginnings and with the establishment of the first kibbutz Deganyah—now Deganyah Alef—in the Jordan Valley in 1910, they advocated transformation of Jewry through a secularized religion of labor. It was their goal to supersede the diaspora Jew with a new type of Jew—the urbanized Jew who had an uncertain economic base, with a rural Jew who worked on the land, believed in "the moral value of labor,"[10] and developed a new relationship with nature. After 1948 their influence declined, their heyday was over. They have passed—as all social move-ments must, according to Max Weber's brilliant insight—from charis-ma to routine.[11]

Though agriculture is no longer the central fact in the economy of Israel, "the kibbutzim constitute a unique socioeconomic structure unparalleled in any other part of the world."[12] Through voluntary collectivization of production and consumption they impart a socialist flavor to the country and even to its literature. They are still searching for new forms—for a central instead of a federative organization, for abolition of administrative autonomies of individual kibbutzim, for closer contacts with intellectual leadership and industrial communities.

These are indicators of a movement that has not lost its robust powers of development. Though it thrived in intimacy in a society that was negligible numerically, it did not decline with the dramatic growth of population—a growth which exceeded all expectations. In 1900 there were only 50,000 Jews in Palestine, one half of one percent of world Jewry. Even when the State was established on May 14, 1948, there were only 650,000 Jews in Israel—less than six percent of world Jewry. By 1968—during twenty years of the existence of the State—1,288,000 new immigrants came to Israel. The upward trend of the population in this century was—and still is—accompanied by a constant debate by the governing organs of the kibbutzim on production and consumer services. It is not only an economic debate; it involves the ultimate aims of society which are rooted in prophetic texts and point to millennial futures.

The establishment of Israel had an impact on Jewry, in general, and on every Jew, in particular. It crystallized new relationships and established a sense of interdependence: world Jewry needed Israel in order to survive, Israel needed world Jewry in order to exist. But a revolutionary transformation of Jewry on a global scale has not occurred—to the great chagrin and disappointment of the Zionist movement. It had failed to materialize half a century earlier. The Balfour Declaration, a statement of the British government in the form of a letter to Lord Rothschild,[13] dated November 2, 1917, marked no startling change in the history of Jewish attitudes to their ancestral home. The document, a single sixty-seven-word sentence and an offense to the English language,[14] led to the establishment of the Jewish State. This was Balfour's intention: "Conversations I held with Dr. Weizmann . . . convinced me . . . that if a home was to be found for the Jewish people . . . it was vain to seek it anywhere but in Palestine."[15] The timing of the Declaration was perfect. On the day the War Cabinet approved the text, on October 31, 1917, Allenby captured Beersheba; on December 9, 1917, Jerusalem. The convergence of these diplomatic and military events was providential.

The Balfour Declaration was not a boon to the Ottoman Empire, which ceased to exist on October 29, 1923, when Turkey became a republic. Weizmann—farseeing statesman that he was—sought viable relationships with the Arabs, and on January 3, 1919, he reached a formalized agreement with Emir Faisal who became King Faisal I of Iraq on August 23, 1921. In its very first article the agreement stated that "the Arab State and Palestine . . . shall be controlled by the most cordial good will and understanding. . . ."[16] It is an ironic footnote to history that the liberation of Arabs was an indirect effect of the Balfour Declaration. A victory of Germany—and her ally Turkey—would not have helped the Arab cause, and certainly would not have led to the establishment of Arab states, since Turkey would have seen to that. At the end of the First World War, when the treaty of peace was discussed in Versailles, such Arab leaders as Faisal, the future King of Iraq, and his father Hussein, later to become King of Hejaz, did not object to the establishment of a Jewish state. They knew that Arab freedom was a corollary of Jewish freedom.

After the war, Britain began a systematic retreat from the implementation of the Balfour Declaration by, first, tearing Transjordan from mandatory Palestine and elevating it into an emirate; then, through the Peel Commission, proposing the partition of Cisjordania into two states, one Arab and one Jewish. During the entire period of the mandate it failed to explain the realities of the Balfour Declaration to the Arabs; it closed its eyes to Arab unrest or actively fostered Arab enmity to a Jewish state.

In spite of its painful ambiguities, the Balfour Declaration—"the rebirth of a nation" in the words of Lord Robert Cecil—marked a watershed in Jewish history. It was promulgated in the year which witnessed the abdication of Czar Nicholas II, the rise and fall of the Kerensky government, and the emergence of the Soviet regime. In the same year, the Turkish government of Palestine sacked Tel Aviv and deported Jews from Jaffa and Jerusalem. And the United States declared war on Germany. It is perhaps also worthy of note that the father of Esperanto, Ludwig Lazarus Zamenhof, and the creator of the modern Hebrew and Yiddish novel, Mendele Moker Sefarim, died in 1917. With their deaths two disparate movements came to an end: the movement for the acceptance of a universal language shriveled in the age of brash nationalism; and enlightenment petered out even before the death of one of its most illustrious novelists.

It was an act of historical justice that Great Britain became the involuntary instrument of Jewish statehood. As early as 1840 Anthony

Ashley Cooper, the seventh Earl of Shaftesbury (1801–1885), urged the return of Jewry to its ancestral land as a distinct possibility of British *Realpolitik*. He was aided and abetted by millenarian interpretations of the meaning of the French Revolution which proliferated in England in the early decades of the nineteenth century. The expected end of the papacy and the gradual dissolution of the Ottoman Empire were interpreted as the Second Coming, the millennium, in ingenious exegeses of *Daniel* and the *Apocalypse of St. John*. Political events seemed to justify the wild assumptions; the Papal States were overthrown, Egypt was invaded. The return of the Jews to the ancestral land was an eschatological link in the chiliastic chain.[17] It was used in the later decades of the century by Laurence Oliphant (the man who befriended Naphtali Herz Imber), George Eliot, and Benjamin Disraeli in their works, independently of such disparate Jewish thinkers as Moses Hess and Zevi Hirsch Kalischer.

In the anxious years of the First World War, Great Britain had good reasons to cultivate friendship for Jewry. It welcomed Jewish volunteers—the so-called "Jewish Legions"—from America, England, and former Palestine and incorporated them in three separate Jewish units: the thirty-eighth, thirty-ninth and fortieth battalions of the "King's Archers."[18] It sought to combat or neutralize Jewish hostility to Russia, to use Zionism as a springboard for a British mandate over Palestine,[19] and to counteract German overtures to Jewry—for Germany, like Britain, was obsessed by the phantom of Jewish power. It even made political promises to Jewish leaders though it never published them. It would, perhaps, be correct to characterize British attitudes to Jewry in the nineteenth and twentieth century as an amalgam of various romantic aspirations with practical overtones. And it justified a reported remark by Weizmann that "to be a Zionist it is not perhaps absolutely necessary to be slightly mad, but it helps."[20]

Literary Background

The literary effect of the Balfour Declaration was instantaneous. It gave a sense of immediacy to Hebrew letters in mandatory Palestine; it superimposed realism on vague romanticism. At the end of the previous century a sense of practicality in Palestinian literature had already replaced the excessive spirituality of literature in the diaspora.

Yehiel Michael Pines (1843–1913), a literary pioneer in the Holy Land, published books which were dictated by social rather than by personal exigencies: a textbook of physics[21] and, in collaboration with his son-in-law David Yellin, a book on Ottomanic law.[22] Together with Eliezer Ben-Yehudah he founded a short-lived society *Tehiyyat Israel,* "Revival of Israel," which, among other things, aimed at the transformation of Hebrew into a living tongue. His most important book, *Children of My Spirit,*[23] which was published before he settled in the Holy Land in 1878, maintained a conservative outlook: the inseparability of nationalism from religion. Linguistic traditionalism was a corollary of Pines's rigid orthodoxy. Neither the philological innovations of Eliezer Ben-Yehudah nor the nationalistic innovations of Ahad Haam met with his approval. As a realist he tended to propose narrow curricular aims for Jewish education in Palestine as early as 1896:

There is here a need for the study of Arabic and Turkish . . . . But for the study of European languages there is no place here at all.[24]

Pines also endeavored to introduce natural sciences and world history into the curriculum of Palestinian schools, all these to be taught from a religious point of view.[25] In spite of Pines's constraining goals for Jewish education, one goal was and remained sacred to him:

Each yard of ground that comes into our possession in the Land of Israel brings us nearer our goal by several miles.[26]

Another author at the turn of the century, Zev Jawitz (1847–1924), a disciple and brother-in-law of Pines[27] as well as a founder of Mizrahi, was born and died outside the Holy Land. But life in the new country, where he settled in 1887 and lived for a decade, filled him with wonder.

I came to the gate of Jerusalem. God, my God, who am I that you have brought me hither? How many great and good men longed to come here and were not found worthy. But my feet stood within your gates, Jerusalem, in the valley of vision that all prophets prophesied about, that all prophets came from . . .[28]

Here was humility, here was exaltation, here was rejuvenation. But Jawitz was not only an antiquarian. The new life—always veined with old associations—had an irresistible attraction for him:

Had anyone in the old country told me that we should eat on the fifteenth day of the month of Shebat[29] in the open, that our sons would bring branches of fruit trees and our daughters pick flowers of the field, I would have regarded him as a liar. For what do we see on this day in the countries of the north? Ice and frost, blasts and snow, rain dripping from the roofs, gloom and sleet. And what do we hear? The whistling of the storm and the whining of the hurricane. And here, before our eyes, the olive stands in its glory and the birds sing. Yesterday, when I passed the orange groves of Jaffa, I was almost blinded by the dazzling gleam of hundreds of thousands of lemons and oranges that shone like the stars among the branches of the trees.[30]

This passage is, perhaps, a crude example of the storyteller's art. But its lack of polish is compensated for by a disarming love of the land.

Jawitz's poetry is worse than his prose. In page after page of hexametric dactyls, he recounts the first and second destruction of the Jewish commonwealth. And his chef d'oeuvre, *The History of the Jews*,[31] written with orthodox bias during thirty long years, is an almost forgotten work, for as a historian and as a writer he exemplified the naive, unsophisticated, unrefined mind. What he wanted to accomplish, the juxtaposition of Greek and Judaic cultures, was beyond his limited powers. He even ventured to construct a table of opposites for Judaea and Greece. It was simplistic, false in the extreme. Judaea represented knowledge of God, Greece fostered knowledge of nature; Judaea urged love, Greece aspired to power; Judaea emphasized free will, Greece preached coercion. This was generalization of the worst kind, arbitrary and crude.[32] But, together with Pines, Jawitz pioneered realism in the Holy Land. Romantic portraiture of Palestine became a thing of the past. It was superseded by descriptions of land and landscape which reflected intimate knowledge rather than intimate nostalgia.

Of greatest importance for the future of Israel was Eliezer Isaac Perlman (1858–1922) who wrote under the pseudonym of Eliezer Ben-Yehudah and made, almost single-handedly, a living tongue out of Hebrew. In his very first article, "An Important Problem,"[33] he urged the Jews to live in Israel and speak Hebrew. With fanaticism that brooked no compromise he taught his wife Hebrew and never talked with her in any other language.[34] After her death he made his second wife study and speak Hebrew. And his first-born son, the journalist Itamar Ben-

Avi, was perhaps the first child in hundreds of years whose mother tongue was Hebrew.[35] Eliezer Ben-Yehudah imposed on Israel the so-called Sephardic pronunciation which he probably heard for the first time from the author of *Topography of Jerusalem*,[36] Abraham Moses Luncz (1854–1918), whom he met in Paris during his student days. He taught Hebrew as a living tongue and paved the way for other Hebrew teachers: David Yellin, Simhah Ben-Zion who wrote not only carefully styled stories but also progressive textbooks for elementary schools, Gur [Grasovski], the author of a practical and popular Hebrew dictionary,[37] and Isaac Epstein, the careful phonetician who settled in Israel in 1886—the man who, in theory and practice, introduced the pedagogical method known as "Hebrew through Hebrew."[38] With no money and no financial backing, Ben-Yehudah founded newspapers and periodicals and fought, quite alone, clerical conservatism which was rampant in Palestine in the early years of the century. Originally observant, he abandoned orthodoxy for secular love of land and language. Such heresy amidst the stifling traditionalism of the day brought about excommunication and, with the aid of slanderous machinations of religious fanatics, brief imprisonment. But the pioneer of spoken Hebrew was not broken. And he lived to see the realization of a dream—the conversion of a literary language into a spoken language.

During the First World War, in America, he wrote somewhat prematurely in the introduction to the pamphlet *How Long was Hebrew Spoken*[39]: "New York, at the end of the days of exile in the month of Shebat in the second year after the liberation of Palestine by the armies of England in cooperation with the Jewish legions."[40] "The end of the days of exile" was a figment of his imagination. But on his return to Palestine he felt the immense satisfaction of a man whose primary goal in life had become a reality: Hebrew was recognized as one of the three official languages of Palestine. Before his death he devoted his entire time to the two major projects of his philological career: the scientific dictionary of the Hebrew language[41] and active work in The Academy of Hebrew Language[42] which he founded, in 1890, together with David Yellin, Hayyim Hirschensohn and Abraham Moses Luncz.[43]

Eliezer Ben-Yehudah will be remembered as a lexicographer and father of spoken Hebrew. Streets and institutions in Israel bear his name, the language of the young state bears his imprint. But, since intellectual achievements are not chronicled with the same alacrity as political events, he is a lesser-known figure to the world at large than some high-echelon, insignificant statesman.[44]

The Eliezer Ben-Yehudah myth—the tale of a man who revived a dead language with the magic wand of stubborn persistence—is accepted as an unimpeachable fact. The fanatical zeal of the man was undoubtedly responsible for the wide diffusion of Hebrew among Jews. But he is not the first Jew in two thousand years who used it as a vehicle of oral communication. The hasidic rabbi Samuel Abba, the disciple of Nahum Sokolow's grandfather, spoke Hebrew on the Sabbath.[45] Dov Sadan reminds us that emissaries from Palestine to Jewish communities abroad spoke Hebrew. And so did Smolenskin and his friends in Vienna as well as three Hebraists in the town of Brody in Galicia.[46] Many teachers and professors of Hebrew, notably Samuel David Luzzatto, communicated with their students in Hebrew. Some of the early settlers in Palestine spoke Hebrew. Hillel Rivlin, who settled in Palestine in 1809, was known as "the Hebraist"[47] because he insisted on Hebrew as a means of communication and asked his interlocutors to respond in Hebrew. And every Hebraist from Eastern Europe remembers that his parents and grandparents used Hebrew words and phrases in conversation. It is a known fact that the business of daily living was conducted in Hebrew in myriads of responsa from the beginning of the gaonic period to our own day. And the depths of human experience have been explored by Hebrew writers in an uninterrupted period of creativity for three thousand five hundred years.

Ben-Yehudah transferred, as it were, Hebrew from the solitary study of the scholar to the streets and public places. And he was responsible—through his periodicals—for the vulgarization and the vitality of modern Hebrew. By 1914 students and faculty in Palestine refused to accept German as the language of instruction in physics and mathematics which a technical school wished to provide under the auspices of a German-Jewish organization, Ezra. By 1916 thirty-four thousand Jews—out of a population of less than seventy thousand Jews—declared Hebrew as their language. The fight for spoken Hebrew, pushed by the dynamism of Eliezer Ben-Yehudah since 1879, was won in 1916—after a struggle of thirty-seven years. That was the great achievement of Eliezer Ben-Yehudah.

The literary pioneers in Palestine—Pines, Jawitz, and Eliezer Ben-Yehudah—were reinforced by a large influx of writers who, with one or two exceptions, came to the country at the beginning of the century. One notable exception was Moshe Smilansky (1874–1953) who settled there as a boy of sixteen. From his nineteenth year till his death he lived in Rehovot. And he was the first Hebrew writer to reproduce faithfully, almost photographically, the life of the immigrant Jews in the early pioneering stage: their working days, their Sabbaths, their holidays, their new colloquialisms, their new Hebrew place-names and their dangerous neighbors. As a recorder of renascent Palestine he has earned a place of honor in Hebrew literature. The Palestinian landscape lives in his descriptions and impresses itself on the reader:

> The Mound of Love, Tell-el-Hub, lies in lone eminence in the heart of the wide fields of Gilead. . . . Infinitely immense and infinitely wide is the plain at the feet of Tell-el-Hub. . . . It is virgin soil. From the days of Noah it has neither been tilled nor sown. . . . And in the winter, when the sky grows dark with black clouds and drenches the soil; when the sun shines and warms the earth, the whole countryside clothes itself in verdant growth. The grass rises to the knees. Caravans of camels, cattle and sheep come from south and east, from beyond the Dead Sea and the wilderness they come; they cover the face of the earth like locusts and lick up the grass of the fields which is upon the plain.[48]

Smilansky depicted not only the Palestinian landscape but also the Palestinian inhabitant. His stories teem with possibilities of peaceful coexistence between Jews and Arabs. So enamored was he of the Arabs that he assumed an Arabic pseudonym, *Hawajah Mussah*, "Mr. Moses." And three volumes of his collected writings bear the name *Arabs*[49] and depict Arabic types—their tribal ethos and rural rootedness—in their relations with Jews, and, in their own milieu, in their relations with each other. Smilansky was the first Hebrew writer who made a serious attempt at neighborly rapprochement between Arabs and Jews. He preached it in his speeches, he practiced it as a colonist, he implemented it in story, in essay, in memoirs. Aware of the oppressive rule of the Turks, he created a character in his play *Rohele*,[50] who suffered torture and humiliation during the well-known Ottoman reprisals in the First World War but did not betray her friends and managed to escape the brutalities of a Turkish commander. In his articles he was able to advocate a sober realism which was unmatched by Zionist leaders in the diaspora:

> The revival of Israel on Israel's soil means acquisition of the area which stretches along the eastern Mediterranean and which is called in history The Land of Israel; acquisition by Jews and settlement of a great part of our people in the ancestral land where they will build villages and cities, till the soil and develop commerce;

where they will live under their own government like any other free people on its own land.[51]

This was practical Zionism as opposed to diplomatic Zionism with its few victories and many sterilities. In his *Memoirs* Smilansky provided the sombre background of early colonization which was the butt of Ahad Haam's merciless attacks in his two essays "Truth from Palestine." But he also described the thrill and torment of the first day of work on a farm, hoe in hand instead of Halakah in the head.[52] This was a new dimension of life for most arrivals in Palestine in the summer of 1882. It was shared by the young immigrants of the Second *'Aliyyah,* the pre-First World War wave of immigration. David Gruen of Plonsk, better known as Ben-Gurion, emphasized their devotion, diligence, rootedness and idealism which did not flag in the face of stern realities. Like Smilansky, he never forgot the impact of his first night in Petah Tikvah:

> The wailing of the foxes in the vineyards, the braying of donkeys in the stables . . . the croaking of frogs in the ponds, the full-bodied scent of the acacia tree, the sound of the sea in the distance . . . all this intoxicated me.[53]

It was not merely neoromantic contemplation of a village which has become a bustling city in our time; it was an enthusiasm born of the consciousness that redemption of the land changed the course of Jewish history. Small wonder that, in spite of wearisome toil, he and his fellow workers often danced in the evening and filled the air with the popular songs of those days: "Ya-Hai-Li" which was published in *Ha-Zevi,* and the less popular "Sadness and Happiness" by Solomon Weinstein.[54]

Delight in the Palestinian landscape, in productive work and in the Arab neighbor mitigated the hardships of the pioneering life. Not only Smilansky but his younger contemporary Yehoshua Barzilai [Eisenstadt] (1855–1918) showed uninhibited admiration for the Arab, especially the exotic Arab woman. In a fictional encounter with an Arab girl he expresses regret at his "inadequate knowledge of Arabic" and joy when, eight years later, he meets her again with her Jewish husband.[55] This longing for symbiosis was to characterize Jewish attitudes to Arabs even when differences led to armed clashes.

Arab-Jewish coexistence was not idyllic togetherness even in these early years of the century: the Arab was the indigenous inhabitant, the Jew the historical claimant of his ancestral land. With the larger influx of Jewish immigration, relationships were exacerbated. The massacres of 1920–1921 and 1929, the outbreaks of 1936–1939 which amounted to civil war—these were extreme forms of tension and the four wars with the Arabs since the establishment of the State of Israel—in 1948—1949, in 1956, in 1967 and in 1973—are crying evidence of an anomalous situation. When relations between Arabs and Jews deteriorated, some intellectuals—under the aegis of men like Y.L. Magnes and Martin Buber—formed a party called *Ihud*, "Unity." Among those who joined enthusiastically were university professors, such as Samuel Hugo Bergman, and writers, such as Moshe Smilansky. They wanted peace and a bi-national state. Perhaps the later philosophy of Buber, the I-Thou philosophy, is essentially a projection of an impossible situation onto an ideal plane. When the I is defined as the person, the free subject, the other is not a thing or a mere exterior reality but also a free person. And the I-Thou relationship postulates liberty or, in Buber's terminology, salvation. For every Thou is a stage toward the absolute Thou: God. But salvation is far from realization. The present divergence in attitudes of Arabs to Jews, of Jews to Arabs indicates an almost unbridgeable distance.

The confrontation of Jews and Arabs is the unsolved problem of the century. It is exacerbated by the fact that both Arabs and Jews are in quest of a new identity. One can only hope that the Judaization of Jewry and the Arabization of Arabs will lead to mutual appreciation in depth, for the reorientalizing tendencies of Jewish and Arab intellectuals can become focal points of convergence.[56] While Arabs and Jews face each other in overt or covert hostility, oriental and occidental Jews themselves are searching for a modus vivendi with each other. Until the establishment of the State, oriental Jewry was an exotic minority; in recent years it accounts for more than one half of Israelis. That change in the demographic composition of Jewry in Israel is an event of primary importance.

Like the founders of Israel, the founders of its literature also belonged to the so-called second wave of immigration that settled in Ottoman Palestine in the twentieth century, during the period prior to the First World War. They were a paradoxical generation of idealists who insisted on a practical conquest of the land through hard labor on the soil; they created new types and new protagonists for their literary artifacts—the revolutionaries, the workers, the pioneers, and later, the soldiers. They also created a new feel for the land. The heroes of

Hebrew literature—the *Hasid* and the *Maskil*—vanished slowly but not completely; they continued to irradiate the new hero and the new landscape with their traditionalism, their piety, their commitment, and even their intellectualism. Their literary spokesmen were, with the exception of Shimoni, not poets but writers of prose: Jacob Rabinowitz, Alexander Ziskind Rabinowitz, Simhah Ben-Zion, David Yellin, A.A. Kabak, Joseph Hayyim Brenner, and Brenner's young protégé, Samuel Joseph Agnon.

The most important figure among them was Joseph Hayyim Brenner (1881–1921), the father of modern Israeli literature.[57] A man of sincerity and integrity[58] who was regarded as the literary conscience of his generation, a journalist and editor of importance, a novelist of modest dimensions, he revitalized Hebrew literature in the first two decades of the century. When he settled in Palestine in 1909, he was already a well-known man of letters, a pessimist à la Dostoevsky,[59] whose dark outlook on life was fed by poverty and intensified by the abortive Russian Revolution of 1905. In spite of his vaunted realism he was a late echo of Byron, a Hebrew edition of the English bard, an individualist and a romantic par excellence.[60] Whatever the locale—Russia, as in his novel *In the Winter*,[61] or London, as in his play *Beyond the Borders*,[62] or former Palestine before the First World War, as in *Breakdown and Bereavement*[63]—Brenner's protagonists were deracinated Jews in an alien land, which never relieved their quixotic gloom. They were forever on the move but the change of locale did not change their innate futilitarianism; and they reflected the tortured and twisted anxieties of their author who, unlike his heroes or nonheroes, worked out his salvation through his faith in labor. His negligence in choice of words and in syntactic structure was a deliberate attempt to free the Hebrew language from classic incrustations and to invent a folk idiom. This, too, was an act of faith in an ancestral idiom capable of renewed vitality.

Even for his translations he chose works that contributed to his own inner development: four plays by Gerhard Hauptmann, including *The Weavers*, two stories by Tolstoy, Dostoevsky's novel, *Crime and Punishment*, Arthur Ruppin's *The Jews in Modern Times*. Serious, saintly, humorless—this was Brenner as a writer of fiction, as a theoretician of labor, as a literary critic. His sweeping generalizations about Hebrew literature are not without interesting aperçus. He claimed—and it was an original insight—that the poetry of the enlightenment was interested in the individual but knew little about him; the poetry of nationalism was interested in the nation, but it was poetry of individual sorrow and joy. As for Hebrew prose, Berdyczewski carried the burden of national responsibility even when he was seemingly interested in the individual alone.[64]

As an editor Brenner will be remembered for two important periodicals. In London his short-lived monthly, *Ha-M'eorer* (January, 1906–September, 1907), rallied the best Hebrew writers of the period when other periodicals were completely silenced after the revolution of 1905: *Ha-Zefirah* in Warsaw, *Ha-Zeman* in Vilna, and *Ha-Shiloah*, which was published in Cracow. Although Gershon Schoffmann and Isaac Dov Berkowitz were not happy with the pretentious name, they supported Brenner without reservation.[65] His monthly, *Ha-Adamah* (1919–1920),[66] emphasized productive life in Palestine, a new bond between man and nature. It had a formative influence on socialism and socialist writers such as Yehoshua Barzilai and Meir Wilkansky. The very first issue of *Ha-Adamah* sounded a note of newness.

This is Jewish socialism: colonization of Palestine on a collective basis. The colonies will not be utopian socialist colonies which seek God or teach wisdom . . . There is in these cooperatives a question of life and death.[67]

Nothing could be more Brennerian and more Byronic at the same time: the tone is challenging but pessimistic, provocative but desperate. And in the title the parochial point of view blends with a thrust at universality: *Ha-Adamah*, that is to say, "attraction to the source of life and growth, to the source of renewal, to the source of human truth.[68] Besides the two periodicals, Brenner also edited six miscellanies under the title *Revivim;* two were issued in the capital of Eastern Galicia, Lemberg, between 1908 and 1909, three in Jerusalem between 1913 and 1914, and one in Jaffa in 1919.[69] The important writers of the day contributed to them: Zalman Shneour and Jakob Fichmann, Isaac Katzenelson and David Shimoni, Micah Joseph Berdyczewski and Gershon Schoffmann, R. Benjamin [Joshua Radler-Feldman] and Jacob Rabinowitz. Younger writers were also drawn to them: Uri Zevi Gruenberg, Yeshurun Keshet [Koplewicz]. Mordecai Temkin, Abraham Ben-Yizhak. Even writers from America found a hospitable welcome in the miscellanies: Ephraim E. Lisitzky, Hillel Bavli, and Naphtali Herz Imber.

Periodicals played an important role in shaping a new image of Jewry in the world: ingathering and integration of oriental and occidental communities in the Promised Land. Long before Brenner, papers and periodicals dotted the literary landscape of Palestine—first in Jerusalem, then in Tel Aviv and other localities. Although 1863 is accepted as the year of publication of the first periodical,[70] it has been proven that as early as 1854 attempts were made to publish a periodical in Jerusalem. In 1907 Simhah Alter Gutmann, better known as Simhah Ben-Zion (1870–1932), and David Yellin founded *Ha-'Omer*, the progenitor of the labor periodicals *Ha-Po'el ha-Zair* and *Ha-Adamah*. And Jacob Rabinowitz (1875–1948) together with Asher Barash edited the bimonthly *Hedim* (1922–1928)—a periodical which created a vogue for the younger contemporaries of Hayyim Nahman Bialik and Saul Tschernichowsky in the 1920s.

The writers transplanted to Palestine in the period prior to the First World War experienced considerable difficulty in their adjustment to the new environment. *Rich Man's Daughter*,[71] an early novel by Alexander Ziskind Rabinowitz, reflected its author's socialist beliefs. And so did his articles and stories on labor. His translation of Wilhelm Bacher's massive investigation into rabbinic legends illuminated a new area of knowledge for the Hebrew reader. Jacob Rabinowitz wrote a novel on the life of a watchman.[72] He, too, befriended labor-oriented writers. Asher Barash found his subject matter in his native Galicia on the threshold of the twentieth century. Later he created an intimate picture of life in Tel Aviv, particularly in his novel *The Gardeners*. An air of yesterday—the title of one collecton of his lyrical poems—permeates his historical stories which have few equals in that difficult genre.

As an anthologist of modern Hebrew poetry, he has shown impeccable taste. His choice of Hebrew verse is a fair example of what is best in Hebrew lyric poetry in the past two hundred years. It has influenced anthologies of Hebrew poetry by Meitus, Toren, and Habermann.

A prolific novelist like Kabak adapted himself to the new environment with difficulty. At his best, he escaped into the realm of history and after a long series of undistinguished books of fiction, he produced a novelized life of Solomon Molko and, even more important, a life of Jesus, in his novel *The Narrow Path*. But one of the seminal novelists and the first Nobel Prize winner in the history of modern Hebrew literature, Samuel Joseph Agnon, was richly nourished by the Palestinian milieu, as was that assiduous implementor of the Zionist[73] dream and most important poet of the Second *'Aliyyah*, the Second Wave of Immigration, David Shimoni.

2
Singer of the Desacralized Land: David Shimoni

DAVID Shimoni (1886–1956)—originally Schimonowitz—may be characterized as the Singer of the Desacralized Land. He was twenty-five when he published his first volume of neoromantic poems, *Desert*.[1] Hackneyed themes in hackneyed forms dominate its pages. Inevitable sunsets, laced with notes of obliging alienation, veil the neat, traditional stanzas. Melancholic moods of Pushkin and Lermontov, whom the poet translated in later years, impart a derivative stance to his first literary ventures. Even his wistful elegy on the rapid extinction of the Samaritans, "The Last,"[2] which was published before the volume appeared in print, was not likely to make any lasting impression. But the poet matured in the course of the years and developed his remarkable ability to create character in poems of epic length. Even in his first volume he revealed an embryonic talent for portraiture. What seasoned traveler could fail to recognize that typical Englishwoman who generously, though unknowingly, supplied the ironic relief to the monotonous crossings of the seas?

Flooded with light and covered with numberless coats
An old British lady dotes on the Psalms and dotes . . .[3]

In his idylls which were modeled on the idylls of Tschernichowsky, Shimoni found his appropriate genre and his thematic strength. The

16

first effort of the poet in that direction, "The Jordan Girl,"[4] was a charming tale in verse of two lovers who spend happy hours by the banks of the historic river. Shimoni succeeded in bringing to life a day—with all its rich variety and changeability—in a small corner in the north of Palestine. He was also the first modern poet in Hebrew literature who derived regional differences in character from geographical divergences: "The girls of Judah are learned but the girls of Galilee are wise." This chance remark bridged somehow a gap of two thousand years: Judah, at the end of the second commonwealth, represented cultural refinement while Galilee symbolized simplicity and even coarseness.[5]

In the idyll "War of Judah and Galilee"[6] the poet explored lingual differences in Palestine. The war between the north and the south was merely a contest of pronunciations between two youths who hiked from the valley of Sharon to the mountains of Galilee. In an idyll of the same period the poet sounded a somber and serious note. The subject matter—work in the malarial swamps of Sharon—highlighted the stern task which confronted early settlers—reclamation of land from the wilderness. Gravity dominated other idylls of that period. Out of his experience as a watchman in Judea Shimoni created types of watchmen whose loneliness was matched by their melancholy. He drew his figures of speech from their moods and modes of life.

Rural Palestine attracted the poet even after he settled in Tel Aviv in 1924. At first he despised the city, "the scent of sea and offices, of busybodies and oranges."[7] Gradually he began to realize what immense toil went into production of goods and he developed tolerance and even fondness for Tel Aviv. But he never wavered in his allegiance to the village and its fields, to the toilers and the watchmen. In two of his best idylls, "Ziyyonah"[8] and "Tombstone,"[9] he created types of biblical simplicity. The heroine in "Ziyyonah" yielded neither to family pressures nor to temptations of city life but stayed in her village out of love for the wide open spaces and out of a sense of responsibility to the soil. In a visionary passage toward the end of the idyll the poet depicted his country as a limitless field peopled by characters who were modeled on Amos and Gideon, Ruth and Shulamit. And he succeeded in translating a prevalent ideal into mature art. The redemption of the Jews without the redemption of the soil was rejected as a fraud and a sham.

In his idyll "Tombstone" the poet created a pioneering type of singular devotion. Katriel, the Russian Jew who was exiled to Siberia for Zionist leanings, escaped to China, and then to Palestine. In the sub-urbs of Jerusalem and in the city itself he reclaimed land from the rocky soil. Working day in and day out, he managed to build two huts, one for his farming needs, one for himself and his wife. When she died in childbirth, he left the city for the dangerous life of a watchman and met his death at the hands of two Bedouins. It was not Byronic grief which drove him from Jerusalem after the death of his wife; the intense desire to erect a tombstone of marble on her grave forced him into the more lucrative occupation of a watchman. He thought he would return to his former plot of ground as soon as he had amassed enough money. But he died and willed his land to anyone who would undertake to till it. As for himself, he preferred to merge with the earth because "it is good to mingle with the dust of the earth without leaving a trace."

Shimoni has not written *the* proletarian idyll nor has he been able to make a hero out of a collective. But in "Tombstone" he has created a type of pioneer who welds the dream of his own welfare and the dream of national resurrection.

The longest idyll of the poet, *Drops of the Night*,[10] revolves around the civil war of 1936–1939 in the blood-drenched soil of Palestine. Though it shares the landscape and the protagonist with other idylls, it is a narrative poem rather than an idyll, a tense tissue of inner events rather than a blissful scene of rural tranquillity. The poet seems to say that the fratricidal strife marks a new epoch of national heroism as contrasted with individual heroism of the preceding fifty years. But in the fifty-six-page long, restless recitation of the thoughts of a watchman during an anticipated Arab attack at night the poet fails to sustain the pitch of tension. On the whole, Shimoni maintained a relaxed stance in his art. He was the spiritual kinsman of Dutch painters whose clean-swept interiors and landscapes presuppose a clean, simple heart. Like Pieter Brueghel the Elder who painted scenes of rustic life with wholesome humor, verve, and drama, Shimoni, the painter of rural Palestine in verse, cherished the simple life in his idyllic work and to a certain extent in his dramatic work as well.

In prose Shimoni produced an interesting dramatic fragment: *Night in a Vineyard*[11] and an imaginary diary *The Wanderer in Time*.[12] The former dramatized an incident: a welcome to a Zionist leader in a Palestinian vineyard. It has historical rather than literary value: it calls attention to the presence of Yemenites in Hebrew literature before the First World War. It also stresses, for the first time in a Hebrew play, a love relationship between workers. But not only the love relationship interested Shimoni. Two of the workers function as writers in the play because "graphomania is a very common disease in the Land of Israel."[13] The second dramatic fragment is the effusion of a worker who commits suicide: he cannot bridge the gap between the vulgarity of Palestinian realities and the nobility of his own dreams. An incidental character from *The Wanderer in Time,* Rabbi Phinehas, reappears in the idylls of the poet: in his "In the Forest in Hadera"[14] and in "Tombstone". This character is an elderly type, a pure and simple lover of the Holy Land who seems to have been modeled on Aaron David Gordon. Interestingly, an erudite, elderly character by the same name appears in many stories of Hayyim Hazaz many years after the publication of *The Wanderer in Time.*

The dramatic fragments introduce for the first time in Hebrew literature the living idiom of the Yemenites, the chatter of children with quaint mutilations of Hebrew phrases and inventive play with words; yet the language does not bristle with neologisms. Shimoni's poetic drama, *Idolaters,*[15] is as simple as a Greek tragedy. The effect is produced by Abraham's daring destruction of his father's idols, an act which, like a stone thrown into a clear pool, engenders ever widening circles of sorrow. Terah, the father of Abraham, is deeply apprehensive. He decides to emigrate with the entire household to Canaan. The women of the household, Milcah and Yiscah, remain faithful to the idols. But Sarah, the wife of Abraham, is afraid of Canaan and its gods, and Nahor, his grandfather, is too old and unwilling to emigrate. He alone remains in Ur and weeps over the dead gods. In its brevity, in its economy of portraiture, in the compactness of its theme, in the melancholic poetry which is the necessary accompaniment of this twilight of the gods, the poetic drama *Idolaters* is one of the finer efforts of the poet.

The biblical poems of Shimoni balance his idylls. Except in "The Jordan Girl" and "Ziyyonah," the heroes of the idylls are men. In the biblical poems the protagonists are predominantly women. This is especially the case in "The Wife of Job."[16]

While Job has been fully treated in the Bible, his wife has remained an insignificant appendage to his tale of woe. Shimoni reconstructed her, as it were, from a few biblical verses and endowed her with the gift of ample reminiscence. In her misery she contrasts her past with the present—Job's courtship, their ride through the desert to his native Uz, the birth and growth of the children. And she becomes painfully aware that a temperamental difference between the fatalist Job and her rebellious character created the marital rift. In his deepest misery Job was incapable of her blasphemy:

> God! Where are my children,
> Big and small?
> Perhaps you don't exist,
> And Satan's all?

Since she cannot and does not want to hate Job, she despises his crawling friends. But theophany in the storm, which convinced her husband of the all-pervasive power of God, has no effect on her. Even if God were to resuscitate her children, he would be incapable of reviving her wounded heart.

The poet who dares to choose a biblical theme must, of necessity, complement the ancient text. He must develop plot and character, suspense and shock, out of a mere hint. Thomas Mann has done it on a vast scale in his tetralogy *Joseph and His Brothers*; Shimoni, on a more modest scale, has accomplished it in "The Wife of Job."

Of the longer poems which are not inspired by the Bible, "A Winter Night's Dream"[17] takes undoubted precedence. It is a series of northern vignettes: a vision of white forests, white cities and white days. With unconcerned impishness the verses flit from forest to field, from sea to city and, finally, arrive at their starting point: the room of the poet. The musicality of the lines, the dancing rhythm, the light touch—these qualities combine to make "A Winter Night's Dream" one of his best dramatic efforts.

But fatal weaknesses marred the poet's work. Like most Hebrew poets he must have absorbed a large quantity of inferior Slav poetry which had a detrimental influence on his oeuvre. Lermontov can be blamed for some of his glaring defects.[18] Among the writings of the Russian poet he found those interminably long effusions like "The Demon" and "Ismail Bey" which he translated and imitated. When he came to render Pushkin and Heine into Hebrew, he significantly chose the former's dramatic poems and the latter's *Die Harzreise, The Journey to the Harz Mountains*. Their lyrical contributions eluded his facile pen. In his translation of Tolstoy's *Khadzhi-Murat* and *The Cossacks* he showed the same long-windedness as in the poetical translations. Precision was not his virtue, concision was not his hallmark. His sketches which go by the name of *Homeland*,[19] and his satires which are thinly disguised fables with a moralizing attitude towards Palestinian life, hardly add to his stature. But the diary jottings in the series called *Secretly*[20] reinforce his poetic output with unexpected illuminations of the hidden processes of his thought. For he was essentially the poet of the commonplace and the anti-hero: his lines communicated for the first time in modern Hebrew literature the Palestinian slang of the early Palestinian pioneers, the taste of their frugal meals, the feel of the desert sands, the wail of foxes and jackals in the night. It was a pioneering achievement of the poet of pioneers.[21]

3
Rediscovery of Landscape: Jacob Fichmann

BIBLICAL poets were not interested in landscape per se: they were singing the glory and the power of the creator of the landscape. The sea and the sky, the earth and the fulness thereof—all these were mere manifestations of an all-powerful deity. In other words, there are no pure landscapes in biblical poetry; there are only theological landscapes. Psalm 104 or chapters 38 and 39 of Job are notable instances of nature poems in the Bible. But they extol God as the Power over nature, not nature itself.

Medieval poets were twice removed from the Palestinian landscape—by virtue of theological bias which they shared with biblical poets and by virtue of geographical distance. Palestinian landscapes, seascapes, cityscapes were mere names, hallowed names like the Byzantine portraits of haloed saints. In the famous "Zionides" of Judah Halevi the litany of Palestinian place-names has the power of magical evocation or incantation.

The early writers who came with the first and second wave of Eastern European immigrants—Smilansky and Jawitz, Brenner and Agnon—began to divest the Palestinian landscapes of theological accretions; they de-theologized them. Later writers completed the process. One of the most prominent landscape painters in verse, Jacob Fichmann, (1881–1958), was also the most careful craftsman in modern Hebrew poetry. Bialik surpassed him in his poetical assessment of Jewish life. Tschernichowsky outdid him in the catholicity of his cultural interests. But no other Hebrew poet in the last hundred years had an equal sensitivity to the value of the word.

If it is true that the minor poet concentrates on landscape, then Fichmann must be regarded as the minor poet *par excellence*, the itinerant landscape painter who feels at home wherever a garden blooms under a tranquil sky and a river flows in graceful curves. In his book *Shadows upon Fields*,[1] a collection of lyrics which range over three decades, there is hardly a poem which does not depict a landscape. The titles are indicative of the content: "A Summer Night," "Blue Flowers," "Night Rain," "On a Winter Evening," "Evening Wind," "Hoarfrost," "Vapor," "The Song of the White Bud," and dozens of others. What makes Fichmann receptive to the charms of nature remains a secret he does not confide, unlike A.E., who chose to write as revelatory a book as *Song and its Fountains*. As a boy of seven, Fichmann fell in love "with lovely blue flowers,"[2] their mute companionship a compensation for the lack of the boisterous companionship of boys of his age. And he was so obsessed with landscape that even sadness appeared to him in the guise of a protective tree.

The quiet aspects of nature are the proper domain of Fichmann. But he weaves his personal reactions into the changing moods of the day and the season—the haunting languor and sadness which are also characteristic of a French contemporary, Paul Verlaine. Yet it is difficult to quote poems or verses of Fichmann that owe their imagery directly to outside sources. Only "Night Rain" is traceable to Verlaine. The conclusion of the poem-night creeps slowly, tears fall upon the window panes-alludes to the beginning of Verlaine's famous poem:

Il pleure dans mon coeur
Comme il pleut sur la ville.

A poet like Fichmann never feels at ease in the city. The favorite book of our age, the *Odyssey*, is the book of his heart's desire.[3] Like the Homeric hero, embodiment of restless search, he wanders, both out of necessity and for his own pleasure, through many lands and climes. But, the impact of Palestine shakes to the very depths the still surface of his personality. In a cycle of sonnets on Judea[4] which, together with Tschernichowsky's sonnets "To the Sun" are among the most perfect in the Hebrew language, he has erected an imperishable monument to himself. Even the cities of arrested antiquity—Jaffa, Jericho, Jerusalem—share the characteristics of landscapes. Jaffa is depicted at noon, when the intense heat sheds a blissful lassitude upon the town and the muezzin wastes his musical voice upon an unheeding flock—not unlike the poet who is "accustomed to sing to the wilderness." Jericho is de-

scribed against the background of night: the gardens dip into the lux-
uriant sky and the Bedouin's campfire licks the hem of darkness. Jerusalem, under the clouds of a gathering storm, resembles Toledo which
El Greco has immortalized in somber paintings.[5]

What the idyll did for Shimoni, the sonnet did for Fichmann; it liberated his specific sensitivities. As for his longer poems, he began to
write them at forty—deliberately but not happily.

> At a very late period of my life. . . I can justify the long lyrical
> poem, strengthened by dramatic elements, as a form of transition.
> Yet this form is, in the main, the development of the lyric and the
> description of the landscape.[6]

Fichmann is mistaken, his longer poems are, at their best, cycles of
connected or unconnected lyrics which he has tried to weave into a
whole.[7] Even in his long dramatic poem *Ruth*, one of the finest in the
book of his longer poems, *Sunny Days*, [8] he shows lack of dramatic ability. Temperamentally, the characters of the poem—Ruth, Naomi,
Boaz—do not differ. They are good people, gentle and genteel, little re-
plicas or ideal images of Fichmann.

But the poem is seriously flawed by its lack of dramatic suspense. In
a long and beautiful monolog the heroine seeks to justify to herself
her new love. She remembers her old love for Chilion, the stranger
from Bethlehem, who bade her, with the gentle insistence of the dead,
return to his land and live with him there again on a plane of pure
imagination. This psychological motivation of Ruth's journey to Palestine throws a new light on her loyalty to Naomi. There is no doubt that
Fichmann imagined her as the embodiment of the stranger who awak-
ens to a new life in Palestine. But he was too much a poet and too little
a chauvinist to insist on the nationalistic theme.

Fichmann stated explicitly that he wrote a great part of his long
poem *Samson in Gaza* at the time when he composed his version of the
story of Ruth.[9] Gentle women, who are temperamentally more congenial to him than men, dominate the poem. Samson's mother who, according to the Talmud, was called Zelelponit,[10] reminisces at great
length about the angel's visitation, the childhood and boyhood of her
son, and his disconcerting passion for non-Hebrew women. Her monolog is followed by the discourse of Yael, the young Judean woman,
who cannot hold the love of Samson. She is true to Fichmann's psychological pattern. She does not curse Samson nor does she pursue him
with violent passion. Samson himself is not the powerful hero from the

Book of Judges; his national victories are bought at the price of personal defeats. For he symbolizes the Jew who, in spite of his attachment to his own country, is haunted and distracted by foreign lands, foreign landscapes, and foreign women. In a vicious circle of xenophobia and xenophilia Samson spends his great strength.

The two long poems are closely related. The problem of the stranger's attitude to Palestine in *Ruth* is the obverse of the problem of the Palestinian's attitude to the stranger in *Samson in Gaza*. Similar historical backgrounds and meters are used in both poems.

A similar relationship exists between two other biblical poems of Fichmann: "The Mourning of David" and "Joab." In both of them the poet uses iambic pentameter, the meter of Greek tragedy. In both, he depicts the biblical period of Kings. "The Mourning of David" wrestles with the periods of uncreativity which hamper and baffle every creative mind. David suffers from atrophy of the imagination in the poem and in homiletical literature. He has been deserted by the Holy Spirit for twenty-two years according to an ancient Midrash.[11] The sustained monolog of the protagonist is deeply felt; it may have been inspired by the protracted cessation of the poetic output of his friend and mentor, Hayyim Nahman Bialik, who produced only a few poems in the last two decades of his life. Fichmann's imagination easily bridged the gap between the best known Hebrew poet of the century and the alleged author of the *Psalms*.

"Joab" is a sequel to "The Mourning of David," a poem that presents the misfortune of David as viewed by persons who are more or less closely associated with the king: his officers who miss the sweet sounds of his harp at night and his wife, Bathsheba.

Fichmann's "Sea Idylls"[12] in *Sunny Days* are seascapes with an occasional personage in them. They have neither Tschernichowsky's exuberance nor Shimoni's breadth. They are personal reflections against the wide vistas of the sea. And the words of Maupassant with which Fichmann prefaced his "Sea Idylls" read like the *leitmotif* of his entire poetical career:

> J'ai vu de l'eau, du soleil, des nuages,
> Je ne puis raconter autre chose.

Fichmann is not only a poet; he is also one of the most prolific critics in modern Hebrew literature. The calm tone which characterizes his poetry suffuses his criticism.[13] In poetry he is the master of the lyric, in criticism he is the master of the essay. Usually he chooses a foreign or

Hebrew writer, sometimes a book, seldom a literary problem as a subject for his criticism. Within that limited field, his interests range from the Bible and Homer to the ultramoderns. His criticism, like his poetry, is measured, cadenced and well-balanced. His essays probe the abilities of writers who resemble him—Abraham Mapu and Micah Joseph Lebensohn.[14] Their unique charm lies in the use of personal recollections and in the loving analysis of the writers' work. They are sufficiently weighty to attract the scholar and sufficiently interesting to hold the attention of the general reader.

Characteristically, Fichmann's essays are neither thoroughly impressionistic nor coldly objective; they are exercises in associational criticism, and they stand halfway between the lyrical poem and the autobiographical story. When Fichmann is impelled to write a disquisition on an abstract theme, he generalizes dangerously and sometimes incompetently. Thus, in "The Concept of Lyricism,"[15] he states that Hebrew poetry after the period of the enlightenment was chiefly and almost exclusively lyrical. Certainly two poets of importance, Tschernichowsky and Shimoni, could not be included in the category of lyric poets. But he is right in his general appraisal of lyrical poetry:

> It is not known that the world becomes known not through what we think about it but through what we sing about it. This lyricism . . . is more of a miracle than any other literary genre.

This is not a statement of objective significance but a measure of the earnestness with which a craftsman evaluates his own craft.

Fichmann aims at immaculate writing. His repeated revisions of poems and essays betray an inner restlessness beneath the calm surface of his poetry, a dissatisfaction with himself and, above all, a love for the right expression—the *mot juste*—which is the mark of the true poet.

As a critic and especially as an editor of many periodicals throughout his life he was an incomparable teacher of literary taste. As a poet he educated—by precept and example—a generation of younger contemporaries to respect poetic expression as the most reliable indicator of human experience.

4
Poet in Prose: Jacob Steinberg

In his early, neoromantic poetry Jacob Steinberg (1887–1947) resembled his contemporaries. Only in his self-lacerating satires did he differ from them—in these seemingly cynical poems which ridiculed his and other people's amours. Love, especially love with charged, erotic overtones, wealth, and happiness were reduced to the sorry rank of mere delusions. Doubts have been resolved, mysteries have been unveiled: the vanity of vanities has become a reality. Man begins with "Hallelujah" and ends with "All is vain."[1] In his poems about children, however, Steinberg reached a measured wisdom, a harmony beyond the pessimistic formula of Ecclesiastes: "the serpent of understanding" is neither poisonous nor deadly; he is, perhaps, no serpent at all but a benevolent, beautiful pet at the service of the poet.

In his "Satires" and in his narrative poems Steinberg endeavored to widen the scope of his involvement in human situations. But instead of creating an objective character he only managed to project his own personality into his poetry. The dreamy and lonely youth in "Voyage of Absalom"[2] is a replica of the young Steinberg. Like Bialik's *Ha-Matmid*, he likes to spend the winter nights in the company of books and shadows. The poem did not advance beyond the twin moods of dreaminess and loneliness which were characteristic of the early poems. Technically, it showed no innovation: it was cast in the trochaic tetrameter which the poet probably borrowed from Tschernichowsky's narrative poem "Amnon and Tamar." There was an altogether inordinate number of similarities to contemporary Hebrew poets in the poem[3]—a surprising characteristic in a man who was later to fashion such an exqui-

27

site and original vehicle of expression as the poetic essay. But, as another poetical documentation of Jewish youth in transition, it has its place in modern Hebrew literature beside Bialik's more potent poem on a similar theme.

Steinberg's ballads are too labored to merit critical approval. In rhyming couplets, surpassed by Alexander Pope in magnificence of expression but not in rhythmic monotony they tell such melodramatic stories as that of a goldsmith who fashions his jewels with the help of Dame Care. An unexciting stranger, Vanity, is a frequent visitor in the house. The two sons, Imagination and Power, run away and are finally captured in the Valley of Life.

This unfortunate bent for allegory reappears in the poem "The Judgment"[4] which is inspired by the twenty-third chapter of Ezekiel's famous parable of harlots—Oholah and Oholibah. The two harlots in Steinberg's poem, the Daughter of Judah and the Daughter of Europe, stand before the eternal judgment seat without settling their difficulties.

The poet's use of allegory is a throwback to the period of the enlightenment, when moralizing verse in allegorical form was in full bloom. The Hebrew drama of the seventeenth, eighteenth, and nineteenth centuries was especially partial to allegory. The outstanding examples, neglected by ordinary readers, are still forced on involuntary readers in Hebrew institutions of learning: *Set Hell* by Moses Zacuto, *Praise to the Upright* by Moses Hayyim Luzzatto and *Truth and Faith* by Abraham Dov Ber Lebensohn.[5]

Steinberg's poetry is rarely first-rate; in quantity and in excellence prose dominates his creative efforts. Of the three volumes of his collected works, the first contains poetry, the second short stories and the third essays.[6] In his stories as in his poems he is essentially a conservative artist. Since the dominant theme in the early years of this century was the ghetto town, Steinberg used it *ad nauseam*. But he was too much an introvert to reach the epic calm of a Shalom Asch, the humor of a Shalom Aleyhem or the sharp-witted piquancy of a Mendele. Nevertheless, in addition to the common types of rabbi and ritual slaughterer, merchant and broker, he succeeded in portraying also the neglected lovers in the Jewish towns of the Ukraine. Thus, in "The Daughter of the Rabbi"[7] he created a female character who read Russian novels, shook hands with the man who was to be her betrothed, and wrote Russian letters to him. But this "emancipated woman" could not bear the consequences of a premarital pregnancy and, rather than expose herself to social ostracism, she preferred suicide by hanging.

In one of his longest stories, "On the Border of the Ukraine,"[8] Steinberg described the gentle relationship between a gentile girl and a Jewish medical student. Smolenskin, in one of his last stories, *Vengeance for the Covenant*, also dealt with the love of a Jewish student for a Slav girl. But his tendentiousness spoiled the artistic effect. Steinberg's hero is conscious of the unbridgeable gulf between himself and the outside world. He obeys the blind forces of desire and love but he knows that he is destined to a tragic fate in spite of the girl's affection. In one of the deeper passages of the story, her brother-in-law, the sympathetic doctor who suffers from marital troubles, explores the difference between the Jew and the Gentile:

> You are a Jew . . . I am a Russian. The Russians . . . from the peasant to the nobleman, are children of the earth; it is natural for them to look with suspicion on a man who is merely a man and not a child of the earth, a son of the land. I like you but a natural feeling in my heart tells me this is Boris Solomonowitz, handsome, understanding and honest, but merely a man by the name of Boris Solomonowitz, nothing else. Here is the secret of revulsion which we Russians feel in our relationship to the Jews.

In a level-headed and sober analysis the passage indicates the essential incompatibility between the man of the earth and the uprooted individual. With the pride of a man who belongs to an ancient race the Jew asserts that he, too, has a homeland of his own. It is not on the map but it is real: it is the realm of the spirit and thought, the Jewish state before the establishment of the State of Israel.

The problem of intermarriage has been posed in all its stringency in Steinberg's story: could the Jew have shared his life with the blond-braided Russian girl? When he leaves her in a sombre moment, he acts with atavistic resolve. Yet he has come dangerously near to uniting his life with hers; and here lies the deep difference between the generation of the enlightenment and Steinberg's generation—what was impossible then has become possible in the twentieth century. Nazism and fascism eliminated the danger of mixed marriages with brutal legality. In the post-hooliganized world, Judaism has been groping, with predictable failure, for a solution to the insoluble problem of intermarriage.

"On the Border of the Ukraine" is Steinberg's best story. It manages to convey a Russian atmosphere: the boring existence and the diversionary loves on one of the vast estates in czarist Russia follow the pattern of Turgenev's tales or Chekhov's plays. And the story is western in style; its Hebrew reflects an occidental syntax and rhythm. An adequate translation into a western language will probably read better than the original.

While Shimoni and Fichmann conquered Palestine in verse, Steinberg transformed it in so-called *Sketches*.[9] They are essays which, in even cadence and balanced thought, resemble the essays of Walter Pater and speak in a medium which is neither prose nor poetry but partakes of the language of the two. To them he entrusted his impressions of the ineffable landscapes of Palestine: the ancient cities, the hoary villages, the remnants of half-forgotten peoples. And in them he adumbrated his attitude to the world. While Fichmann restricted himself to literary themes in his essays, Steinberg extended their scope to include anything that had even a remote connection with Jews.

Jerusalem has not lacked writers who endeavored to capture its mystic charms. But Steinberg's long essay on the ancient city penetrated into its very heart, evoked the ghosts of ancient memories and bared its present burden of fate. The very first paragraph strikes the mellowed chord which, like a motif in a symphony, reverberates again and again:

> Every ancient town looks like a riddle to the wayfarer. The early ways of living are preserved in the tangled streets, the scent of nameless days clings somewhere to a buttressed wall, to the edge of a trough hewn out of stone, to the lintel of an age-old prayer-house. And yet a feeling of oddity and amazement grips you when you walk in Jerusalem. Mound upon mound the city is built; the spirit of bygone days hovers over all of them. The deeper you enter into the walled city, the more it will seem to you that each stone is dry with age and every crevice in the wall is as dark as an ancient secret. . . What is the nature of the sadness that also clutches at your heart when you walk in the areas outside the wall, a bitter and intoxicating sadness which feels like a faint residue of the ancient hatred of its zealous defenders? The traces of time were not covered by the dust of destruction in Jerusalem, that dust of passing days upon which every wayfarer treads in any other ancient town.

As for the source of sadness in Jerusalem:

> There the most delicate beauty in the world was created: the beauty of longing.

Steinberg has also seen with the eye of a poet that special segment of humanity which has almost its own laws and its own ways:

> The blind dwell among the seeing in proud separateness, their attitude to all that is being done around them is that of light mockery; the seeing people cannot possibly know the truth. . . They push their canes against the stones of the street with a bothersome noise. It awakens something that forces you to stand and listen for a moment to that strange sound which also tells of the wonders of Jerusalem.

In a compact sonnet Baudelaire immortalized the blind of his hated and beloved Paris. But he had to segregate them from the pleasure-loving city as a distinct entity, as a foreign element that cannot be absorbed in the seething metropolitan life. In Steinberg's essay the blind, in spite of their separateness, merge with their surroundings and express, unknowingly to themselves, the tremendous symbol of Jerusalem. That is undoubtedly the reason why he chose to finish his essay on the ancient city with the blind. Only one quality, the subtle hauteur of the blind, both poets have observed in common.

> *Leurs yeux, d'où la divine étincelle est partie,*
> *Comme s'ils regardaient au loin, restent levés*
> *Au ciel . . .*

With his prose hymn to Jerusalem Steinberg outstripped both his verse and his prose tales. At one stroke he achieved maturity, he penetrated into his real self. Only the undue length and the unctuous tone disturb the modern reader who suspects artificiality in pathos because he prefers the poetry of trivialities.[10]

In his essay on Jerusalem Steinberg intimated the close connection between the Book of Books and the City of Cities. In his essay on the "Three Lofty Books" Steinberg endeavored to show that prophets like Isaiah and Amos were the exception rather than the rule, unrepresentative yet characteristic of their people. Only three historical works, Judges, Samuel, and Kings, have resurrected the epic life of the Jewish people.

> We, distant and strange progeny of that race, regard now the circumstances of its life in order to boast and not in order to under-

stand or enjoy. And this is the clear mark of the impoverished epigone.

All the strong qualities of the people—the heroic and the lowly endeavors—have been portrayed in these three books with a conciseness which harmonizes with the genius of the people. Whether the characters face each other as enemies or friends, they understand each other to a terrifying degree. Thus, when the implacable foes Ahab and Elijah meet, they only have this to say to each other: "Have you found me, my enemy?" "I have found you." Such brevity, in Steinberg's estimation, illumines relationships of people like the Palestinian sun itself. Hence the immense psychological and pedagogical value of the three lofty books which, together with Ruth, Genesis, parts of Exodus, Numbers, and Deuteronomy, form the Jewish *Iliad* and *Odyssey* and permit the Jews to reconstruct the soul of their people.

Steinberg noticed a seminal similarity between the Greeks and the Hebrews. Both were able, in a stroke of genius, to bare their grandeur in a literary work: the Hebrews in the Bible, the Greeks in the Homeric epics. The biblical people no longer exist, but biblical literature feeds Jews with spiritual strength. Hebrew literature throughout the ages is merely a reinterpretation or "reincarnation" of the Bible. It may reach unsuspected heights but it will never lose its derivative character. The Bible is an awesome inheritance.

These fatalistic views on Hebrew literature do not exclude the possibility of new departures and new beginnings; they do not necessarily convert the blessings of heritage into a curse. The Bible is the consummation of the Jewish people's first love. But there is the possibility of a second love. The people who wrote the Bible, the "divine novel" in Steinberg's phrase, may yet create the "human comedy." For the Bible is the indicator and originator of creative endeavor among Jews.

In two essays, "Rain" and "End of Summer," Steinberg asserted that the understanding of the Palestinian climate may lead to a better understanding of the Bible. The ancient legislators and prophets were aware of the uncommon value of rain in a parched land. The memory of cascading drops affected their concept of God who ceased sometimes to be King of the Universe and became simply God of Rain like the Roman *Jupiter Pluvius*. In a strained comparison Steinberg traced the connection between the clarity of Mediterranean days and the clairvoyant biblical half-verses of the ancient Hebrews.

Steinberg devoted many essays to the evaluation of Hebrew literature. Almost alone among Hebrew critics, he preferred analyses of poetical lines to glib generalities. He even went as far as to say that "modern Hebrew poetry redeemed the Hebrew spirit: it created the line." With the sure touch of a seasoned critic he stressed purple passages in the works of medieval and modern Hebrew poets. But he also made some valuable observations of a general nature. When he argued that the chief malaise of modern Hebrew literature stemmed from the decline of religious feeling among Jews, he pointed to a well-known phenomenon of decadence in world literature.[11] He went a step farther and maintained that the pursuit of current themes would lead to the Americanization of Hebrew literature. For Steinberg America was the present. The elimination of the past presented possibilities of impoverishment for Hebrew literature.

In his essays, which read like prose poems, Steinberg arrived at an esthetic attitude to the world and a classic balance in style. Some of his poems and stories will stand the test of time, but many of his essays will be timeless treasures of Hebrew literature.

Neither the Hebrew plays of Steinberg—*Reb Leb Goldman and His Daughter, Hankah,* and the one act drama *The Blemished,* nor the two Yiddish plays *Mother* and *Temptation* appeared in his collected works. A reading and re-reading of the plays vindicates his judgment: exclusion was deserved.

5
The Avant-gardists: Avigdor Hameiri; Uri Zevi Gruenberg; Jacob Horowitz

THE three avantgardists between the two world wars shared a common homeland—the Austro-Hungarian empire—and an innovative thrust which was prevalent in Vienna since the early years of the century.

In Hungary, far from the beaten tracks of European civilization, Menahem Avigdor Feuerstein, who changed his name to Hameiri (1886–1970) began his literary career with a conservative volume of poems. Throughout his life he was fascinated by the exaggerated romanticism of his native land. Translations into Hebrew from the works of Imre Madách (1823–1864), Endre Ady (1877–1919), and Sándor Petöfi (1823–1849)[1] give ample testimony to the strength of this attachment. In his old age he wrote a narrative poem *Yosele Teglashi*[2] about a boy who grew up in a Hungarian village. Unlike other Jewish boys—bloodless, emaciated, studious—he was a paradigm of physical strength. Although the niceties of the Talmud were over his head, the trees of the forest talked to him in a language of sheer exhilaration. When an act of courage was called for, he saved a Jewish beggar from the clutches of a wolf. This deed, so untypical of Jewish emphasis on scholarly prowess, was probably intended as a symbol by Hameiri: regenerated Jewry must stand up against its wolfish enemies. The redeemer of Jewry—and Yosele's parents had cast him in that role in their dreams—must be a man of physical prowess.

34

This unfinished poem—literally and figuratively unfinished—shares the theme of muscular strength with his greater contemporary Saul Tschernichowsky. Hameiri also resembles him in praise of national heroism in ancient Judea: both in "Samson's Last Song"[3] and in "Before the Statue of Apollo" there are elegiac evocations of muscular strength. There is another similarity between these poets: they carried their Jewish ancestry with inordinate pride. Tschernichowsky boasted that his blood was "the blood of the conquerors of Canaan," Hameiri vaunted his priestly stock.[4] And he went beyond Tschernichowsky in his commitment to Jewish heroism in the present. His play *Blessed is the Match*[5] may not be great drama. But it is a paean of praise for Hannah Szenes who gave her life for her people in the Second World War. The dissimilarities between poets are more revealing than their similarities. Tschernichowsky, the master of poetical form, chiseled his lines with sculpturesque dexterity; Hameiri made poetry out of charged emotionalism. Most of his poems were structurally too narrow to contain their author's avalanche of feeling. They had no end; they seemed to continue in some emotive centre of the poet; they gushed in Swinburnian self-forgetfulness and swept the helpless poet into their vortex; they degenerated into repetitious chants. Work for a newspaper—as journalist and as editor—also contributed to the dilution and flabbiness of his style.

The First World War released new energies in the poet. All its horrors swam into his ken—battlefields, imprisonments, Siberia. In his novel *The Great Madness*[6]—the Hebrew counterpart of Remarque's *All Quiet on the Western Front*—he captured war in its stark brutality. In the poem "Document of Death"[7] he wrote the imaginary will of a Hebrew soldier who was also a poet:

> His name: unknown and blurred by gore.
> His rank: captain of wandering crews.
> His birthplace: an eastern land of yore.
> His faith: the faith of the Jews.

> His work: artificer of rose-red verse.
> His age: two thousand years.
> His social status: friends who disperse . . .
> His sign: Cain's sign of tears.

> His will: Go forth to my dream-girl, my dream,
> And tell her it is my belief

That she will escort me to Lethe's stream,
She—and the people of grief.

Death on the battlefield—as Hameiri saw it—undermined the life of the individual, the nation, the world. But his poetry, so reflective of the cruelty and brutality of the age, was also capable of infinite tenderness. The mother of the poet, symbol of Jewish motherhood in general, represented that refuge of love and pity in a maddened world. In his inimitable hyperbolism Hameiri compared her forehead to the firmament, her hands to the hands of the God of pity and her total being to the moon. No painter could possibly translate this verbal portrait into color on canvas. And yet the poet succeeded in evoking a half-angelic, half-human image of "mother" in the minds of his readers.[8]

This compound of reverence and blasphemy was to have a profound effect on the younger poets: Gruenberg's worship of his mother, Lamdan's invocations of his parents, Shlonsky's cycle of poems "To Father and Mother" and his innumerable imitators who suddenly discovered their fathers and mothers—they all owe a debt of gratitude to Hameiri who released a flood of odes to father and mother. The loss of faith in the father of creation may be regarded as an additional cause of parental romanticism in contemporary Hebrew literature. But Hameiri created the vogue for filial piety among the pioneers who left their parents in Europe and suffered from frustration of filial love.

Just as the Jewish mother was more than mother, so Palestine was more than Palestine to Hameiri. In the poem "Redeemed Zion"[9] which resembles the famous "Zionides" of Judah Halevi, the poet envisages a liberated people which is, at the same time, a liberating force for social justice in the world. The idea is reorchestrated in the song of the road which is being built by pioneers:

In the name of the God of the Past we will make the future
For nations and individuals, for the living and even the dead.[10]

The Holy Land, which became Hameiri's adopted land after the First World War, developed his nascent mysticism. Jeremiah, Ezekiel, Rabbi Akiba and Bar Bar-Hana became daily companions of the poet, friendly figures rather than historic personages. The immense past broke into the budding present.

In English poetry only Blake showed such easy familiarity with biblical prophets, such deliberate lack of polish, innocence and visionary prowess. Hameiri was probably unconscious of that spiritual kinship.

He was more likely aware of Jacob Cahan's "From the Songs of a Bright-Eyed Youth" when he wrote his sequence "Schoolboy Dreams":[11]

> I am a little child.
> The world is big and bad.
> The world is a wheeling whirl.
> How can I keep from going mad?
> How can I keep from going mad?
>
> I am a Jewish child.
> The world is a gentile place.
> The world is full of hate.
> I love all, and all
> Turn from me in disgrace . . .
>
> The hound is on my trail.
> A voice yells: give up, lad.
> The world is a wheeling whirl.
> How can I keep from going mad?
> How can I keep from going mad?

Just as the child is a favorite subject, the dog is a favorite animal, a sentient being, a lover of Jews, a Messiah, a poet.

> Like you I am a barker and a prophet,
> A dog . . .[12]

The prophetic dog became the beloved symbol of Hameiri's younger and greater contemporary: Uri Zevi Gruenberg. Both poets suffered from overemotionalism, both poets delighted in verbal overindulgence. Like his earlier countryman, Solomon Löwisohn, author of the beautiful and original myth of creation in *The Poetry of Israel* and of the first Hebrew translation of a Shakespearean fragment, Hameiri impressed his time with the stamp of his élan and originality. In poems and essays, in stories and novels, he articulated an unrestrainable hyperbolism. In the Teapot, which he founded, he organized and produced grossly satirical theatricals[13] with salutary effects in Palestine. Like W.P.A. dramatizations of actual events in the United States, and like the satirical monologs in European cabarets and nightclubs, Hameiri's ensembles ridiculed outworn institutions and personalities.[14] But in the little lyric poem "My Two Souls"[15] he revealed himself more thoroughly than in the stories, novels, and theatricals:

> By the rivers of the East dwells my first soul
> And turns to thoughts of peace
> And dreams her dreams of peace.
> By the rivers of the West dwells my second soul
> And dreams a blood-red dream.

The primeval East and the civilized West struggle with each other in his work. That is why he feels a deep kinship with the Hebrew poets of the Golden Age in Spain: they have experienced that dichotomy more than Hebrew poets in other countries. Like Samuel Ibn Nagdela, Hameiri knew how to wield sword and pen. And like most Hebrew poets of the Middle Ages he dedicated poems to rich patrons, friends, relatives and fellow authors. Even his bombastic hymns of redemption resemble the effusions of the poets of the Golden Age: thematic similarity bridges the gulf between them. On closer scrutiny Hameiri emerges as a lover of the national past and national aspiration for the future rather than as an individualistic maverick, a trumpeter of personal alienism and an ideologist of national identity.

Uri Zevi Gruenberg (1894–   ) is the product of the new poetry which made its debut in Europe before the First World War under the aegis of Marinetti and Apollinaire.[16] From them he borrowed metaphorical acrobatics and daring figures of speech which succeeded in shocking the idyllic tenor of Hebrew literature. When Dada and surrealism made their noisy appearances in the West, Gruenberg showed sympathy with their efforts and identified with their excesses.[17]

Gruenberg's first book which appeared in large format and with the enigmatic title *The Great Terror and the Moon*[18] presented a challenge to an unsuspecting public. Since the appearance of *Job* no such obscure passages had been published in Hebrew as the first paragraph of the introduction in prose to Gruenberg's first book:

> In the sole of the right foot—the soul, in the sole of the left foot—the heart. On the tablet of the bare breast I strike with crushed hand saying: I deny! Electricity in the head, light of all the lanterns and all the lamps which are on sea and land. Man is full to the very toenails. The entire landscape . . . wrestles because of

the blood. The great dry land and all the seven seas are worrying in one head. I know that I am in the twentieth century.

These words that were intended to give vent to abysmal grief were supplemented with boasts about "a change of guard" in Hebrew poetry and phrases of such Nietzschean arrogance as "I am not modest . . . I know well the value of this book of mine." The shock of content was encased in the shock of form: rhyme was almost completely abandoned, rhythm was distorted by lines of unusual length. Dryden had maintained, centuries earlier, that rhyme was essential for elevated poetry; Gruenberg achieved the sublime in rhymeless verse. This was not a startling innovation; this was a reversion to masters of the epic who, consciously or unconsciously, did away with rhyme. More than three hundred years ago, in a few introductory lines to *Paradise Lost*, Milton stated that rhyme was "the invention of a barbarous Age, to set off wretched matter and lame Meeter . . ."

Gruenberg ignored rhyme in most of his poetry. His first book, almost totally rhymeless, opened with the cold and cruel assertion that rural life and idyllic peace have come to an end. Not unlike O'Neill in *The Hairy Ape* Gruenberg claimed that romantic ships and romantic seas have been stripped of their allure. And this was not his only point of affinity with American literature. Although he made only one cursory visit to the United States, he was profoundly influenced by its literary trends. Even if he had not confessed his indebtedness, it would have been easy to surmise the source of his long lines and the unorthodox meters in his work. From the point of view of form his poems stem from Walt Whitman, "that singing bundle of blood and flesh who deifies corporeality."[19] It was not only form which Gruenberg borrowed from the American poet. His glorification of the Palestinian pioneers owed an immense debt to the author of "Pioneers! O Pioneers!" But the two poets parted company in their attitude to life. Joyous exaltation, so characteristic of the work of the American poet, changed to gloom in the work of the Hebrew poet. The pioneers of Gruenberg are an aggrieved army of despair.

Gruenberg's generation grew up in agnostic carelessness. And his poetry documents a crisis of faith no less than the poetry of Baudelaire. But it is also the poetry of Jewry—its past uniqueness, its present suffering, its future greatness. In his romantic attachment to the past, in his attitude to the present, an amalgam of infinite pity for the victims of the holocaust and infinite disdain for the blind leaders who did nothing to avert the catastrophe, in his messianic certainty of a redemptive future, Gruenberg has merged his individual self with the national self. His choice of Palestine as a new home was an act of protest against the decadence of Europe and a search for moral revival on the ancestral soil. For Europe meant deceit and Palestine pointed to a new truth: regeneration through pioneers who were devising just structures of social living. The polarity of Jew and gentile—an absolute fact of European civilization—was to be avoided in the Land of Israel through a naive apotheosis of the Jew and a thoughtless derogation of the gentile. This retrogressive isolationism led Gruenberg to idealize the nationalistic pioneers who, in his verse, became pioneers of a new Hebrew nation as well as pioneers of a new world. He cast his lot with them:

> Therefore I will always be a poet wandering among you
> Southward, northward, under shadows of the cactus and the palm.
> I don't know how I made my verses under crosses and rejoiced,
> Even whispered to a girl there: you're the world and all the
> beauty.[20]

These verses, full of verve, teem with resentment; they also vaunt their pride in the new generation. The tumult and the shouting—this is the prevalent characteristic of Gruenberg's initial poetry where true ecstasy can rarely be separated from mere rhetoric. The light of calm, the brevity and the brilliance of traditional Semitic syntax—these are absent from his first book. In a later book he boasts: "I am not a master of conciseness."[21]

The howling incantations in raw, rasping verses were repeated in succeeding volumes. Even the motifs, the symbols, and the expressions did not change perceptibly. Pioneering dominated as the major theme, militarism effected some modification. The peasant-pioneer changed into a soldier-pioneer in his book *Belt of Defense and The Word of the Son of Blood*,[22] a reaction in poetry to the Arab attacks on Jews in 1929; and the soldier-pioneer is again the hero in *The Book of Accusation and Faith*,[23] a reaction to the civil war of 1936. The poet, a former Laborite in politics, became a Revisionist; the tenor of his work veered more and more into political pamphleteering. His poetry became political poetry.

But political poetry is a paradox. Poetry strives for permanence; politics thrive on transient achievements. Political poetry, like an old newspaper, loses its efficacy immediately after publication. A single sample can demonstrate how obsolete such poetry can become.

> Poland rose from the dead. Her white eagle screams from
> the Baltic to the Black Sea.
> Czechs and even Estonians, smallest of nations, have nationhood,
> Also Lithuanians and Letts, and Albanians, smallest of nations.
> This is the time which proclaims resurrection to peoples;
> It also calls us to rise in singing might,
> To fulfill the vision in the land of kings.
> We could have established alongside the Hebrew Sea,
> From Gaza to Tyre, the golden threshold of dreams
> To millions of Jewish exiles who would have returned with joy.[24]

These lines read today like a political speech of a remote past. Poland and Czechoslovakia and Albania are not the freest countries in the world. The Estonians, the Letts and the Lithuanians have lost their independence. The Hebrew Sea, like the Fascist *mare nostrum*, is a concept laden with superannuated and disastrous associations.

Political poetry cannot avoid critique of contemporary events. Gruenberg's is as merciless against Jewry's enemies as against Jewry's leaders: both neglect their duties to the spiritual center of humanity. Jewish leaders in the guise of Judases, sons of Josephus Flavius, and, especially, Sanballats, bear the brunt of the poet's opprobrium. Against them he ranges the new Sicarii: the pioneers. This sharp division of the nation into traitors and loyalists is not only an over-simplification of contemporary Jewish history; it is an unjust perversion of actualities.

In reminiscence of Klatzkin, who regarded the decline of Jewish religion in the nineteenth century as the third destruction of Jewish nationhood, Gruenberg used the term "third conflagration" for the abortive Jewish home which existed between the Balfour Declaration and the establishment of the Jewish state.[25] The Jews, according to the poet, have missed an opportunity which may not occur again in the next two thousand years: the immediate establishment of a viable state through mass immigration. The Balfour Declaration could have become the turning point in their history; it degenerated into United Jewish Appeals for money and into glorified ventures in philanthropy. The vision of Herzl paled; the pioneers persevered in their arduous task. Jewish youth turned in disgust from senile Zionism and flocked to aggressive communism which demanded personal inconvenience and sacrifice. Jewish bankers spent money on orphan asylums without distinction of race and creed, on synagogues "in Gothic style" but turned a deaf ear to the call of youth for a renascent land.[26]

Such is Gruenberg's indictment of Jewry in his political poetry: sneering, harsh, uncompromising. In the overwhelming majority of his poems he poses as a prophet:

> And I say unto your rocks: limbs of Jerusalem!
> Listen to the word of your prophet in Judah.
> Live and wait because it is meet to wait.
> With Ezekiel's vision of the valley of bones I see you, my rocks.[27]

Gruenberg persistently compared his lot to the lot of a new Jonah who had been driven away from his compatriots or of a new Jeremiah who was to be imprisoned by the British or of someone who was about to hurl his unheeded voice upon the entire diaspora. Belief in his prophetic gift led him to a hollow originality which consisted, for the most part, in reversing famous dicta or changing accepted symbols. Thus, in contradistinction to Spinoza, who maintained that "pleasure is man's transition from a lesser to a higher state of perfection,"[28] he wrote that joy is the ascent of the soul for the sake of descent to sadness. And he likened the leaders of the people, in perverse use of the legendary thirty-six saints, to thirty-six hidden incendiaries.[29]

Gruenberg's forced metaphors—the holy city of Jerusalem as the phylactery of the head and the valley of Esdrelon as the phylactery of the hand—are difficult to absorb.[30] And his efforts to shock are in questionable taste. All the houses of Tel Aviv are not "gluttonous and licentious retreats."[31] And the Hebrew writers of the twenties are worthy of higher esteem than that accorded them by Gruenberg in his pamphlet *Against Ninety-nine*. Gruenberg may have been right in emphasizing the extreme conservatism of contemporary Hebrew literature—the love of the poet for lyric inanity and the preference of the storyteller for the *Shtetl*, the little town. But in his vitriolic condemnation of all Hebrew writers he perpetrated an act of literary injustice.

> Perhaps this hard world will change in the far future—after my death and the death of the other good Hebrew writers. Perhaps this hard world will become softer than velvet. Then, perhaps, the Lord of the Idyll will appear and praise these ninety-nine Parnassians who persevered with the heroism of tenderness in the Hebrew tongue even in that difficult era.[32]

With unconcealed contempt for his confrères Gruenberg posed as the one author who felt the impact of the revolutionary times in the Holy Land and in the world at large. But all his contemporaries have been aware of the changing times and the changing environment, and some like Hazaz and Agnon made more enduring contributions to Hebrew literature out of their confrontation with contemporaneity than did Gruenberg.

> The peoples of the world have nine muses but we have a tenth one:
> Fragmented Judaism in the light of Messianism.[33]

This obsession with Judaism is Gruenberg's limitation and strength.

> I am not a poet for poetry's sake. On the anvil of
> the world stand the feet of millions of Jews.
> Their grave sorrow is my sorrow, their awesome majesty
> my majesty,
> And their end my end.[34]

The holocaust engulfed his poetic sensitivity and inundated his poetic output. It numbed Shlonsky and Alterman, Bertini and S. Shalom and the martyred Isaac Katzenelson. But Gruenberg consecrated a whole book of poetry to the holocaust: *Rehobot ha-Nahar*. Students of the Bible know that this is a place name[35] associated with princes of Edom, and that in Hebrew literature Edom symbolizes Rome, then Catholicism, finally Christianity in general. The place name may therefore be regarded as an indictment of the Christian world.[36] The impact of the indictment can be felt even in a feeble translation of a few verses:

> Nations have slain us with merciless wrath
> And ruined our remnant in the valley of woe.
> The beautiful sky and the pasture below
> Is terror to us. The violin's voice
> Is a rending of heart. If whitest snow
> Were to fall, we would think it was black
> Like black stripes on the prayer-shawl's field
> Of our father who is dead.[37]
> For now has come true what we dared not dread.

Rehobot ha-Nahar presupposes a spiritual experience and solidifies it into a value. For the Jew can never be the same after Dachau, Birkenau, and Ravensbruck, after Maidanek, Auschwitz, Treblinka, and the dozens of extermination places all over Europe. He is holocaust-branded. And, perhaps for generations to come, he will live with that experience both as a *memento mori* and a *memento vivere.*

Before the First World War the youthful Gruenberg published a poem on the inevitable theme of the sunset and the equally inevitable theme of love.[38] Ten years after the publication of that poem he had become the avant-gardist par excellence, the radical exponent of Hebrew militarism and—*mirabile dictu*—of Hebrew imperialism. It may be a forced and wild exercise in criticism to compare Uri Zevi Gruenberg with Virginia Woolf: his is the strident, hers the muffled voice; his is the anger, hers the resignation; his is the antiliterary pretense, hers the mannered, literary attitude to life. Yet, both enriched the national heritage with the undoubted originality of their quasi-prophetic insight: Virginia Woolf widened the resources of the English language and literature as surely as Uri Zevi Gruenberg widened the scope of the Hebrew language and its literature. She was uneven in a new prose technique just as he was uneven in his new poetic technique. She belongs, with Dujardin and Joyce, with the experimenters in a new type of novel: the stream-of-consciousness novel and the novel of dissociated sensibility. Gruenberg is the innovator of a new type of poetry—Whitmanesque in structure and texture, neoprophetic in the immediacy of perception and verbal communication.

Both Gruenberg and Woolf were occasionally great writers—she as a writer of poetry-in-prose, he as a writer of prose-in-poetry. The *Waves* is unique in English literature: common, almost disembodied emotions of personal and cosmic fear are expressed in a rich profusion of images. *Rehobot ha-Nahar,* Gruenberg's translation of the holocaust into poetry, is unique in Hebrew literature: an anguished, angry, sustained howl which will reverberate through the empty corridors of mankind's drugged conscience. That the genteel member of the Bloomsbury Circle should resemble the rough individualist and scion of a hasidic dynasty is, perhaps, an unexpected result of literary confluence. For Uri Zevi Gruenberg could have applied to himself—if he had the detachment of a Virginia Woolf—her evaluation of her own defects: "Watery and flimsy and pitched in too high a voice." Perhaps he would have had to change only one adjective: "fiery" for "watery."

Jacob Horowitz (1901–   ) who studied in Vienna and graduated as a Ph.D. from its university, became a simple laborer in mandatory Palestine in 1919, immediately after the First World War: a builder of roads, a construction worker, a fruit picker. But literary ambitions, developed under the aegis of expressionism prevalent in Austria and Germany, reasserted themselves and, eventually, took shape in a series of novels and stories and plays. The best of them, *Sown Light*,[39] borrowed its title from the Bible: Light is sown for the righteous.[40] In chronicling the tragedy of the expulsion from Spain, it conceives its characters—Jewish and non-Jewish—in larger than life dimensions; it lends them semilegendary stature; it commends utopian love as the ultimate solution to all evil. For this earth of ours, this "evil cedar" is potentially an island of light[41] where even Christian and Jew can live in harmony, where even an unholy love like that of Famula and Miguel can be sanctified.

The format of the novel—a supposed reproduction of medieval manuscripts in Hebrew and in other languages—lends itself to the expressionist stance. Protagonists and lesser characters have their disjointed moments of presentation. And the reader can mould them—in partnership with the author, the imaginary discoverer and publisher of the forgotten documents—into a coherent whole.

Sown Light is an epic of love; the *Gates of Defilement*[42] is an unholy aspiration to love. *Sown Light* is escape from defilement to purity, a sort of embarkation for the Island of Love; the *Gates of Defilement* are no more and no less than the title states: entering accommodations to a world of erotic decadence. Like so many Hebrew novelists from the days of enlightenment to our own days, from Peretz Smolenskin to Hayyim Hazaz, Horowitz indulges in exchanges of ideas among his characters or in long monologs which are disguised essays on the cultural malaise of the twentieth century. In *Gates of Defilement* culprits and originators of decadence like Tolstoy share the spotlight with the heroes of decadence in Max Nordau's *Degeneration*;[43] some are added to the gallery of intellectual perverts: Hamsun and Grosz, Weininger and Freud.

Deromanticized Eros in *Gates of Defilement* is paralleled by deromanticized Zionism. The pioneers who come to redeem the Land of Israel have to contend with harsh realities—tents instead of decent housing, porridge instead of satisfying meals, tea without sugar. In brief, they face hunger and fever and the unsavory realization that they are merely the fertilizing dung for the fields in the Land of Israel.

In another novel, *The World Which Has Not Yet Been Destroyed*[44] the tendency to discuss and philosophize almost destroys the fictive integrity of the author. Time and space lose their identity, continuity is violated in favor of discontinuity in quick, nervous assaults on art and life and immortality. In such a world, somewhat incongruously, the hope and the future lie in the hands of the young sabra in the Land of Israel and the young American in the United States: both are direct, realistic, unromantic and unsophisticated. Horowitz was probably unaware that he fathered a new romanticism. The young sabra and the young American have not redeemed the world. And the simplification of life, lived by both types on different levels and in totally different circumstances, did not lead to the millennium.

The four volumes of Horowitz's collected works[45] were awarded the Brenner Literary Prize. The linkage is not fortuitous: both writers were aware of Jewish and non-Jewish decadence, both despaired and hoped against hope.

6
The Neo-liturgical Poets: Isaac Lamdan; Judah Karni; Joseph Zevi Rimmon; Jacob Rimmon

THE severance of conjunctions which endanger the individuality of authors is a legitimate function of criticism. An inestimable amount of harm has been done to Goethe and Schiller, Keats and Shelley, Bialik and Tschernichowsky, because they have been lumped together by heedless historians of literature. In modern Hebrew poetry Gruenberg, Lamdan, and Shlonsky are jointly considered a triad of similar talents. It is true that the burden of Lamdan's poetry is pioneerism but his manner lacks Gruenberg's flamboyance or Shlonsky's verbal virtuosity. Stolid seriousness weighs upon the main body of his work.

Lamdan (1899–1954) who witnessed the disintegration of Russian Jewry, the pogroms in the Ukraine after the First World War and the incipient communization, was able to impart an intense ardor to his experiences of despair. When he settled in Palestine in 1920, he became a laborer on the land for a brief period of time. The experience accelerated the blend of personal and national hope in his poetry. It is this identity of personal and national stance which marks him as a neo-liturgical poet.

Fame and popularity rewarded his early efforts in Hebrew literature. The title of his first book, *Massadah*—a grim reminder of the battle which the last Judean zealots waged with Rome between 70 and 73 C.E.—became an ominous symbol for Jewish youth. Structurally, the book is a series of lyrics which combine into one long poem in six parts—a prolog, four vignettes of Massadah, an epilog. In the prolog a young man—perhaps the poet himself—escapes to **Massadah**

47

from the pogroms in the Ukraine after the First World War. He meets—not unlike Job—three friends who react in three different ways to the sufferings of Jewry. The first calls for vengeance, the second identifies with communism, the third, a traditionalist, is determined to wait for redemption. The refugee—or the poet—undeterred by his friends, pursues his way to Massadah and arrives at its gates.

In the succeeding parts of the poem, despair dominates the mood of the refugee poet and the other victims of persecutions which followed the First World War; there is even some slight temptation to return to the Ukraine. Yet the people around Massadah dance in an exaltation of despair. And the dancers represent the chain of tradition forged by the spiritual fire of Jewish generations as well as the heroism of pioneers who must avert the fate of Massadah from the Land of Promise:

> The dance of Massadah is aflame
>   And aflare.
> Clear the way, O destiny,
>   Beware.
> The fire of our feet will burn the stones,
>   As it must.
> The rocks will fall with a heavy fall
>   And turn to dust.[1]

In the penultimate part of the poem despair is at its highest, prayer at its intensest. And in the concluding section—"Yet"—the fighters for Massadah prepare for the final battle which is, in reality, the beginning of the endless battle for continuity.

This, then, is the plot of *Massadah*: the poet escapes in complete penury from the Ukraine to the Land of Israel, the new Massadah, in spite of Communist temptations in his native land. While Gruenberg's pioneers shout their defiance to the whole world, Lamdan and his pioneers sing their despair in muted strains. Behind their despair lurks hope. It is this divergence in tone and mood which constitutes the major difference between Gruenberg and Lamdan. But points of similarity are not lacking: both are deeply moved by Jeremiah; both are inspired by Hasidism; both believe that there is no road for Jewry except the road to Massadah; both are aware of the indifference of the diaspora to the ancestral land.

When *Massadah* was published in 1927, it was immediately recognized as the poem of the generation, the symbol of the third Aliyyah, the third wave of immigration which followed the First World War.

The last bastion of Jewish freedom became identified with national aspiration to a new freedom; the desperate reminder engendered a desperate hope. And when after Lamdan's death, the rubble of Massadah
was removed by the spade of the archeologist, possibly as a result of the
persuasive force of his verse, the visible reminders of the last battle for
freedom inspired an entire people to new resolves of endurance. Even
non-Jews—thousands of young people from Europe, Asia and Africa—
helped in wresting the pathetic treasures of Massadah from its rocky
soil.[2] And the head of the expedition, Yigael Yadin, who had been the
Chief of Staff during the battle of independence in 1948, became the
living symbol of the past-present syndrome of liberty.

It is interesting that the reactions in prose to the Ukrainian pogroms
made only a minor impact on the Hebrew reader. Neither *1919*, the
massive novel by Abraham Friemann, nor *The Stone Shall Cry Out*,
the collection of stories by M. Siko (1876–1949),[3] moved him as a literary experience of personal or transpersonal vigor.

Massadah was Lamdan's first and best literary venture. His succeeding books marked either a decline from its muffled pathos or a
tired repetition of its main motif. In his second book *In Triple Harness*[4]
Lamdan deplored the isolation of Palestine. A short trip to Europe
fortified him in his conviction that there was a gap between the new
center of Jewry and its moribund periphery. The disintegration of unity among the various segments of the people inspired in him a romantic certainty that *the triple harness* of Abraham, Isaac, and Jacob represented the cohesive mainspring of Jewish tradition. From that triad
there was no escape.

There is almost an erotic quality in Lamdan's prayers:

> O God! Like a miserable wren shivering with cold
> Take my heart into your big hand and warm it
> In these autumnal days . . .[5]

It is true Lamdan deliberately avoided love poetry;[6] but yet, his invocations of the Deity often resemble the frustrating advances of a rejected lover.

The books that followed, *In Triple Harness* and the volume of poems
From the Book of Days,[7] showed no change in the scope of Lamdan's
poetry or the means of expression. With monotonous insistence they
repeated the moods of *Massadah*. Only a few poems in Lamdan's last
book *At the Scorpions' Ascent*[8] signified an important departure. In his
identification with biblical and rabbinical personages—Jacob, Jonah,

Honi—he achieved an admirable empathy with the past which, at the same time, represented somehow the immediate present. Thus, Honi was not merely an ancient Rip Van Winkle, a relic of the past, in spite of his benefactions when he returned to his people after a long sleep of seventy years. He was, above all, the tragic leader who gives all to his charges and receives nothing in return.

> And what you loved here and what you lived for
> Vanished. Not a smile around.
> The distant sky—it heard your prayer.
> The earth—it killed its echoing sound.[9]

Thirty years after the composition of Lamdan's poem on Honi, Nathan Zach devoted two poems to "Honi the Circle-Drawer" and revived his imaginary experiences.[10] For Lamdan's generation Honi symbolized rejection and renunciation, for the present generation, he is the prototype of alienation. The monthly periodical *Gilyonot* which was founded by Lamdan in 1934 and ceased publication after his death reinforced his monolithic interest in the tragic fate of Jewry. The periodical was hospitable to a generation of younger authors who had wider interests. It served a loyal group of writers who hoped to become "a decisive and changing factor in literature . . . and even create a [new] era. . . ."[11] But for Lamdan Jewry was the focal force in the universe.

> I know we have a different sun.
> Why, then, do we lift our eyes to search it in the four corners of the earth
> When it is not there?
> We possess, outside the four, a fifth corner of the earth.[12]

The fifth corner, like Gruenberg's tenth muse, is Jewry in the throes of redemption, the only legitimate concern of Hebrew poetry in Lamdan's view. His poetical work abounds in the grace of faith but it lacks the grace of musical articulation.[13] Flat and colorless in tonality, it manages to survive by the sheer intensity of its inspiration and by the serious dedication to a single theme.

In the neo-liturgical poetry of Judah Karni (1884–1949) the fate of his people and the fate of his personality are as indistinguishable from each other as in an ancient psalm or in a medieval poem of Yannai.[14]

Before he settled in Palestine in 1921 he was always on the way to Palestine:

> You ask: Wanderer, what do you ask?
> I answer: For my homeland . . .
> I ask for homeground under my tired feet,
> A spiritual home for my exiled spirit . . .[15]

Karni seems to have known with surprising exactitude what home is, what home means:

> Homeland is form
> And hoard
> Where man clings to the earth,
> To the speckled earth of the Lord.[16]

The sights of the Holy Land inspired Karni with prayer poems about its tortured people and the unredeemed country. The heat of summer is the subject of a poem which reads like the recitation of a blessing:

> Blessed are you, summer day, burning with furnace heat
> On ancestral soil,
> Giving the fig and the date their honey
> And the grape its purple foil.[17]

Jerusalem is Karni's object of admiration in forty poems.[18] Even his love poetry, tinged as it is with national sorrow, lacks that personal note which is the soul of Eros. Conversely, when he writes about Chagall's picture "Death" or about the Labor leader Hayyim Arlosorov or about a historical personality like Rabbi Akiba, he cannot confine himself to objective portrayal, but describes his reactions to the picture, the man, and the ancient sage. It is rarely that he succeeds—as he does in the poem on Menahem Ussishkin—in translating correct observations into genuine portraiture:

> I see him march with pride and trust.
> Beneath him burns the sand.
> I see him hug the humble land.
> We've redeemed a span of its crust.[19]

Thematic monotony, unrelieved by novel technique or mature expression, mars Karni's poetry. The language and melancholy of Bialik inform his entire work and give it a derivative character.

Joseph Zevi Rimmon (1889–1958) is the purest neo-liturgical poet in modern Hebrew literature; Israel Najara, with his almost sensual perception of the divine rule and role in the world, is his closest poetic kin. As a traditionalist Rimmon manages to merge his personal idiosyncracies with his ancestral religion. But his religion is permeated with an unsophisticated pantheism. His mission as he sees it is to search for the echoes of God in the sea of the world's voices. The earth and the sky, the sun and the moon are drenched with such echoes.

> I lift my eyes to the mountains.
> To the mountains I lift my eyes.
> Hosts of angels soar on high.
> God's own glory bends with longing
> And descends upon the mountains.[20]

God is everywhere in Rimmon's God-intoxicated world. Without God the world is worthless:

> What's the music of days without God?
> What's the song of men without love of God? . . .
> What are sun and what are stars
> And what is all to me without you?[21]

Rimmon created numerous variations on the valuelessness of the world without God, on divine ubiquity in the universe. In a daring image he repeated an ancient insight:

> God glows on the lock of a girl.
> And God is love.[22]

The language of liturgy is even more metaphorical than the language of poetry. In its bold associations it transcends temporal limitations and reaches eternal expanses. In its perpetual movement from the timely to the timeless, from the timeless to the timely, it blurs the boundaries between becoming and being, history and eternity. Prayer, in Rabbi Kook's opinion, flows from the divine source and returns to the divine source. It is "a thirst for the living God,"[23] whose spirit "dominates all the possessions of the nation: the land, the language, the

history, the customs."[24] And Rabbi Kook, the mystic and potential
poet, was a close friend of Joseph Zevi Rimmon, the poet who was not
untouched by mysticism.[25] As a pre-First World War immigrant to the
Holy Land in 1908, he associated with Brenner and Alexander Ziskind
Rabinowitz[26] but, unlike them, he was untouched by socialist aspirations.

> When I arrived in the Land of Israel, I experienced a change. The
> gentile world grew distant. I was scented with a holy spirit in the
> air of the Holy Land.[27]

In a God-suffused universe Rimmon was content to pursue his vision
of holiness, as it was reflected in the sages of Israel and Babylon, Spain
and Italy, Poland and Germany. In his book *Trees of Life*[28] he jotted
down his musings about them, his random thoughts about their lives
and their teachings. And what he said about Rabbi Moses Alshek applies to him equally well: "Alshek makes a special impression because
of his holiness."[29] And yet, in spite of the protective wing of the Deity,
Rimmon was not an unregenerate optimist. In a posthumous poem he
deplored his loneliness in the unhappy strains of a secularist:

> I am alone in the Fall.
> I want to cry with the world.
> What is it to me—this sun of charity
> Which scatters indiscriminate rays.
>
> If spring hides
> And God hides,
> I fear man,
> His evil inclination since his youth.[30]

The mood of modernity—stark in its alienated despair—strikes the
unbeliever and the believer with equal impact. But the believer has a
refuge: God; and His word: the Torah. That is why Rimmon could pen
hymns to the Torah with the fervor of the enlightened when they ex-
tolled Hebrew, the holy tongue:

> When I searched for God,
> I found you, Daughter of the Heights.
> In a corner they covered you,
> But your lovers looked for your presence.

> You reign in mansions of grandeur
> While I am alone.
> I want to delight in your face,
> To find your love like happiness.
> All will know you in time to come.[31]

For Rimmon that time had come; he lived in a state of grace.

Jacob Rimmon (1903–   ) has not escaped the influence of his elder brother Joseph Zevi Rimmon. In the introduction to the volume of poems *Bush*,[32] S. Daniel remarks justly that "all his [Jacob Rimmon's] poems are a pure prayer with the prominent characteristics of a prayer: devotion, a still voice. . . ."[33] Medieval liturgy—especially the poetry of Judah Halevi—permeates their form and content.[34] What distinguishes them from his brother's poems is the greater variety of their themes. Not only the Creator and the created in their dramatic interrelationship but people and landscapes for their own sake fascinate Jacob Rimmon. Not only redemption in the religious sense but pioneerism in its secular aspect excites his imagination:

> I saw the worker's sweat on the plow's blade:
> My homeland shone in labor's beauty . . .[35]

Love, too, is Rimmon's favorite theme: it centers around his wife and it does not lack a religious strain:

> Give back to my spouse the familial joy,
> To my little ones, laughter.
> May my home bloom
> In your calm kindness.
> May your sun shine there,
> May shadows shun it.
> Would that my spouse did not weep,
> Did not suffer in furtive gloom.
> Would that your light did not dim
> In my little ones' eyes.[36]

That combination of familial and theological stance is probably the most characteristic feature of Jacob Rimmon's poetry. It appears and reappears in simple lines:

Protect my home, God.
I love you with a true love.
Out of the eyes of my little ones
I see your greatness.
Out of the heart of my spouse
I feel your heartbeat.
Protect my home, God,
And don't abandon it
Forever.[37]

Children come in for special attention in Rimmon's poetry; a whole book is devoted to them. Its title is fully justified: *Dawn Sings*.[38] The world is young, the heart of the child throbs with delight at the sight of planes, at the sound of a pipe played by a Galilean shepherd.

The poet's involvement in social problems as Secretary of the Department for Social Work in the municipality of Tel Aviv widened his horizons. In prose sketches entitled "From the Diary of a Social Worker"[39] he identified with the poor, the sick, the distraught, the shattered, but his undistinguished prose—beginning with a monograph on Rabbi Benzion Uziel and ending with a miscellany of characters[40]— must yield to the deep humanitarianism of his poetry.

7

The Poets of Jerusalem: Asaf Halevi; Jacob David Kamson; Ari Ibn Zahav; Zerah Halevi; Isaac Shalev

THE capitals of world culture, Athens and Jerusalem, were fixed in the memory of mankind by the phrases of poets: Athens, in Pindar's verse, was immortalized as the "violet-crowned city."[1] Jerusalem, in the Psalmist's verse, was "beautiful in elevation, the joy of the whole earth."[2] The Greek poet delighted in mere description, the Hebrew poet emphasized his elation at the sight of "the holy city,"[3] "the city of truth."[4] Even in talmudic times Jerusalem fascinated the beholder: Jerusalem took nine out of the ten measures of beauty which descended on the world.[5] Later generations spiritualized the city and endowed it with transcendent significance; the terrestrial city was changed into a celestial city. In Arabic tradition it was one of the four cities of paradise.[6] In Christian tradition and in Jewish sources it was the golden city;[7] and as late as 1973 the American novelist James A. Michener was moved to write about Jerusalem in these ecstatic words:

> . . . this noble city was intended from the moment of its inception to be a central source of light for a very wide community reaching from Cairo to Babylon. Here should be the great universities, western and eastern alike . . . great libraries should center here. . . . Religious experience would also center here, as it does now, and from Jerusalem would go forth Arabs and Jews and Druses and Circassians and all the citizenry of the various nations, to the profit of each.[8]

No major Hebrew poet neglected to extol the city—from Judah Halevi
to Moses Hayyim Luzzatto, from Solomon Ibn Gabirol to Saul Tschernichowsky. And no other city has been as frequently anthologized in
verse as Jerusalem.[9] In times of stress Jerusalem epitomized the hope
and the despair of Jewry. After the Six-Day War a mediocre song,
"Golden Jerusalem," by Naomi Shemer became number one on the Israeli hit parade[10]—perhaps because of skillfully incorporated talmudic, medieval, and modern elements which were instantly recognized
and cherished by masses of people. First sung publicly on May 15,
1967, in Jerusalem three weeks before the Six-Day War, it won immediate approbation and applause. It captured the audience with its
lively tune and mourning words—an unbeatable combination for a
Jewish audience. The empty cisterns, the deserted marketplaces, the
unvisitable remnant of the ancient sanctuary: these images broke all
the dams of sentimentality. The learned, a common breed in Israel, enjoyed the title and its allusion to a talmudic legend: Rabbi Akiba, in
his more affluent days, had given his wife a golden brooch in the shape
of Jerusalem in memory of the years of penury which she shared with
him. The learned also enjoyed the allusions to the Psalmist's vow never to forget Jerusalem[11] and to the well-known "Zionides" of Judah
Halevi. When Jerusalem was captured by the victorious soldiers in the
Six-Day War, the song was on everybody's lips. The modifications, authored by Shemer, transformed the song into a hymn of exaltation:

> We have come back now to the water cisterns
> And to the market place.
> The sound of the ram's horn resounds
> At the Wailing Wall in the ancient city.

"Golden Jerusalem" monopolized the singing and poetic mood of Israel for a year while Dalia Ben-David mourned the loss of the "beautiful boys" who conquered the city with their blood.[12] Four poets had monopolized Jerusalem as the almost exclusive domain of their poetry for
half a century: Asaf Halevi, Jacob David Kamson, Ari Ibn Zahav, and
Zerah Halevi. Asaf Halevi (1883–1933) seems to have been inebriated
with the Holy Land in general and with Jerusalem in particular. The
ancient capital has not lacked admirers for the past three thousand
years; but Asaf Halevi dedicated himself to the worship of Jerusalem
with the zest of a fanatic. A Russian Jew by birth and Alter Lewin by
name, he added to his pseudonym the proud sobriquet: *Ish Yerushalayim*, the Jerusalemite. This was the adopted city of his love from

the time he settled there as a boy of eight and this was to be the place of his ultimate rest.

> I want to be buried within your gates, golden city.
> At the foot of a proud tower or towering cypress,
> Within the shadow of the Sanctuary, under the wings of the Deity,
> To the echoes of a prayer melting in the sunset
> And the hymnal litanies of generations.[13]

Since death and burial in Jerusalem have been associated with the Mount of Olives, the thoughts of Asaf Halevi naturally turned to the sacred hill:

> This mount is the mount of revival and redemption.
> The builder of the land establishes a cemetery first
> To the pioneers who fall while they build;
> He raises monuments to the dead upon the high mountains,
> A testimony to coming generations.
> This is the mount of revival and redemption, this mount of mine,
>   the Mount of Olives.
> A voice at the end of days shall be heard on this mount,
> The sound of the ram's horn summoning the redeemed.[14]

The love of the poet for the mountainous terrain of Jerusalem was of such intensity that it left him with contempt for level terrain:

> I hate the plain. I love the mountains,
> The kings of the land and the kings of my heart.
> There dwells the vision, there prophets spoke.
> Therefore my heart is in the mountains.
>
> I hate the plain. I love the mountains.
> The mountains of Israel reign forever.
> I know new prophets will rise on the mountains.
> Therefore my heart is in the mountains.[15]

The all-pervasive influence of Bialik in form and language colored the high exaltation of Asaf Halevi's verse. And deliberate identification with ancient sun worshippers is strongly reminiscent of Tschernichowsky's sonnets to the sun.[16] But conscious orientalism—the palm as a sacred candelabrum for instance—was his own:

Who lit the lamps at night?
It was the High Priest on high,
The Moon in his glory who lit
Your beautiful candles, my palm.[17]

The poet even craves a palm on his grave so that he may sleep his eternal sleep under soothing sounds of the palm tree.[18] Orientalizing tendencies are so numerous in Asaf Halevi's poetry that he appended a vocabulary to his book[19]—the *diwan* as he significantly called it in imitation of Arabs who thus designated a collection of poems.

The eternal freshness and the immense appeal of Jerusalem permeate the poetry of Asaf Halevi. The city is his symbol of the land, the eternal aspiration of its people. And it yields its mystery only to the Jewish soul.[20]

Jacob David Kamson (1907–   ) captured in a minor key the elusive mysteries which hover over the sacred city and especially over the Western Wall:

Doves flutter above the Wailing Wall.
One is white.
Pious old men whisper withal:
God's light.

The white one flies all day on high
Above the holy stones.
Weary and faint, when night draws nigh,
It stands and moans.[21]

The dove, traditional symbol for suffering Jewry, has been transformed by a bold stroke of the imagination into the Deity itself and has acquired a mystical quality; yet the poem retains that simplicity which has characterized all the poems of Kamson. While Bialik, in "The Scroll of Fire," embellished the simple legends of the first destruction of the Sanctuary with labored allegories, his younger contemporary preserved faint echoes of the national tragedy in unpretentious verse. He may have lacked the soaring imagination and the technical skill of Bialik but he created a few poems of incomparable tenderness about the Holy City.

The ancient splendor of Jerusalem was only one aspect of Kamson's poetry. Modern Jerusalem—its occupation, its liberation—was also of intense interest to the poet.

> The women of Zion
> Kissed the tires of cars and tanks.
> Wrapped in shawls of prayer, with tears of joy in their eyes,
> The elders of Zion embraced
> And kissed the defenders,
> The conquerors of Jerusalem.
> Happy the eye that saw that sight
> Not seen even by the men of vision,
> The prophets in Jerusalem.[22]

These simple verses were representative of the unsophisticated dedication of Kamson to Jerusalem. No other subject aroused his poetic sensibilities, his sense of humor, his anecdotal strength. A nonagenarian lady reacts to the establishment of the State of Israel with typical self-mockery:

> But I am ninety . . .
> And if, in a little while,
> Messiah will come,
> How will I find the strength
> To live forever?[23]

For twenty-two years—from 1926 to 1948—Kamson wrote his poems about the Holy City and collected them in a volume which he entitled *Jerusalem*. No other name would have done them justice.

> When I remember your name, Jerusalem,
> Like God's name,
> My soul is on the wing.[24]

The art of Kamson combined biblical reminiscences with idolatrous adoration. And it remained, magically and miraculously, in the realm of pious poetry.

The popular novelist Ari Ibn Zahav (1889–1972), the author of the historical novels *David and Bathsheba* and *Jessica, My Daughter*,[25] focused his poetic oeuvre on Jerusalem and entitled one of his five books of poetry on the eternal city *Within Jerusalem*[26] because, for him, the world did not seem to exist outside its walls. Like Asaf Halevi and Jacob David Kamson he produced surprising effects of depth with unsophisticated verse. Like them he was not born in Jerusalem; he adopted it with unrestrained love.

> Be blessed, Jerusalem, you have fulfilled my dreams of childhood:
> To belong to a land of my own . . .
> When I tread on your threshold, my eyes light up:
> This is the city of the Bible.
> When I look at your sky and your earth I feel:
> You are mine and I am yours.
> The Book of Books is holy to all the nations,
> But it is my book, my Bible.
> Foreign masters rule now; they may rule in the future,
> But you are betrothed to me and you are mine.[27]

Jerusalem was not merely the symbol of the past; it was eternally present:

> For the city is not the capital of yesterday, the capital of a day
> before yesterday,
> It is the princess of cities,
> The capital of the eternal people, the goal of longing
> Of immemorial generations . . .[28]

Jerusalem languished in desecrated occupation, but it would become the mother of a future nation:

> You are about to bear a nation, and a nation is not born in a day.
> Suffer your pangs in joy and exaltation.
> In a little while your little one, your nation, will hug you.
> Jerusalem, don't mourn, don't mourn, Jerusalem.[29]

What lends special piquancy to the poetry of Ari Ibn Zahav is its style. Ancient and medieval allusions to Jerusalem are so well integrated into the texture of his art that they are almost unnoticeable. With disarming modesty the poet confesses that he does not pretend to be even the minor poet of Jerusalem. The spirit of the past and the anonymous guardians of the walls hover there in "a pillar of cloud of tears" and "a pillar of fire of hope."[30]

In sum, the poet was a stranger in the world until he settled in Jerusalem. And when he first set foot in the Holy City, it was not as a new-comer but as someone who has returned and knew each path and each hill in its heart from the time of his birth and before his birth.[31] It was an adopted home that became more than home.

> I don't know at home as I know abroad what you have given me.
> Small of stature and spirit, I am like a giant among the thousands
>   of brothers in exile.
> They are cast down, I ride on the heights of clouds,
> I breathe your air of redemption, they inhale the alien air.
> When I come back to your gates, when I stand before your eternity,
> I bow down again as always—small, very small, a mere firefly,
> A mere speck against your mountains, a passing butterfly before
>   the one who lives forever.[32]

This intensely autobiographical poem is permeated with biblical phrases from Isaiah, the Psalms, Daniel.[33] They are skilfully woven into the text, they give it the proper patina of age. The minuscule sta-ture of the poet—a physical fact—is exploited with abandon: in the diaspora he is a giant. This antithesis begets another: the air of prom-ised freedom in Jerusalem, the air of slavery abroad. Finally the third antithesis with its triple metaphor: the smallness of the poet's sta-ture—a speck, a firefly, a butterfly—against the mountains of Jerusa-lem, before the Almighty Himself whose word came out of Jerusalem. In its simplicity, in its compactness, in its brevity the poem is a monu-ment to the poet and to Jerusalem.

The intense identification with Jerusalem on a subjective plane: this is Ari Ibn Zahav's contribution to the poetry about the Holy City. In rare instances of collective identification he appropriates material from Jewish liturgy. When he does—as in imitation of a Falasha pray-er—he creates a poem of such ritual significance that it resembles a prayer by a medieval poet for use in the synagogue:

> All hearts hope for Jerusalem.
> All souls ask about Jerusalem.
> From the banks of the Vistula,
> From the shores of the Danube,
> From the edge of the Rhine,
> From the ends of the Mississippi
> To the ends of the Ganges . . .
> From every hell

And every heaven
All hearts hope for Jerusalem,
All souls ask about Jerusalem.[34]

Small wonder that David Yellin, the Jerusalemite par excellence, paid Ari Ibn Zahav the supreme compliment: "Jerusalem has found its poet."[35] Perhaps more than any other contemporary he deserved the sobriquet: Poet of Jerusalem.

Zerah Halevi is an intriguing phenomenon: scion of a hasidic family and a volunteer in the Jewish Legions after the First World War, a tinker by occupation[36] and a native third generation Jerusalemite. Remote from literary coteries and close to Old Jerusalem where he spent his entire life, he enjoyed a double advantage. For others Jerusalem was many things: nostalgia, tradition, ancient glory, promise of redemption. For him

It's the city of my birth, the city
That cradled my earliest years.
It's the city where I heard in the dawn of my days
Its wondrous music in tears.[37]

Sensitivity to music,[38] thirst for knowledge: both inclinations were stifled by a strict father who was a recipient of welfare and feared the loss of possible income through future earnings of his son. He was self-taught and he owed no one the deeply felt quality of his verse with its twin theme—the holocaust, which he did not experience personally, and Jerusalem, which he experienced daily. More than any other spot in the city the Wailing Wall has been held in special affection by Zerah Halevi. And to the Wailing Wall he dedicated seven poems.[39]

The heroes of Zerah Halevi—like his grandfather's heroes—are the mystics of the Holy Land: Rabbi Solomon Alkabez who appears to him in a vision and asks Rabbi Simeon bar Yohai to intercede on behalf of his people and hasten its redemption.[40] But unlike his grandfather, Zerah Halevi also worships Naphtali Herz Imber, the author of the national hymn.

Some poets have lived in Jerusalem physically or spiritually. Zerah Halevi is both in the Holy City and of the Holy City.[41]

Of the two Jerusalems—the celestial and the terrestrial—it is the former that was the object of greatest love. But in recent times the Jewish and the gentile worlds witnessed a despiritualization of the city which has found its most articulate expression in the poetry of Isaac Shalev (1919–   ). As one who grew up in Jerusalem, he was familiar with its nooks and crannies as well as with its architectural treasures and kaleidoscopic landscapes. He gave expression to that familiarity in his simple verse that did not stunt the narrative while it concentrated on the lyrical overtones.

O city, my city . . . city of tin and slush
Of fallen fences, tottering walls, peeling plaster . . .

But in a moonlit night, there's no beauty, no solace like
                    that of your asphalted want

For the moon is good, very good to you; it covers what
                    has to be covered

And swaths your wound in white and spreads the white
          tablecloth on the grey table of your dailiness . . .[42]

It is for this city that the poet reserves his secular hosannas and hallelujahs:

Praise it with slamming of doors,
With banging breakage of panes.
Praise it with fluttering laundry
Hung by the poor of my city . . .[43]

For Shalev Jerusalem is a tangible reality—Jerusalem as seen from the Castel, from the approaches of Abu Gosh, from the automobile road which leads from the lowlands around Tel Aviv to the high plateau, to Jerusalem "the mountainous, strong and stony"[44] which was already cherished by the Psalmist when he invoked the city "beautiful in elevation, the joy of the whole earth . . ."[45]

So much for Jerusalem observed from a distance. Seen from inside, it teems with poor neighborhoods like Romemah and Mahaneh Yehudah as well as more affluent enclaves like Talbiyeh and Rehavyah. The smells and the scents of the pungent foods—kabab and falafel—as well as the aromas of fruits in season—cactus and pomegranate, grapes and melons—seem to send the poet into transports of delight. Yet his Jerusalem is not as terrestrial as he pretends. He is aware of the biblical city, of the "lone, biblical eagle"[46] on the mountains and of the biblical camel; the city where every tree is a harp which blooms and puts forth "fruit of tender melody."[47] But even this ancient Jerusalem is somehow part of the new city that has been redeemed by the gallant young fighters who have died that it might live, who have been kissed by the Almighty when he closed their dream-filled eyes.[48]

In a pungent parallel in prose, the poet Hayyim Guri describes the Battle of Jerusalem in the Six-Day War. This is a vivid document from the first faint realization that the fighting has begun through the grim account of the bloodshed to the cessation of fire.

> The war has begun, I said to the people who congregated in groups on the road. I think that a bit of excitement crept into my voice . . . The people did not budge. They seemed very calm, matter-of-fact—as if something which had been in the realm of hypothesis for a long time had become clarified to them. For that morning all Israelis received the news of the war as something which had to come—without joy and without fear. . . . Yet here and there a chin trembled or color changed in the face.[49]
>
> That was Monday, June 5, 1967, in Jerusalem, that was the inevitable beginning of individual tragedies which are seldom reported by newspapers. An old Arab. Not far from him a killed goat . . . He said that when there was bombing all around, his wife ran to save the goat. But the goat was killed. His wife was also killed.[50]

And then the grim dénouement on Wednesday, June 7, 1967: "Now begins a new chapter. The name: Israeli Army of Occupation in an Arab City."[51] That chapter is the axis; everything turns around it, everybody clings to it with desperate fascination, Jew and Moslem and Christian. Impotent ire was the common response to the desecration of graves by Jordanians on the Mount of Olives. But there was also the uncommon response of Ezra Sussman, a poet more sophisticated than Shalev.

> That split
> Cadaver
> I stand by
> I look
> I fear
> I hide my face
> I flee

From the woman in black
With the seven black sheep
Like seven gates—
Black
From this brightness
From this glory
From this desolation
From this mistiness
From this calm
From the glory of losses
And not to come back
And not to see
And not to phantasy
Any more.[52]

In the nervous lines, emitted like sobs, senseful and senseless, the agony of one poet at the sight of the desecrated dead has been transmitted to all the living.

8
The Revolutionizer of the Hebrew Language: Abraham Shlonsky

THE lingual genius of Abraham Shlonsky (1900–1973) has revitalized the Hebrew language. Many of his poems, even those which will not stand the test of time, may eventually serve as research material for future investigators of Semitic philology. Deftly, almost magically, he coined neologisms and related unrelated words with bold artifice. Sometimes he grafted sexual expressions onto non-sexual objects:

> Swollen with pregnancy the black earth lies on its back
> And the wind with his hairy palm pats her bare belly.[1]

Sometimes Shlonsky joined such disparate objects as trees and money:

> The trees put out their hands and threw their pennies
> To the autumnal charity-box.[2]

Sometimes Shlonsky indulges in language for language's sake and eliminates all conative and emotive content. This is a literary abuse which the mercurial poet shares with most virtuosi of language. Swinburne sacrifices meaning to music, Joyce plays havoc with English for the playful pleasure of destruction and invention.

Like Gruenberg, Shlonsky deliberately set out to shock and surprise in his work and in the literary reviews under his editorship.[3] Unlike Gruenberg, he was not exclusively interested in Judaism. He paid his debt to pioneerism and holocaustism.[4] But in dramatic poems which made his debut in Hebrew literature he celebrated the decadence of European civilization. Linear time was not essential in these strange eruptions of grotesque morbidity. Tubal Cain and Job, Moses and Elijah, Jesus and the Messiah showered messages of doom and desolation on the reader. In later poems Shlonsky would confront such disparate entities as Maimonides and Bakunin, Rabbi Shneur Zalman of Liady and Alexander Sergeevich Pushkin.[5] And just as he dared to wrest impossible antitheses from alien cultures, so he burdened his metaphors with bold indecencies.

> Here lies above us . . .
> A filthy, wilted sky.
> Its soiled buttocks
> Pour on us autumnal drizzles.[6]

This pretentious vulgarity enjoys a vast vogue in modern literature. It can be illustrated by numerous effusions of a similar nature in all the literatures of the West. Such a poem as "Song for the Clatter Bones" by an Irish contemporary Frederick Robert Higgins forms a perfect counterpart to the verbal acrobatics of the Hebrew poet.[7]

Deep pessimism pervades Shlonsky's poetry. Our days run on without purpose, our work is void of meaning: this seems to be the burden of his song. With dulling emphasis he reiterates his desperate refrain: we come from nowhere and to nowhere we return. Europe crumbles in the dollared hands of America; Columbus, like a new Noah, rides in his ark to nondestinations. In a stanza which borrows religious vocabulary from the Psalms and metaphor from rabbinic sources he sums up his philosophy of life:

> We pursue the gazelle of mere
> Vanity. We place our gold on the horn of the hunted deer.
> We carve God's name on the horn of the deer in the moor.
> For the Leader. A Psalm of the Poor.[8]

The triteness of a theme was no deterrent to Shlonsky who furnished it with new content and refurbished it completely.

> The sun is the driver of the world.
> His rays—the reins.
> The cosmic chariot runs on and on.

Is there an end to the roads, to the lanes?

All of a sudden the driver's orphaned.
Soon, very soon he will have said
Kaddish. The casket is brought from somewhere.
And in it—the dead.

The reins drop. The wondrous driver
Wraps himself in his coat.
The night comes out and hangs its lanterns
By rote.

All of a sudden all feel the shudder,
The keen dismay.
In widowed clothes the night leans gently
Over the corpse of the day.[9]

Sunset is a banal theme in the literatures of the world. Yet Shlonsky
has succeeded in shedding a new sorrow on the death of day and infus-
ing a new vitality into the Apollonian myth. The unusual metaphors
change a well-known phenomenon into an unusual experience. But
Shlonsky has done more than that; he has applied funeral rites of the
Jews to the nonhuman world. When the sun says its mourning prayer
over the dead body of the day, the whole creation seems to be cast into
an abyss of gentle despair.

Like many contemporary Hebrew poets who have read Avigdor Hameiri Shlonsky, too, indulged in parental romanticism. In sharp antithesis to his melancholic sophistication he praised childish naiveté
and achieved genuine lyricism in his cycle of poems *To Father and
Mother:*[10]

We had tiny feet.
We were the chicks of God, the joy of mom and dad.
And how we loved to wade
In every puddle,
In every pond.

The rain is good to those who wait for rain
In quiet fields.
But rains are even better
To those who have those tiny feet.

For what is better than—unnoticed by the gaze
Of mom and dad—to sneak outside and run
With bare and tiny feet, when rain stops in the street,
On pavements washed by rain.

And then, when somewhere far away
The puddles hurry,
The puddles huddle,
To knead earth's dough
And feel the tongues of mire in all the fingers.

Blessed be the tiny feet
On the deserted, distant roads.
And blessed be God,
Who gladdens infants' hearts with rain.

Love and devotion and self-pity were unmarred by the artificiality of
lingual innovations which prevailed in other poems, but were absent
from the cycle *To Father and Mother*. The lyricist withstood the temptations of the master of language.

In numerous translations Shlonsky used his lingual acumen to great
advantage. He paid, with interest, the debt he owed modern Russian
literature. For he grew up in a Russian environment and could not escape the impact of Mayakovsky, the brash and official poet of the incipient Soviet Revolution, and Yesenin,[11] the more subtle, suffering
and frequently maligned hooligan-poet of the twenties. The former's
artificiality and the latter's Villonesque bohemianism were the twin
stars which illumined his poetic journey through life. It was out of a
deep sense of gratitude, then, that he recreated Russian poets in Hebrew. His masterful translation of Pushkin's *Evgeni Onegin* earned
him recognition in Russia. He was feted in Moscow after the appearance of his revised version of *Evgeni Onegin* in 1965. While his original poetry effected a lingual rejuvenation, his translations enriched
modern Hebrew literature with Russian classics, and with French and
English masterpieces like Romain Rolland's *Colas Breugnon* and
Shakespeare's *Hamlet* and *King Lear*.

Shlonsky was the only Hebrew poet of the twentieth century who
may be said to have created a school. In this respect he resembled Ezra
Pound who, although not a major poet himself, did more for the development of modern English and American poetry than any of his con-

temporaries. Lingual excesses, sensational imagery, punning pyro-
technics, obscure allusions, daring neologisms—all the devices which
distinguished both poets, made Shlonsky the great representative of
l'esprit nouveau. But our shockproof generation is no longer shocked by
Shlonsky, and his preoccupation with decadence is foreign to the embattled Israel of the seventies. Shlonsky has become a classic; admired
but not read, honored but not heeded.

9
In the Wake of Shlonsky: Nathan Alterman; Raphael Eliaz; Abraham Halfi; Joshua Tan-Pai; David Rokeah; Solomon Tanny; Noah Peniel; Jacob Orland; David Avidan; Alexander Pen

CONTEMPORARIES of Shlonsky felt the impact of his poetry on their work: Pen, Talpir, Eliaz, Pomeranc, Halfi, Tan-Pai, Almi, Rokeah, Peniel, Orland, Avidan. The roster could be swelled by lesser and less-known poets. Only two emancipated their later poetry from Shlonsky's preponderant influence: Leah Goldberg (1911–1970) and Nathan Alterman (1910–1970). The latter—under the spell of Shlonsky's lingual innovations and Gruenberg's preoccupation with the fate of Israel as a country and as an ethnicity—became the poetic spokesman of his generation. From the forties till the end of the sixties his voice was the predominant poetic voice in the country. As a poet, he outdistanced all his contemporaries in popularity—with the possible exception of Agnon. But his claim to greatness cannot be substantiated by either his poetry or his plays, his journalistic efforts in verse like *The Seventh Column*[1] or his newspaper essays which advocated absorption of Arab lands under the domination of Israel after the Six-Day War.[2] His contribution to Hebrew poetry—a variation on Shlonsky's daring modernism—excelled in lightness of touch, deftness in versification, ease of rhyme and rhythm. Though technically Ogden Nash may be regarded as most nearly related to him in American literature, Alterman had

72

no ambition to tickle his reader's funny bone. It is possible that France where he studied agriculture in Nancy imparted a certain Gallic grace to his poetic oeuvre. And it is no mere accident that, among his numerous translations, plays of Racine and Molière take their distinguished place.

Like Shlonsky, his younger contemporary created novel effects in his nature poems. Clouds are elephants of heaven who "wallow . . . in the roseate mud of the sunset;[3] the moon appears sometimes "on the spear of the cypress,"[4] and sometimes "clothes the window with waxen masks."[5]

A genuine sorrow informs Alterman's nature poems.

> Out of the lakes the waters look at us.
> The tree stands still
> With its red earrings.
> God! I shall never forget
> The sorrow of your immense toys.[6]

The mad rush of days and nights is one pole of Alterman's poetry; young love with its inevitable end is its other pole.

> All of us, my child, shall rest without ourselves . . .
> All of us shall be the time which passed away.[7]

The mystery of the female body: like all true poets Alterman seems to have made the original discovery of its pristine charms:

> Your legs are a hymn to the goldsmith's art,
> Your figure—cuddled and bright.
> The constellations observe you,
> The polar bears roar at your sight.
>
> The fields that have paled, the trees with their trains,
> They stand in your light, in your breeze.
> Night, dizzy with doves in their cote,
> Lights for you cherry trees.[8]

Even in his nationalist poetry Alterman utilizes daring metaphor with pleasing obscurity:

> Who can look at you, my country, with obtuse

Eye? You bare like lightning names and things.
The all-blue giant, caught in your sweet noose,
Languishes. The Golden Scalpel stings.[9]

The solemn clarity of Israel lives in these lines in spite of their excessive burden of imagery. Originality atones for the congestion of metaphors: the all-blue giant, the sky, and the golden scalpel, the sun, point to the inexorable ferocity of the tropical day which threatens all living things with extinction.

There is an immense din in Alterman's poetry, a wealth of provocative expressions, the sound and smell of circuses and marketplaces, inns and innkeepers' daughters. This clutter and clatter—especially in his light verse—is a delight to the senses. It charms with its musicality and shares a certain inventiveness in thematic felicity with Ogden Nash and e.e. cummings.

The first volume of Alterman's poems, *Stars Without*, was followed by *The Joy of the Poor, The Songs of the Plagues of Egypt, Summer Party, The Oppressing City*, and *The Book of Riddles*.[10] In them he accomplished the transition from the personal to the transpersonal: he raised nationalist symbols to universal significance. The ten plagues, for instance, became representative realities of wars which visit humanity in eternal recurrence. *The Oppressing City* and *Summer Party* celebrated the Jewish people, its excellence, its martyrdom, its uniqueness; the former, in narrative forms, the latter through dramatic and allegorical personages. And through irony. At the end of *Summer Party*, for instance, the poet warned his readers against eisegesis, against conversion of explicit verse into arcane profundities. But he nullified his own warning with charming counterwarning:

. . . Not every verse is intimation.
The city is a city. The street, a street . . .
The city is a city. Though it's obvious that, at times,
The city is a man, the man is time, the time is summertime . . .
. . . There is no denial
That, without symbols and metaphors, the poem is no poem.

In the posthumous *Book of Riddles* Alterman made two observations which encapsulated his *Weltanschauung:* man as mystery, the world as mystery. In his own phraseology: "Man is a riddle that solves riddles" and "The world is a riddle but the riddle is a world."[11] For Alterman the mystery was the thing; the solution, the resolution mattered less. The antiquity of the riddle, the enigma of existence—these were fascinating realities for a poet who delighted in the acrobatics of the human mind but often bent his verse to nationalist exigencies. This was, perhaps, the unique source of tension in Alterman's poetry—a conviction of the eternal mystery of existence and a compulsion to cope with the harsh realities of his people. Like Jorge Luis Borges, but less sophisticated than the South American spinner of tales, Alterman was an adroit manipulator of the unmanipulatable: the mechanism of perception, the associative leap, the intricacies of such farraginous processes as thinking, feeling, imagining.

The riddle was the ideal vehicle of versification for Alterman. It made less rigorous demands than the ballad which was his other favorite genre or the elegy which provided no latitude for his humor. It transcended national boundaries—a welcome relief for a poet who was totally committed to nationalist aspirations. For the riddle, like the folktale and the folksong, wandered from nation to nation. And it was brief, transparent: "The Hive and the Bees," a text of four lines, sufficed to impart originality to a standard parable of diligence:

> A city closed, enclosed.
> No locks, no
> Bars. All citizens knead in endless toil
> Flower-dough.[12]

The hive is an enclosed city like Jericho before Joshua's conquest. The bees are the citizens who knead the booty taken from flowers, flower-dough, with breathless industry. Sometimes two lines—as in the riddle about a man with an enormous hat—satisfy the poet's requirements for an original parable of vanity:

> Here stands a man and can't be seen.
> His hat is bigger than his mien.[13]

Ancient riddles were the prime possessions of humanity. They were peopled by the ram, the goat, the donkey, and primitive utensils like hoes and saws, bells and barrels. That fact was another incentive for Alterman who used the genre with abandon and achieved in it and through it transition from complication to simplicity. In that sense the *Book of Riddles* can serve as a *point d'appui* for the reevaluation of the poet's work. And not only the *Book of Riddles*. It seems that, a few years before his death, the poet searched for new departures in his work. The need for expression in prose manifested itself with increasing intensity. A satiric story, interspersed with a few poems, *The Last Mask*,[14] served as a new beginning in fiction although the theme might have been a fitting subject for one of the longer pieces in *The Seventh Column*. Is it a satire on the bureaucracy of Israel or does it imply ironic contempt for human frailty? The arrival of the one hundred thousandth immigrant from the rich West is blown up to a grand exercise in public relations. A state celebration, banquets, empty speeches are being prepared with feverish diligence. But the exact count yields only ninety nine thousand nine hundred and ninety nine immigrants. Since all arrangements have been made at Haifa to receive the ship and the nonexistent lucky number with state honors, falsification of the records is the only remedy for this embarrassing situation. Somehow the truth surfaces and presents the citizenry with an occasion for hilarious contempt of the authorities. It is a thin tale: the chief characters are slogan-mouthing caricatures rather than real people, the plot is a mess of slapstick situations.

At his death Alterman stood on the plinth of public attention. Little wonder that posthumous publication of his unpublished work proceeded at a brisk pace in Israel. Even ephemeral pieces like book reviews and landscape impressions which originally appeared in newspapers were collected in a book.[15] The prose bordered on journalistic jingoism; it was the culmination of Alterman's political poetry which was collected in the two volumes of *The Seventh Column*. Both the political prose and the political poetry were deeply rooted in daily events and could not be fully understood today without recourse to the yellowed pages of the press of former years. The ephemeral remained ephemeral and often died with the death of the event. Alterman tried to convert this disadvantage into an advantage:

> Learn from the daily paper:
> Your life is a single day . . .
> And this your reward and your gain:
> You hear how the press impresses
> Tomorrow's page.[16]

Rarely does Alterman's poetry in *The Seventh Column* rise above the ephemeral as in "The Silver Salver,"[17] which is a clever paraphrase of a dictum by Weizmann: a state is not given to a people on a silver salver. In the poem a young man and woman combine in their stark existence the ruggedness of pioneers and the arduous labors of defense.

They stand before the people and say: we are the silver salver on which you were given the State of Israel. Usually Alterman eschews the purely serious stance in the poetry of *The Seventh Column*. The ironic or satirical comment on an event is his favorite ploy, the ballad or near-ballad his favorite genre. Set to music they become a popular substitute for art.

It is not an accident that Alterman's vast work of translation includes not only plays by Racine and Molière and Shakespeare, but also Scottish and English ballads. That genre fascinated the poet throughout his life. It imparted folk piquancy to the poems in *The Seventh Column;* it filled almost a fifth of *The Oppressing City* with a single ballad, "The Song of Ten Brothers," based on a popular folk song in Yiddish.[18] In Alterman's version it is set in his favorite locale—an inn—and, in rambling circumlocution, it purports to sing of wine and the din on the roads and in the market places which are "the bridge and not the wall."

The art of the ballad hovers over the entire *Book of Hurdy-Gurdy*[19] written for children and absorbed by adults with special delight. To cite but one single example: the poem on the "Travels of Benjamin of Tudela"[20] depicts the departure of the medieval traveler for foreign lands and the wondrous sights, including the fire-spitting dragon. In the rush of its breezy lines, in a mixture of the miraculous and the real, in the singing refrains the poem can only be characterized as a ballad:

> He saw the giants prowl and prance,
> The dwarfs of smallest stature.
> He saw uncouth barbarians dance
> A dance like tarantella.
> He saw their queen: a captive by
> The name of Miss Adela.
> Ah, what a brilliant traveller
> Ah, what a brilliant traveller
> Was Bejamin of Tudela.

The art of the balladist informs even Alterman's plays written in the last decade of his life: *The Inn of the Winds, Kinneret, The Theorem of Pythagoras,* and *Queen Esther.*[21] The first play dramatizes the artist's conflict between loyalty to his art and loyalty to his love. At the hour of mystery between the death of night and the birth of day, the chief protagonist of the play, Hananel, decides to abandon his home and his sweetheart, Naomi, in order to fulfill his mission. The parallel between the fates of the two individuals—the man as artist, the woman as object and subject of love—is carried out throughout the play in the form of allegorical characters: the beggar and the female innkeeper who impinge on the life of Hananel; the money-changer and the money-changer's son who dog the life of Naomi. The hurdy-gurdy, beloved object in Alterman's poetry, acts as substitute for a Greek chorus and, at the same time, as a grotesque imitation of art.

The second play bares reality with merciless realism. It is the portrayal of the cooperative movement in its inception in the second decade of the century, the dramatic tale of the hard and harsh adjustments of the individual and his needs for privacy within the imperatives of the collective. The third and fourth plays convert reality into absurdity—a common practice in the work of Ionesco and Beckett, Pinter and Genet. What the last two plays lack in subtlety, they compensate for in obscurity. *Queen Esther* may be regarded as a sort of musical which plays havoc with the notion of time; the past impinges on the present, the present informs the past; simultaneity of time replaces succession of time. And the hilarity of the ancient *Purimspiel*, a model for the play, is twisted and bent to the none too hilarious exigencies of Alterman's muse. Even Mondrish—the Jewish harlequin—is more tragic than comic in this play. *The Theorem of Pythagoras,* Alterman's only play in prose, poses the problem of confrontation between man and machine. It is a difficult play and according to the author, it has been misunderstood. In a long epilog[22] he endeavored to clarify his intent. The computer Pythagoras, in imitation of his distinguished namesake, the philosopher of Samos, represents the scientific interpretation of the world and sees the world as a number. But there are things which a number is impotent to express; and it is this conflict between the measured and measurable on the one hand, the unmeasured and immeasurable on the other that is the plot of the play. Alterman, unlike critics of technology, regards the computer as "a positive character," as a "precise and disciplined and loyal and powerful tool." Science, represented by the computer, does not deny "what is beyond logic . . . but beats out of logic a path to what is beyond it."

All of Alterman's plays suffer from overallegorization and the consequent emasculation of plot and tension. The characters lack vitality; they resemble marionettes which are doing the will of their author. But his Midas touch converted everything he wrote into popular successes. Even an early play, *Solomon the King and Salmi the Cobbler,*[23] adapted from a text by Sammy Gruniman, became the rage of Israel in the sixties in the new form of a musical.

The articles written in the last three years of the poet's life were collected in a book *The Triple Thread*[24] which is the very antithesis of his poetry: turgid, redundant, serious *ad nauseam*. But they contain shrewd analyses of contemporary problems and they expose a certain flaccidity of the national fibre after many frustrating years since the Six-Day War:

> The prophets of Zionism saw reality—the true reality, not one falsified and fabricated by our enemies and by ourselves today. They saw a poor Arab settlement without ethnic and political identity in a land subject to all sorts of boundary combinations . . . If Zionist colonization struggled with this problem, it struggled for the Arab settler who had to be compensated and whose existence had to be secured but not for the Palestinian Arab nation. Such a nation did not exist. Herzl who said that the problem of Zionism is to return a people without a land to a land without a people was not shortsighted; he saw the truth and articulated it, the eternal truth . . . which made the return possible and restored to it its historical and practical justification.

After the Six-Day War Alterman became the mouthpiece of the political struggle for a Greater Israel that was to include the liberated lands. For he regarded untruncated Israel as the redemption of a pledge in a remote past and an obligation to future generations. The poet who invented a popular verse technique in *The Seventh Column* and created the slogans and the symbols for the native and the immigrant for three decades became the organizer of "The Movement for the Redemption of the Entire Land of Israel," a chairman at literary and nonliterary meetings, a pleader and cajoler on behalf of expansionism. In the moving tribute to the poet at the first anniversary of his death, Moshe Dayan said what was in everybody's mind: he was the voice; we were the echo. In the age-long search for redemption Alterman was the poet of an embattled generation, the arbiter of its aspirations and the evaluator of its achievements. But was he a poet of surfaces or a poet of depths? Was he the first political poet who worried about the state of the State? The dynamics of his poetic antinomies— simultaneous mystification and demystification of reality in his work—can only insure ambiguity rather than inerrancy in judgment.

The poetry of Raphael Eliaz (1905-1974) is burdened with the lingual heritage of Shlonsky and accepts, consciously or unconsciously, his unquestionable authority. The imagery is traceable to the same source: people rise "at the well of dawn,"[25] "trees dip their white feet in the river,"[26] the poet runs in the fields "like a red flower."[27] The articulation of filial devotion is also an import from without rather than an inner experience. The indubitable individuality of Eliaz expresses itself in his story-telling poems which resemble ballads in content though not in form. Their rhyming schemes are often enriched by assonance, their themes presented with charming informality. In the most sensitive of his ballads "Abel Weeps Over Cain"[28] Eliaz portrays neither a revolutionary Cain à la Byron nor a bourgeois Abel à la Baudelaire[29] nor a philosophical pair of brothers à la Regelson, but an intensely human youth who stands in complete bafflement before the elemental fury of the first-born. Only such an Abel can recite from his grave verses of love to his brother:

> God will remember your pure disaffection
> For storms have loved you with might and main.
> Would that your white soul inspired my inaction.
> In the grave I am little brother again.[30]

In the two narrative poems, "Vladimir's Letter" and "Answer to Vladimir," Eliaz created a modern parallel to "Abel Weeps Over Cain." In the latter, brotherly love triumphs in spite of psychological differences; in the former friendship thrives in spite of political differences between the revolutionary Vladimir and his poet-friend who has settled in Israel. In a letter the Russian urges the Jew to return to his country from the land of "palms praying against a Canaanite sun."[31] In a long answer Eliaz justifies his preference for the ancestral land in spite of its shortcomings. Like Lamdan, the poet realizes that it is the last stage in the long wanderings of his people. He ends with a hymn to the city of Jerusalem:

> Jerusalem of mine.
> Take me as a sinful child.
> I will swallow your great sorrow with my little body:
> I will ripen in your bosom.
> Your heritage lives in my blood like a dagger in the chest.[32]

In spite of the inordinate length of the poem, "Answer to Vladimir" is an interesting poetical document. It mirrors the confusion of Jewish youth between the two world wars: the magnetic pull of communism and the magnetic pull of the Land of Israel. It also explains the intensity in the love of the non-native generation for the ancestral land as a filial attachment that fulfills an elementary need.

In his attitude to tradition Eliaz deplores the loss of ancestral security:

Long ago we have renounced our fathers and our mothers.
With the fervor of their simple, dying faith
We cannot warm our hands again . . .[33]

Like so many other poets and non-poets Eliaz sought in love substitutes for religious security. In the form of a letter—a form he seems to cherish—a woman writes that she lives for the one presence in her life. Always at her side is that "strong and humble head when dawn walks in on tiptoe."[34] It is a believable stance for a woman—even in the twentieth century. But is individual love the all-satisfying need for a man?

Translation has absorbed most of Eliaz's creative time. Five plays of Shakespeare owe him their Hebrew versions: *The Taming of the Shrew, The Tragedy of King Richard III, Romeo and Juliet, Twelfth Night, The Winter's Tale.* And so do plays by Lope de Vega and Ibsen. Eliaz even wrote verses for the children's theater Bubatron: *Zivah the Doll.*[35] He is also one of the few translators of Lorca: a representative selection of Lorca's poetry in Eliaz's rendition has enriched the meager treasury of Spanish literature in Hebrew.[36]

The pessimism of Shlonsky and the nihilism of Yesenin cradled the poetry of Abraham Halfi (1904-   ).[37] Ballads about nothing and thoughts about nothing—these are the characteristic indications of his themes. There is nothing more to ask; Halfi's desperate summation of imaginative impotence seems to echo the hero of Ibsen's *The Wild Duck.*

As Shlonsky's disciple, Halfi does not fail to surprise, confuse and bewilder. The night is characterized as a creeping eternity invalid in one leg, God is a blind man with a lantern in search of a path. Halfi also lends Hebraic color to cosmic phenomena:

The moon like half a loaf lies in the sky.
The sky is set for the meal.
The soul of the world says grace over calm
And over the light of the stars.[38]

In changing a visible object into a gustatory object Halfi transfers the ageless intimacy of home and family from the earth below to the sky above. The simplicity of the device and the adroit use of imagery combine to produce a memorable effect.

Unlike most disciples of Shlonsky, Halfi wrote lyrical poetry exclusively. And the master theme was death. In one of his maturer poems he could write:

> A day will come
> When I shall not come again
> To what I used to come day by day.
> Then I shall lift the voice of laughter louder
> Than all my laughters
> That I laughed.[39]

But death was regarded as a reward rather than a punishment, release from alienation rather than infinite nothingness.

> Thank you, God of life, for death that will arrive
> And lock the doors and let the shutters down.
> Thank you, God of Life, for death that will contrive
> To atone for all without a frown.
>
> Thank you for the open spaces which we saw before conclusion
> Of life; for gold that gushes in the field to entertain
> The eyes; for air that's full of microbes of seclusion
> And pain.
>
> Thank you for whatever you have burdened soul of man
> With, for our stammering lips when we confess in gloom.
> Our bride, our well-beloved, lost her jewel and fan
> When she ran to the imaginary groom.[40]

Death is the leitmotif of Halfi's poetry—death in general, death of poets, his own death, and even the aftermath of his own death.[41] "Everything, everything is only a poem that always ends abruptly"[42]—this is the sad refrain of a modern Ecclesiastes. Nothingness and emptiness: this is the persistent refrain of his muse, a model of brevity and pure lyricism. Even in an original "Poem about the Parrot Yosi"[43]—an amusing dialog with the echoing bird—the last line reads: "My heart is hollow today." Such a poet as Halfi finds comfort in an unlikely place: at the grave of Baudelaire from whose tomb "the flowers of song will come to comfort the mourners of life."[44] This morbidity is coupled with a love for interiors, for solitude in the recesses of one's room. The title of one of his books, *From Corner to Corner*,[45] is an indicator of a mood, an attitude, an activity: the poet wanders from corner to corner in a tight and terror-stricken universe.

> The universe is indifferent
> And so divine.[46]

For a poet like Halfi death is the only certainty, life is an uninterpretable dream:

> Life I give
> To all my dead.
> They live again
> For ever.[47]

Two forces vie for supremacy in the mind of Joshua Tan-Pai (1914–): the force of confession and the force of surprise. A predilection for rags is also an unusual characteristic of the poet: his soul is a rag which absorbs the waters of the sea and is squeezed drop by drop; the night descends upon the poet like a moist rag; the young day arrives like a dry rag; life itself is a tattered garment.[48] In rare instances Tan-Pai is capable of the unsophisticated approach to life:

> A web of muscles and feelings is man. He endures for a breath.
> A web of seconds and hours and darkness and light is day.
> And I am a web of tiny pleasure and great dismay.
> And I weave the warp of life and the woof of certain death.[49]

Like Eliaz, Tan-Pai seeks security in love. But it is an unsatisfactory search which, at best, adds to the anguish of the seeker.

> Friendship of bodies by night
> Is concord of sorrow and sorrow
> And blend of shadow and shadow.[50]

The poetry of Tan-Pai may be characterized as poetry of desolation—especially after the death of his son in the defense of Israel. But decades before that event he called a collection of his poetry *Songs of Darkness and Vision*.[51] He was only half-right: the darkness was all-pervasive; not so the vision.

David Rokeah (1916–   ), one of the most prolific and most translated poets,[52] is a native of Galicia who settled in Israel in 1934. The new homeland—especially the sea and the wilderness—had an immense fascination for the poet who, in rhymeless, unadorned lines, sought and won progressive liberation from Shlonsky's influence. In a typical poem "Negev" he described the exotic landscape, without sentimentalization or mystification, and transformed it in the very act of description:

> Waving wilderness again.
> Whirl of eagle wings
> Among the desert rocks.
> Light of noon in heaven
> Blinding with primeval force.
> Revelation of the Deity
> On copper mountains
> In greenish rust.[53]

In contradistinction to Alterman, who cultivated the ephemeral, Rokeah cherished the eternal, landscape and love first and foremost.

> I saw
> Your voice
> Leap in the dark
> Like a firefly
> Among the willows:
> Nightend's voice which walked on the shore of the sea
> Like the painter's brush
> Saturated with vermilion.[54]

Among the eternal themes of Rokeah's poetry childhood—"the vineyard of childhood"—[55] plays an important role. And so do the passing seasons, time past, and time present. But he delights, above all, in that hallucinatory imagination which colors reality with surrealist sparseness:

> The city took a trip.
> It reached a dark grove by evening.
> And as then, in the days of the flood,

From the aperture of Noah's ark
Man escaped
To light the firesignals
On mountaintops.

There was night—
Black like the river of forgetfulness in Greek legends.
Man was so small, he could not be seen.
Only his shadow crept like the brush
And painted on the walls' canvas
The city's tremor at night.[56]

Like Voznesensky with whom Rokeah shares a common profession, engineering, the poet uses stark and strange imagery with startling originality. Imagination is not enough: the poet aspires to realms "Beyond Imagination":[57]

When my imagination soars
To unearthly spheres
I hone my sense of hearing for your word
Is real reality
Beyond imagination.

From the tower of my dreams on the sea shore
I call for you
As a ship calls the land
Waving longing flags.

Messages of your love:
They are purple waves at the edges of sunrise
For one who wakes at dawn.

In this poetry the style is the image: embers whisper, spring prophesies, God in the gorges of Kidron sports many needles.[58] With his cosmopolitan interests Rokeah appeals to his contemporaries, Jews and non-Jews alike. The fact that his poems present fewer challenges to the art of the translator than do, say, Gruenberg's poems, accounts for the wide diffusion of his poetry in Germanic and Anglo-Saxon countries. That a poet should enjoy greater receptivity abroad than in his own country is no surprise: Poe, for instance, has acquired—thanks to Baudelaire—a greater reputation in France than in America. The old saw about the neglect of the prophet in his own land is not without foundation in fact.

Solomon Tanny (1919-   ) has learned from Shlonsky to write poetry on the verge of prose, but he struggled to achieve selfhood and simplicity. In one of his best efforts, "To Learn to Part," he has achieved a poignant lyric without the device of metaphor and simile:

> To learn to part:
> To cross the river
> And not recross;
> To shut the shutter
> And shut off light . . .
> To learn to part:
> Not to fear,
> Not to collect days;
> To squander a bit
> From the treasure of years;
> To divide, to give
> Out of the whole soul;
> Till nothing remains.
> To part. To be still.

The tone is quiet, relaxed, almost smug; the theme universal. The title of one of Tanny's books of verse *Till the Day Arrived*[59] gives a clue to the non-national personal quality of his work. Though a Galilean wind may blow through his verses, though Eilat may show its harsh face in them, though Sharm el Sheikh may lend them its mother-of-pearl glitter, they have little of an Israeli flavor.

Tanny rarely touches upon his childhood, but he compensates for this omission with books and records for children—his bond with the world of childhood,[60] the roots of a rootless poet.

In the best tradition of Shlonsky, Noah Peniel (1906–   ) deplored the decadence of modern Europe. It was "a heap of rubbish," "an aging Jezebel, sated with harlotry."[61] Later, it became "the treacherous soil," "the continent of the holocaust that had not swallowed its hangmen, the land where . . . snakish men run amuck to erase God's writ with their polluted hands."[62] Europe effaced the image of God which was man's glory and revealed man's arrogant, howling dogdom.[63] "Proof: the slaughter of infants—"each infant stirring like an Isaianic vision."[64] The poet hoped for personal rebirth in Israel. In the landscape with its historic associations, in national memories of a distant past he sought and achieved a certain equilibrium and serenity at last. Like Jephthah's daughter he accepted his lot.[65]

Jacob Orland (1914–   ) strikes a familiar note in the introduction to the book of poems which he calls *Tree in the Wind*.[66]

> To
> The month of May
> I give these poems,
> To the month of May
> And to me.[67]

It would be wrong, however, to infer from these lines that Orland is a poet of spring and joy and the ecstasy of his own heart. In one of his books, *Poems from the Land of Uz*,[68] he has ventured into the tragic landscapes of Job. Because he has adopted no definite stance he escapes easy classification. He can be mercurial, mockingly playful, feigning ignorance of his own personality and a Socratic lack of knowledge:

> Four trees are in my paradise:
> The tree of forgetfulness
> And the tree of drunkenness
> And the tree of slumber
> And the tree of death . . .
> Why do I know
> That I don't know?[69]

Like Hameiri, Shlonsky, Lamdan, and Gruenberg, he indulges in filial romanticism. And, like Shalom, he ventures into mysticism:

> We do not sing the songs of anger and joy to the world.
> Our name is not on the lips of this vain generation.
> Calm, like an ancient song, bursts from our unsung lives.
> We are the sounds from an organ that has not been heard.[70]

In his deep attachment to Israel Orland resembles no one but himself. Simply, straight from the heart, he records his sensations on the roads of his ancestral land:

> To walk on your roads, O motherly earth,
> Like an animal at dawn's birth,

With arched breast and breathing nose
Breathing the light, the tree, the water, the rose,
To bleat like the lamb in reverent calm,
To bray like the ass in passing the palm,
To knock with the hollow animal knock
The head on your furrow and on your rock . . .[71]

This is not an isolated fragment in Orland's work. The landscapes of Israel appear and reappear in the pages of his poetry with the seductiveness of a dream and the freshness of reality. The children of the land, who have experienced the terrors of fratricidal war, move with the same insecurity as their elders because bullets sing to them "a cradle song no other child knows." With disarming naiveté Orland assures us that men cannot aim their deadly missiles at these children. But in the brief time that elapsed from the date of the composition of Orland's poems, millions of European, Asiatic, and African children served as innocent targets of carnage and thousands were butchered without qualms of conscience.

Even in his mature work Orland was fascinated with childhood. And he combined that interest with his love for Jerusalem, which had hosted Amorites and Phoenicians, Philistines and Egyptians, Assyrians and Babylonians, Greeks and Romans, Byzantines and Arabs, crusaders from many lands and Turks from many regions, and the British before the establishment of Israel. In the descriptions of his beloved Alley of the Ethiopians in Jerusalem he showed keen perception of the telling detail. There was, for instance, when he was growing up, a certain Doctor Feigenbaum, an eye specialist, unseen by his neighbors. But his invisibility was compensated for by the high visibility of his daughter, Hemdah, who blinded all onlookers with her white skin and raven-black hair and converted them into patients of her father who should have been a heart specialist.[72] Orland retold his childhood in the rhymed prose of the *maqama* with a queer mélange of refreshing irony and nostalgic pathos. And he may be regarded as one of the few poets who strove to create an Oriental style for his unique experiences.

The vociferous animadversions of David Avidan (1934–   ) and the style that—in English and Hebrew—teems with neologisms and jargon, do not inspire confidence in his sincerity or ability. When a publication on the holocaust is announced as "notes towards a psychoethnical theory of the etiology of the holocaust, diagnosing a binational magnatrauma,"[73] the reader's interest is immediately repelled or an-

agonized. Another publication-to-be is preceded by an impossible fan-
are: *"Ha-Yahid ha-Mitno'e'a (Homo mobilis), Early Notes Towards a
Dynamic Psychosomatosophy and an Active Sociomysticism . . . "*[74]
And so on ad infinitum. The poet characterizes his verses aptly: "Ex-
periments in Hysteria."[75] Or in stridency:

> Had I been born fifty years earlier
> Perhaps I would have nodded acquaintance with myself . . .
> Too late. Yet
> right now
> I'm safely selfed. My self for myself. Selful of myself.[76]

That Avidan also succeeds in writing a touching poem shows that he
s a poet who has deliberately misconceived his mission and misrepre-
sented himself. Thus, a brief, epigrammatic poem on the war, a constant reality in Israel, reveals a pathetic moment in the eternity of modern clashes and counterclashes:

> The soldiers asked a cigarette, a cigarette.
> The woodlegs marched on sulphur, wearing skates.
> Wood to wood. Spark to spark. And then a voice
> Was mildly introducing a dead choice:
> "If nothing turns up now, my dear men,
> We shall advance into defeat again."[77]

Except for the "was mildly introducing" in the fourth line and "my
dear men" in the fifth line, the poem conveys the horror and the pathos
of war in appropriate imagery and pathetic stance.

Avidan has absorbed modern English and American poetry indis-
riminately. He has even written a poem on "The Matter of the Unfortunate Love of J. Alfred Prufrock."[78] Like his master who sometimes
used German and French in his verse, Avidan did not hesitate to in-
ert a poem of five lines in English into a Hebrew poem—a sort of
uggestion for a hymn of Jewish beatniks in New York:

> Ya, ba, ba, ba, bum!
> Ya, ba, ba, ba, bum!
> I'm a Jewish, a Jewish bum.
> Frankly I wish, frankly I wish
> To have Friday night my *gefilte hashish.*[79]

But unlike Eliot, Avidan has not gone beyond nihilism and purpose lessness to win a new faith for himself:

What justifies loneliness
More than anything . . .
Is the simple, decisive fact
That we really have nowhere to go.[80]

In this nihilistic abyss the act of creativity is assessed in cold, quasi prosaic verse:

And writing is nothing
But strange mélange
Of drives and consciousness,
Of suffering and knowledge.[81]

For this vicious circle of repetitive nonsense which marks the hu man world repetitive verse is the ideal vehicle. Like Zach, the maste of repetitive technique, Avidan has learned to use it effectively even in Latin, even as titles for poems: *"curriculum vitae," "curriculum mor tis," "curriculum vitae et mortis," "curriculum post mortem," "cur riculum curriculi."*[82] But where Zach is light and playful, Avida affects a seriousness of content which contradicts his form. An strangely, the many international locutions—"vegetative love," "se appeal," "psychotherapy," "nonconformism"—lend his verse a provin cial air.

The ultramodernism of David Avidan was a deliberate stance tha was meant to disturb the alleged placidity of Hebrew verse; the u trabohemianism of Alexander Pen (1906-   ) was an almost instine tive attitude to life and letters. Poet and drunkard, Communist an Zionist, translator and boon companion of the Russian poets Maya kovsky and Yesenin, friend of Shlonsky and Halfi—such was Alexar der Pen. His poetry, especially his political poetry, was tinged with radi cal ideology. But his ideal was universal brotherhood rather than uni versal hate. When he was asked to choose for an anthology his mos significant poem, he selected the "Ballad of Thirty-five,"[83] because i expressed struggle against chauvinism and pursuit of love between th two nations of Israel. In a dialog between the resurrected Abraham and Sarah, it is Abraham who prays for peace in his anxiety:

God of Peace, put your healing hand

On my wound. Hear my prayer in the desert sand.
For the sake of the blood of my sons,
Sons of Eve, I would
Ask only this: brotherhood.

The naiveté of the prayer is matched by the sincerity of the poet. And weight is given to his words which are uttered by Abraham, the alleged father of Jew and Arab.

10
The Canaanism of Ratosh

ABRAHAM Shlonsky marks a watershed in the development of Hebrew literature. A gradual radicalization in form and content characterizes the poetry of Alterman, Amichai and the lesser luminaries who drew their literary sustenance from his work. With Jonathan Ratosh[1] (1909–   ) a new impatience with the diaspora and its creative forces came to the fore. In 1948, with the establishment of the periodical *Alef*,[2] the so-called Canaanite movement or the movement of the Young Hebrews was launched on its brief career. Jewish history after the termination of the unsuccessful revolt of Bar Kohba against Roman dominance and might was declared to be "an irrelevant intrusion into the present," Jewish literature including the Talmud, an aberration, Zionism, an episode. Only Hebrews in Israel constituted the true Israel; Jews outside Israel were to be relegated to the status of second-rate Israel, as people without roots and without significance.[3] In the terse formulation of Ratosh: "Not a Jewish people, a Land of Israel, a Hebrew language, and a nationalist-Zionist movement. This is caricature."[4] As for the new Israel, it must become Greater Israel and include the Fertile Crescent. It must conclude an alliance with the Druse and the Lebanese, it must proceed to occupy Damascus and Cairo and impose a *pax Hebraica* on the entire region, a peace with responsibility—not with the aid of politicians but by the authority of a dictator. It must abandon Zionism and clericalism, especially clericalism which has transformed the Jewish State into a medieval theocracy, a Jewish ghetto, and a branch of world Judaism. It must give complete equality to all its citizens regardless of their religious affiliations and impose on

92

them Hebrew culture that has no roots in the so-called Jewish heritage or Islamic heritage but in the pre-Jewish civilization of the ancient land. The new Israel must proclaim the Hebrew language as the only cohesive and common denominator of Hebrews, Arabs and the existing minorities. Such a far-reaching revolution in Judaism and Islam can only be achieved by violence—the normal way to independence and cataclysmic change.

This atypical aberration had its birth in the thirties when Jewish resistance to the mandatory government and Jewish reaction to Arab hostility crystallized into military and paramilitary opposition with such extreme versions as the National Military Organization, *Ezel,* under the leadership of Menahem Begin, and Fighters for Liberty of Israel, *Lehi,* under the leadership of Yair Stern, the poet and friend of Jonathan Ratosh. In the sixties, after the Six-Day War, it reached its peak though it never numbered more than a thousand adherents. Its literary repository—*Songs of the Sword*[5]—contains Ratosh's pertinent poetry of more than three decades. Its message: war, or rather, peace through war.

This propagandistic theme is matched by the poet's insistence on the reconstitution of a Canaanite literature in the neo-Canaanite land. Hence his preference for imagery and vocabulary which date back to biblical times. In his poems the altars of Astarte, goddess of love, still crave the animals and the incense. She is invoked as protectress of young lovers:

> You are the sorrow and the scent,
> Love-flower bosomed, love-flower borne.
> Lover came and lover went.
> O house forsaken and forlorn.
>
> Futile freedom. Poverty.
> Lonely head on lonely pillow.
> Queen Astarte, pity me.
> Will my lover come tomorrow?[6]

The later poetry of Ratosh views the fragile sex with quasi-realistic cynicism:

> Woman . . . needs
> Three in all seriousness:
> One in bed,

One in the heart
And one to bear the yoke of daily life with.[7]

Banality characterizes the later love poetry. The poet's spent passion
relies on common simile and common speech for poetic effect:

Strange, how you became
The superfluous, disturbing factor.
Only yesterday—
And even more so a day before yesterday—
The world
Was full of you.
So much so that even today
I cannot free myself.
It's like a headache,
A stomach ache . . .[8]

Even a poet in hot pursuit of the novel stance can finally be overcome by fatigue. When he tries to summarize his philosophy of life, he
achieves a few trite and trivial observations:

Perhaps, in the final resort,
It is really not
So important
What we probe
And think so much about—
Perhaps, all that is really
A matter of age
And character
And education
And some warp of prejudices
And some woof of complexes . . .[9]

Ratosh, who advocated abandonment of tradition, could not free
himself from the tyranny of traditional metaphor like the biblical
"dark dread,"[10] or a medieval line like Judah Halevi's "My heart's in
the East,"[11] or a hasidic phrase like "divestiture of corporeality."[12]
Sometimes a stanza by Ratosh is a mere mosaic of quotations from biblical literature as in the poem "Love":

Be lifted up, everlasting gates, that the king of glory may come.

Tear the ascetic cloak that He may spread the canopy of peace.
Come, my beloved,
We will go out in blossom.[13]

Perhaps Ratosh's poetry is essentially erotic with violent variations
on the theme of love. A lusty heathenism dominates his early poetry, a
reflective stance suffuses his later poetry, a lone nonconformism characterizes his entire oeuvre.[14] The superpatriotic views on Israeli expansionism parallel his ecstatic pitch in the thirties and in the forties
of this century. Flamboyant, exhibitionist bravado marks these early
poems as surely as, say, meditative prayer distinguishes the poetry of
Temkin. In a sense Ratosh was exploring the Canaanite substrata of
Jewish civilization in his lyrics as John Millington Synge was discov-
ering the pre-Christian civilization of folkloric Ireland in his plays.
The result, in Ireland and in Israel, was mythologization of the past.

11
The Tranquil Poets: Temkin; Meitus; Wolfovsky; Keshet; Lichtenbaum; Lander; Bass; Kariv; Mohar; Rosen; Goldenberg; Solodar; Span; Homsky; Braudes; Benshalom

THE shouting poetry of Hameiri and Gruenberg, Shlonsky and his disciples, the innovative techniques of Alterman and Amichai drowned the subtle voices of their contemporaries between the two world wars. Tranquility, the condition of creativity according to Wordsworth, was banished from the highways of literature. But in the byways delicacy of perception, refinement of expression, a mood consistent with the Psalmist's still waters and green pastures, flourished in unobtrusive grace.

Sincerity in a minor key: that was the hallmark of Mordecai Temkin (1891-1960) in all the six collections of his verse[1] which were published between 1927 and 1965. It was not patriotic fervor which prompted him to settle in Israel; it was the realization of a spiritual kinship between him and the land of his dreams:

> You are gray and lonely
> Like my soul.
> You are my land, my only
> Land, my goal.[2]

Like a lover, transformed by his beloved, Temkin discovered the ever-widening horizons of his happiness in the Holy Land transformed into a cosmic force. His longest poetical effort "When the Chariots of Victory Roar"[3] indicates more than it expresses; the tragedy of a little, peace-loving nation, threatened by belligerent, victory-loving nations. But it voices the fact of Palestinian life in a mood of quiet grief rather than loud indignation. Temkin's *Poems of Jerusalem,* published posthumously and culled from previous books, especially from *Muted Voice,* contain twenty-six lyrical pieces. They are primarily reflections on holy places, expressions of moods engendered by the long history of the city and the present vestiges of ancient glory.

Like Rilke, Temkin sought out the poor; their company filled him with silent resignation. And like his great contemporary he saw human grief and hate against a background of love in the animated landscape.

> House near house
> And fence of woes.
> Two neighbors
> And two deadly foes.
>
> Door against door:
> Cave against cave.
> On each side stand
> Two trees and wave.
>
> Two deadly foes
> That fret and frown
> But friendly trees
> Bow crown to crown.

"House near House"[4] is one of Temkin's few objective poems. The bulk of his work consists of scarcely audible utterances and half-uttered complaints about the gulf between the poet and the outside world, the poet and the Land of Israel, the poet and the nearest of kin—wife and son.[5] Prayer is his genre, his form, his content.

Eliyyahu Meitus (1892–   ) also preferred prayer to other forms of poetry. But he lacked the warm intimacy and the natural simplicity of Temkin. In his love poetry he achieved an airy perfection:

> I am happy tonight!
> Stars, do you know? I am happy tonight!
> Do you know what the heart sings in its might?

I am happy tonight!

Light in my limbs.
Stars, fade out! Light in my limbs!
I'll make light when starlight dims.
Light in my limbs.

Fields of night, ends of earth!
I hurry to you, fields of night, ends of earth!
I carry my love, I radiate mirth,
Fields of night, ends of earth![6]

Unrestrained happiness seems to burst the bounds of these verses: the exaltation of love has shaken the poet to his depths.

As an anthologist of modern Hebrew poetry and as a translator of European poetry, Meitus has shown taste and ability. Numerous poems of Baudelaire, Mallarmé, Verlaine, Rimbaud and Verhaeren owe their Hebrew versions to his pen. It was Baudelaire, however, who was his master and his idol; and to him he dedicated a sonnet and a triolet. He even tried to emulate the master's favorite genre but composed un-Baudelairean sonnets—light in tone, ironic, almost mischievous.

Meitus is one of only two Hebrew poets to have published a book of triolets—104 of them.[7] And he managed, in that succinct and artificial eight-line mould—where rhyme and rhythm are rigid, the first, fourth and seventh lines are identical and the second line reappears as the last—to face the unknown with restrained awe,[8] to paint a late summer landscape,[9] to revive naiads and sylphs[10] and even the sad triangle of Columbine, Harlequin and Pierrot.[11] Reminders of Villon[12] color his homage to womanhood. And a triolet in praise of triolets prefaces the book,[13] a charming *tour de force* not unlike Tschernichowsky's sonnet in praise of sonnets. Roumanian folk music, well-known through the symphonic elaborations of Enesco, and Roumanian folk poetry, have also affected the work of Meitus who not only translated Roumanian folk poetry into Hebrew but absorbed its quasi-oriental moods.

Menahem Zalman Wolfovsky (1893–   ) published his first lyrical poems before the First World War. Some of them were daringly unrhymed, but in thematic stance they resembled the romanticized sunsets and ennui and fashionable pessimism which characterized the poetry of the West at the end of the nineteenth century. Early in his poetic career he also tried his hand and talent at narrative and even historic poems, but the mystic fury of an Ezekiel, for instance, does not come alive in "From Visions of Ezekiel."[14] Many years later, Wolfovsky published an interesting historical novel on Jeremiah,[15] on his early years in Anatot, on his relation to the Rechabites and on his mission in Jersualem.

The poetry of Wolfovsky is predominantly Palestinian: the cities, the cooperatives, the Valley of Esdrelon are recurring themes. Like Lamdan, he regards Israel as the last refuge of Jewry and the prime guarantor of national regeneration. A poem like "In the Last Fort"[16] resembles Lamdan's *Massadah* in title and content. And if the book *Pathends*[17] may be said to owe its mood to Lermontov, it borrows its pathos from Lamdan and its theme from Gruenberg. But Gruenberg endowed the pioneers with the raw strength of his personality. Wolfovsky's vignettes of their difficult existence have that touching sympathy and eloquence which Vincent van Gogh lent to his "Potato-Eaters." Though not a master of poetical technique nor an imaginative wizard, he made up by stubborn adherence to the drabber aspects of life for what he lacked in inventiveness. Not only as a poet but also as a short-story writer and an essayist he owes a primary debt to the Russian realists of the nineteenth century. A prolific translator, a melancholy poet, a matter-of-fact writer of narrative prose: this seems to be a fair evaluation of his oeuvre.

Jeshurun Keshet (1893–   )—in the Hebrew transformation of his original name, Jacob Koplewicz—characterized his poetry as "growth in wasteland." Perhaps the poet suffered from a double wasteland—that of his environment and that of his own selfhood. Hence the reiterated wails of loneliness in his poems, the delight in the desolate light and desolate heart.

In a time of social upheavals Keshet cultivated his own individuality.

What am I? Only a mine of precious stones!

"Only" which is intended as a touch of modesty, intrudes upon the metaphor with disturbing hauteur and, incidentally, recalls the modest verse of Fichmann:

Who am I? Only a lone, white sail.[18]

Fichmann appeals with moving simplicity; Keshet repels with unintentional arrogance. The success or failure of a poem can depend on the proper use of an adverb.

Keshet's loves are bodiless apparitions rather than women of flesh and bone. They live in "fields of jasper," they recline in "meadows of purity," they move in an atmosphere of somnolescence. When emptiness threatens to engulf the poet, he prays in desperation:

God! Create something, a little something for me
Out of the great nothing which is in my heart![19]

But the something failed to appear, the nothing grew out of bounds, dangerous overindulgence in dreams robbed the poet of substantive reality. Frischmann may have been too harsh a critic when he characterized the work of Keshet as "empty estheticism, inflated art,"[20] but there was a grain of truth in his appraisal. Even Keshet's autobiography *Between the Chestnut and the Lilac*[21] does not dispel the acute observation of the older critic. The sensitivity of the boy in the little town at the turn of the century—and this is the gist of the author's evocation of his early years—is a vague thin-skinned reaction to the harsh realities of the world.

In *A Conspicuous Horn,*[22] a book of essays in national self-criticism written over many years, Keshet indulges in numerous self-confrontations. Youth, community, Land of Israel, culture: these themes preoccupy his endless musings. In one of the essays, "Judaism and the Future,"[23] he arrived at an interesting aperçu: "The function of future Judaism is to inherit the culture of the West . . . Judaism was not designed to be a continuation of Asia . . . it was destined to be the beginning of something new: the culture of the West; it participated in the creation of that culture together with Greece and Rome . . ."

The re-Westernization of Judaism—this idea and ideal with a high potential and prime importance—is an antithetical foil to Feierberg's hope for the re-orientalization of Hebrew literature.[24] Keshet may have discovered it in the work of Berdyczewski which fascinated him for many years and prompted him to write a valuable monograph on that author. As a prolific writer and a critic of the arts he has no equal in Israel: he authored forty-three books—twelve original volumes and thirty-one translations. When the final estimate of his oeuvre is made, it will become apparent that he is a cultured poet whose potential sophistication lacks subtlety of expression; an essayist whose flashes of insight are marred by lack of coherence; a translator who rarely rises above mediocrity.

The two outstanding German poets of the twentieth century, Rilke and George, fascinated Joseph Lichtenbaum (1895-1968) to the extent that he never was able to free himself entirely from their influence. The volume of poems *In the Shadow of the Hours*[25] echoed the title of Rilke's *The Book of Hours*[26] and, to a certain extent, its content. Though Lichtenbaum lacked the religious and musical depth of the German poet, he succeeded in capturing the monkish, almost ascetic atmosphere of *The Book of Hours* in his book. And George, translated by Lichtenbaum into Hebrew, invested his own poetry with gravity:

> From velvet vistas gentle evening parts.
> The branches drip with roving reveries.
> On carpeted paths the longing day departs.
> The wing of night flutters among the trees.
>
> With no exultant heart, with no exultant speech—
> How good to love all, o how good to wrap
> All in love, to wander out of twilight's reach
> When night calls like a girl unto her lap.[27]

This cadenced poem imitates the well-balanced poems of George's *The Year of the Soul*.[28] The cold verses depict the evening as a remote phenomenon and proclaim an intellectual love of all that lacks the effort of the heart. Lichtenbaum seems to have been cowed by foreign influences; he has failed to rise to his own heights. That was, perhaps, the reason of his repeated clamors for death: he has not discovered his own life. Even his exaggerated love for the night was not merely a neo-romantic affectation or poetic stock-in-trade; it was a conditioned escape from clarity and light.

As a landscape addict Lichtenbaum probed with enviable dexterity the soul of the mountain; he sang its song in the first person as if he himself were "an old mountain, desolate to the top"; as if the complaint of the mountain were also the complaint of the poet:

> I am dreary, numb, wrapped in dreams of woes.
> Sing to me, buoyant forest, the song of budding boughs.[29]

Longer poems never tempted Lichtenbaum's creative powers. It was the short lyric or sonnet which helped him conquer his inner ennui. In his translations from modern German and Polish poetry, in his essays on Hebrew and non-Hebrew writers and, especially, in his original poetry he achieved a purity of expression rarely equaled even by major poets.

Phinehas Lander (1903-   ), who bears a close poetic resemblance to Lichtenbaum, also aspires to classicism in the lyrical poem, in the sonnet, in the long poem. That is why he contents himself with conservative themes and conservative language. In his poem about Gomer he recreates a biblical character with imaginative élan. She is a poor and passionate girl, "a garden of flames" in Lander's characterization. Her princely lover is the victim of jealousy; the chariot of a rival maims his body. What one misses in the poem—as in the book by Simon Ginzburg on a similar theme—is the complete absence of mystery. Too great clarity in poetry is as grave a fault as too great obscurity.

Temperamentally and thematically, Samuel Bass (1899-1949) was the very antithesis of Lichtenbaum. A warm intimacy characterizes his prose and poetry. But the cadenced line and the perfection of expression which adorn the work of Lichtenbaum rarely grace the work of Bass; and imagery or ideas imported from foreign sources rarely intrude into his work which is a pure product of Hebrew poetry. The influence of Bialik, Lamdan, and Shlonsky amounts to a tyrannizing power over his imagination. In the little poem "Moon,"[30] for instance, Bass endeavors like Shlonsky to inject the startling metaphor and the unexpected simile into his description of ordinary moonlight:

The jug is on the wane.
Mother-milk pours
On thirsty ways.

They are full of sleep—
The tiring eyes of
The wanderer.

Over dead willows
The sky lights its candelabra.
And on guard
Stands night
Alone.

In a poem on the sunset Shlonsky also utilized the obvious motif of death. But he did it with such spare and consummate skill that he produced a miniature work of art. Bass, on the other hand, has piled several figures of speech on the "dead willows" and diluted several poetic ideas in a very brief poem. This ostentatious wealth of imagery has succeeded in creating the paradoxical impression of poetic poverty.

Bass toyed with the idea of alienation. By mere enumeration and juxtaposition of place names he tried to achieve what he expressed in yearning lyrics:

> How your alms call unto me, Parthenon.
> But I am a stranger in your midst . . .
> For Lycabettus, Colonnus,
> Hymettus, Olympus,
> Are neither Tabor nor Hermon,
> Neither Carmel nor Gilboa . . . [31]

It would be unjust to Bass, however, to relegate him to the category of Shlonsky's disciples. He is an eclectic poet in the sense that Cicero was an eclectic philosopher. Both are known to have studied their contemporaries and predecessors with great profit to themselves and both lacked originality. Cicero compensated for his defect with an elegance of style which was the paradigm of scholasticism and humanism. Bass endeavored to cover his defect with the thin leaf of unobtrusiveness. For poetic material he ransacked the landscapes of North America, the Middle East, and almost all of Europe. Thus, in Waterbury, Connecticut, he wrote his "Prayers from an Alien Land for My Little Homeland."[32] The miniscule size of the country fascinated him. "Little" became his favorite expression. Even his verses were "little windows looking out upon the fullness of the world;[33] the palm of his beloved was "a little, soft palm" or "a little, warm palm" or "a little, good palm";[34] the stranger was "a little brother";[35] and what he missed in the entire universe was "one little heart:"

> Only one little heart I propose
> To woo in this world of woes.
> Only one little heart, aching
> For me, in my dreams, in my waking,
> Like a diamond, brilliant, unbreaking.
>
> Only one little heart I propose

To woo in this world of woes.
Only one little heart will command
Me to strive with the world and stand
On my own in any land.

Only one little pulsating heart
Will save me from vanity of art.
But this little heart I miss
Though this little heart I kiss
In vain in my dreams of bliss.[36]

This is one of the most charming poems of Bass—unpretentious, almost childlike.[37] Gentle sorrow, moderate condemnation, ultimate resignation—all these themes combine to produce unadorned brilliance, sojourn in "The Landscape of Yeterday"[38] as he so aptly characterized his poetry.

Bass wrote undistinguished feuilletons, educational articles, and literary sketches with a facility which consigned them to instant oblivion. Even his short novel *Era* which was supposed to be the monument in prose to the Jewish Legions of the First World War remained an insignificant love story. But the lyric has become an instrument of balanced grace in the hands of Bass. And as a lyrical poet he has a distinct place in contemporary Hebrew literature.

Abraham Isaac Kariv (1900-   ) made his appearance in the decade which followed the First World War: he was one of the few Hebrew writers who remained in Russia after the Bolshevik Revolution. When he emigrated to Palestine in the beginning of the thirties, he gradually turned to criticism and achieved a solid reputation with his essays on the Bible and on modern Hebrew literature. Neither the great social upheaval in Russia nor the great national experiment in Israel left a marked impression on Kariv's poetry which was essentially personal. When he generalized, he used such categories as "Jew and non-Jew." These were real antitheses to him; nothing had changed his medieval outlook.

Non-Jew rules with mighty arm.
The booty and the beauty of the world are his.
The Jew has his voice, nothing else.[39]

The biblical dichotomy of Esau's hand and Jacob's voice reappears with frightening sameness.

Another favorite image of Kariv is the Eternal Jew who has suffered indignities from Christians in un-Christian acts of cruelty and oppression.[40] The burden of Jewish inheritance weighs heavily upon him:

Listen, son, listen, my son!
Inherit all you can inherit
From me with my blood and name.
But scatter far and scatter wide
The aftergrowth of my own fate,
Follow not in my footsteps,
Seedless on fieldless tracks.
Come not near me, not within loveshot,
Drop no anchor into my days on a stormy day.
Let your star not meet my star
In the heavenly constellations.
Selah.[41]

Inner composure hovers over city scenes and village scenes in the poems of Meir Mohar (1888-1968). His predilection for lyric brevity is uncomprising in the face of modernist poetry. For him "the little poem" is "a childhood melody" in the American jazz jamboree."[42] Seldom does he permit himself the stormy outbursts of dialog as in "Samson." He is at his best as a paysagist, a landscape miniaturist, in the delineation of a tree, for instance, which seems to collect so much sorrow and despair under the autumnal rains that even the peasant passing in his cart becomes infected. Pages and pages of his prose also depict landscape scenes.[43]

In the last years of his life Mohar experienced a change of mind in his attitude to the world. The sweetness and the charm have vanished from his work; the harsh realities of totalitarian regimentation appeared in his poems. Since he lived in Berlin for many years, he reacted to the misfortunes of Jews and non-Jews in his native city with understandable vigor. Unfortunately, Mohar's poetry of this period rarely rises above the incidental value of the *pièce d' occasion*. The tired simile of the "foolish dove"—a symbol of Jewry borrowed from Hosea and repeated in medieval Hebrew poetry—also reappears in Mohar's work: the world is a stormy sea, humanity—a stormy ship. In such a ship a foolish dove builds her nest.[44] As for his short stories and essays, they are conservative at best, undistinguished at their worst. Sentimental scenes of childhood, nationalist musings cast in unoriginal molds, bland sketches of Jerusalem: these are the predominant themes of his prose. And they fail to add any importance to his stature.

Abraham Rosen, originally Rosenzweig (1888-), shared the idyllic manner of Mohar. Both were subject to the influence of Tscherni-chowsky. But Rosen failed to transmit the sights and sounds of a village in the diaspora in a long poem "To the Field of the Fathers."[45] His types, unlike Tschernichowsky's, are blurred; Slav expressions fail to reproduce the local color; the background does not stand out with sufficient clarity. In the poem "Three in the Homeland,"[46] an enlarged version of "To the Field of the Fathers," Rosen transferred a young couple, a Jewish young man named Hayyim and a gentile girl named Mary, from a village in the diaspora to a village in former Palestine. Unlike the classic masters of the idyll he burdened his protagonists with numerous complications. Hayyim and Mary live peacfully and share the joys and sorrows of their Galilean village while their son grows into sturdy manhood. But Hayyim's death marks a break in the life of the family. Mary returns to her ancestral faith, the son volunteers to fight in the Loyalist ranks of republican Spain. Then, the final irony of antisemitism: the Jews—of all people—are blamed for failure in the Iberian peninsula. Then and only then does the son recapture the strong ties that bind him to his people and to his country. When rumors of Arab-Jewish strife on the eve of the Second World War reach his ears, he hurries to defend the land of his love. The East has gained the victory—not only over the protagonist but also in the case of the poet, whose verse has become as firm as the clear outline of a hill in the valley of Esdrelon that excited his imagination.

> The East is afire, the light is on its wings.
> The driver drives his machine and sings
>
> The song of the man who returns to the earth,
> The song of the people in the land of rebirth,
>
> The song of yearning for life without tears.
> Singers have sung it for two thousand years.
>
> The East is afire, the plowing is done.
> Man and machine and sunlight are one.[47]

Rosen produced memorable lines and even memorable lyrics on his new homeland. Among the numerous songs on Tel Aviv his verses on the first Jewish city stand out in oriental splendor:

You're clothed with burning, beauteous light.
Like Sheba's queen you shine in the bejeweled night.
A sailor's song dies on your knee,
A lonely star falls into your sea.[48]

Tel Aviv lacks the charisma of Jerusalem. But modern poets, especially Rosen, have bestowed a splendid dignity on the new city that borrowed its name from a biblical prophet.[49]

The poetry of Mordecai Goldenberg (1889-1941) on the village of the diaspora left faint echoes in Hebrew literature. It was overshadowed by the stronger poetry of Tschernichowsky who mastered that theme with consummate skill. When the latter's massive idylls appeared, Goldenberg's lyrics about shepherds and gypsies lost the appeal of newness and freshness. Goldenberg clings to the open spaces with the simple devotion of the peasant:

My heart goes out to field and sea
Where the lonely tree is dreaming,
Where the softest, sweetest glee
Of chirping, wandering birds is gleaming.

My heart goes out to seas of corn
That, when winds are blowing strong,
Rise from sleep like early morn
In endless waves and restless song.[50]

The monotony of Goldenberg's theme renders his work ineffectual. And the even tenor of his feelings which neither rise nor fall deprives his verse of the vitalizing factor of variety.

After his sudden death the friends of Abraham Solodar (1890-1936) collected the meager harvest of his poetry in a small volume of verse. The few longer poems on Galilee[51] and "The Throes of Messiah"[52] lacked the power of narration and the gift of observation. The lines which describe a day in a Jewish village move with pedestrian prosiness, the lines of "The Throes of Messiah" that endeavor to express the mystic yearning for redemption teem with unmystical clarity. Solodar's short poems created fine impressions of Jericho and Safed. They lacked the artistic maturity of a Fichmann, who penned immortal lines on urban landscapes, but they managed to express devotion to the Palestinian cities in simple verse. Under the impact of modernistic poetry Solodar composed artificial, offensive metaphors like "on the hill of my night grows the cedar of my longing."[53] But this is the exception rather than the rule. The simple sincerity of Solodar was, on the whole, impervious to such aberrations.

Solomon Span (1898-1962) confesses in an elegiac poem dedicated to Emmanuel Ben Gurion that he has not added wisdom to ancient wisdom, and that he has not deviated from the understanding of the sages.[54] It is a just and humble evaluation of his poetry. For it is romantic, nostalgic, melancholy, wrapped in soulful loneliness to such an extent that they bear the signature S. Nefesh, the Hebrew for soul. Like Bialik who guided his poetic pen, Span yearned for childhood, the golden age of his life. But, unlike Bialik, he cast his poetry in the conservative forms prevalent at the end of the nineteenth century. The few lyrical and almost autobiographical stories which he contributed to Hebrew literature were molded on the brief stories of Schoffmann. But his essays on Greek prosody, on Greek authors, on problems of translation are still useful.[55] It was mainly to the field of translation that Span made his permanent contribution. Though he rendered poems by Balmont and Frug, and some lyrics by Goethe and Frost into Hebrew, he will be mainly remembered by his Hebrew versions of such Greek classics as Hesiod and the Homeric Hymns, the fables of Aesop, the idylls of Theocritus. He even translated Ezekiel's *Exagoge*. The brilliant translator of Greek and Latin classics, Solomon Dykman, eulogized him in a hellenizing elegy and characterized him as a Semite who wielded the Hellenic lyre.

At the beginning of his poetical career Homsky was inspired by the political poetry of Uri Zevi Gruenberg.

> I am
> One of an army of myriads, the unknown soldier.[56]

This desire to submerge one's identity in the mass of the people indicated perhaps an unconscious drive to escape the burden of one's individuality. One missed in the youthful poetry of Homsky the personality of Homsky.

Suddenly the poet made a complete *volte face* in his work. A love experience deepened and perfected his means of expression; in *Veils* he achieved maturity. Verse, scintillating with the warmth of life, began to gush from his pen:

> To the yearning buds of my heart be dew,

Be the good sun, be support, be root.[57].

With bated pain Homsky told the evasive love of his heart in the elegant idiom of Pierre Ronsard. He transposed verses of the French poet which Yeats had already so beautifully paraphrased in one of his sonnets.

Here are my lines, a gift to you.
Do not send them away in disdain.[58]

Despair, born of love, is not the end of the road for the poet but the transition to a new world, an absorption in new themes. Thus, in the poem "Eliezer"[59] the manager of Abraham's household struggles with his love for Rebekah and brings her to her destination in spite of his wild desire to lead her away from Isaac into his native city of Damascus. Loyalty lends him a new dimension, a new stature. It was in this poem that Homsky achieved what was denied him in his youthful work: the revival of a biblical figure in a biblical landscape.

A hesitancy, charming in its helplessness, informs the later verse of Homsky.

You spread your hands: they are ready to press.
What happened below and what happened above
Is so hard to express.[60]

In the beginning of his poetical career Homsky had no difficulties. He acquired them in his maturity—when he bid his storms to subside, his heart to acquiesce, "to regard the accompanying pains as permanent guests . . . to enjoy the hypothetical joys that would come perhaps in the future."[61]

The formal conservatism of his poetry did not change. Even the holocaust was subjected to rhymed lines, to hushed expression:

The smoke vanished with the gusts of wind.
In the hollows of the night, in the caves of the day
Time rages and does not rest.[62]

It is the poet's contention that the holocaust must be avenged by an orgy of construction: Noah built his ark before the flood and did not despair after the flood. Similarly, the tragedy of the final solution merged into the apocalyptic re-establishment of Israel as a political entity in an independent state.

Demographic superabundance seems to mark a great number of human beings for extinction—or perhaps, the poet muses, he alone is the victim of superfluity?[63] The consequence of such psychological disarray: alienism which borders on loss of identity—as in the case of Honi the Circle-Drawer. But the loss need not last seven decades. Even seven days or less will suffice "to absorb all that is audial, all that is visual."[64]

In the miasma of threatened extinction the poet struggles to new imagery:

> The leaves of night strum on fiddles
> Of shadow. A choir of grass and trees
> Breaks into thousand silences.[65]

This is a new romanticism which the poet adopts as a way out of despair. Or to put it differently: severance of self from self, a schlemihlism, pioneered by Adelbert von Chamisso and given a modern interpretation.

> Suddenly a man bares himself
> Of himself without shame
> And severs himself from the essence
> Of his selfhood which is the way of his life.[66]

The mature poet has not relinquished the mannered stance of his youth entirely. The effortless ease of artificiality frequently submerges the artist—especially in his parodies of sacred texts.[67] But, at his best, Homsky is a poet who has learned to adapt modernistic leaps into incongruity to the sincerity of his inspiration. Austere and classical, he can also be lyrical and confessional, sensitive to love and to landscapes of many lands. For he is—to use his self-characterization: "an immigrant to many lands."[68]

When, in 1965, Abraham Braudes (1907–) published an anthology of his own poetry, *Quarry*,[69] his readers made the astonishing discovery that his poetic personality had not changed in forty years. The brief lyric, the brief line, the rhymed simplicities of a poet who had earned his bread by manual labor: they had an identical stance in 1925 and in 1965 though they might have lost innocence and immediacy. In 1925 Braudes mourned the iniquities of his own people in his own land: the suffering of the oppressed at the hands of the oppressors, the dignity of man crushed by fellow-man.[70] In 1965 he sang about his private Messiah—wounded but inspired by his "orphaned truth."[71] In the time span between these poems he composed lyric intimations of a small, hard and beloved land wooed and won in daily sweat; parental effusions of singular charm; romanticizations of familial relationships.

Few know the Land of Israel as intimately as Braudes—from Safed, the seat of the mystics in the north to En-Gedi, in the vicinity of Massadah, in the south. Yet that land is as elusive as his poetry which plays hide-and-seek with him, and is compared to a rose crowned with thorns.[72] Braudes catches in his verse the surface sadness, the lonely longing. Sometimes he slips into banalities and sentimentalities, but most of the time he guards his rockbound roots with care.[73] At the same time he likes to think that he sails "a flagless ship."[74] The metaphor of the ship—a tired metaphor—pursues the poet with relentless insistence: it deludes him into feeling that he is a pioneering sailor in the eternal current, and steers him into a romantic vocabulary which he has not succeeded in exchanging for new and exciting modes of expression. Like a Victorian poet Braudes pens his seafaring lines with an unselfconscious aplomb:

> What if the captains are many,
> If ships have preceded my trips,
> I shall be the lone sailor forever,
> The first to chart paths
> In the recurrent currents.[75]

In his singular preoccupation with fatherhood Braudes seems to be obsessed with an almost pathological love for his son. Even in his landscape poems he rarely forgets his son. This unparalleled devotion produces unforgettable poetry.

> In my narrow world of delight
> Your image shines
> With greatest light.

> More than the ecstasy of throngs
> You transport me
> With simple songs.

Your breath and your touch
Console and redeem.
In your soul flowers
Your father's dream.[76]

In his latest volume—*As Long As I Am*[77]—Braudes added to his poetry a new dimension in familiar, conservative form. Age has caught up with him, infirmities plague him, the hospitalized life has superseded the familial milieu. A world of men in white, women in starched uniforms, an ambience of drugs and pills and moans dominates his world. A feeling of superfluity gnaws at the very center of his being. Occasional visits of friends offer a welcome distraction but wifely loyalty is an abiding source of strength. And the ability to compose verse which verges on homespun philosophy:

His unique blend of being
Man can't perceive.
He is sealed and unsealed,
A riddle inside a riddle.[78]

Benzion Benshalom (1907–1968) deserves the sobriquet as the most tranquil poet in Israel. His interest in poetics and classics enriched Hebrew literature with studies on forms and scansions as well as first translations of *Prometheus Bound* and *The Persians* by Aeschylus and even the *Rubayat* of Omar Khayyam. But he was a poet of modest dimensions. Pursuit of lingual preciosity and search for the unusual genre were the outstanding characteristics of his art. In "A Frightened Ray,"[79] a sonnet which consists—with the exception of the first line—of one-word lines, the eye is arrested by the brevity and sparseness of words on the page rather than by the fragile content—the frightened ray on a branch, the frightened bird, the sick leaf falling, the calm weeping. In the five sonnets on the death of a dog[80] sympathies fail to be aroused: the desolation of the neighborhood after the canine demise is told rather than translated into poetic idiom.

Most of Benshalom's poems are landscape poems, more chiseled but less animated than the landscape poems of Fichmann. Only in his poems on Jerusalem does the poet reach a serious maturity of expression.[81] In them—as in many other poems—he resorted to uncharacteristic rather than characteristic aspects of his theme: the wintry landscapes, the stormy skies, the fogs of Jerusalem. That the poet dared to produce a book of rhymed, formal, formalized verse as late as 1965—in the teeth of fashionable modernity—that was an act of courage. Or, perhaps, a stubborn conservatism that would not bend under the blowing winds of change.

12
Holocaust

THE holocaust has become an international experience, a metaphor of horror. But contemporary events of titanic proportions seldom achieve more than ephemeral significance in contemporaneous literatures. Only distance in time and even in space—historical and even geographical perspective—may lend mythical strength and verbal valor to cataclysmic occurrences. More than fifty years elapsed between Napoleon's invasion of Russia and Tolstoy's *War and Peace.* And more than a hundred and fifty years separated the Thirty Years War from Schiller's dramatic trilogy on Wallenstein. The holocaust, the bankrupt infamy of Western Christianity, produced a literature of massive quantity, but uneven quality. Memoirs, documentaries, poems, plays and novels have partially explored the gory theme. Outside Hebrew and Yiddish literature the eight novels by Elie Wiesel, from *Night* to *A Beggar in Jerusalem,* the *Fugue of Death*[1] by Paul Celan, *O The Chimneys*[2] by Nelly Sachs, *The Deputy*[3] by Rolf Hochhut, Peter Weiss's *Oratorio,*[4] *Babii Yar*[5] by Yevgeni Yevtushenko, *The Wall* by John Hersey, *Dance of Genghis Cohn*[6] by Romain Gary, and *The Last of the Just*[7] by André Schwarz-Bart may be counted among the important literary documents of the holocaust. In the poetry of Sylvia Plath it survives with stark unimaginability. The locomotive and train speeding to the death camps, the mountains of shoes without the wearing victims, the chimneys, the ravines, the smoke and the ashes: these are the disparate debris and detritus of a grim heritage.[8]

Special Jewish and non-Jewish research institutes and periodicals are exploring that tragic era scientifically.[9] Some poignant fragments of human misery in the forms of diaries and letters are constantly coming to light.[10] Single events of overwhelming significance are researched again and reevaluated in the light of documentary evidence: the uprising in the Warsaw ghetto, the extermination of 33,771 Jews—

114

according to the low figures of German sources—in the ravine of Babii Yar on the outskirts of Kiev on September 29 and 30, 1941. And the Eichmann trial by the Jerusalem District Court encouraged a new wave of books and articles on the holocaust.

In Jewish literature the most poignant expression of the sorrows of the holocaust was the poetical oeuvre of the martyred poet Isaac Katzenelson in whose memory one of the research institutes of the holocaust was founded: the Ghetto Fighters' House in Memory of Yitzhak Katzenelson in kibbutz Lohame ha-Getaot near Haifa. No other document has the poignancy and immediacy of Katzenelson's poems which were written in Warsaw, in Vittel, in Drancy—in Yiddish, mostly, in Hebrew occasionally.[11] Other Yiddish poets—H. Leivick, Abraham Sutzkever, and Peretz Markish, martyred at the hands of Stalin's executioners in 1952—have wrestled with holocaustism in potent verse and impotent rage. In Hebrew literature the grand elegy in the form of a book, *Rehobot ha-Nahar* by Uri Zevi Gruenberg, is probably the most abiding document of the holocaust. The younger writers who are survivors or memoirists of concentration camps carry the traumatic experience with them into their creative work—Yonat and Alexander Sened,[12] Moshe Shamir and Hanoch Bartov, Amos Oz and A. B. Yehoshua, Uri Orlev and Ben-Zion Tomer, Shammai Golan and Katzetnik, and, in a sense, Amichai and Alterman, S. Shalom, and Leah Goldberg, Hayyim Guri and K. A. Bertini, Kovner and Gilboa and Zalka, have been associated with the holocaust. But it was, above all, Aaron Appelfeld (1932–) who, in story and novel, depicted the process of slow dehumanization by the holocaust. In a poignant story like "The road to Myself" he described the growing up of a refugee, perhaps himself, in Israel. Like other refugees, he has acquired the art of fighting the enemy without, but "we knew that the enemy was entrenched within us, that he ambushed us from within." That enemy was memory.

Almost any story by this haunted writer presents processes of creeping deterioration. Two human beings live in a forest—afraid of the natives and intermittently in touch with them, afraid of the enemy who lurks invisibly and potentially as a threat to life, afraid of the seasonal severities. The result is animalization. These two individuals almost cease talking to each other, almost become enemies to each other. In sadistic or devotional excesses they live their miseries and separate. This is the gist of the story "Process of Changing."[13] It is no accident that one of Appelfeld's books—a collection of stories—bears the title: *Frost on Earth.*[14] The wintry landscape of the soul is his habitat or rather the terrain for the endless wanderings of his protagonists. His novel *The Skin and the Gown*[15] begins with the characteristic Appelfeldian sentence: "Winter's end at night flowed in the streets, slow as in a transparent bell."[16] Another beginning: "At the end of winter they [fowl] appeared as if they had been made of pliable metal."[17] And again: "Winter like a dark band of birds landed at night. . . ."[18]

The stark landscape of Appelfeld's stories is the poignant reminder of the holocaust in modern Hebrew literature. Human lives driven by the visible and invisible enemy to insecure shelters in woods and caves and ruined huts: these are monuments of misery in a dark world. Autumn or winter adds intolerable burdens of near freezing and near starving. Sometimes foraging raids are organized by some escapees from a certain death to an uncertain life-in-death, and the mere expectation of food turns into a creative event of overwhelming magnitude.

> Mad energy pounded in their veins. . . It would save them, give them again the gift of light and food. . . Everything was behind them already: the tribulation, the sacrifice and the successful escape at last.[19]

One of Appelfeld's stories "Siberia"[20] reads like an epitome of his creative work. The impossible landscape makes impossible promises— ironic expectations of immortality: "He who arrives here does not die." When liberation comes, it is powerless to liberate. The human beings, debilitated by hunger, torture, and constant danger to life cannot adjust to normal existence. They suspect benefactors: the Joint Distribution Committee, the religious organs—Jewish or non-Jewish. They suspect each other—though they are capable of sacrifice for others, though they are motivated by a deep sense of communal responsibility that defies expectation. They behave logically or illogically as in a surrealist nightmare. If frost of winter is Appelfeld's favorite metaphor, smoke is his ultimate metamorphosis—as it is in Nelly Sachs's *O the Chimneys*. "The Waste Land," the vatic poem of the generation ·between the two wars, prefigures in its title the literal consummation of barbarization at the end of the Second World War.

It is an astonishing fact that Appelfeld's protagonists are capable of self-irony rather than self-pity. A cripple can brush off his infirmity as a "cheap experiment of nature;" a man in a legal entanglement can remark: "For people out of luck, even a lawyer is of no help."[21] The infinite pity—nothing less is permissible—that accompanies the halt and the wan and the gaunt in their processional to their individual Golgotha: that is Appelfeld's gift of creativity born out of the reality of hell. Softness, like the first snow, covers their ambushed minds and their contorted emotions.

Even the non-holocaust stories of Appelfeld glow with human detritus: foundlings reared in monasteries and incapable of adjustment to the rigors of religious life, the retarded who are barred from companions of their own age forever. To enter Appelfeld's world is to enter a Dantesque hell. Not only must all hope be abandoned; all despair must be experienced and recycled in ironic self-mockery or self-immolation

The oeuvre of Appelfeld cannot be dissociated from holocaustism. But there is hardly a major or minor Hebrew writer who has not reacted extensively or intensively, or both, to that apocalyptic event: the young who were too young to realize the immensity of horror when it exploded on mankind, the mature who experienced it as victims or desperate participants at a distance. Some like Yonat and Alexander Sened teamed up to produce an interior monolog on the holocaust. In their novel *The Added Experience* [22] the chief protagonist, Martha, builds her life on the shattering experience of the holocaust and the added experience of Israel. These major twin events in recent Jewish history are the two major events in her personal life. In spite of her total lack of Jewish identity she suffers as a Jew, she comes to Israel by chance and she shares her life in unconscious participation with the life of the people. The lot of the individual as an ethnic molecule in an ethnic compound of tragic proportion—this dichotomy lends special significance to the book of both Sands.

Dan Zalka (1936-) who was born in Warsaw and spent the years of the Second World War in Siberia chose two main characters for his first novel, *Dr. Barkal and His Son Michael*.[23] Progenitor and progeny seek to build a firm base for their lives after the experience of the holocaust: a spiritual home in Athens, a new commencement in Israel. The father adjusts but the son, rootless in Judaism, remains equally rootless in Israel.

The rootlessness of the younger generation is also the burden of Uri Orlev's work. In *Leaden Soldiers* [24] and *Till Tomorrow*[25] children of assimilated parents, totally unaware of their Jewishness, have to cope with the raw brutality of the holocaust. In spite of his personal "sabraization"—he was born in 1931 and came to Palestine in 1945—Orlev harps on the holocaust theme and singes his stories with holocaust embers.

The shattering experience of the holocaust seems to have invested survivors with impotence or madness. In *Wounds of Maturity*[26] Hanok Bartov (1928–   ) joins his vivid skills as a journalist concerned with the ephemeral to his undoubted talents as a novelist concerned with the permanent. What he strives to achieve is a *modus vivendi* for Jews in the post-holocaust era. What he actually accomplishes is a tacit admission of failure: no individual can cope with the enormity of the disaster. The swaggering soldiers of the Jewish Brigade in prostrate postwar Germany are scorched forever by their multiple exposure to the aftereffects of the holocaust. This is also true of Yoram in *Children of the Shadow*[27] who, like the author Ben-Zion Tomer, came with the mass youth immigration by way of Teheran to Israel. Educated in a cooperative, engaged in the War of Independence, he remained an outsider in spite of his seeming integration into Israeli life. The scar of the past has not healed in the therapeutic present.

Only Yehiel de-Nur(1917–), better known by his pseudonym Katzetnik 135633,[28] manages to make an adjustment to life for himself and his protagonist after the horrors on "the flaming planet of Auschwitz."[29] In *Phoenix Over the Galilee* [30] he emerges—like the legendary bird—from the fire which had consumed him and given him rebirth. Love between a man from Auschwitz, Harry Preleshnik, and a native girl of Israel, Galilea, is the theme of the book. Symbolically, though not melodramatically, the two are united in wedlock on the night of November 29, 1947, when the U.N. voted to establish the Jewish state. The political significance of the date adds a unique dimension to the private ceremony: after the recitation of the joyous blessings under the bridal canopy, the traditional prayer for the dead is chanted—the prayer which summons the martyred relatives of the groom. But the repeated threat of annihilation hovers over the happy pair, over the entire populace of Israel. The two make a fateful decision: they dedicate their private love to a larger love—to the idea of symbiosis between Arabs and Jews. The book ends on an ominous note: Harry carries away the mangled body of an Arab girl from the debris of a truck to uncertain safety. Though surrealistic techniques obscure the author's art with the gaudy trinketry of pseudopsychology, a hope emerges in lucid splendor: inhumanity of man to man may change to empathy and sympathy. Love, not weaponry, is the key to humane metamorphosis.

A survivor of the horror, Abba Kovner (1918-) managed to escape and remember the stark events in episodic and spasmodic verse. As a leader of the resistance in the ghetto of Vilna and as a leader of partisans in the forests of Lithuania he was transformed by the holocaust.

When he settled in Israel after the termination of the Second World War, he hardly had time to adjust to the new freedom. In the War of Independence, he experienced overt warfare as cultural officer on the southern front.

Holocaust-branded and battle-scarred, such was Kovner as man and poet. In *My Sister Is Little*[31] which earned him the Brenner Prize, he fashioned a poem of the holocaust; in *Face to Face*[32] he articulated his anguish in prose, in *Parting From the South*[33] he told in verse what the Six-Day War meant to him.

In *My Sister Is Little* the brother of the little girl narrates a few episodes of her life in a convent which shielded her from the fury of the Nazis.

> One bell
> For prayer.
> One bell
> For danger.
>
> One hangs on a long rope.
> One holds
> The life of my sister.[34]

In abrupt, disconnected lines the brother tells the story of the girl: how she grows up among nine sisters of charity and the mother superior in a strange world with an incomprehensible idiom. The language is permeated with the imagery of the Song of Songs—from the title page to the end of the poem. The love song par excellence becomes an ironic travesty on a world without love and without pity.

> You were not privileged to die.
> You were not covenanted in blood.
> On the day you will be spoken for [35]
> You will be
> Sanctified
> More than eagles
> And cherubs. [36]

The effectiveness of Kovner's poem can be attributed to the contrast between the grandeur of tragedy and the restrained pathos of the poem about one little human being. In lines of one or two words, almost monosyllabically, the poet moans rather than sings that one personal tragedy which is a symbol of six million tragedies, and of all the millions of tragedies on this unhappy planet.

Eighteen years before *My Sister Is Little* Kovner published his *Parting From the South*, a poignant poem about the cruelty of war and the liberation of a land. But he renounced patriotic posturing and the rhetoric of militarism and chose, as in *My Sister Is Little*, a series of disjointed verses on comrades in the field; their anguish before, during and after the battle and, above all, humanity ravished by inhuman deeds:

> Guernica on every hill. We listened to David.
> But David did not rise.[37]

David did not rise, many did not rise. But out of the Guernicas of the world at war a new liberty was born.

In prose—and on a much broader canvas—Kovner wrote his semi-documentary novel of the War of Independence. It begins with the birthday party of a twenty-four year old girl, Beruriah, on December 19, 1947. The confusion in mandatory Palestine after the U.N. resolution on November 29, 1947—the resolution which assured statehood to Jewry—serves as the point of departure for the poet. Out of the confusion—the inimical reaction of the Arabs, determined to frustrate the international decision with armed might, the obstructionism of the British in their last governing spasm, the lack of weaponry and provisions among Jews—a new nation surfaces, to its own astonishment, to the astonishment of the world. And this birth with its birthpangs, refracted in the vision and the action of a few youngsters, is the burden of Kovner's novel. In a new language—in a picturesque slang with many lingual arabesques borrowed from the hostile neighbors—they articulate their agonies, their defeats in the vicinity of Jerusalem and, finally, their victory. Only a small segment of the country comes alive in the novel—the southern front, the vital Jerusalem-Tel Aviv sector. In an encounter between British soldiers and Jewish members of the underground a terse dialog illumines Jewish determination to wrest a homeland out of the wilderness:

> —How do people live here? . . .
> —How they live? You can see: from the soil . . .
> —What's all this worth? . . . Why don't you give up the place?
>   If it's such a damned place, why don't you leave?[38]

The British leave the country torn by fratricide and still unborn to its humanizing tasks.

The unfriendly milieu of the desert and the protective cover of the forest fascinated Kovner and conditioned his attitudes to man and nature. In *A Canopy In the Desert*[39] he is no longer an active soldier but a man who travels at a leisurely pace in the Negev and in the Sinai and reflects on primal events in the area: the patriarchal history and the revelation. But these are not in the center of his attention. Belatedly, the mystery of womanhood enters his tense world and his short poems. The juxtaposition of woman and desert elicits a new technique. It is still narrative but it dares, at times, to abandon Hebrew for the universal, mechanical, nonpoetical dots and dashes of Morse, a poor substitute for words.[40]

Kovner is at his best as a documentalist. He made his debut in Hebrew literature with a poem, "Before Light"[41]—a poem about one night with partisans in the forest. In seven episodes, haunted by saboteurs and spies and constant danger, he presents the harsh reality that veers spasmodically to tenderness or to inarticulate cries that rise to controlled anger. The real hero of the poem—the forest, symbol of shelter and awe, danger and mystery—appears at the very beginning:

> It was not the falcon of steel that has kindled the
> >   wide open clearings.
> It was not the flame of perdition that fed the horizon.
> But the forest burns and the treetops burn. . .
> It's the sun that furls its flag. . .[42]

Toward the end of the poem the forest wakens to dawn:

> Darkness hovers over the forest. . .
> Pines don't stir. . .
> Resin freezes in dew.
> A cry, a hoarse cry.
> The last wolf returns to his lair.
> Famished.[43]

Within that awesome majesty of the woods human lives are never far from hunger, torture, death. But they possess the dignity of freedom, rebellion, resistance. That is the lesson Kovner the partisan has acquired from their checkered murmurings and mutterings. The philosophic stance, the leisurely pace: these qualities do not characterize either his poetry or his prose. A nervous dynamism, a confused tension informs his work, which draws its sustenance from a macabre world—before light.

Like Abba Kovner, Hayyim Guri (1923—) fought with the Southern Brigade in the War of Independence. And the title of his first book *Before Dawn*[44]—an allusion to Jacob's struggle with the angel—carries the same connotations as Kovner's first book, *Before Light*. Although moved by a similar struggle for dignity, he was conditioned by a dissimilar fate. As a native of the Land of Israel he faced the obstacles of the mandatory government to his country's independence. To thwart these obstacles—that was his mission in Europe as an organizer of illegal immigration to mandatory Palestine. Then, as a soldier of newborn Israel, he was involved in the defense of his country; only after the War of Independence did he acquire an academic education at the Hebrew University and at the Sorbonne. But his real education he received in the wars which were part and parcel of "the hundred year war."[45] And, as an experienced reporter, he left an unforgettable account of the Six-Day War as seen from the vantage point of a fighter for Jerusalem. [46]

This soldier-poet conceived his first book, part prose part poetry as the story of "the infantry which wrote with its footsteps the great poem on the burning land of the Negev."[47] But it was also a book of *Betrothal*[48] with an ancient land through reminiscences of the ancient Canaanite pantheon (especially Anath, the Goddess of War),[49] and o the current fight for redemption. Gradually, between the four wars o Israel, Guri evolved a private stance which reached its culmination in *The Rose of Winds*.[50] Repose and restraint were to be the twin characteristics of that new development.

I heard about calm
I haven't met yet.

Calm belongs to a land
Whose name I don't know.

Calm belongs to a town
Where I have not walked.

Calm dwells in a house
Whose windows are strange.

I think calm is
Where things end.

But I am penultimate.
Like hunger.[51]

Perhaps he articulated the fate of a generation when he wrote on his thirty-fifth birthday:

I had no time.
Now it's clear
That I had no time.

Half of my life.

Now one may
Keep quiet.
My shadow lengthens
With the steps of the sun.

I am the man
Who had no time.[52]

In *The Rose of Winds* the memory of battles recedes; the private world asserts itself in hushed lines. The poet is an Odysseus who has returned home after the wars and discovered "the sea and the fish and the floating grass on the slow waves."[53] This identification with the Homeric man of many modes, reiterated in another book of poems,[54] is not casual but emblematic: the poet, like Odysseus, has to rediscover his home and his destiny. In his ambitious *Odyssey*, Nikos Kazantzakis sought to enclose his search for a personal and national identity in an epic of inordinate length. In a pithy poem Guri summoned the wanderer from Ithaca to symbolize his own life, and, in spite of the dissimilarity in cultural backgrounds and in levels of artistic attainment, their work uncovers identical compulsions of self-analysis and reevaluations of ethnic goals.

The Glass Cage[55] and *The Chocolate Deal*[56] attest to Guri's attraction to the theme of the holocaust. *The Glass Cage*, a report on the Eichmann trial in Jerusalem, is the poet's document of identification with the holocaust. *The Chocolate Deal* is a fictionalized transformation of his experience as organizer of illegal immigration[57] to Palestine. It involves two friends who are imprisoned in their experiences of Auschwitz. One tries to escape total despair, the other accepts total defeat. Both are the unfinished victims of the final solution; both live on in the ruins of a German city after the Second World War. One of them, Mordi Neuberg, dies prematurely; his death is, as it were, a symbol of solidarity with the 6,000,000 dead. The other, Rubi Kraus, inflates the price of chocolate, an import of the American Army, through shady deals consummated by a German doctor. And the German doctor is the victim of blackmail by Rubi. Guilt by association: is this the form of survival in the post-holocaust world? The title of the novel seems to force on the reader this melodramatic conclusion. In spite of spicy sexuality and cumbersome plot entanglements, the novel moves in a dreamy pace between the living and the dead. In this sphere the past impinges on the present, imagination reenforces reality, language serves as a special tool for a special exigency. The result is an important novel of the holocaust among the many mediocre products on an impossible theme. Such a novel is possible for a man who has observed madness at close range and composed a book that mixes fact and fiction, prose and poetry, fragmentary autobiography and biography, Israel-to-be and Israel-as-it-is: *The Crazy Book*.[58]

Amir Gilboa (1917–), who settled in Israel when he was twenty and lost his father to the Nazis when he was twenty-five,[59] had already experienced the aftereffects of the First World War in his native Poland; in the conflict of Arab and Jew in mandatory Palestine in the thirties he was a volunteer in the Hebrew Brigade, and he fought as a soldier in the War of Independence at the end of the forties. For him, as for many young men born in the first three decades of the century, war was the central event of his life and work, identification with the biblical Isaac and the near-sacrifice a personal necessity.[60] Unlike other poets—Guri for example—he did not have to establish a personal stance for himself. He was from the beginning of his poetical career an intensely lyrical poet with a personal style embedded in the style of Shlonsky.[61] The wars of the century—especially the War of Independence—were his anguish, his anger, his release.

> Winds of my wrath will sweep the world.
> Tongues of my fire will lick the wrong.[62]

The outburst is not rhetorical pathos; it is the justified cry of impotence in the face of a comrade's death, the deaths of all comrades, as in the moving poem "The Speech of the Dead Before Their Time:"[63]

> Our day has set. Not appeased.
> We cry for we did not sin.
> See our sorrow which can't be grasped.
> Before we smiled, we were finished.

No wonder Gilboa can say without self-consciousness:

> I think iron
>   I sing iron
>   For I want iron
>   For this is soul.[64]

But the repetitive technique detracts from the impact of these and other poems.

> And my brother keeps quiet.
> And my brother keeps quiet.
> And his blood yells from the earth.[65]

For a poet like Gilboa, Isaac is not only a prototype; he is a brother, an eternal victim. And the father, unlike the biblical Abraham, is also a victim. The persona of the poet and his ancestry merge into a synthesized unit—into the unity of nationhood.

As for the world, the poet has a two-line poem to the world:

> If my people will forgive the killers of my people, there
>   will be no forgiveness for my people.
> Mother, my mother![66]

The poet's anguish is felt even in confrontation with the landscape:

> Alone. Like one not from here,
> Not from there.
> Between roads, in the fields
> Each stalk higher than he.

> Mountains in mist all around. They have closed the horizon.
> The valley is full of bones.
> And a puny point melting in sadness like sadness

Caught in the twilight.

I am the point. But I will rise
And embrace the mountains.
I will send forth, with the rustling leaves
Which sing the song of the first day each day,
That spirit of mine.[67]

This haunting experience of war abates only in the experience of
love. For love is Lethe.

You are proud unto death.
For your breasts are firm
And the eve of your lids is warm.
For a verse burns in your moving lips,
For summer gallops around you, a slave
Who faces his master, God.[68]

But even a love poem is not a new departure. The poet may say—
ironically—that he discovers a new America but he concedes after a
while it has already been discovered. Yet Americas that no one has discovered appear to him from time to time. But he does not hold on to
them; he lets them go.[69]

For a poet like Gilboa poetry is more than the translation of experience into verse. It is experience itself, it is the desperate affirmation of
impossible life and inevitable death. And that is why he can address
his "wild song" with confidence: he can always return "to it, to himself."[70] And that's why he can delude himself with the assumption that
"greater than poetry is seeing and sensing."[71] No, not even for Gilboa.
For poetry is seeing and sensing and storing the booty of sensation and
reflection in verse.

Ben-Zion Tomer (1922–) who made a name for himself with his play
Children of the Shadow has almost conquered his nightmarish obsession with the holocaust in his poetry which is lyrical and extremely
economical. His poems are paradigms of brevity.

I am not guilty, father.
I am the flower on the wreck.
Your house fell, father.
I remained, the island.

It's terrible, father.
To be a flower on a wreck,
To be an island in the blood.

Had I, at least, been guilty, father.[72]

In a few words, manipulated with admirable economy, Tomer succeeds in an evocation which may be a reminiscence of the holocaust.
But the evocation is unsubstantiable. And the paradoxical title of the
poem, "Guilt"[73] is a proclamation of innocence. Perhaps his "Love Poem"[74] also alludes to the holocaust:

When my heart reaches out to you,
The dead disappear.
When my mouth rests on your lips,
The dead vanish,
The dead vanish,
My love.

How many streets
And dead men
Must I see,
Hear,
Bless,
Till my mouth rests on your lips.

That Tomer uses his favorite title "Children of the Shadow" for a poem—that is evidence, perhaps, that he is haunted by the obscenities
perpetrated on his people in the Second World War. Perhaps he has
characterized himself best when he said in an earlier poem, in an earlier book, that joy does not mix with his blood.[75] This stranger to the
happy life has also produced a simple metaphor for his life:

A black river
Is the river of my life.[76]

Itamar Yaoz-Kest (1934–), Hungarian by birth, experienced the horrors of the concentration camp at Bergen-Belsen as a child and, understandably, never forgot the impact. Like Nelly Sachs who was haunted
by the chimneys, he lived in a landscape of smoke,[77] in the acrid fumes

of the crematoria. In a poem of four lines and merely seven Hebrew words he succeeded in evoking what he could not relinquish:

An old day.
My face bent
On your life
Like smoke.[78]

Of such stuff are the poems in *Landscape In Smoke*. In a short verse drama, "Fences of Night,"[79] two young people, Daniel and Eva, return to a village in Germany and search for clues of holocaust victims. They roam the anonymous world of the dead where incinerated remnants of a past reality play on the imagination. The concentration camp emerges in stark phantasy—the moon is women's hair which is caught by the barbed wire and touches off a fire in the fence. The inheritance of the eyes—the title of one of Yaoz-Kest's volumes of poetry—[80] is also the inheritance of the imagination. And imagination runs amok in *Light Growing Dark*,[81] where visions of redemption and mystifications of the Sabbath are barely hinted at by verses which consist of one word and by a locality, Safed, a cynosure of mystery in Jewish lore and history.

As a holocaust victim the poet clings to tradition with gloomy desperation. Tradition becomes a personal possession, represented by the father, "my father—the root."[82]

My father—the root in the earth.
I am the tree
Trembling for fruit.
Fowl perch in the evening
On my head
And storms.
And I bend toward the root.

It was inevitable that the mother should also become a major theme—the widowed mother who, in a series of verse monologs, mourns the loss of father in fear, in sorrow, in loneliness.[83] In a holocaust novel, *The Luminous Line*,[84] the poet depicts the tragic confrontation between mother and son in a postholocaust atmosphere. And in the "Ballad of the Locked Door"[85] the child knocks but the mother does not answer. The child flees from some terrible disaster, the mother lies on an unmade bed "with nontherapeutic pills by her side." The father-mother syndrome is the powerful pillar which supports the edifice of Yaoz-Kest's work: "A mixture of mysticism and realism accompanies my entire life. I think that the mystical element is mainly embodied in my mother, the realistic in my father. My difficult problem is to synthesize these two elements—the realistic and the mystic—in my writing."[86] It was in search of the realistic element that the poet turned to the novel.[87]

Like other contemporary Hebrew poets Yaoz-Kest is haunted by the Abraham-Isaac syndrome. While the son represents sacrifice, the father is the thicket.

> The tombstone
> Moves.
> Father's head floats
> In the milky way.
> —My son,
> He calls in parting,
> You are the sacrifice,
> The thicket am I.[88]

In a short novel, *In the Window of the Traveling Home*,[89] the poet also remembers the holocaust. The father of one of the protagonists, a boy named Peter, dies in Israel after all the obscene horrors in trains that went to the destinations of violence in concentration camps. The boy clings to the memory of a father whom he knew inadequately and immaturely. And that minimal inheritance must serve him as a foundation for an uncertain life. The widowed mother is merely another aspect of the irreparable loss. The biographical and imaginative elements merge in the novel and obliterate the line of demarcation. In another novel, *Bird's Shadow*,[90] Yaoz-Kest again remembers the holocaust through the internal conflicts of a young poet. And again he writes a semi-autobiographical novella. Awesome recollections of a broken identity in the era of the holocaust; search for a new identity in Israel: such is the stuff and texture of the poet's prose.

As a poet and poetic novelist Yaoz-Kest produced a commendable quantity of work. As a translator he ransacked the literatures of the West and the East: German and Hungarian, English and French, Latin and Japanese poets owe the Hebrew versions of their work to him. A study of Dylan Thomas, Rimbaud and Horace—a few of the translated poets—reveals subtle influences which have been thoroughly absorbed and transformed into an original stance.

When the poet republished and refurbished his first volumes of poetry in a collected book of *Poems*,[91] he said in a brief introduction that they were united by a common thematic thread: "the destruction, the transplantation from clime to clime and the biologico-psychological inheritance." What he gave to Hebrew literature was a new illumination of the havoc wrought by the Second World War.

13
Dissociation and Discontinuity in Contemporary Hebrew Literature: Yehuda Amichai

PROSE poems—short pieces in prose couched in sublime language—delighted generations of readers in the nineteenth century. The aphoristic chapters of Nietzsche's *Thus Spake Zarathustra* are the culmination of this genre and the trivial, frivolous *maqama* marks their inception. Since Eliot a reverse process has taken place in literature: prose-in-poetry. Sublimity has been replaced by drabness, rhyme by unrhymed verse, rhythm by faint echoes of rhythm, association by dissociation, logical sequence by arbitrariness, rural imagery by technological imagery, preoccupation with the past by the cult of the now and the *dernier cri*.

For the past fifty years—roughly since the publication of *The Waste Land*—prosiness dominates the poetry of the West. In Israel the ancestor and grandmaster of the new direction is Yehuda Amichai (1924–). *Now* is his favorite vocable: *Now In Noise*[1] is the title of a volume of his poetry; *Not Of This Time, Not Of This Place*,[2] literally, *Not From Now, Not From Here*, the title of his surrealistic novel. Even Jerusalem is the city of *now* rather than the city of *then*:

> On a roof in the Old City
> Hangs the wash illumined by the last ray of day:
> White sheet of a she-enemy,
> Towel of a he-enemy
> To wipe the sweat.
>
> And in the sky of the Old City

Flies a kite.
At the end of the thread
A child
I cannot see
Because of the Wall.

We fly many flags,
They fly many flags,
To make us think they are happy,
To make them think we are happy.[3]

And in a five-line poem—a reminiscence and transformation of a rabbinic parable on the lame and the blind[4]—he has meshed his own personality with the personality of Jerusalem in a parallel parable of incomparable beauty:

I and Jerusalem: the blind and the halt.
She sees for me
Till the Dead Sea, till the end of days.
And I lift her on my back
And wander blind in my darkness below.[5]

An ordinary parable has been elevated to an extraordinary parable of interrelationship between the figuratively blind poet and the seeing, stationary city. She scans the physical horizon for him and sees as far as the Dead Sea. This is geographical reality; one can see as far and even beyond from the hills of Jerusalem. But she has also surrealist eyes; she sees as far as the golden age—the end of days predicted by Isaiah and Jeremiah and Ezekiel and the minor prophets. This is the city's simultaneous sight on two levels. The poet, representative of his people, carries the physical and metaphysical reality within him and wanders blindly, unconsciously toward his unknown destiny on earth.

It is because of its close kinship with the poetry of the West that Amichai's poetry has been translated into English, not only sporadically in periodicals like *Atlantic Monthly,* and *Mademoiselle* but also in book form.[6] It was, in fact, easy for Michael Hamburger, the American author, to write an introduction to Amichai's poetry in translation, though he had no knowledge of Hebrew. He sensed that the German-born Amichai was only accidentally a Hebrew poet:

If in 1936 Amichai's family had emigrated not to Palestine but to

Britain or America, he would have written in English, as I do, or in German, as his near-coevals Paul Celan and Erich Fried continue to do, though one lives in Paris, the other in London.[7]

And that is why Amichai as an Israeli seems to remember Jerusalem with the Psalmist's fervor,[8] and reverses the Psalmist's injunction: "If I forget you, diaspora . . . " The remembrance of the diaspora by the Israeli in the present, the remembrance of Jerusalem by scattered Jews in the past: here is the root of Amichai's idea and image of simultaneity. It underlies the novel *Not Of This Time, Not Of This Place* in which the hero lives in Israel and in Germany simultaneously; it underlies the poems and gives them, in the happy phrase of Hamburger, "multiple awareness." It juxtaposes human beings and landscapes, as in the poem "Indian Summer in Princeton"[9] where the first line converts Indian summer in New Jersey into Jewish summer in Jerusalem. Even confrontation with a biblical character like Jonah or Saul is an exercise in simultaneity:

Once I escaped, but I do not remember why or from which God.
I shall travel through my life like Jonah in his dark fish . . . .[10]

In "King Saul and I" the idea of simultaneity reaches a startling magnificence:

I am tired,
My bed is my kingdom.

My sleep is just,
My dream is my verdict.

I hung my clothes on a chair
For tomorrow.

He hung his kingdom
In a frame of golden wrath
On the sky's wall.

My arms are short like string too short
To tie a parcel.

His arms are like the chains in a harbor

For cargo to be carried across time.

He is a dead king.
I am a tired man.[11]

But nowhere has simultaneity been expressed with greater conciseness than in the poem "The Place Where I Have Not Been:"

The place where I have not been,
Where I never shall be.
The place where I have been
Is as though I had never been there. . . .

And what I shall never in the world return to
And look at, I am to love forever.[12]

In "Luxury" the why and wherefore of simultaneity become painfully clear. The father was buried in Jerusalem, an uncle in the Carpathian mountains, the forefathers in the villages of Lower Franconia in Germany:

So many tombstones are scattered behind me—
Names engraved like the names of long-abandoned railway stations.

How shall I cover all these distances,
How can I keep them connected?
I can't afford such an intricate network.
It's a luxury.[13]

Simultaneity is the need and, in an ironical twist, the luxury. It covers and connects the distances in geography and in history and in personal history. That need and that luxury make for simultaneity of pain that must be banished in order to remain. Simultaneity informs even Amichai's love poems; simultaneity of time and place is taken for granted by lovers:

We were together in my time, in your place.
You gave the place and I the time.[14]

And, as always, Amichai furnished an example of perfect simultaneity in a few lines in "The Songs of Resignation:"

> I resign.
> My son has my father's eyes,
> My mother's hands
> And my own mouth.
> There is no further need of me.
> Many thanks.[15]

The longest poem of Amichai, "The Travels of Benjamin The Last of Tudela," plays with variations on the theme of simultaneity:

> . . . My son
> Is a war orphan of three wars.
> I was not killed in them,
> He was not born in them yet, but he is the war orphan.[16]

Finally, in his book *Now In Noise*, poems on New York follow the poems on Jerusalem in simultaneous antithesis.

Amichai is not only a master of simultaneity but also a master of irony. With tongue in cheek he can excoriate the three monotheistic faiths:

> I'm tired. And curse the three Great Religions
> Which won't let me sleep at night
> What with bells and howls of muezzins and loud shofars and noisy
> > atonements.
> O, God, close your houses, let the world rest.
> Why hast thou *not* forsaken me?[17]

While the deeply devout may feel offended by such lines, the nondevout will enjoy them and pity the religious for their notorious deficiency in humor. Still, it is a fact that Amichai's poetry borders on the blasphemous; only irony prevents a poetic line from crossing the border surreptitiously as in the poem which echoes the most solemn prayer for the dead: "God Full Of Compassion."

> God full of compassion.
> If it were not for the God full of compassion,
> There would be compassion in the world . . .
> I, who have brought mounds of bodies from the hills,

I can tell you that the world is void of compassion.[18]

Irony also informs "A Sort of End of Days:"

All nations (united) will flow to Jerusalem
To see if the Law has come forth.

Since it is spring now,
They will gather flowers all around them.

And they shall beat the sword into plowshare, plowshare into
sword
And so on and again, ceaselessly.

Perhaps from many beatings and sharpenings
The iron of strife shall cease.[19]

The Isaianic vision is repeated, changed, ridiculed and, finally, substantiated by the poet's parallel hope for a world of peace. But irony is aware of tragedy and has, in fact, its birth in a tragic view of the world. And Amichai's poetry is almost tragic irony—an ironical paradox:

One half of mankind in the world
Loves the other half.
One half of mankind
Hates the other half.
Because of these and of those
Must I wander and change endlessly?[20]

In the ironic world of Amichai "a young he-star marries a she-star";[21] the poet's father sees "traces of angels" in the "sands of prayer,"[22] presumably in the notoriously artificial prayers for the holidays which flowed with such profusion from the pens of Yosi ben Yosi and Eleazar Kallir; sentences are left unfinished because the business of the world is unfinished.

The poems of our mercurial poet seem to be written with deceptive ease. Perhaps they are, perhaps they are not. Heine's smoothest lyrics required long hours of composition, and so did the graceful poems of Yeats. But Amichai's facility borders on superficiality. He refuses to discipline the rush of inspiration, to weed out the wilder growths of his imagination.

Amichai's fictive and dramatic works complement the poetic work. The protagonists of his stories saunter in the streets of New York or Jerusalem, meet casually, say a few words indicative of a mood or a passing thought and dissolve as in a film on the screen. In the title story of the book *In This Terrible Wind*[23] the protagonist, the thinly disguised poet, walks in Chinatown and notices a Chinese on the other side of the street. A red-haired Irish girl between them struggles with the wind and the dog on the leash.

> Had a chessplayer come or Fate with enterprising ideas and a sense of humor, he would have grabbed all three of us and joined us and bound us in many strange combinations. But, since he did not come, the three of us were unharmed. Three driven by the wind, three accidental entities, three freight cars on a siding. Each one on a different track. . . .

This is a sample of a fragment of a story by Amichai: the casual encounters which have no continuity, the plot which begins and ends abruptly, the dissolution which is a solution of some sort. As for the story, the protagonist makes his way to Coney Island, meets a girl in a tattered dress and, after a brief dialog, accompanies her to her tiny room:

> We sat on bedcovers and on books . . . I heard her breathing. Her breathing was the little sister of the terrible wind outside. Her face was beautiful. I remembered my mother who used to interpose her hands between her and the Sabbath candles when she pronounced the blessing . . . I also wanted to do that but the girl held my hands in her hands. Outside doors were opened, doors were struck. A big tin sign crashed with a terrible din. I thought the wind was the soul of this place . . . When I was small, I imagined the soul was a white thin rod alongside the whole body. Or a shoelace. At night one takes off the shoes, one liberates the soul, the body can rest and dream.

The protagonist tells her about a summer in his childhood, she tells him about a sea captain. They talk in disharmony, but they complement each other: "The logic that turns water into clouds, clouds into water, operates in us." They walk out into the streets of Coney Island again; they enter a diner.

I looked at my watch. All times inside me were different. The time of thought and the time of memory and the time of feet and the time of my wife who waited for me.

Outside they were separated by the awful wind. The protagonist took the subway to Times Square and wanted to telephone his wife.

There were ten booths—all taken. I waited till one would become available. Suddenly I was overwhelmed by a great joy. The telephoning people seemed to be bees who made honey in the cells of their hive. The sweet honey of conversation between man and man. All the ten telephoning people made sweet honey in public telephone booths on the day of that awful wind.

This is the end of a story which is not a story but a tale of chance encounters, philosophical musings, mystical aperçus, poetic imagery—mélange like life itself. And so are the other seventeen stories in the book, *In That Awful Wind*, all nonstories, all rewarding, all full of that honey of life which people make unconsciously for themselves and for others.

The novel *Not of This Time, Not of This Place* is similar in essential technique but the proportions are on a grander scale. Joel, the archeologist and the protagonist, is told at a party that he should return to his native Germany and find hatred; but he should also stay in Jerusalem, at the same time, and fall in love, in spite of the fact that he is happily married. The Empedoclean syndrome, hate and love, divide Joel's mind and the book about Joel as well. He returns to his native Weinburg and tells, in the first person, about his vicarious revenge that is never consummated. At the same time he also stays in Jerusalem, meets an American doctor named Patricia and falls in love with her. In Weinburg he is caught in a filming scene by Melvin, an American who is trying to memorialize the tragic deportation of Jews from the town. Melvin complicates the plot, for he is the American officer who had ordered the destruction of the town to save his men. And he is the husband of Patricia, Joel's love in Jerusalem. The intricacy of the plot is episodic rather than schematic, casual rather than foreordained. There is no catharsis of Melvin's feeling of guilt through his cinematographic venture as there is no catharsis of Joel's hate through love for Patricia.

In his confusion Joel retires to work on Mount Scopus and is killed by an unexploded mine. But he returns—after death as it were—to

Germany and comes back to Jerusalem again. At the airport he meets Patricia who is returning to America. As his plane descends on Jerusalem he asks:

> How will my life be from now on? Will it be stormy and fateful or calm with endless peaceful thoughts?[24]

This abrupt, unfinished *finis* to the novel is as undecisive as the remark a few pages earlier:

> Once I awoke with the cry "My God, my God, why have You forsaken me?" And immediately after I cried, "My God, my God, why have You not forsaken me? Why didn't You leave me in my peace, without vengeance and without love?"[25]

The novel is a blend of phantasy and realism as all good novels are. What distinguishes it from other works of fiction is a total blurring of boundaries between the real and the unreal, between perception and imagination. The principle of simultaneity which had too little scope in a lyrical poem had found its ample role in an ambitious, full-length novel. The unstructured structure of *Not Of This Time, Not Of This Place* crumbles sometimes from the heavy weight of detail—especially in the original edition.[26] But even in its shattered fragments it shines with the opalescent brilliance of a large diamond.

One has the feeling in reading Amichai's work that one is sitting in a theater and participating as an audience at a play where unimaginable gaffes alternate with inspiring suspense, where irresponsible reality performs impossible events. But, then,

> All the world's a stage,
> And all the men and women merely players . . . [27]

Amichai's talents lie in the domain of lyrical poetry and possibly in the short story. In these genres he accomplished a breakthrough; a new vision, a new technique. The novel *Not Of This Time, Not Of This Place* may be merely a series of short stories interconnected or rather disconnected by a broken thread of simultaneous narrative in two countries. The latest novel, *Hotel in the Wilderness*,[28] is unworthy of his talent. It is, as it were, an insight into the inner life of an aging Israeli poet living in New York. He is plagued by a prolonged creative drought. His remedy: a series of flirtations with pornographic overtones. In his two successive jobs he is a failure; an overt failure as an official of the State of Israel, assigned to induce Israeli émigrés—members of the academic community—to return to their country; a covert failure as a disgustingly successful writer of advertising copy for a manufacturer of women's lingerie. All told—a depressing character with a supporting cast of dismal Israelis who live in a hotel that is more of a flophouse than a hostelry, and equally dismal Jews who have made a fortune in New York and give generously to Israel.

Hotel in the Wilderness is not only a stopover for bankrupt Israelis; it is a symbolic asylum for the bankrupt protagonist in the wilderness of New York who decides to return to Israel on the eve of the Six-Day War.

Amichai's plays do not measure up to his lyrical poetry: neither the dramatization and modernization of Jonah for Habimah, the National Theater of Israel, under the title *Journey to Nineveh*,[29] nor the radio play *The Day Martin Buber Was Buried*,[30] nor *No-Man's Land*,[31] nor *Bells and Trains*.[32] They sparkle with *nonsequiturs*, they amuse with extraordinary situations. The best—*Bells and Trains*—is a miniaturization of the grand theme of Amichai's novel: the protagonist visits his native town in Germany after the holocaust and relives moments of his childhood in the awful glare of the national and personal tragedy. The setting—a home for the aged where a relative and acquaintances of his youth reside—adds grim tension to the dramatic episode.

In his early fifties Amichai is still in the prime of his creative vigor. And he may still surprise his wide readership with works which probe the unsuspected recesses of the human imagination.

14
Disengaged Poetry: Carmi; Mar; Zach; Rübner; Pagis; O. Hillel

T. CARMI (1925–), a New Yorker by birth, came to mandatory Palestine as a boy of six and stayed there three years. He returned to the United States, studied at Yeshiva University, and acquired a degree at its Teachers Institute. In 1947 he settled in Israel and fought in the War of Independence. In his life, as in his poetry, he may be said to have shared and not shared the experiences of his contemporaries. In the daring modernity of his style he belongs to the Alterman-Amichai generation. But he is a pure lyricist, a poet's poet, a man in confrontation with the eternal themes and verities.

> Come, pass your hand across my mouth.
> I am not accustomed to this light.
>
> Our love is batlike, is a round of darknesses.
> It will not miss its mark. Your face explains
> My hands to me. What shall I understand in the light?
> Rise, pass your hand across me.[1]

A love poem? Not in the ordinary sense of the word; rather, an original transfiguration of a worn theme in six lines—the involuted love accustomed to batlike flights in darkness; the lovers in unaccustomed, uninterpreted light. Perhaps this is enough; perhaps it isn't. And you, dear reader, can supply the missing data in the love equation.

In his greatest intimacies the poet invites you to a participatory communion. The bat is the favored bird:

141

> I have not understood that the yearning of the bat
> Flies blindly to the darkling city-night.[2]

The bat graces an original concept in the poem "How Many Days, How Many Years:"[3]

> My forehead's bats hummed dizzily
> Round and round . . .

The child is a flower, a playmate:

> Child, child, flower of mine,
> Can one play words with you now?[4]

Bat or child—both are entities which involve the poet's investigative, imaginative quest. Carmi makes poetry—as so many modern poets do—out of a quotation from the prayer book[5] or an ancient incantation preserved in the Talmud[6] or a paraphrase of a quotation from the Bible.

> She is asleep. But her hand is awake
> More than the palm of the surgeon.[7]

The allusion is unmistakable,[8] but the verse in Song of Songs is used for another purpose than love. It has changed its grammar—first person singular into third person singular—and lost some of its intimacy. In the sleeping-waking syndrome, the emphasis—as in the Song of Songs—is on the waking. But the waking state is suffused with the sensitivity of a surgeon who depends on his hand for that precision which may mean life or death to his patient.

It it only natural that a poet of Carmi's imaginative bent should attempt novel techniques. In collaboration with an Israeli painter, Jacob Agam, a musician, Frank Pelleg, and a film technician, Aryeh Mambush, he created a nine-minute art film with a text that underscores the eternal verities of the Israeli landscape: desert and sun, camel and sandstorm, sheep and shepherd.[9] It was also a vital need for a poet like Carmi to translate poets after his own heart[10]—Wallace Stevens, Dom Moraes, Nazim Hikmet, Sophocles and Shakespeare. He is always fiercely original; but he does not strain to be so; he comes by his gift naturally. In "Transition"[11] the seeming subject of the poem is a tree. But is it?

The eucalyptus tree tore the autumned nights.
O what a shameless wail
With the moon looking on.
It cleft the silence of the windows,
It plucked the sleep of birds.
O what disgrace
To drive into our borders
The tatters of its days.

And now,
After all the lamentations,
It stands
On the mounds of its calm skins
Ruddy and gentle
In the midst of another season.

The two seasons of the Israeli year stand out in vivid vignettes, not because of generalities but because of one characteristic tree. The eucalyptus experiences— and invites all who observe it to experience— the storms of autumn, the gentleness of spring.

Such is the stuff of Carmi's poetry: love, landscape, even war, or snow in Jerusalem. It is made durable and it will survive more popular and more famous poems. As he himself says in a beautiful paraphrase of a biblical verse:[12] "Don't mind if I am not seen."[13]

When father and son or sons ply the art of poetry or prose—as did the Lebensohns in the nineteenth century, the Mohars and the Steinmans in the twentieth century—the generation gap is apt to assume sharper contours. First, outwardly, there is a change of name. The younger Mohar writes under the name of Mar (1921–), the younger Steinman under the name of Shaham. Then there is a complete departure from the father's ideas or imagery, style or content matter. Yehiel Mar was aware of the generation gap, filial reverence and the need of secession from parental tutelage: "I grew up in a home of artists. My father was a writer, my uncle [Schlanger–Mohar] was a writer, one of my brothers studied singing, another was a painter . . . I knew the name of Bialik before I knew how to talk . . . I developed within me a resistance to all that atmosphere."[14] Resistance meant a total break with a mode of life. At sixteen Mar came to Israel, worked as a pioneer in rural surroundings, and as a laborer in the city. He suffered poverty and hunger; and he wrote a new kind of lyrical poetry. In 1951, he published his first book of verse.[15] Like his father's verse it was rhymed at times, but unlike his father's it was daring in content, elusive, "a handful of wind."[16] Even when it attained a certain solidity, it rarely rose above the consistency of a watercolor. The poet was happiest with what was neither discernible nor tangible.

All that I have
Is a handful of wind,
A gift for the kingdom of birds.

All the silences—
A throatful of tiny silences—
A gift
For the stone and the doe.

All the light—
A phial of light
For the sea of rising dawn.
An offering

With a full heart,
With all the strength
Like the innocent and the guilty.

But my eyes will not see
When the sea
Overflows the shores.[17]

Interpretation of such poetry must end in failure. For the elusive cannot be caught, cannot be dissected. It must remain whole in its elusiveness. In "All That I Have" there is an intimation that silence of man cannot equal and cannot feed the silences of stone or doe; there is also a hint that the bit of light in the poet's possession may make a difference, may be a gift to the dawn though he would not see the result of that gift. There are other hints in the poem and they may or may not be interpreted, but they have their place and their value.

Mar is a poet who uses the Bible for his purposes with exemplary skill:

All the girls stream to the sea,

Yet my heart is not full.[18]

These lines from "Summer 1966" paraphrased Ecclesiastes 1:7:

All the rivers run into the sea,
Yet the sea is not full . . .

An observation borrowed from the pessimistic philosopher becomes in Mar's manipulation an allusion to futility and frivolity. Another observation from Ecclesiastes 11:1 is given a playfully ironic twist which points to man's utter disillusionment and inadequacy:

Cast your bread upon the waters,
You shall not find it.[19]

Is Mar's poetry heightened appreciation of the vanity of all things? It is. But the act of articulation is a release from abysmal despair. In Mar's case, a release based on "truth, talent and individuality."[20] By truth Mar undoubtedly means emotional honesty. In a beautiful poem, significantly entitled "Man,"[21] Mar sums up the limitations and the grandeurs of *homo sapiens:*

That's all his strength. To know, to sing,
To see his abysses and not to retreat.

Mar can be as good in generalization as in particularization:

Let your hand go.
The hand is wiser than you.[22]

Pars pro toto, the part for the whole: Mar rides this kind of conceit with subdued aplomb. For death is at his beck and he, the bitter one, as he named himself incongruously, drinks "the bitter wine of his way" with sweet resignation.[23]

Nathan Zach (1930–   ) is a master of uncertainty with a vocabulary that is a mosaic of perhapses and ors and ifs. Alienation is his badge. In his poems on "Honi the Circle-Drawer"[24] he recreates the background and foreground of an ancient Rip Van Winkle; he also revives the imaginary experience of Honi—the prototype of alienation.

But Zach is also a manipulator of words for the mere pleasure of manipulation. And, in such cases, he is performing rather than creating, playing tricks rather than making serious attempts at poetic experience:

> She is dead—the wife of my math teacher.
> Woe to the wife of my math teacher.
> Woe to the math teacher himself.
> She is dead—the wife of my math teacher.
> Woe to the wife of my math teacher
> Woe to my math teacher himself.
> She is dead—the wife
> Of my math teacher
> Woe to the wife
> Of my math teacher
> Woe to my math teacher himself.
> Himself.[25]

There are, in fact, only three lines in the whole poem. After the first three lines the next three lines repeat the previous words. And the next six lines are merely the first three lines with all their repeated words again in a cozier verse arrangement. This repetitive technique— also used by David Avidan, Meir Wieselthier, and Avot Yeshurun—is supposed to produce a hypnotic effect. But it doesn't; it is a stillborn poem—as, unfortunately, so many of Zach's poems are. Perhaps this repetitive technique, which can be a blessing, is Zach's curse.

> Saul hears music.
> Saul hears.
> What sort of music does Saul hear?
> Saul hears music
> Which is therapeutic.
> Saul hears music.

And this is, presumably, the "precise description of music which biblical Saul has heard."[26]

Repetition does not produce the desired effect; it is a sterile *perpetuum mobile.*

> I can paint
> But I don't know

I know how to play
But I can't

And if somebody should come and say to me
That all the world's a stage

I would spit straight into his mug.[27]

When Zach forgets his modernism he can write charming lines on
that northernmost outpost of Israel, Metullah, which was a sort of spa
for American and Israeli tourists:

No ancient majesty,
No Jerusalem. But very
Beautiful,

Very. Here a bird flies
With a smaller bird. Perhaps a daughter-bird.

A tourist whispers in her husband's ear
In the rocking chair, in English.
So that I won't understand.[28]

There is a saving irony here—as in many of Zach's poems—and a
charming immediacy. And these are the paths to his future glory, if he
succeeds in dumping uncongenial Anglo-American prototypes in poetry, such as C. Day Lewis, and in criticism, such as Wellek and War-
ren.[29] With an acrobatic skill which verges on mastery he can perform
the balancing act between the ultramodern and the ultranaive. And it
is not only patriotic duty that draws him to the folksong; it is deep self-
knowledge, right use of his poetic abilities.[30]

A typical poem by Tuvia Rübner (1924–) and, to a certain extent,
Ozer Rabin, reads like a word game; it depends on the relation of word
to word, syllable to syllable; it achieves its success or failure through
their fortuitous coalescence into meaning or non-meaning. As he put it
so aptly himself: "Birth of man and birth of language are one."[31] Pun
and repetition are the orthodox, disjointure of words and far-fetched
neologisms the unorthodox devices in that game. Lack or economy of
punctuation is, of course, *de rigueur* since the days of e.e. cummings. A
whole poem like "Walking in the Streets"[32] consists of four lines:

I sent my eyes
Her clear face
Passed my face, my hand, my back, my face
Which remained like a bush without birds.

This is probably the effect of a passing girl's face on the poet's face. Man, it is said, is a playing animal; no reason for not playing poetry.

Dan Pagis (1930–) has earned his reputation as a poet and translator and Senior Lecturer for Medieval Hebrew Literature at the Hebrew University of Jerusalem. As a scholar he has published distinguished editions of medieval Hebrew poetry. As a translator he has cultivated mainly German literature which was familiar to him since childhood in his native Bukovina. His mastery of the Hebrew idiom is apparent on every page in the three volumes of his poetry—*The Shadow Dial, Late Leisure,* and *Transformation.*[33]

The poems—brief and lyrical, austere and severe—reflect the malaise of an individual who has experienced the horrors of the concentration camp and the alienation of the poet which has become so familiar a trait of modern poetry as to be almost a commonplace. Themes culled from English literature such as "The Epilog to Robinson Crusoe"[34] and themes from biblical and post-biblical literature such as "Ararat,"[35] "The Cycle"[36] or especially the sensitive "Honi"[37]—the Hebrew Rip Van Winkle who dozed for seventy years—are cast in a sparse, rhymeless mold.

As a poet with a definite personality and a penchant for exotic themes, Pagis deserves his place in modern Hebrew poetry. A field-mouse[38] hoards food; the granary is full, the passageways cunning, but above lurks the hawk. This is prudence and violence in uneasy confrontation. A laboratory experiment presents a dozen scorpions in a beaker; an experimenter blows poison inside; the scorpions struggle, "begging the glass wall for one more moment;" the superfluous sting; the non-understanding pincers; the approach of the final shudder. And the laconic, wise ending of the poem: "It's only an experiment . . . Not a judgment/of poison for poison."[39] In "The Cycle," the parable of the ant[40] is given a startling interpretation. The naiveté of biblical didacticism turns to nihilistic sophistication: the sluggard and his ways; the eternal recurrence of life and death; the return to dust; the bin to store the grain of a harvest which is yet to come, and the straw that is one's body.

O. Hillel (1926–) narrates brief, pungent episodes in charged lyrical language. Deliberate departures from traditional themes and vocabulary: these are characteristic features of his poetry. A good example: "The Butchershop."[41] Three women are wending their way to the butchershop and indicate their compassion with another woman—a victim of her husband's infidelity. "I would gouge out his eyes"—says one. "I would poison his drink"—says the other. "I would set his house afire"—says the third. In the refrain the butcherwoman dips her hand in blood: gory accompaniment to an unfortunate event. And then, the appearance of the child in the street, the offspring of that accursed father. New burst of compassion from the mouths—if not the hearts—of the three women with wasps in their eyes.

Feigned compassion in ironic verse against a brutal background: this is not a mean achievement. Eroticism also commands violence. The body of the simple daughter of a tailor with the innocent name Joseph is wracked on the wheel of inquisition; two swarms of bees consume the nipples of her spring; the torch of her womb burns. Her prayer: to be the victim on the pyre of her master's couch.[42]

These poems could have been written by any modernist poet in France, Germany, England or America. They are the non-rational, nihilistic posturings of the young and not so young throughout the world. The capitals of Europe and the Americas are filled with their arid shouts of impotence.

15
Mysticism in Poetry: S. Shalom

At the end of the second decade of this century a young poet, S. Shalom (1904–), began to publish poems which lacked Bialik's sweetness of language and Tschernichowsky's strength of form, but vaunted original and studied crudeness. Like all true poets he studied his predecessors in order to find the thorny path that leads from one's self to one's self. Within a decade the novelty of his poetry became part and parcel of modern Hebrew literature.

His originality was not noticed immediately; it was hiding under a cloak of conservative form and expression. In a youthful poem he chose the hackneyed subject of the sunset as his theme:

> In the evening, when sparks
> Flash on the mountain,
> Someone leaves me
> For the landscape of unreturn.[1]

Except for the last word everything seems conventional in the four lines: the expressions, the stanza form, the melancholy mood of evening which, since Sappho, has never failed to find the poet responsive. Yet everything is new in the four lines: the lack of rhyme in a stanza where rhyme is a customary embellishment, the enigmatic departure of the guest.

As Shalom grew in strength and maturity, the mists of mystery spread over most of his poems: "Wonder of wonders, all is wonder"—he says in a clever paraphrase of Ecclesiastes.[2] More than any of his predecessors and contemporaries he drew his inspiration from insignificant objects which had come into their own with the advent of Rilke.

> A house, a ladder and perhaps a tree:

150

This is my world.
The rest is mist.[3]

The feet of a bird, the slice of a pear, the remnant of an altar served Shalom equally well. The pathos of the inanimate world, the moods of flora and fauna, found their first adequate expression in Hebrew poetry through Shalom.

There is another point of contact between Shalom and Rilke. Both poets viewed death with a certain equanimity; they even looked upon life *sub specie mortis*. Small wonder that Shalom created a quiet elegy of great intensity on the men who gave their lives in the defense of the homeland:

When a man dies in the valley of Esdrelon,
The ears of corn keep calm.
The Holy of Holies is the valley of Esdrelon;
One doesn't weep in the Holy of Holies.

When night descends upon the valley of Esdrelon,
The stars tremble.
They are the candles for the dead in the valley of Esdrelon
For those who have no *Kaddish*.[4]

Only the death of millions, the holocaust, evokes a different response from the poet—especially in the play *The Diary*.[5] But to view mass murder with equanimity would be madness compounded with blasphemy.

The belief that death is not the end, not for Shalom nor for anybody else, must be expected from a mystically inclined poet. Since "the soul is everything and everything is its echo," nothing really decomposes. Death is thus a rung in the ladder of existence, a foretaste of immortality.

Like death time loses its arithmetical significance for Shalom: "Our time cannot be counted among the years." Space is non-space, the burden of life is no burden. On the boundary line of the immense Nothing the poet stands in contemplation and wonders how to clothe his visions in verse; hence an almost stuttering helplessness which adds charm to his poetry. Like one who has lifted the veil of mystery and seen unusual sights, he projects the unaccustomed experiences into the most ordinary words and, in doing so, deprives them of their common connotations.

If he has an unusual predilection for the dream and the dream world, it is because there, as in death, the differences vanish between man and man, between man and beast, between being and being. In a poetic reproduction of a dream about a cat, he drops a weight on the paw. The cat utters a cry and pierces his heart with its nails. Instantly the partitions between the world of man and the world of animals and the inanimate world disappear as in a phantasy by Cocteau. The poet becomes the weight, the paw, the leap in space, the frightened cry.

In dreams Shalom achieved the disintegration and the mysterious reintegration of his personality. And it was by virtue of his dream-power that he was able to extract new subtleties from the Bible in his biblical ballads. What fascinated him, above all, in the Book of Books was the wealth of unexplained lore which reached down to the very depths of humanity. In "The Slain Heifer" he illustrated an ancient custom[6] with a concrete example. A man was killed by an unknown hand in the field. Thereupon the elders and the judges measured to the nearest city and wrung the neck of an innocent heifer according to pre-scribed ritual. But in Shalom's poem the dead man rises after the cere-mony and charges the sanctimonious priests and elders with man-slaughter. They have performed their ritual and proclaimed their in-nocence but they had spilled his blood because he, the victim, had dis-covered the treasure that would have deprived them of their high posts had he shown it to the people. Shalom does not reveal the nature of the treasure but he succeeds in enlisting sympathy for the slain individual and antipathy against the official representatives who always trample upon the people and upon their true benefactors.

Shalom also infused an element of surprise into the biblical ballad "The Scapegoat." It was not the goat, as custom prescribed for the Day of Atonement,[7] but the "appointed man" who was sacrificed in expia-tion of the sin committed against all the scapegoats in all times. There is dramatic intensity in the lone walk of the "appointed man" and the goat:

> They walk with silent step
> And do not turn around.
> Fear goes before them
> Like the fear of the Ineffable Name.[8]

The sudden metamorphosis of the "appointed man" into the goat, and the goat into the "appointed man," the accuser into the accused, and the accused into the accuser, plays havoc with the accepted notions of sanctimonious morality. Vengeance of the goat on the man is retribution of right against might. The disconcerting death of the "appointed man" disrupts the ceremonial on the Day of Atonement but leaves no legacy of far-reaching consequences. The fast lasts somewhat longer than usual, the prayer of the High Priest suffers a delay. In the years to come, the ceremonial of the Day of Atonement in the Temple will go on with its prescribed ritual, unchanged and unchallenged except by the dim memory of an unpleasant incident.

The mystical and mysterious tendencies of Shalom extend also into the area of sex. Like many modern poets Shalom minces no words; he prefers the explicit image and the plain statement. In his erotic poetry as in other spheres of poetical endeavor he likes to break barriers. In a series of sonnets he pursues the mystery of woman with the zeal of a lover and a philosopher. While Tschernichowsky imparted a sculpturesque quality to his sonnets and Fichmann spread the warm colors of his palette on his sonnets, Shalom was the first to use this form in Hebrew as a vehicle for mystical expression.

Man is the trope. The trope is the sound and the sight.
We are fed on fanciful tales: we never existed at all.
Books are written in vain, in vain the years pass withal.
The unreal bags are devoid of happiness, pain and blight.

Earth is not fashioned of clay nor heaven of azure light.
And all our wisdom is merely the stutter of dwarfs in the squall.
The heretical mime is a fool, a fool—the creature of gall.
Words and words without end, and silence governs in might.

Calling on you in distress, I am only a whirl in the wind,
A sound that was torn from its source and suddenly found its palls,
The pall of flesh and desire, the pall of sorrows and sins.

Until you open the window that faces the halls
Of the deep, and my being return to the font and sink in the stalls
Of chaos, I'll not comprehend like the prophet until he begins.[9]

This is, perhaps, the most enigmatic sonnet in the Hebrew language. Yet the general idea seems to be quite clear: the unreality of man, the uselessness of books, the imaginary pains and pleasures, the pathos of heresy and rebellion in a world of uncertainty, and the possibility that love opens the window onto the abyss of destruction and knowledge.

This proliferation of ideas in the compact form of the sonnet has, at first, a bewildering and disturbing effect. But, on second and third reading, the full impact of imaginative wealth produces lasting pleasure. With Shalom the sonnet was liberated from the frivolity of Immanuel of Rome and Ephraim Luzzatto. What he lacked in smoothness, he compensated with seriousness. In discarding the iambic pentameter of the sonnet—a feat accomplished before him by the American-Hebrew poet, Hayyim Abraham Friedland—he freed it from metric petrification.

In spite—and perhaps because—of his mystical idiosyncrasies Shalom clung to realities. When mandated Palestine was drenched with the blood of civil war between 1936 and 1939, he accompanied the anxiety of his fellow citizens with memorable work. The cycle *From the Flames,*[10] the long poem *On Ben Pele,*[11] and the play *Shots Into the Cooperative*[12]—*Dan the Watchman* in a later edition—reproduce the period of fratricidal strife with poetic precision. In the language of penitential prayers which, because of the numberless misfortunes suffered by Jews in the middle ages, became stereotypes for the expression of sorrow, Shalom mourned the death of a girl in the cycle *From the Flames;* and he did not forget Hanitah nor the tenseness of the sowers by moonlight and gunlight. At the same time he managed to project his unique sense of mystery, his major claim to originality in modern Hebrew poetry. The days of bloody strife were merely days of reckoning for "the army that has gone to the unknown." As for himself, he knew that "the soul of the unknown echoed in his soul." Little wonder that an event like the establishment of the State of Israel unlocked new hermetic sources in the poet. In the form of a love poem—against the enflamed backgrounds of the final years of mandatory Palestine and the first years of independence—S. Shalom projected a new, allegorical image of his people. Kohavyah, the Star of God, is a mere pretext for new national nomenclature: "Each Jew is fathered by the Star of God." The beloved is the Rose with the biblical overtones of the Rose of Sharon, the external symbol of spring and awakening.[13] And the union produces the son Ami, my people. In spite of the simplicity of this tale in rhymed stanzas, a deeply felt participation in the national awakening marks every line of the poem.

There is no incident in the life of Shalom that has not elicited a mystical commentary. In his only long poem *On Ben Pele* he depicts the agonies of a watchman in pre-independent Israel. At the same time the poem illuminates his own life with an autobiographical account: the days of childhood in a village, the days of youth in the house of the town rabbi, the escape to Vienna during the First World War, the transition to Jerusalem and to the Valley of Esdrelon, are stages in the life of the watchman and the life of Shalom as well. But the reflections on the incidents are the poet's and not the watchman's.

> And all that will happen to me the child had known.
> For it was like a sound on a godlike string.[14]

In the same manner the Irish poet A.E. wrote about the child and the terrible responsibility of the world to the child.[15] But A.E. emphasized the fatality of the early impressions; Shalom concentrated on the fatality of inheritance and predestination.

Even when, in the early years of his life, Shalom observed the penitential midnight mourning prayers, he asked the typical question: "What is sin and who are the guilty?" The mother lacked the power to alleviate the inexplicable yearning of the child for "the arm of mystery." National misfortunes strengthened Shalom's sense of the mysterious, the wonders of Jerusalem deepened it considerably. His heart, as he so beautifully expressed it, was sharpened "on the rock of despair." In its swift movement, in its short chapters of two four-line stanzas, and in its autobiographical interest *On Ben Pele* is one of the loveliest lyrical compositions that have come from Shalom's pen. In his attempts at drama, Shalom was less fortunate than in his lyrical work. In the dramatic poem *Elisha and the Sabbath,* (changed in a later edition to *The Sabbath of the World*),[16] he had already failed to rise to the exigencies of living speech. The hysterical note that mars many of his poems destroys the plays. In *Elisha and the Sabbath* the characters shout rather than speak. Elisha strays from his faith because of his love for the wife of Rabbi Meir; Ben Zoma rages because of the blood of the victims of Betar[17]—hallowed by Bar Kohba's victory; the mother of Elisha goes mad after the apostasy of her son. In this assemblage of maniacs the souls of the individuals are as blurred as the soul of the period. This is also true of the play, *The Cave of Joseph*.[18] Shalom did not succeed in recreating the tense times of Josephus Flavius. Nor did he try to establish any logical links between the various characters of the play. In an autobiographical essay "On My Creative Ways" he confessed frankly:

> In the play *The Cave of Joseph* all the characters . . . in the cave of Jotapata are, with all their reality, especially in the first acts, visions, voices, wills and dreams of Josephus Flavius . . .[19]

But Josephus is a mystical dreamer, an unrealistic leader in the poet's vision. He is Shalom, pure and undisguised. Yet Max Brod characterized the play as possessing "great metaphysical depth."[20] The play, *Dan the Watchman,* is another excursion into the field of autobiography. For Yehiel, the watchman who ponders the fate of the Jews, is none other than Shalom. His worries about the homeland and about the girl who loves his friend are pretexts for self-laceration and self-analysis. The end of the play falls back on the naive device of the *deus ex machina:* Yehiel, who wants to shoot his friend, abandons this bloody resolve; the friend marries another girl. Other girls of the cooperative play a negligible role: their mockery of the hero is self-mockery of the poet. The parents have no active influence on the progress of the play. As in *The Sabbath of the World* and *The Cave of Joseph* hysteria loosens rather than binds the scenes and the acts. Shalom may have been right: the dramatic tension of *Dan the Watchman* is the tension "between man and himself." This is the essence of all dramatic tension. But the dramatist must deepen it with clashes between the hero and the other characters. For Shalom other characters do not exist. The voyage from self to non-self is an impossible adventure.

In his *Galilean Diary*[21] which has been translated into Norwegian, Dutch, German and English, and in *Storm Over Galilee*[22] the poet attempted to do in prose what he failed to do in poetry: he told the story of a cooperative poetically and he described some unforgettable types. He also depicted the sowing at night—a necessity occasioned by the inimical attitudes of the indigenous population—with poignancy and restraint:

> Go gentle, moon, go gentle. We sow by your light in the field of
> > Galilee.
> Enemies rise against us on all sides . . . so we sow at night.
> For we only want to sow, our soul yearns for wheat.[23]

Shalom's voice is a distinct, major voice in Hebrew poetry. Veined with mysticism, open to realism, he reflects the eternal and the ephemeral in Jewish life.[24]

16
Poetry and Prose of Women: Rahel; Bat Miriam; Amir; Goldberg; Raab; Rabikowitz; Zeldah; Tur-Malka; Baron; Hendel; Karmon

FEW women writers of rank grace world literature. The exceptions only confirm the rule: Deborah—if she authored the victory song[1]—in biblical literature, Sappho in Greek literature,[2] Gaspara Stampa, the reincarnation of Sappho in the Italian renaissance, Louize Labé and Elizabeth Barrett Browning who cultivated the love sonnet, Edna St. Vincent Millay who shed a new glory on American poetry, and Anna Akhmatova who enhanced contemporary Russian poetry. Theirs were the lonely voices; they repudiated the prison of silence and escaped from its intimidating darkness.

Women writers were scarce in Hebrew literature; women scholars were a rarity. Paola Anav copied Hebrew manuscripts in thirteenth century Rome, Pomona da Modena excelled in talmudic studies, Deborah Ascarelli wrote Italian verse in the sixteenth century. And so did Sarah Coppio Sullam, a famous beauty and lover of learning. In the period of enlightenment Rachel Morpurgo published a volume of mediocre poems; and Nehamah Puhachevsky (1869–1934) wrote a few mediocre stories. They were the pampered exceptions in modern Hebrew literature.

Jewish tradition was partly responsible for the paucity of women writers. A famous adage of Rabbi Eliezer deprecated the education of women: "If any man imparts knowledge of the Law to his daughter, it is as though he taught her lechery."[3] Against such views Judah Leb Gordon raised his fervent plea for the liberation of women and David Frischmann, as early as 1887, advocated the importance of teaching women Hebrew. Their voices were heeded. In this century Hebrew prose benefited by such writers as Deborah Baron and, in more recent times, Judith Hendel and Amalia Kahana-Karmon. In the difficult field of translation women made notable contributions: Puah Toren, for instance, continued the work of David Frischmann with her Hebrew versions of Tagore. The lasting impact of women on poetry is an acknowledged fact of contemporary Hebrew literature.

The spiritualized chastity of Rahel (1890–1931), pseudonym for Rahel Bluwstein, was more than an individual characteristic; it was the trait of a large section of Jewish womanhood. Three thin volumes, reassembled after her death in a single book,[4] hold her entire lyrical output—an uninterrupted hymn to the fields and the hills and the waters of the Holy Land.

The poems in manuscript and the selected letters afford intimate glimpses into her life. Her gift for friendship drew into her orbit the eminent figures of the Second Wave of Immigration—Berl Katzenelson, Moshe Sharett, A.D. Gordon[5] and, above all, Zalman Shazar who met her in Galilee three weeks after his arrival in Jaffa and who regarded her presence as a major experience in his life.[6] With particular tenderness she expressed her love for the Sea of Galilee, "the blue eye of the homeland."[7] She yearned for the lake and for the palms which raise their high heads above the shores, the mountains of Golan and Hermon in the distance. And on the banks of the Sea of Galilee she found her last and lasting resting place—in accordance with a wish expressed in a poem. It was only right that another lover of that landscape—Levi ben Amittai—should immortalize her grave in a poem.[8]

The tragic fate of Rahel cast a tragic splendor over her poetry. A grave illness, tuberculosis, dogged her life from the days of her youth—before she left Russia for the Promised Land in 1909. Like Böcklin in the famous picture, she seemed to respond to the macabre music of the sullen fiddler, Death. In time, she became reconciled to the inevitability of an early end. Grim renunciation of love and motherhood became a painful theme.

> If I had a son, a little child,
> Black-curled and wise;
> A son to take by the hand and guide
> Through the garden paths;

A son—
Uri I'd call him, Uri mine.
How soft a name, how dear and short.
A flake of light.
My curlyhead boy
Uri
I'd call.[9]

As a woman she regarded her barrenness as a curse. Happiness and immortality meant reincarnation in the flesh of her flesh. In the unrealizable hope for progeny she contented herself with a plea to a friend to call her daughter Rahel:

Give my name to your girl
That I may stay.
It is so sad to pass away.[10]

Rahel adopted suffering and ailing unlike wrathful and blaspheming Job as a symbol of her acquiescence. She identified with the man who knew how to receive good and evil at the hand of God. From the desperate lines of the biblical protagonist she absorbed only soothing stimulation: "He wounds and his hands make whole."[11] In the poem "My Dead," written shortly before the end of her life, she succeeded in expressing the melancholy consolations which the dead give to the living:

They alone are left me in my life,
They will not be cut by death's sharp knife.

When the day surrenders to the night,
They surround me with mystic light.

We have made a bond which will not fray.
Only what is lost is mine to stay.[12]

Illness, deprivation, death: this terror-inspiring trinity wrested poems of gentlest acceptance from her wracked femininity which sported an exotic garb. Russian was her native language, Hebrew became the language of her heart. In her translations of Pushkin and Yesenin, Moravskaya and Akhmatova, she partly repaid the debt she owed Russia. In her own poetry she paved the way for a galaxy of women writers—for "Miriam's daughters" in the apt phrase of Bialik.[13] Far from being "emotion recollected in tranquillity," her poetry presents an immediacy of reaction to an experience. This may be the poetic mystique of a woman poet. But speculation on the distinctiveness of the feminine mind is a hazardous task replete with guesses and devoid of solid information.[14]

The first poems of Elisheva (1888–1949), pseudonym for Elisaveta Ivanovna Zirkowa, were imbued with Zionist ideology and written in Russian. She thought in Russian and spoke Russian throughout her life. Her inflated reputation—the result of a biographical accident rather than the reward of any real merit—rested on her spiritual conversion to Judaism and Hebrew poetry.[15] An early interest in the Jewish people led her to the study of the Hebrew language from a Hebrew grammar, the gift of her brother, an Orientalist. Schoffmann, Brenner and Gnessin, whom she translated into Russian, and the Russian poet Alexander Blok,[16] were the formative influences on her work. But echoes of Heine, who had taken the opposite road and become a convert to Christianity, reverberated in many of her poems; they were palpable in "Green Pines":

> Green pines in the woods full of scent.
> Guard my repose, my heart's content.
> Of the numberless trees in this land of balm
> Only you know the widsom of calm.
>
> At sunrise to the sunlit sky
> You raise your bright-green hands on high.
> Thus, in God's ancient temple, swayed
> Your brothers—the cedars of exquisite shade.[17]

In his poem "Pinetree"[18] Heine had expressed the longing of the northern pine for the disconsolate palm of the south with inimitable passion and sweetness. In "Green Pines" Elisheva created a lyric of tranquillity in a similar though less artistic vein: she changed the palm to cedars, the distance of space to distances of time, the longing into liturgical gestures. It was a poetical *tour de force* which verged on originality.

Echoes of other poets reverberate in her poems:

> Come, brother wind,
> Embrace me once more![19]

Like St. Francis of Assisi who, in the beautiful "Hymn to the Sun," called the wind *frate ventu* (brother wind) and like Charles van Lerberghe who called the rain "brother rain,"[20] Elisheva humanized the forces of nature. She imparted to them, in drab verse, intimacy rather than sublimity.[21]

In her prose Elisheva dwelt on two themes: alienation and love. She understood the horrors of maladjustment because, she complained as early as 1919 she had "two souls: one Russian and one Hebrew."[22] And she was obsessed with a passion to merge with her new environment.

In her story "Sabbath Candles"[23] a gentile girl falls in love with a Jew, and develops a growing fascination for the rites of the Sabbath, the idyllic calm and the festive stance with their vast implications for humanity.

In "Queen of Jews"[24] Elisheva reverses the process: a Jewish girl, falls in love with a gentile, makes a pathetic attempt to rid herself of her Jewishness and loses her lover. Fear of an imminent pogrom raises a wall between her and her man—a wall that cannot be breached.

A similar theme informs the "Unimportant Incident."[25] An assimilated girl, Mania Libin, acquires fluency in Russian and a taste for Russians. Before Easter an old Jew is imprisoned in her native town: he is caught with the body of a child in a sack. "Blood libel" becomes the main topic of conversation everywhere and, especially, in Mania's own circle in Moscow. Even her closest friend begins to show symptoms of antisemitism. The change plays havoc with her relationship: it is not broken off completely, but it is considerably loosened.

The lack of reality in the deeply rooted prejudices and superstitions in Russia led to very real persecution and bloodshed. The "liberated" Jew, free from traditional ties, suffered for a Jewishness which he neither knew nor cherished. That tension was often ended in conversion. Elisheva took the opposite road. In her only novel, *Alleys,*[26] she again used a variation on the theme of alienation. The plot centers around the love of a Hebrew writer for a Russian woman poet. They think and speak like relics of the Victorian age, though they live in Soviet Russia. The meagre resources of Elisheva's language and imagery and thought were not equal to the creation of a novel. Only in a few stories and poems does this modern Ruth capture the nostalgic joys and woes of the alien who, since 1925, resided with her Jewish husband, Simon Bichowsky, in the Land of Israel. Like Rahel she was destined to find her last resting place on the banks of the Sea of Galilee.

The work of Bat-Miriam (1901–   ) is a memorial to the disappearing woman of the past. The soulless modernism of the twentieth century disgusts her; the half-forgotten world of Jewish traditionalism fills her with delight. Love for the Sabbath and the Sabbath chants is no romantic affectation; it is admiration for a waning form of Jewish life which has not been replaced by an intense spirituality of a corresponding nature. Bat-Miriam seems to caress such words as *Tallit* and *'Atarah,* the prayer shawl and its silver-braided border, *Mahzor and Siddur,* the prayerbook for holidays and ordinary days. Even her metaphors and similes are drawn from a bygone age. Her shoulders are "a book of prayer and praise to the Lord"[27] and the door to her father's house is "an illuminated title page of the hymnal."[28] Hers is a Judaized landscape, a Judaized universe. Memories of patriarchal types she had known in childhood haunt her poetry:

My father's house rose peacefully
Like a prayer—pure and bright.
Saintly men illumined it
With religious light.

Spacious windows, towering windows
Looked upon the land beneath,
Upon the infinite expanses
Of the heather and the heath.[29]

Contemporary woman fails to elicit Bat-Miriam's poetic attention. The woman who follows the traditional pattern of life—the housewife and the mother who devotes herself to lowly duties with modest dignity—this is her heroine. Even in modern Tel Aviv ancient women sit on the threshold of the house of study and dream out their dreams, their prayer books open.[30] In the preparation of meals, in the clatter of dishes, in the traditional chant of hymns and prayers Bat-Miriam's woman finds true comfort. To soothe and to please—this is the highest attribute of womanhood.

This is our gift of gifts:
To ease for a while
Man's grief with a song
And a motherly smile.[31]

And not only man's grief, but also woman's burden, mother's agony. Bat-Miriam sought relief from her unimaginable loss in a series of poems dedicated to her son who fell in the War of Independence.[32] He lived on in her memory—just as her own "childhood forgot to close its book."[33]

The personal poems of Bat-Miriam—the love poems—lack the immediacy of appeal of her nonpersonal poems. It is out of the tapestry of the past that she draws golden strands and weaves them into poetic patterns. On the soil of the Land of Israel where she settled in the early thirties, she longed to identify with the nationalist aspirations of her people. Yet the country remained for her a distant vision in spite of physical propinquity.[34] It was the land "on the threshold of mysterious worlds." And she yearned to convince herself that nothing existed before her arrival in Israel.[35] Neither love of land nor love of man matched her overpowering love for the woman of the past. Bat-Miriam became—through the sheer force of empathy—her recorder, her annalist, her historian in verse.

Flourish and fulmination: this is the poetic habitat of Anda Pinkerfeld-Amir (1902–   ):

We, women,
Pass through the world
Like torches of love.
Our dresses burn with the warmth of our bodies.
We, women,
Call hungrily for lovers
With eyes, with mouth, with heaving chest,
With each motion of the body
We call.
And this is life
To us, women.[36]

Anda Amir shows a deep understanding for mothers—black, white, yellow, red: they bear in sorrow and they understand nothing except "the fears of life and death" when they give birth.[37]

Like other modern poets, e.e. cummings for example, Anda Amir experimented with geometric patterns of symmetry:

I will sing,
    I will carol,
        I will weep,
            I will pray,
                I will go mad.[38]

Neither these lines nor the subsequent lines in triangular form made memorable poetry:

> From all the gardens of the town you gathered roses for me,
>   And there is no other rose in town,
>   And my room is very strange,
>   And so am I,
>   And my eye
>   And my mouth.[39]

These lines fascinate, at best, with total lack of premeditation or labored resolve.

All ten books of her poetry teem with woman and womanhood: their enormous need for love, their maturation through motherhood. It is only natural that a woman poet should be preoccupied with the female personages of the Bible: Eve, Lot's wife, Hagar, Leah, Yael, Jephthah's daughter, Delilah, Abisag, Astarte. Their common denominator is sensuous intoxication and violent passion. The cycle of poems *The Geisha Liam Tang Sings*[40] throbs with femininity in a lower key; it tells the unhappy love of the geisha for Judge Tsung-Tu:

> When your eyes met mine, Tsung Tu—
> Your eyes, two scarlet cherries—
> I knew it was for you I waited.
>
> Your glance sank in me
> Like a pearl in the depths of the sea
> With no hope of recovery.
>
> On that day I said to my serving girls:
> Note the day with bright colors
> On white parchment.[41]

This is charming orientalism in form, in feeling, in imagery. And the entire cycle of poems would have given Anda Pinkerfeld-Amir an abiding place in Hebrew literature even if she had not written anything else. In her later poetry she achieved again a certain serenity:

> And now I am a garden.
> My arms are flowers;

My eyes gleaming violets,
Laughing violets,
Flirting with the sun's gold.[42]

The collected edition of her poetry *Shocks and Sheaf* highlights her faults and all her considerable talents: the noise, the unbridled romanticism, the Slav patterns in Hebrew garb. In her youth she wrote in Polish. And she never lost her attachment to the three vatic poets of Poland—Mickiewicz, Słowacki, Krasiński—and to the Polish poets of Jewish extraction—Tuwim, Witlin, Słonimski.

Anda Pinkerfeld-Amir earned a just reputation as a writer of folksongs and children's songs. As a writer of folksongs she is at her best when she identifies with women. In "An Evil Omen," for instance, a black cat crosses the path of a young lady, and the day becomes a succession of minor misfortunes: the hearth smokes, the roast is burned, the soup is spoiled; and worst of all, these mishaps threaten her marriage. In a fit of fury, her husband may send her back to her father's house.

As for children, she delighted them with nimble fancies in nimble verse. The very title of a representative volume of poems for children appeals to the imagination: *Stars in a Bucket.*[43] Younger poets like Dalia Rabikowitz and Nurit Zarki modeled their children's songs on her craft, her technique, her imagery. In her collection of poems for children *I Like To Whistle in the Streets*[44] Nurit Zarki depicted a woman who lived in a watermelon and, after the watermelon season, fitted herself into a carrot. The poem about the noodle which performs acrobatic tricks in the soup will charm adults as well as children.

Leah Goldberg (1911–1970) has also done well by children—especially in partnership with the sensitive artist-photographer Anna Rivkin-Brick. Riding a tractor or scrambling over archeological ruins or facing up to camels—this amalgam of fun and exuberance in *Adventure in the Desert*[45] will never fail to charm the youngest. In *The Zoo*[46] she chose a number of animals and rhymed their characteristic attitudes in memorable verse. She also experimented with children's stories in prose.[47] But she earned her greater reputation as a poet for adults. Austere, lusterless, half-prosaic language burdened with an excess of imagery was her preferred manner.

A rug of roofs is spread before my window light
Like a childhood story storing the expanse.
Perchance some guests will come to me tonight,

A star will fall into my cup perchance.
The street spread all its rugs before my glance.
Perchance some guests will come to me tonight.

The antenna clutches like a mast
The hem of heaven heaving on the sea.
Melancholy night is coming fast
With light and bitter mist, with sleepy melody.
Someone, in a ship, will sail at last,
To some non-existent land, aghast.
Melancholy night is coming fast.

The lucid cloud from the scarlet sky
Will settle on the nearest canopy.
Wrapped in a cloak of vapors, fleecy, high,
It will kneel before the azure sea,
Before the waves that seem to hum and sigh,
Before the night that surges with expectancy—
The lucid cloud from the scarlet sky.[48]

The three disjointed stanzas, connected by a unifying mood rather than by logical sequence, present a novel evening. With such startling images as "a rug of roofs" and such daring lines as "A star will fall into my cup perchance" Leah Goldberg shocks the reader to poetic awareness. Sometimes she carries elements of surprise to the point of blasphemy. Thus, by an impossible feat of the imagination, the Palestinian buses sing "psalms with a Yemenite chant." In search of revolutionary techniques Leah Goldberg experimented with satirical verse in the performances of Broom—a theatre that attracted attention in Tel Aviv between 1928 and 1953.[49] But Leah Goldberg never forgot or repudiated her considerable reserves of conservatism. In the poems of her maturity she developed the fine art of discourse.[50] Epigrammatic terseness coupled with long poetic experiences, lent a sharp brilliance to the many poems which were collected in the posthumous volume *Remnant of Life*.[51]

A young poet grows silent suddenly:
He is afraid to tell the truth.

An old poet grows silent: he is afraid
That the best in poetry

Is its lie.[52]

The very title *Remnant of Life* is given a quixotic interpretation. "Remnant of life: it means understanding or folly. You have the choice."[53] Official honors from academic sources like the Irving and Bertha Neuman Literary Prize in 1969, which is administered by the Institute of Hebrew Studies at New York University, highlighted her fame. As Professor of Comparative Literature and the Head of the Department at the Hebrew University, she has been active in the field of criticism,[54] especially dramatic criticism and short story criticism, and in translation, especially from the Russian. A volume of essays on Russian literature in the nineteenth century attests to her life-long interest in the culture of her native country.[55] Disparate authors, Shakespeare and Petrarch, Tolstoy, Gorki and Brecht, have been translated by her. And a Hebrew poet, half-forgotten, has been restored to Hebrew literature because of her critical appraisal: Abraham Ben-Yizhak (1883–1950).[56] Though only eleven poems were published by him during his lifetime—and a few posthumous fragments after his death in Tel Aviv—he was a real precursor of modernity. Without traditional forms but in traditional language he managed to impress Hebrew poetry of the early decades in this century with the stamp of his aristocratic apartness. In ascetic distance from his contemporaries he wrote sparsely and almost ceased writing before the First World War. Characteristically, he was one of those happy sowers who do not reap but wander far.[57] It was Leah Goldberg who, through reminiscences, recalled Abraham Ben-Yizhak—his loneliness, his vast cultural background, and his perennial value. When she died prematurely in 1970, twenty years after Abraham Ben-Yizhak, the Hebrew world realized that it had lost its best Hebrew woman poet.

Esther Raab (1899–) draws her strength from the earth. As a native of the Holy Land and as a farmer's daughter she is in love with the wild eucalyptus trees and the orange groves, the mountains of Gilboa and the Golan:

Golan, Bashar.,
Hermon, Kinneret:
The entire land
To hug with a glance.

The majesty of the mountain, the dream of the sea.
God of the Fathers

Is in these skies.
I tremble, I shudder.[58]

This is a typical poem by Raab: a number of brief, sparse, direct lines—unaffected, glamorless like prose which has been cut to the proper length of the improper poetical line.

Beginning of wisdom:
To be with you—
Like the wind
In the tree.

Beginning of wisdom:
Obey you—
Like the bird that obeys
Its flight.

Beginning of wisdom:
To be yours—
Like the vine that is
The earth's.[59]

This "Portrait of a Woman" is not exactly the dream of Woman's Liberation. But it is characteristic of Raab's poetry, her conservative outlook on life, her traditional femininity. Even the original subject, "She-Fox,"[60] resembles, on closer inspection, a worn theme: the hungry she-fox feeding her cub in a cold night is uncannily similar to a Jewish mother in a forsaken hamlet of Eastern Europe. Prose is perhaps the right vehicle of expression for her talents. In a short story, "In the Orchard,"[61] she succeeds to portray a Jewish peasant. In the short poem she creates neither memorable types nor memorable images but only a vague impression of love for her native land.

Dalia Rabikowitz (1936–), a city-bred sabra, is a rebel against reality. In her poetry the dead come back to the living, fish fall in love, oranges lust for their consumers, a little woman fashions a cradle out of the whole, big, spherical earth. In this strange world she herself is metamorphosed into a mechanical doll; or, with less consistency:

Today I am a hill,
Tomorrow I am a sea.[62]

But the image of the doll persists. It is a longing, an aspiration:

To be a marionette,
A porcelain doll, thin and pale . . .[63]

And she mixes mathematical mock-precision with outlandish phantasies:

Four years of honey and milk.
I walked on the beach in the sunny isles.
The fruitstands were laden,
The cherries gleamed in the sun . . .

Four years round like an apple
I strung my string of coral beads.
Merchants and peddlers in the sunny isles
Spread curtains of red silk.[64]

Such poetry—like the subterranean springs of the imagination which feed its lines—has neither a beginning nor an end: it begins abruptly and ends inconclusively. For "imagination is a limitless thing."[65] In consciously, ungrammatical language, in unfinished sentences, in stylized slang she produces a new kind of poetry in a new syntax, a succession of poems with undefinable meanings like semi-abstract pictures of Braque or Picasso in their first cubist adventures. Even in her portraits in verse, as in the poem "To the Memory of St. Exupéry,"[66] she produces an unrealistic image of the writer-aviator who, had he been saved in the month of March of the year 1943, would have been "a shining grain, a rose in the wind, laughing in the clouds."

"What is this wondrous thing?"[67] she asks in one of her poems, incongruously entitled "Mahlon and Chilion."[68] And though the line sounds like a poetic bit from a song on the hit-parade, it characterizes her questioning personality: it is her life, everybody's life which is a query with multiple, unsatisfying answers.

While Dalia Rabikowitz rebels against reality, Zeldah (1914–) accepts it with traditional religiosity. Her genuine orthodoxy is a refreshing antidote to rampant agnosticism. As a daughter of a hasidic rabbi, Shalom Solomon Schneurson, she is possessed of an inner security: "The Lord is for me—I have no fear. What can man do to me?"[69] The "perfect faith" of her grandfather is likened to the faith of the patriarch who was ready to sacrifice Isaac.[70] The Sabbath is still a major experience for Zeldah:

> Sabbath has plucked
> The setting sun.
> Sabbath descends slowly.
> The rose of the firmaments is in her hand.[71]

The rose holds a special fascination:

> Each rose is an island
> Of promised peace,
> Of eternal peace.

> In each rose lives
> A sapphire bird
> With the name: And they shall beat their swords.[72]

The rose is metamorphosed into a symbol of the messianic era. And Sabbath is the silent participant in the love of woman for man, in her love:

> I and you and the Sabbath.[73]

That "the moon teaches Bible"[74] is perfectly natural in Zeldah's world; yet her femininity is an object of wonder and awe. In confrontation with contemporary society it is almost incomprehensible:

> Strange to be a woman—
> Simple, housewifely, weak
> In an arrogant, violent generation . . .
> Strange to wither before clouds of enmity
> When the heart is drawn
> To mysterious worlds without end.[75]

In spite of her flights to the empyrean, Zeldah enjoys mundane reality. Perhaps it is a bit different than ordinary reality, but it certainly is peopled with recognizable objects and living beings:

> We had a hidden treasure of leisure
> Gentle like morning air—

Leisure of tales and tears and kisses
And holidays.
Leisure of mother, grandmother, aunts
Sitting in a gleaming, peaceful
Boat,
Drifting slowly
In the fishing boat of peace
With the moon and the constellations.[76]

Zeldah oscillates between the visible and the invisible—the visible which is everybody's and the invisible which is her own. Hence the title of a volume of her poetry, *The Invisible Carmel*.[77]

The poetry of Ayin Tur-Malka (1926–) invites inevitable comparison: does it reflect the influence of her husband Uri Zevi Gruenberg, does it avoid its powerful seductions into the quasi-prophetic idiom? The equivalence of italicized lines in Hebrew, the exclamatory and declamatory expressions, the combination of three instead of the usual two nouns in a Hebrew construct: these are telling indicators of shared external techniques. In content Ayin Tur-Malka preserves a more subdued stance than Gruenberg, even a feminine coyness at times.

You were the treasure of my heart,
But I was not the treasure of your heart.

I forgot I was not your treasure,
Though I was a field as all women are.

In my misery I would go
As thoughts go toward the wide expanse.

I would draw the words, the washed ones,
From the wells' depths.

I would seek to clear the heart with the sunrising song.
I would prize the spiritual idiom of the elements.

The wells of clinging clouds
Were ready for the depths of heaven.

How often my heart had knocked at heaven's walls.[78]

This poem about the "Heart's Treasure" is typical of Ayin Tur-Malka's poetry in general. It achieves its transmittal of an unrequited love through repetitive, unadorned simile and metaphor.

The poems of Ayin Tur-Malka are short, lyrical, unrhymed, innovative in language but not on an ostentatious scale. In the expression of love as mother, but especially as wife and sweetheart, she achieves her best lines:

> When you met me, I was an instrument
> Untuned with the harmony
> Of femininity.[79]

It is with the intimacies of love that she also charges poems which are not love poems. Thus, in "Announcers of the New Jerusalem"[80] she asks:

> Were there among us bridegrooms and brides
> For the New Jerusalem?

Ayin Tur-Malka insists that the alphabet of the heart must be acquired before the acquisition of spelling.[81] In the Samson-Delilah syndrome she found a myth which she could adapt to her own femininity; Delilah, at best, is a broken instrument to Samson, son of the sun.

Deborah Baron (1887–1956), a traditionalist in the fullest sense of the word, pampered the *shtetl* with motherly devotion. As a rabbi's daughter in Uzda, not far from Minsk, she grew to love the small town with a delicate compassion. When she settled in Turkish Palestine in 1911, she merely continued her budding career as a writer in intimate association with her husband, Joseph Aharonovitz who edited the important Labor weekly, *Ha-Po'el ha-Za'ir*. For she had brought to her new homeland a wealth of vignettes of small-town life and transposed them into stories as she had done in Russia. What was equally significant for her literary growth: she brought a knowledge of biblical and rabbinic literature, Jewish customs and ceremonies and, above all, a sensitivity to the Hebrew language which was—and still is—unequaled by any woman writer in Israel. As a bedridden invalid for the last twenty years of her life she strengthened her inborn feelings of compassion for human and nonhuman life.

In her narrow thematic framework Deborah Baron knew how to extract an inner dynamism out of a comatose existence, an almost indiscernible movement out of durable imperturbability. Though she situated some of her stories in Palestine and a novel, *Exiles*,[82] in Egypt where she spent four years of involuntary exile during and immediately after the First World War, she returned invariably to the milieu she knew and felt best: the small town in Eastern Europe. And she peopled it with a gallery of portraits that have lost neither color nor freshness. For her restrained style harmonized with the small, suffering existences and, especially, the difficult burden of Jewish womanhood. At times she hovered dangerously over the swamps of sentimentality. But her sober realism—a trait shared with contemporary writers and with the massive masters of the novel of nineteenth century Russia—saved her from artistic failure. The baker behaves like a baker. He draws water from the well for kneading the dough, he stands near the oven and watches the product of his hands with the inborn care of the artisan.[83] The diffident miller, ill at ease with the rabbi, his son-in-law, cares for Pshoika, the cow, with tender warmth.[84] The boy Abraham— Rami in an affectionate diminutive—manages to get lost and found in the course of a day filled with exciting adventure.[85] But, above all, the girls and the mature women and the grandmothers seem to have achieved a quiet immortality in her stories: the untutored Mina and Zivah, tragic Nehamah and motherly Naomi.[86] Perhaps in no other story of hers does womanhood appear in such soft, self-effacing light as in "Fradel."[87] She was possessed of "a sweet but melancholy charm," the quiet bravery of the traditional woman who bore the sorrow of a failed marriage with a dignity that didn't waver even when she was compelled to institute divorce proceedings. She faced the death of her only child with stoic resignation. She showed inoffensive aloofness to a lover who never married because of his love for her. Even when she deferred to the prescribed laws, such as the ritual baths after days of so-called womanly defilement, she differed somehow from her co-religionists—those saintly mothers who nourished boys on sorrow and washed them "in maternal tears" and fed them "on the ambrosia of melancholy love." Fradel may be said to symbolize orthodox Jewish womanhood in all its splendid purity and modesty. Yet she remains human and individual in spite of her extreme adherence to ancestral rites which had been sanctified by general usage for centuries. To sum up: the vaunted realism of Deborah Baron did not prevent her from becoming an idealizing writer. Her *shtetl*, her characters, her plots were touched by the light of compassion; and even when she tackled "Wickedness,"[88] she suffused it with the inner glow of her creative personality. Perhaps this personality concealed unsuspected depths; she translated Flaubert's *Madame Bovary* out of an inner need for identification with unfulfilled womanhood.

Less than forty years separate the world of Deborah Baron from the world of Judith Hendel (1926–   ). But the time factor could be counted in centuries. Instead of the somnolescence of the *shtetl* she presents the pulsating recrudescence of Jewry in Palestine and in present-day Israel; instead of tradition, a trial of socialist ideas in rural and urban milieus; instead of Jewry in Eastern Europe, a confrontation of Jewries from many lands. As a matter of fact, *The Street of Steps*,[89] the book which catapulted Judith Hendel to fame both in its original and its dramatized form, was a novelized problem in acculturation. Eastern and Western Jewry meet in the old-new land—Eastern Jewry with its medieval outlook and exotic customs, Western Jewry emancipated from tradition and almost secularized. The inevitable clashes, the tensions, the misunderstandings are dictated by that circumstance. Yet Judith Hendel also came from Eastern Europe—from Warsaw, as a matter of fact. But since she arrived in infancy in mandatory Palestine, she was "sabraized," and that made all the difference—in spite of similarities to Deborah Baron in novelistic techniques. The realistic style of Hendel did not prevent her from noticing otherness, to use her terminology. That otherness may be the result of holocaust experiences, as in the case of Sheftl Rubin who is keenly aware of the fact that people who were not subjected to that infamy differ from other people. Whatever the case may be, otherness—deeply felt and adequately realized—characterizes Hendel's stories; otherness of people who are about to die like Saul hit by a sniper's bullet; otherness of people like Zili, Saul's loving wife, and his devoted friend transformed by the experience of death;[90] otherness of women in widowhood;[91] otherness of people who live in the constant shadow of death.

In her realistic technique Judith Hendel may resemble Baron, in her themes and in her style she is totally different. Not only does she not have command of Baron's lingual resources; she is also innocent of the whole "burden of inheritance" which was the mark of the Hebrew writer for centuries. As a new voice of Israel she represents a generation which struggles amidst unceasing danger for a new life in Israel.

Amalia Kahana-Karmon (1930–   ) is the prose poet of ordinary human beings who seek and find poetic extraordinariness only to lose it again in prosaic ordinariness. In a sense she is the untraditional story teller and the traditional Jew who seeks "sanctification of his daily routine: and, within that sanctification, the mystic moment of revelation."[92] On a religious plane this is the object of Joseph Karo in his massive code of Jewish law; on a secular plane this is the object of the characters in Kahana-Karmon's stories.

The introspective tone of Amalia Kahana-Karmon suggests the voice of a Valéry or a Rilke. Like the French poet she intellectualizes her aperçus or those of her protagonists; like the German poet she turns inward both in her native land and in the foreign milieus of England and Switzerland. In the exotic titles of her stories she approximates the felicitous inventiveness of Odilon Redon: "The Heart of the Summer, the Heart of Light"[93] or "Neimah Sason Writes Poems"[94] or "Basic Ideas."[95] And she does not hesitate to borrow a poetic phrase by Abraham ben David for the title of her story "I Thirst for Your Waters, Jerusalem."[96] In her episodic craft, a sort of original poetic epistemology, Amalia Kahana-Karmon approximates, paradoxically, the least introspective writer in world literature, Ernest Hemingway. But Hemingway creates heroes, and heroes resolve their predicament in climaxes; Kahana-Karmon creates antiheroes who rush in her stories toward anticlimaxes. Her writing technique is a studious exercise in the unusual simile: "The wondering city was recuperating like a psychopath smiling to hide a terrible secret."[97] This is her buoyant beginning of a story—buoyant in spite of its allusion to illness. She also characterizes people in pithy phrases: "See what you have become. A doll. A porcelain face."[98] Women are her specialty; she knows them with perceptive empathy:

> The years passed. I can't believe. I am a mother of two big children and I can't believe. Am I that? Perhaps I am only that part within me which stands and looks at this worn woman who is perpetually busy . . . perpetually trying and not always succeeding.[99]

Amalia Kahana-Karmon wields a bold brush and paints a city and a region with a few bold strokes. In "Beersheba, Capital of the Negev"[100] she succeeds in depicting the merciless landscape and the merciless nostalgia of a woman for the city:

> She wanted to be in Tel Aviv—with her husband and her child. . . . It was sheer chance that brought her here. Blond dust. Dusty roads. A cloud throws a shadow on the flat, strange city. On a mourning mosque. . . . a pepper tree. A mosque changed to a museum. And the sun sinks. A blond ball of sun, burning and sink-

ing. The earth is pink. With a monotonous pinkishness under the violet sky. Already it is night, translucent and cool. Frozen light . . .

This paragraph, almost at the very beginning of the story, strikes the mood, the pose, the situation. The meager plot will only add or modify or shape the people in the image of that exotic landscape. Perhaps the credo of that fictive writer in her story "Basic Ideas" is Karmon's own credo:

The thematic arc is modest . . . A, the mood of the place, the seasons of the year, the hours in a day. B, the character of the individual's belonging to the world and to himself . . . C, the super-reality which dictates actions to man . . . [101]

This is a narrow world. But within that world there is room for originality, and Amalia Kahana-Karmon achieved it. Hence her unique significance in present-day Israel.

17
Antecedents and Contemporaries of Agnon; Samuel Joseph Agnon; Hasidism in Hebrew Poetry; Seminal Impact of Hasidism

Antecedents and Contemporaries of Agnon

MOSES HESS (1812–1875) in *Rome and Jerusalem* and Eliezer Zevi Zweifel (1815–1888) in *Peace to Israel*[1] heralded new attitudes to Hasidism. Hess, a former admirer of Marx, sympathized with its communal attitudes; Zweifel lavished praise on the three Jews who conferred originality and even greatness on eighteenth century Jewry: Mendelssohn, the Gaon of Vilna, Baal Shem Tov. But these were lonely voices in the sixties and seventies of the previous century. Even Judah Leb Peretz (1851–1915)[2] who was to change Jewry's attitude toward Hasidism with his enticing stories, published, as late as 1875, an anti-Hasidic poem, "Partnership,"[3] in which, in the best tradition of the enlightenment, he ridiculed the Hasidim's excessive enthusiasm in prayer, their addiction to alcohol, and their pursuit of miracles. Later, in his memoirs, he remembered a Hasid who would down his brandy "in one gulp" but munch his cookie meditatively.[4]

It was not until 1894, when Peretz began to write his *Hasidic Tales*, that he effected a turning point in people's attitudes toward Hasidism. This complete reevaluation is one of the most curious phenomena in the development of the shifts in ideas and emphases in social and religious movements. The swift conquest of the field of psychology by psychoanalysis, the emphasis on intuition by the influential works of Henri Bergson, the refined techniques of anthropology—these fostered a new receptivity to the nonrationalist movement of Hasidism. The re-

177

searches of Simon Dubnow and Samuel Abba Horodetzky into the historical backgrounds of Hasidism, the seductive paraphrases of Hasidic stories by Martin Buber and Micah Joseph Berdyczewski and, above all, the poetic tales of Judah Leb Peretz and the realistic tales of Judah Steinberg—all these savants and men of letters effected a new approach to Hasidism. It culminated in *The Bridal Canopy* by Samuel Joseph Agnon who recreated the world of Hasidism with reverent piety.

The revival of Hasidism was more than an act of romanticism on the part of some writers and scholars: it filled a deeply felt need for religious regeneration and it lacked the faddist overtones which characterized the introduction of Zen Buddhism into the West by non-Jewish authors. The rationalist bias of the "enlightened" had blinded them to the virtues of Hasidism. They had lost faith in religious regeneration from within, they had committed themselves to secular transformation from without. The opposite climate of opinion prevailed a hundred years after the initial attempts at discrediting Hasidism. The psychic void, left by the deterioration of religion, had to be filled by nonrational movements: intuitionism, mysticism, Jungian archetypes, and the whole angelology and demonology of men, uncovered by psychoanalysis.

Peretz, who was anti-hasidic initially, became the prime mover in the reassessment of Hasidism. Like Janus he faced backward and forward. He began with an anti-Hasidic stance à la Erter, and he pioneered pro-Hasidism. From his deep interest in the folklore and imagination of simple people he fashioned a new trend in Hebrew literature: neo-Hasidism.

Peretz's short story "If Not Higher" is a perfect example of the new attitude toward Hasidism. The Zaddik of Nemirov disappeared every morning in the period of penitence preceding the High Holidays. His adherents believed that he had flown to heaven to intercede for his people. But a skeptical Jew from Lithuania was determined to explode the myth. He stole into the Zaddik's room, hid under his bed, watched him rise and put on peasant's clothes, and followed him to the forest. There the skeptic saw him wielding an ax to fell a tree, bringing the wood to a sick Jewish woman, and lighting a fire for her. But the poor woman was worried: "How will I pay?" The rabbi answered reproachfully: "Fool, you are a poor, sick woman. I trust you for this bit of wood. I have faith that you will pay. But you have a powerful God, a mighty God, and you don't trust him. . .[5] The Zaddik, in the guise of a peasant named Vassil, managed to convince her that she could pay later and that he would trust her. That did it: the Lithuanian Jew when he heard the Hasidim say that the Zaddik flew heavenward, added: "If not higher."

All the ingredients of this story would have been mercilessly satirized by a Perl or an Erter, by a Levinsohn or a Gottlober: the miracle-working rabbi, the unattended visit of the rabbi to a woman, the superstitious faith of the Hasidim in their rabbi. But the art of Peretz—aided somewhat by the hush technique of a Maeterlinck and the mystifications of French symbolists who were in vogue at the end of the nineteenth century—reduced the allegedly superhuman miracle to a mere human situation and by reducing it, by making it believable, actually elevated it again into the metaphysical realm.

Nothing aroused the ire of the "enlightened" as much as the myth of metempsychosis. Erter castigated it mercilessly. But Peretz knew how to infuse a new vitality into the hoary myth. In his story "You Shall Not Covet," a saintly, learned, ascetic person was about to depart this life. But the neglected body refused to release his soul: "I have not lived at all. . . . And each organ struggled with the angel of death. The heart said: I have not felt anything yet. The eyes argued: We have not seen anything yet. The hands asked: What has been ours? The feet cried: Where did we go? . . ." All the other limbs fought valiantly and bitterly. And the saintly person sighed the sigh of envy in his agony: "He envied those who died an easy death." And another transmigration was earned by the transgression against the commandment "you shall not covet."[6]

The saintly person became Reb Zanvele Purisover—rich, learned, hospitable to a fault. He befriended the stranger, even the deformed, even the hunchback. One such guest had argued with him a point of ritual law and seemed to win the argument. Reb Zanvele had to catch his breath outside the door. The wintry night, the fresh snow, the radiant sky: these cleared his mind and showed gaps in the guest's reasoning. He walked in ecstasy, crossed and recrossed the market place, left the street of the town and lost his way. After considerable wanderings he arrived at an inn, entered a room where half-drunk peasants toasted each other and kissed each other and wept with tenderness.

And then Reb Zanvele who was a greater scholar than the Rabbi, a better singer than the cantor, a better reader of the Torah than the Lithuanian teacher, who had the most beautiful house, a woman of valor for a wife, the brightest children . . . Reb Zanvele, the best counselor, the most honest arbiter, the most generous philanthropist . . . lost control of himself . . . and envied in his heart

of hearts each peasant who sat beside the warm hearth . . . And a
new series of transmigrations began for Reb Zanvele.[7]

The juxtaposition of wealth and want, intellectuality and ignorance,
elegance and rudeness: Peretz achieved it in the final passage of the
story "You Shall Not Covet." And he gave a poetic reinterpretation of
the doctrine of metempsychosis, which in that story is not a punishment for a life of crime, but an opportunity to correct, on a different
life plane, one single blemish.

Peretz also pioneered in the domain of Hasidic drama. *The Golden
Chain*, a play in three acts, first appeared in Hebrew under the title
Ruin of a Zaddik's House.[8] Later it was reworked in Yiddish as a complicated portrait of four generations of Hasidim who were given to an
abundance of talk and a scarcity of action.

The hasidic plays par excellence were written in our generation by
Harry Sackler. *The Seer Looks at His Bride*,[9] *Eastward*,[10] *Journey of
the Zaddik*[11] are masterpieces of hasidic lore and dramatic art. But
they could not compete in popularity with *The Dybbuk*[12] which was
written by Solomon Zanvil Rappaport under the pseudonym of S. Ansky (1863–1920). Originally composed in Russian, it was translated
into Yiddish by the author and brilliantly done in Hebrew by Hayyim
Nahman Bialik. It was first performed by the Vilna Ensemble in Yiddish in 1920 and by Habimah—the National Theater of Israel at the
present time—in Moscow in 1922. The meager plot—exorcism of a *dybbuk* from the body of a girl—is given substance by folklore in imaginative profusion. Brilliantly acted by both theatrical companies it became a classic in Europe and America. In the history of the theatre it
marked the end of naturalism as represented by Stanislavsky and the
beginning of expressionism as represented by Evgeny Vakhtangov.[13]

Peretz, Ansky, and Berdyczewski were collectors of folklore, which
enriched their creativity and pioneered their new approaches to Hasidism. Though interdependent they managed to preserve their independence in spite of mutual cross-fertilization.

Berdyczewski, the uneasy revolutionary in Hebrew literature, sympathized with Hasidism because it deviated from traditionalism.[14] In
his poetic craving for change in Jewish life—from fascination with the
book to union with nature, from legalistic surfeit to mystic rapture—
he seemed to find an ally in Hasidism. And Judah Steinberg
(1863–1908) published stories which lack the perceptive, lyrical, almost musical quality of a Peretz and the supernaturalism of a Berdyczewski. But they are permeated with naiveté and with realism and, at

times, they reflect the conflict of Hasidism with nationalism. Thus, for Zaydl the watchmaker, Zionism is a religious movement, a beginning of redemption. He pawns two watches to buy a share of the Colonial Bank, a Zionist institution, and keeps it in a special bag. His faith in Zionism conflicts with the faith of his fellow-Hasidim and he suffers from their obloquy: they cannot condone association with "heretics" like Zionists.[15]

Steinberg is at his best when he integrates Hasidism with the ortho-dox environment as in his folk tale "The Two Brothers of Blessed Mem-ory."[16] With mock precision he enumerates ranks of perfection among Zaddikim. Some are the eyes of the people, the masters of the revealed tradition. Some are the mouth and the teeth of the people; they are the keepers of the keys of livelihood. And then there are those who are the heart of the people; there is no higher rank than theirs. On this hierarchical stratification Steinberg builds his story about two brothers, Rabbi Elimelech and Rabbi Zusya, who wander from place to place in order to reform evildoers—not by edifying sermons, but by taking, as it were, their sins upon themselves and forcing the sinner to repent. Thus, an adulterer would not be shamed by direct assault on his personality. But Rabbi Elimelech would say to his brother within the hearing of the adulterer: "I have committed adultery." And Rabbi Zusya would answer with a question: "When? Where?" And then a re-cital of the circumstances would follow, and Rabbi Zusya would rebuke his brother and admonish him to repent. But how can one justify the lie? This is the mystery. Steinberg uses a similar method in the story "Saturday Night."[17] First he announces an axiom: the best way of serv-ing God is through joy; sorrow is the work of Satan; one has to avoid sadness or fight it. Then he proceeds to tell the story of Baal Shem Tov who arrived at this triple truth after many trials and tribulations.

In the early decades of this century several writers made ambitious attempts at literary transformations of Hasidism. They produced nov-els on hasidic themes and personages.[18] *Yehiel the Hagrite* by Simon Halkin (1898–) is the work of a youthful writer whose hero strives after a living God. The protagonist may be a visitor to the Bohemian haunts of Greenwich Village; he may be unsettling the emotions of a few dreamy girls; he is nevertheless rooted in hasidic ancestry, in Ha-badism. Perhaps he is guilty of a double flirtation—sexual and theolog-ical. In his reveries he oscillates between futility and frustration. But the paucity of action is not entirely compensated for by the inner monolog of Yehiel Hero.

Yohanan Twersky (1900–1967) portrayed Hasidism on the basis of personal experience and historical studies. With the ease and nimble-ness of a Maurois he concentrated in four novels on the piquant epi-sode and the essential characteristic. In *The Inner Court* he depicted his own family background of the hasidic townlet of Chernobil in the vicinity of Kiev; in *The Heart and the Sword* he chose as his theme Rabbi Nahman of Bratzlav's pilgrimage to the Holy Land; in *From Darkness to Light* he painted the period of the Baal Shem Tov and the Gaon of Vilna; in *The Virgin of Ludomir* he concentrated on the unique role of womanhood in the hasidic movement. He brought novelty to his exploration of depth psychology which was fashionable in European and American literature a generation ago.

The Gaon and the Rabbi by Zalman Shneour was essentially a dou-ble portrait of great personages à la Plutarch. The great novel of Hasi-dism was written by the master-novelist of the present century, Samu-el Joseph Agnon.

Samuel Joseph Agnon (1888–1970)

AGNON was born on the eighth day of the eighth month in the year 1888, corresponding to the ninth day of Ab. A triple tragedy is as-sociated with that date: the destruction of the first Jewish common-wealth in 586 B.C.E., the destruction of the second Jewish common-wealth in 70 C.E., and the expulsion of the Jews from Spain in 1492. An ancient legend has it that on the day of the loss of Jewry's political in-dependence the Redeemer was born, the Messiah who would restore the state and bring about an era of uncompromising justice. Agnon, who was permeated with Jewish law and lore, must have pondered on this twin theme of *Galut* and *Geulah,* exile and redemption, from his earliest youth. Indeed, his entire work is a variation on the theme of exile and redemption. In this sense, it is like the work of the great me-dieval Jewish poets, Gabirol, Halevi or Moses Ibn Ezra. In this sense, and in this sense alone, Agnon can be regarded as a medieval poet in modern garb.

Not only the time but also the place of Agnon's birth is important for the appreciation of his work. The gentle chronicler of traditional and transitional Jewry saw the light of day in a small Galician town, Bu-czacz.[19] At the time of his birth Galicia was a part of the Austro-Hun-garian empire which was rather liberal in its policy toward Jews. While the official language of the empire was German, the urban popu-lation spoke Polish, the rural population, Ukrainian. There was thus a multilingual atmosphere which nourished most of the young Jews at the time. Curiously, Agnon was almost unaffected by the multilingualism of his native land. He knew a bit of Polish, some German thanks to his mother Esther, a lot of Yiddish; and he was immensely erudite in the Hebrew language. There is evidence of his knowledge of Polish in his works; he uses Polish phrases in Hebrew transliteration. There is evidence of his knowledge of Yiddish; he speaks it skillfully and he published his juvenile effusions in the Yiddish periodicals of his native land: *Der Yiddisher Weker, Yiddisher Folkskalender* and *Stanislawer Wochenblatt.* In the latter periodical he published his awkward legend in verse, "Rabbi Joseph della Ryena," on June 25, 1903, when he was less than fifteen.

Yet he is not multilingual. His main influences derive from the immense resources of the Hebrew language which were opened up to him by his father Shalom Mordecai Czaczkes, a fur merchant, an ordained though nonpracticing rabbi, and a poet to boot. In the words of Agnon at the banquet for Nobel laureates: "I have been influenced first and foremost by the Bible, Mishnah, Gemara, Midrash and Rashi's commentary on the Bible . . . medieval Halakhic commentators, poets and philosophers led by Maimonides. I also used to read every book in German that came to my hand. I was influenced by every man and every woman and every child who happened my way, both Jews and non-Jews. The same is true of nature. . ."

Hebrew literature up to modern times, German classics, personal encounters with "manscape" and landscape—these are the formative influences in Agnon's life. Another factor in his work may be attributed to the place of his birth: a slow, calm, adagio rhythm of life, a certain urbanity which is usually missing in Hebrew authors of Russian or Lithuanian origin.[20]

So Agnon spent the first twenty years of his life, the formative ones, in his native town of Buczacz. It was there that he equipped himself with all the future tools of his writing and with the immense knowledge of Hebrew literature from its inception to his own day.

When he decided to immigrate to Palestine as a youth of twenty, he was fully formed. In 1908 he published his *'Agunot*,[21] the tale that made him instantly well-known, if not famous, the tale of Ben Uri and Dina, Ezekiel and Freidele, the tale of unconsummated love, the tale which rests on the Halakic term *'Agunah*—the anchored one, the one tied to an absent husband, the grass widow who cannot remarry until her husband divorces her or is attested to be dead. From that tale he allegedly borrowed his name Agnon. Another tale of that period *And the Crooked Shall Be Straight*,[22] published in 1912, established him as an author. A young critic who was to write the first modern history of modern Hebrew literature, Fishel Lachower, noted in his review that "the book is a perfect folk book in language, in style, in comprehension of the world . . . "

When Agnon was made an honorary fellow of the Weizmann Institute in Rehovot—after he had received the Nobel Prize for Literature—he told a story in his inimitable way. Many years ago Professor Edmund Landau, the great mathematician of Göttingen, visited him and greeted him with the words: "How are you, *Herr Kollege?*" I said to him: "How have we become colleagues?" He answered: "We mathematicians try throughout our lives to make the crooked plain. You have done it in your book *And the Crooked Shall be Straight.*" The story of Menashe Hayyim who loses his wife (who marries another man in the belief that Menashe Hayyim is dead) is more realistic than "*'Agunot,*" more mature in style. And it adds—together with "*'Agunot*"—a dimension of tragedy to the disintegrating townlet (*shtetl*) in the Diaspora. The title of the story is based on Isaiah 40:4: "Every valley shall be lifted up, and every mountain and hill shall be made low, and the crooked shall be straight, and the rough places a plain." Bialik, it is known, fashioned his youthful verses with lingual help from Psalms. In early stories Agnon echoed Isaiah, the calmest, the most urbane of prophets—if calm prophet is not a contradiction in terms.

Agnon immigrated into Palestine when immigration into the land was not only an act of daring but an act of faith. For in the first decade of the twentieth century only the hardiest of idealists dared to settle in Palestine. That was the generation of the second *'Aliyyah,* the generation that included Ben Gurion, Ben-Zvi, A.D. Gordon, Simhah Ben-Zion and Agnon. And these were the builders of Israeli literature. With the exception of twelve years (1913–1925), which included the years of the First World War, Agnon spent the rest of of his life in Israel, most of it in Jerusalem, with a single-minded dedication to his work. He was lucky: the late Zalman Schocken, then his late son Theodor, provided him for almost half a century with an income in return for the rights to his works. And that income was his freedom from want and economic worry. He was also lucky in choosing Jerusalem, another powerful influence on his work. For Jerusalem is not only the capital of a tiny state on the shores of the eastern Mediterranean, but undoubtedly the religious capital of the world, the mother-city of Judaism, Christianity, and Islam.

Agnon does not belong with the great immortals of world literature.

Although he has built up a solid reputation in Hebrew literature and earned the Nobel Prize in 1966, the highest literary award and the first to be accorded to a Hebrew writer, he is essentially a *laudator temporis acti*, a singer of the past. This is no detriment except in the eyes of those whose vision of the present is synonymous with the latest headline. Those who see the present as a repository and refinery of the past will accept Agnon's vision of the past as a contemporaneous and futurist adventure.

It is not his preoccupation with the past which denies him greatness. And he is not exclusively addicted to the past. His novel *A Guest for the Night*[23] is the tragic story of a past-oriented town and protagonist in Poland after the First World War when the sole hope for a future was immigration to Palestine. Another novel—*Yesterday, A Day Before Yesterday*[24]—depicts the generation of the second 'Aliyyah (the second wave of immigration); Jaffa and Jerusalem as seen through the eyes of Isaac Kummer who represents in his person both the old Judaism and the new Judaism but who leans more toward the symbol of old Judaism, Jerusalem, and dies in a peculiar way (he is bitten by a dog). Finally, a posthumous work, *Shirah*,[25] which deals with the groves of academe, the Hebrew University of Jerusalem.

Agnon cannot, therefore, be accused of a past-centered outlook. But he can be accused of a simplistic view of man, too simplistic to account for the innumerable complications of man. There is another factor which bars his way to greatness: his use of language. The richness of his Hebrew idiom has been justly praised. Good Hebraists savor an unprecedented sweetness in his idiom which feeds on 3500 years of lingual resources. Agnon is the only modern Hebrew writer who has made good use of the Hebrew language from its biblical beginnings through its rabbinic continuation to its modern efflorescense. Yet his style is not eclectic in the disparaging sense of the word. It is an artistic blend of various strata of language at an unusual pitch of intensity. Any paragraph in any story or any novel of Agnon's teems with half-phrases and quarter-phrases from the Bible, the Talmud, the medieval tract, the hasidic tale, the philosophic homily. And these language pebbles form a mosaic of unusual splendor and unusual brilliance. How they do this is Agnon's secret. In an age which has enriched but also vulgarized the Hebrew language, Agnon stands out as the self-appointed guardian of its purity, its wealth and its Semitic character. He has no equal in that domain. In the past 200 years, two types of style predominated in Hebrew literature—the pseudo-biblical and the pseudo-rabbinic. The pseudo-biblical was the invention of the period of enlightenment as connoisseurs of Hebrew literature know. The pseudo-rabbinic was the invention of Mendele Moker Sefarim. Agnon created a new style for Hebrew prose, a style based on all the resources of the language. That was one of Agnon's major contributions. Yet this burden of allusion is stylized, mannered, and monotonous. It is learned but without daring, without élan.

Within these two limitations, the limitation of psychological depth and the limitation of lingual depth, Agnon has achieved an almost perfect vision of a segment of Jewry as it lived in nineteenth century Europe—mainly Galicia.[26] He is at his best in his translation of Hasidism into a spiritual experience. And he knows it not only from books but from first-hand observation. For Galicia was solidly hasidic at the time of his birth. A medieval way of life which was slowly being shattered characterized his native town, Buczacz. We of today have, almost without exception, a positive attitude toward that movement which was the last major efflorescence of Jewish faith, of Jewish piety. But that was not always the case. When the movement originated some 200 years ago, in the towns and townlets of Galicia and Podolia, it met with fierce opposition from the right and from the left, if one may borrow terms from our political vocabulary. From the right it was assailed by the orthodox as a heretical movement, and no less a figure than the saintly Gaon of Vilna advocated a spiritual war against the Hasidim. At the same time, the opposition of the left, that of the so-called members of the enlightenment, reared its head. Writers of the eighteenth and the beginning of the nineteenth century reviled and satirized the movement mercilessly. Joseph Perl, Isaac Erter, Isaac Ber Levinsohn—they were all unanimous in their hilarious mockery of Hasidism. Then an interesting change took place. As the movement declined at the end of the nineteenth century, historians took a long and charitable look at Hasidism. Simon Dubnow and Samuel Abba Horodetzky devoted many volumes to the unsung glories of Hasidism. And Martin Buber transposed their simple and naive tales into major works of art in an elegant and highly sophisticated German. It is perhaps that transposition, rather than his existentialist philosophy of Judaism, that will be his ultimate claim to immortality. Be that as it may, the historians, plus Buber, paved the way for a new attitude to Hasidism. And then came the writers—Judah Leb Peretz in Yiddish and Agnon in Hebrew, who rediscovered Hasidism and its major contributions to Jewish life. And especially Agnon.

No one has forever enshrined that bygone world as did Agnon in *The Bridal Canopy*.[27] That major work of Agnon—perhaps his most important literary effort—published in 1931—is the Hebrew *Don Quixote*. Both novels presuppose a medieval way of looking at life; man is a wayfarer in a strange world, a *homo viator*.[28] Indeed, man appears already in ancient times as a sublime wanderer, Ulysses, or a monstrous exile doomed to a restless condition. Gregory the Great called Satan the Stranger, *Alienus*.[29] Both novels, *The Bridal Canopy* and *Don Quixote*, are stories about unrealistic, fantastic heroes in adventurous travels to nowhere. But unlike Don Quixote, whose mind is crammed with the romantic heroes of medieval knighthood and whose desire it is to emulate or better them, Reb Yudel, the hero of *The Bridal Canopy*, is sated with biblical, talmudic, and homiletic lore, and his desire is to equal the great saints and sages in piety. Like Don Quixote he has a goal—not "to right every wrong and to expose himself to peril and danger" in quest of the beautiful Dulcinea del Toboso, but to find three husbands for his three nubile daughters. Like Don Quixote, Yudel has his Sancho Panza, Note the Wagoner; and his two horses—not Rocinante but Drawme and Willrun—are straight from the Song of Songs. Again like Don Quixote, the epic of early renaissance Spain, *The Bridal Canopy* is the epic of hasidic Jewry—an epic continued in the story "In The Heart of the Seas" and in innumerable other tales.

The Bridal Canopy—even within the context of his collected works—remains Agnon's *chef-d'oeuvre*. He has a weakness for the concept of *The Bridal Canopy*. He even explained his trip to New York by a bridal canopy parable:

Once there was a young man who had reached marriageable age. The matchmakers came and offered him a wonderful proposition. The young man would not hear of it, and did not even want to have a look at the girl. Said one of the matchmakers: "Even if the girl had only a few of the qualities which are associated with girls, it would be worth your while to see her, and this girl has all of the qualities. Won't you tell me why you refuse to see her?" The young man replied: "I'll tell you exactly what it is. When a man is standing under the bridal canopy, he has to pronounce the words, "*Hare At*,"[30] be consecrated unto me. I'm very bashful and I can't open my mouth in public and I'm afraid that because of my extreme bashfulness I won't be able to utter a word and I'll make a fool of myself." Said the matchmaker: "If that's what it is, then you should have no fear, for the Rabbi and the Cantor and all the relatives and the *Mehuttanim* will be with you at the wedding, and the Cantor will sing his opening piece and the Rabbi will recite the

Seven Blessings and read the Marriage Writ[31] and everybody will say *Mazal Tov, Mazal Tov*[32]—so what are the couple of words of *"Hare At . . ."* that you'll have to say as compared with all the joyous acclamation?"

To apply this to myself: I was afraid to go to America because I thought I would not be able to open my mouth: I don't know English. But my friends came and said to me: "If that's what it is, then you have nothing to worry about. What are the couple of words that you will say compared to all the fine things that will be said about you?" So I took myself and my bashfulness in hand and I came.

No translation, not even the adequate translation of I. M. Lask, can do justice to *The Bridal Canopy*. Its idiomatic language can be transposed, paraphrased or metamorphosed, but it cannot be translated. Neither the Hebrew language nor the idiom of hasidic life of the early nineteenth century reflected in the novel lend themselves to translation into English. For the Hasidim life is almost totally religious—as opposed to our secular outlook on the world. Moreover, it is touched by a mysticism which is not acceptable to our scientific and technological outlook. It is a life of dedication to Torah. And that means not only Pentateuch but the sum total of Jewish law and lore. It is a life of expectation: the Messiah, the future Redeemer of the world and the liquidator of the Exile and all its attendant ills is just around the corner.

The hero of the story, Reb Yudel, is not only an individual, *he is* the Jewish people. His name is a diminutive of Judah, the individual and then the tribe that gave Jews their name. His three marriageable daughters—Gittele, the good one, Blume the flowering one, and Pessele (Bess, Elizabeth)—are the cause of his extensive journeys. For Yudel, spurred by the naggings of his wife Frummet, the pious one, sets out to find three bridegrooms for his daughters. Marriage in those good old days was not the business of the parties concerned; it was the business of their parents. Add Note the Wagoner, a sort of Sancho Panza, and the two horses who are very much a part of the story and you have the main *dramatis personae*. But the cast is inexhaustible. Almost any village or town on the list of Yudel's peregrinations adds a character or two. Like all good stories, *The Bridal Canopy* has a happy ending; the three daughters are married off to learned husbands. Reb Yudel and his wife live to see their children's children and, at the end of their days, they settle in the Holy Land.

The thread of Yudel's journey is a thin thread of narrative. Village follows village, story follows story. Yet the story within the larger context of the main plot develops the characters horizontally rather than vertically. Their virtues and vices, which are known almost from the very beginning, gain in width and sometimes in depth. No unexpected traits illumine their characters. It is a remarkable fact: the stories within their main plot have a life of their own—an independent life and a dependent one. As a matter of fact they have been published separately—in Hebrew periodicals and, in the form of small books, as far back as 1920. In 1931 Agnon published his novel—really a second version from which Lask's translation was made—and in 1953 a third revised version. Like Yeats in modern Irish literature Agnon revised his work endlessly.[33]

These stories within the larger framework of *The Bridal Canopy* reinforce the implicit didacticism, the moral tone of the novel. But it would be unjust—and many of his critics are guilty of that injustice—to regard Agnon as the mere poet of Hasidism. He has devoted a considerable portion of his work to European and Palestinian Jewry in this century. And since this century is often regarded as the century of the alienated individual, much has been made of the alienated types that roam his novels and stories. It is not hard to find examples. *Simple Tale*[34] is the story of Hershel, who loves the socially inferior Bluma but marries the unloved Mina, becomes unsettled in his mind, then comes back to his wife almost cured. In *A Guest for the Night* the anonymous "I" who returns to a ruined town after many years and finds it a spiritual shambles, a past-oriented town with one sole glimmer of hope: emigration to Eretz Yisrael. *Yesterday, A Day Before Yesterday* is the novel of Second 'Aliyyah Jaffa and Jerusalem as seen and experienced through the eyes of Isaac Kummer. He represents both the old and the new—Jaffa and Jerusalem—but settles in Jerusalem, marries an orthodox girl, then is bitten by a dog and dies. *Betrothed*[35] is the story of Jacob Rechnitz, a scientist who earns a living as a teacher in Palestine before the First World War, and indulges in nonsensual love of his charges. *Edo and Enam*[36] tells the story of post-World War II life in restive Jerusalem, and *Shirah*[37] is the posthumous novel about the Hebrew University of Jerusalem. It was but a step to bring in Kafka, that master of the theme of alienation and to compare him with Agnon.[38]

Nothing could be more unjust to both writers. They are worlds apart. Agnon's characters move in a landscape of love and compassion, where the Almighty's protective vigilance envelops them like a refreshing breeze of summer. Kafka's characters are moved by uncertainty, accused without knowing the terms of their guilt, judged without comprehending the intent of justice. Agnon's is a deeply ethical landscape; Kafka's is an amoral landscape. Finally, Agnon as well as most of his characters live by the traditions of Judaism; Kafka and his characters are completely deracinated. That is, perhaps, Agnon's great worth for our generation: in a world of shaken values he stands—together with his works—for the solid principles of moral regeneration. And these principles are not preached: they are lived by men and women raised to the level of esthetic experience by the immortal art of Agnon. It is no mere whim on his part that he published three highly stylized anthologies—*Days of Awe*,[39] with its wealth of sources and resources for the High Holidays, duly "agnonized"; *You Saw*,[40] with its wealth of material for *Shabu'ot*, the festival commemorating the revelation of Jewry and to Jewry on Mt. Sinai; *Book, Scribe, Story*[41]—legends and stories and phantasies about books and their authors. These are the themes of his work: the festivals as the heightened environment of spirituality for Jewry; the Book as the embodiment of that spirituality. Agnon said it simply: "I have written all that God has put into my heart and into my pen."[42] That is why his style has affected old and young, artificers of prose and masters of poetry. One writer, K.A. Bertini, who has experienced the rigors of Stalinist persecution in Siberia for his addiction to Zionism, paid Agnon a supreme compliment; he fashioned "Agnonic Ballads"[43] out of Agnon's works of fiction. The author of *Yesterday, A Day Before Yesterday* has become the harbinger of the future.

Hasidism in Hebrew Poetry

It is a paradox that the eminent poets of Hasidism were writers of fiction—Peretz and Agnon; while the leading poets of the Hebrew renaissance in the twentieth century, Bialik and Tschernichowsky, were almost untouched by Hasidism. Shneour, the author of the *The Gaon and the Rabbi*, did publish one memorable poem on Rabbi Levi Isaac of Berditchev in 1942. Yet most contemporary Hebrew poets sympathized with Hasidism. It was a Hebrew poet in America, E. E. Lisitzky who discovered a hasidic intensity in Negro prayers and spirituals.[44] This linkage, not sufficiently explored, opened a window on interesting resemblances in folk imagination and folk art. Another Hebrew poet, who wrote his most significant poetry in America, created a dramatic dialog, "Ahijah and Israel,"[45] on a hasidic theme. but the preeminent triad of poets in the nineteen twenties—Gruenberg, Shlonsky, Lamdan—expressed Hasidism in soul-searching poetry. Rabbi Levi Isaac of Berditchev appears in Gruenberg's verse as "the dadaist in prayer shawl and phylacteries," a modernized saint whose life was a sacrament, whose love for his people was a passion, and whose homiletical work, *The Holiness of Levi,*[46] was an infinite longing for the Ineffable. Both Shneour and Gruenberg used the intercession of the saintly rabbi against the calamitous background of the holocaust. And both developed the cautious streak of rebellion from the rabbi's famous prayer into confident defiance.

Gruenberg cultivated other saints of the hasidic pantheon: the learned Rabbi Israel of Rizhin, the fiery Rabbi Uri of Strelisk, and the generous Rabbi Meirl of Premishlan. The first imparts "translucent repose" to the poet; the second instructs him in the thunderous voice; the third commands extreme poverty: he never kept his meager supply of money more than a day because he wanted no metal coin barrier between him and his Maker.[47]

Consciously and deliberately Gruenberg used hasidic locutions to enrich the texture of his poetry. And he was one of the first poets of this century to demand of the Hebrew writer that he explore and exploit the untapped sources of linguistic treasures in the totality of Hebrew writings, in Bible and Talmud, in Midrash and Kabbalah, in the liturgy and in the devotional works of Hasidism.

The unbridled intensity which characterized hasidic prayer and dance became a distinguishing feature of Gruenberg's equally unbridled line which often reached sixteen syllables. Whitman, so unpopular at mid-century in English-speaking countries, became Gruenberg's patron saint. "The Hebrew Walt Whitman"—that was the ecstatic call of poet to poet across the years and across language barriers. But "hasidic Walt Whitman" might have been an equally good, if not better, battle cry. For Gruenberg characterized Whitman in hasidic terms: "that singing bundle of flesh and blood who defies corporeality."[48]

Unlike Gruenberg, Lamdan glorified hasidic dances with sophisticated self-consciousness; and that was his innovation. While the original Hasid danced with the abandonment of joy, the Lamdanic Hasid danced with the exultation of sorrow and despair. In "The Chain of Dances," the most popular segment of the most popular book of poetry in the twenties, *Massadah,* there is a constant antithesis of fathers and sons, a confrontation across centuries. Fathers danced thus: one hand clasped the shoulder of a friend, another hand held the Torah. Sons dance thus: one hand joins the hand of a friend in a circle, the other hand clasps the woes of a generation. The poet forces a pattern of unity on the dances of the different generations: in the hasidic dance a feeling was created that the burden of an entire people was borne with love; in the contemporary dance a feeling is created that the dance is one great circle of sorrows. In other words, the forms of artistic expression change, the content of sorrow is a constant, unchanging value. Hasidic intensity remains; hasidic joy has departed.

Shlonsky was the only popular poet of the twenties who was not deeply affected by Hasidism. Like Auden he was trapped by his own lingual virtuosity. And he made a lasting contribution to the development of the Hebrew language through his supple verse. But Hasidism, for Shlonsky, was merely grist to his lingual mill; it became in the thirties a force in the ballads of Samson Meltzer (1909–   )—the most genuine and sensitive interpreter of Hasidism in verse. His storytelling talent converted hasidic tales into genuine poetry. And a folklike imagination enabled him to create unforgettable vignettes of hasidic life. Thus, in his "Dobush and the Baal Shem Tov," to quote an example from his numerous ballads, the poet engineers a meeting between two folk heroes of the eighteenth century—the old Ukrainian robber, revered in legend and song, and the father of Hasidism. Toward the end of his days Dobush experiences a change of heart and seeks to save his soul from damnation. At the advice of Baal Shem Tov he abandons the ax and the gold, two symbols of his power, and looks into the waters of the Prutetz:

> Skies below us, skies above us in this land of limpid light.
> Waters of the Prutetz wander on and on in roving might.
>
> They meander like the days of one who is about to die.
> To the Prut the Prutetz flows—whither ebbs our life away?
>
> Life was given by our Maker, life goes back to Him again.
> Man is like the wave of water, all his deeds are vile and vain.
>
> Man is like the water-mirror, mirroring the will of God.
> Man does what He asks of him, what He commands with gentlest
> nod.[49]

The advice of Baal Shem Tov works; the river soothes the conscience of the robber. On his return to his hideout Dobush scatters his treasures in the best tradition of the folk song. The homespun philosophy is almost biblical in its simplicity and devout humility. And it acquires its proper form and rhythm in the ballad which, as a poetic folk form, is eminently suited to the recital of feats of physical and spiritual valor.

Baal Shem and Dobush are antithetical types and the symbols of two different cultures. In "The Dance of Rabbi Zusya" Meltzer uses antithesis in the context of one culture. The ballad tells the story of two brothers, Rabbi Zusya and Rabbi Elimelech who go into voluntary exile in order to do penance and who stop at a country inn in the course of their journeys. At night a gang of drunkards arrives and pulls Rabbi Zusya out of his sleep and into the whirl of their wild dance. Rabbi Elimelech wakes up and sees a great light and hears "a song like a song of angels." Suddenly he realizes that his brother dances with heavenly visitors. He asks to be drawn into the charmed circle. The sound of the voice dispels the song, the dance, and the vision. Then, at the request of Rabbi Elimelech, the brothers change places for the night. But when the gang of drunkards returns, it draws again, with unmistakable certainty, Rabbi Zusya into the whirl of their wild dance. By that time Elimelech realizes that only his brother has been admitted to supernatural company. And, at this point, the profundity of the parable is told so subtly that it almost escapes notice. Rabbi Elimelech wakes his brother without a trace of jealousy. Twice he had been honored to participate in angelic song and dance. But the recipient of that heavenly bounty is totally unaware of his good fortune. Living in an esoteric state of exultation and illumination he is almost envious of the exoteric mind which perceives, by a special act of grace, what has become almost commonplace to his uncommon sense. In Judah Steinberg's tale of two brothers, Elimelech's subordinate role is a matter of mere technique—the lowly function is assigned to him, the admonitory functions to Zusya. In Meltzer's poem the two brothers live on two different levels of saintliness.[50]

It is of extraordinary interest that some of Meltzer's ballads and verse stories are woven around the central personality in Hasidism—Baal Shem Tov. The poet's early years in the Galician townlet of Tlust which reverberated with legends of Baal Shem Tov's mother and his orphaned youth, of Baal Shem Tov's habits and customs, stimulated Meltzer's folklike imagination. Sometimes he is merely the poetic reporter of a hasidic town. At his best he is the poetic interpreter of a movement which, for him, never lost its pristine freshness. In his native town it was still possible to hear and see Elijah the prophet in the guise of the benevolent Ukrainian peasant who helped push Baal Shem Tov's wagon of provisions out of the mire. And by an interesting interposition, Baal Shem Tov himself appeared as a poor wanderer on the eve of a Seder and saved a Jewish family—and perhaps a Jewish community—from a slandering blood libel.

As in Gruenberg's works, other great figures of Hasidism are also subjected to poetic interpretation in Meltzer's poetry: Rabbi Israel of Rizhin, who flees from the persecution of the Czar and is accompanied by a heavenly orchestra on his way, the Rabbi of Chortkov with his luxurious court and, of course Rabbi Levi Isaac of Berditchev. But their light dims in the bright simplicity of Baal Shem whose intense love of Jewry and whose popular brand of piety appeal to men who are unhappy in their heterodoxy and their sophisticated nihilism.

In his best ballads Meltzer achieves a feat of extraordinary quality. He has learned how to tell a folk tale in verse without debasing its inherent poetry. And he has revived the ancient art of the balladist which has become almost extinct in the chief European literatures and which, until the twentieth century, had never acquired a place of prominence in Hebrew literature. He utilized all the favorite tricks of the balladist with consummate skill: the repetition of individual verses, the refrain, the studied artlessness of rhyme, the faulty prosody, slang, and even current phrases of foreign origin. He succeeded in translating into an art medium his warm concern for the fate of the Jews and his romantic love for the Jewish townlet, its ethical pathos and its hasidic traditions.

S. Shalom, the contemporary mystical poet, also spent his childhood in a hasidic environment and wove his experiences into his long autobiographical poem *On Ben Pele*. In short, musical chapters of two four-line stanzas he manages to allude to the main stations of suffering in his personal life. But he yearns for the hasidic house into which he was born and for the devotional air which hovered over the workday, the Sabbath, and the holiday. His hasidic mysticism is contemporary with the tragic elimination of masses of Jewry during the Second World War. Thus, in a moving ballad, a rabbi is about to be shot together with his Hasidim by a Nazi firing squad; they dig their own grave, they are on the brink of ultimate despair. In the funereal silence the Rabbi asks for water in a loud voice. No one dares to do his bidding; only a humble tailor in chains runs to the spout and brings water for the Rabbi, who washes his hands and recites the Confessional. When the officer gives the fatal command, the Rabbi smiles—there is still a Jew who knows how to die a martyr's death and how to conquer evil with death.

The great Holocaust inspired some hasidic poems of Shalom but it did not overwhelm his poetry. Aaron Zeitlin, on the other hand, was moved like Gruenberg to devote a whole book to the disastrous tragedy of European Jewry. In the ultimate sanctification of humanity, he assigned the role of Baal Shem Tov to every man on earth.

Seminal Impact of Hasidism

On the scientific, on the novelistic, on the dramatic, and on the poetic planes scholars and authors have reassessed their immediate spiritual heritage. Some have sought religious regeneration through Hasidism, some have looked at it with nostalgic regret. All believed in its mystic strength and potent message for our time. That is why Hasidism proved to be a valuable article of cultural export. Theological circles in England, America and Germany found this exotic product of Eastern Europe interesting, stimulating, and even fascinating.

Through the writings of Buber, Hasidism has become a widespread cult, a poetic stance, a mystic energy. His influential *I and Thou* can be regarded as the hasidic poem of the twentieth century, but its language must be characterized as ecstatic discourse in prose.[51] Though it makes frequent allusions to the Buddha and to Socrates, to Dante and to Goethe, it is permeated with the spirit of the Baal Shem Tov[52] and Shneur Zalman of Liady, the preacher of Mezritch, and Rabbi Nahman of Bratzlav. Ultimately, *I and Thou* reaches beyond *I and Thou* and coexists in an organic *We:* the familial circle, the contemporary commune in Israel, the hasidic enclave. Such spiritual communities as the hasidic rabbi and his adoring followers reached at times "one of the strongest fusions of communion with God and communion with man known in the history of religion."[53] This may be the charged language of hyperbole but it is a representative statement of Buber who, in an excellent epigram of self-evaluation, has maintained that he became a filter of Hasidism.[54] How much of a filter can best be seen in the passage on prayer which can be duplicated in many a hasidic source:

> The man who prays pours himself out in unrestrained dependence, and knows that he has—in an incomprehensible way—an effect upon God, even though he obtains nothing from God; for when he no longer desires anything for himself, he sees the flame of his effect burning at its highest.[55]

The whole existentialist stance of the book—an elaboration of hasidic ideas of confrontation between man and man, man and nature, God and man—has influenced theologians like Reinhold Niebuhr, art critics like Sir Herbert Read, and psychiatrists like Leslie H. Farber. The Lutheran pastor, Albrecht Goes, who rose to eminence in Germany after the Second World War, paid tribute to Buber's influence on three generations in Germany. And he maintained that *I and Thou* was as important to him and his contemporaries as bread.[56] It was indeed a seminal work—as seminal for religious transformation as the difficult *Tractatus Logico-Philosophicus* by Ludwig Wittgenstein for the development of logic, linguistics, and philosophy. Both books are difficult, almost obscure. *I and Thou* remains enigmatic even after the summation of the contents by the author:

> The "complete," the legitimately religious existence of man, does not stand in a continuity but in the genuine acceptance and mastery of discontinuity. It is the discontinuity of essentiality and inessentiality that I understand as that of the I-Thou relation and the I-It relation to all being.[57]

In *I and Thou* Buber formulated these relationships in ecstatic imprecision:

> I perceive something. I am sensible of something. I imagine something. I will something. I feel something. I think something. The life of human beings does not consist of all this and the like alone.
>
> This and the like together establish the realm of It. But the realm of Thou has a different basis. When Thou is spoken, the speaker has no thing for his object. . . . Thou has no bounds.[58]

This is what Franz Rosenzweig termed *das neue Denken*—the new mode of thinking—for it involved commitment and participation: "No one can be really devout in relation to God, if he is not devout toward His creation . . . the love of God is unreal, unless it is crowned with love for one's fellow men."[59]

It is not an exaggerated claim: Hasidism—via Buber—has become a dominant influence in the intellectual history of the West. It provided at times ephemeral stimulation; but it also built a permanent base for spiritual regeneration.

18
The Rediscovery of Oriental Jewry in Hebrew Literature: Tabib; Burla; Shami

THE ingathering of Jewry was an instinctive drive rather than a political decision of Zionist leaders in the beginning of the twentieth century. And the absorption of Yemenite Jewry—"the oldest Jewry in the world"[1]—into the web of life in the Holy Land is a modern saga of determined acculturation. The fanaticism of the Islamic sects in Yemen which, under the Zaydi dynasty, established its rule in 897 and reigned with interruptions till 1960, had led to discrimination against Jewry for many centuries; restrictive legislation and cruel humiliation resulted in abject poverty and inner insecurity. Jewish artisans, the bulk of Yemenite Jewry, subsisted on meager rations of food in impossible living quarters. Such was their lot though they could claim proud ancestry and even a king who converted to their faith in the sixth century—Yusuf Asar Yathar Dhu Nuwas of Himyar.[2]

Messianism and mysticism were the twin forces which illumined Yemenite Jewry in the dark night of symbiosis with their Arab cousins. In the twelfth century Maimonides responded to a Yemenite plea for guidance on messianic claims of a Yemenite in his *Yemenite Letter*.[3] And he reminded world Jewry of the presence and existence of Jews in a corner of the Arabian Peninsula. In the same century, Benjamin of Tudela, the indefatigable traveler, also showed interest in the Jews of Yemen. In succeeding centuries sparse information about that remote community reached world Jewry. In isolation it cultivated poetry which resembled Hebrew poetry in Spain. For it modeled itself on the language and style, the themes and the imagery, the prosody and the forms which prevailed on the Iberian peninsula. But it also differed from the poetry of Spanish Jewry: it relied on post-biblical rather than on the biblical vocabulary, it used not only Hebrew but also Aramaic and Arabic as a vehicle of expression.

After the expulsion of the Jews from Spain the Yemenite community drew spiritual sustenance from the mystics of Safed. One of the Yemenite poets who was well-versed in the Arabic and Hebrew literature of the Middle Ages and who produced the famous *Book of Ethics*,[4] Zechariah al-Dahiri (1519–1589), made the arduous journey to the Land of Israel and met Cordovero, Alkabez and Najara. His colorful and erudite personality left an impression on the learned and imaginative literature of Yemen in succeeding centuries. Thus even the nineteenth century poet Saadia Ben-Yehudah would never have produced his *Book of Thought*[5] which lacked his predecessor's grace but not his deep concern with the bitter lot of the Yemenites in Yemen and especially in Sana. There were poets like Rabbi Solomon Adani (1567–1622) who wrote tales in rhymed prose, *maqamat,* and produced a commentary on the Mishnah.[6] And there were erudite chroniclers like Rabbi Said Sadi[7] in the eighteenth century. But the outstanding Yemenite poet was the popular and mystic Shalom Shabbazi (c. 1617—c. 1680) who was held in exaggerated admiration by his contemporaries and was even regarded by them as the Messiah. But he ridiculed the idea and, though he did not bring redemption, "he healed the nation's heart with his songs, for they expressed the bonds of love between God and Israel, the suffering of the Galut and the longing for Zion in words . . . new and precious."[8] In three languages—Hebrew, Aramaic, Arabic—he expressed his infinite yearning for Zion and the ultimate redemption. The nostalgia was so deeply felt and so sincerely articulated that no other Yemenite ever succeeded in emulating or surpassing its fervor. To this day Shabbazi is for Yemenite Jewry what Halevi was for Spanish Jewry and what Bialik was for East-European Jewry: the national poet.

> Grant Salvation to the holy wandering people,
> Restore us to Zion . . . [9]

This ardent prayer was finally and fully granted when almost all Yemenite Jews settled in Israel after the establishment of the State.

Poetry was not the most significant cultural contribution of Yemenite Jewry. That special genre of Hebrew literature known as Midrash found a hospitable home in Yemen. Bibliophiles pored over Yemenite *Midrashim*—such as the *Great Midrash*[10]—which differ from *Midrashim* of other lands. Interest in Yemenite poetry, homiletics and antiquities aroused also an interest in Yemenite Jews. Hardy souls ventured into their land and brought back tales of wonder about exotic brethren. One such was Jacob Halevi Saphir (1822–1885) who visited Yemen in the middle of the nineteenth century and described their mode of life in the capital, Sana, and in the villages.[11] At his suasion Yemenite craftsmen of Jewish provenance—silversmiths, goldsmiths and workers in baser metals—immigrated to the Holy Land before the Bilu pioneers[12] and continued to ply their trade in their new home in Jerusalem in the nineteenth century. They were, as a matter of fact, the first Jewish immigrants who lived by the sweat of their brow rather than by alms, *Halukkah*. They were few in number; some thirty families in all, but they were followed by kinsmen and friends who settled in Jerusalem and in Jaffa as craftsmen, in Rehovot and Rishon le-Zion as farmers.

Another traveler of note, Professor Joseph Halévy (1827–1917), brought back Arabic inscriptions from Yemen to the West and published them in learned periodicals.[13] He was helped by Hayyim Habshush who described his adventurous forays—with or without Halévy—into the interior of Yemen in a book written partly in Hebrew but mainly in the Arabic dialect of Sana.[14] It is regarded as a mine of information on Arabs and Jews in nineteenth century Yemen.

But it was not until Samuel Javnieli (1884–1961) brought the message of national awakening to Yemen that Yemenite Jews began to settle in the Holy Land—first a trickle, then a flood, then almost the entire Yemenite community flew into the promised land in the operation "Magic Carpet."[15] As Bible-oriented Jews they based their influx into the Holy Land and the simultaneous influx of East European Jewry in the eighties of the nineteenth century on a biblical verse:

I will say unto the North: Give up,
And to the South: Keep not back.[16]

By the time of the establishment of the State of Israel more than half of all the Yemenite Jews had immigrated to the Holy Land. With the establishment of the State of Israel all had left Yemen—most of them for Israel, some of them for the United States. They aroused curiosity and respect as artisans and scholars.[17] Their delicate work in filigree, their sumptuous designs of feminine embroidery, their picturesque ways of speech in their Judeo-Arabic and Hebrew idiom, and their graceful dances which were later cultivated by Inbal, an artistic company of their own, became part of the saga of renascent Israel.

First they were written about, then they took their own hesitant steps in the literature of the Holy Land. Though they have not yet produced a writer of stature, they are responsible for major works of fiction—especially in the oeuvre of Burla and Hazaz.

As early as 1883 Imber expressed sympathy in his poetry with the unhappy lot of the Yemenites who were adding poverty to the prevalent poverty of Jewry in the Holy Land.[18] Yellin, on the other hand, stressed their gradual progress from destitution to dignity.[19]

In the first two decades of the twentieth century the Yemenite made his appearance in plays, in poems, in stories, in history. Before the First World War Joshua Radler Feldman—better known by his pseudonym Rabbi Benjamin—had collected and published in a booklet some facts about Yemenites in Yemen and in the Holy Land.[20]

In a clumsy comedy, *The Disdainer*,[21] Yehoshua Barzilai foists upon his prospective public, which had a chance to read but not to see the play, an Englishman named Mr. William, a gentleman who insists on speaking English. The author's English is a travesty of the most elementary rules of grammar: "Hebrew very good, beautiful, but I not speak."[22] The author also delivers himself of the famous adage: "Times [sic] is money."[23] But he is a character in a play which may be regarded as an early attempt at the idea of ingathering: a Yemenite servant graces the galaxy of characters.

In another play, *Night in a Vineyard*,[24] written by a more eminent writer, David Shimoni, the Yemenites appear as exotic specimens of Jewry. They are still nameless types rather than individuals, primitive and picturesque in their modes of expression. But at that early stage, they are already subject to the contempt of Russian Jewry: they are not a constructive "element." Although they do not know the precise connotation of the term they are worried. And they are quick to take advantage of the modest opportunities in the Holy Land before the First World War: one of the younger Yemenites in the play studies "a certain craft with a certain Professor . . . Bezalel." In his play Shimoni not only devotes an entire scene to the Yemenites; he becomes one of their first sympathetic spokesmen. For, like the poet, they are driven by age-old messianic expectations and a modern determination for self-realization through productive work.

Though *Night in a Vineyard*—a series of fragmentary scenes in the poet's own characterization—revolves around a certain character named Korngold, a superficial journalist and professional enthusiast who stays in Palestine for a while and then leaves forever to write at length about the renascence of the Holy Land, the unnamed Yemenites add color and realism to the play.

While Barzilai and Shimoni depicted Yemenites in plays, Nehamah Puhachevsky (1869-1934) was the first to introduce Yemenite women into Hebrew fiction. One of the earliest women writers in modern Hebrew literature she delighted "the lion of the enlightenment," Judah Leb Gordon, with her talent. In Rishon le-Zion where she resided from 1889 on, she had an opportunity to observe Yemenites and devoted five stories to Yemenite characters. In "Rumah"[25] a Yemenite woman reminisces about her immigration to the Holy Land, the death of a baby, and the death of her husband. She herself dies at the end of her tale.

The fate of Rumah and that of many early settlers dot the landscape of Puhatshevsky's early and later stories.[26] Unassuming characters, confronted with the inexorable problems of daily existence in cooperatives, they toil in the fields, in the gardens, in the stables, and eke out a meager livelihood. The women, especially the Yemenite women, play a major role in the national adventure: they are sensitive creatures who suffer from their environment, their men, their own dreams.

The first writers on Yemenites in modern Hebrew literature—Imber and Yellin, Barzilai and Shimoni, Rabbi Benjamin and Puhachevsky—were non-Yemenite. Only when they took root in Israel and matured artistically were Yemenites able to produce writers of their own. A good example of early Yemenite creativity is the Tabib family: Abraham Tabib (1889-1950), one of the early Yemenite leaders and a member of the first *Keneset* in 1949, authored two historical books on Yemenites.[27] His son Mordecai Tabib (1910-) who was born in Turkish Palestine produced poetry and prose on the Yemenite community in Israel. The poetry is sparse but the prose—not in the plays but in the fiction—is alive with stories which convey the exotic pathos of a distant segment of Jewry. "Yosi's Fiddle,"[28] for instance, grips the reader with the simplicity of its reminiscences. Yedidah, a widow who lost her only son in the War of Independence, is left with his fiddle as her most cherished memento and with the memory of his life which she hopes to perpetuate by commissioning his friend to write a book about him. Though neither this story nor other stories with their tender regard for Yemenite women can compare with the Yemenite tales of Hazaz, they are sufficiently interesting as reflections of a Yemenite on Yemenites.

Mordecai Tabib did not suffer the prolonged miseries of adaptation as had his father who immigrated from Yemen. But he observed the older generation with sympathy. And he created his first novel, *Like the Grass of the Field*,[29] out of the friendly conflict of father and son. The traditionalism of the first generation, the slow detheologization of the second generation—this is the burden of the novel. The resentments of the first generation against the European Jews and their superior economic status is overwhelming.

> Those Ashkenazim preceded us in their entry to the Land of Israel. The wealth of the entire country is in their hands. They have the lands, they have the vineyards, they have the houses, they have everything.[30]

The second generation—in the person of Yahia ben Yahia—is eager to lead what is regarded as a superior life style and seeks out the rural cooperative, the kibbutz, as its proper habitat. *Like the Broomtree in the Desert*[31] continues Yahia's story. It begins with his father's death and it projects Yahia's personality against the background of other natives and immigrants of many nations. His love, his work, his joys and disappointments and, finally, his preparation for an entrance examination to the Teachers Seminary in Bet ha-Kerem, are depicted with Tabib's competent realism. The Yemenite becomes an Israeli, and this, perhaps, is the author's chief concern—to trace and illumine the metamorphosis.

A Jew of Sephardic origin whose ancestors had lived for many years in the Holy Land became the major literary spokesman of oriental Jewry, including the Yemenites, and the fictive chronicler of Eastern Jewry:[32] Yehudah Burla (1886-1969). It is a paradox of his art that he is essentially a Western writer. The acknowledged masters of Hebrew literature were his masters: Mendele Moker Sefarim and Joseph Hayyim Brenner. Their realism, their mode of narration, their unadorned style was refracted in his numerous novels and stories. Exotic names and place-names, Arabic or Turkish phrases: these were mere Oriental trappings. The style was occidental. The only conscious—or unconscious—orientalism in his fiction was the untrammeled eroticism of his Jewish and Arab characters. From the first story "Lunah"[33] which depicts a young girl married off to an older voluptuary, through his first novel *His Hated Wife*,[34] through *In Darkness Striving*[35] to the stories in *Women*[36] and to *Lord Among His People*,[37] the unhappy woman in love or the unhappy man in love or both form the central theme. A melodramatic rather than dramatic quality dominates Burla's men and women in their confrontation with the world. David, the central character of his first novel *His Hated Wife,* struggles with oriental fatality against an unloved wife. The Jewish peddler Rahmu—Rahamo in Schachter's translation of the novel *In Darkness Striving*—who also suffers from an unhappy marriage, seeks the love of Shafikah, a beautiful Moslem divorcee, and is blinded by her relatives. Distracted Shafikah loses her mind and commits suicide by drowning. In *The Singer*[38] the roles are reversed. Bediah, a Jewish demimondaine of Damascus, conquers the heart of Rashid, a wealthy Arab. After the First World War she migrates to mandatory Palestine and becomes enamored of its nascent pioneerism.

Love and spring require and replenish each other with cathartic sublimity in Burla's stories:

> Spring came and made me sing with the wheat fields.
> My love grew and my heart swelled at the sight of
> the growing green stalks and ears.[39]

Cooperative life in the kibbutz also serves as a cathartic experience in a voluminous novel by Burla, *Daughter of Zion*.[40] Rose Rodowitz, the heroine, of mixed Sephardic and Ashkenazic stock, is an erotomaniac whose early education in a French missionary school is continued through cheap French novels. She converts to Islam and marries a Moslem, but finds no happiness in her new faith and new milieu, reconverts to Judaism and seeks a new life in the kibbutz.

In *Deeds of Akabiah*[41] Burla attempted to join the theme of love and the theme of salvation in a new combination. The protagonist is a modern Samson whose Delilahs are not mere temptresses but rather romantic lovers in search—not unlike himself—of escape from a humdrum existence. This paragon of prowess is a dreamer in hot pursuit of God and salvation. In his sensitivity to nature and human suffering he is the exception rather than the rule in Burla's novels. And his humiliation, degradation, and lack of fulfillment in Jerusalem exemplifies the inexorable logic of his life's events.

Burla struggled to abandon his obsession with the love theme in his last works, in the fictive biography of Judah Halevi, *The Travels of Judah Halevi*[42] and in *On the Horizon*,[43] the biography of Judah ben Solomon Alkalai (1798–1878) who is regarded as a precursor of Zionism.[44] What he could not and would not abandon was the oriental milieu of his novels—Jerusalem in the early years of the twentieth century in *His Hated Wife*, Damascus in the novel *In Darkness Striving* and in the *Singer*, the Anatolian landscape in the *Deeds of Akabiah*. Again and again he places his plots in Jerusalem, the city of his birth and his affection. It is his undeniable merit that he is the first oriental novelist of stature in modern Hebrew literature. For he cast his net not only over the exotic Yemenites and over Jews of Bukhara, but also over Syrian and Persian Jews and over Arabs.[45] And he unveiled the veiled woman of the Orient—Jewish, Druze and Bedouin. In a style that was the epitome of occidental realism he enshrined his oriental characters in their erotic passions and in their religious fervor which, under the influence of a Western veneer, was slowly becoming a disintegrative rather than a constructive force. Burla, the scion of a rabbinic family that had lived for two centuries in the Holy Land, was almost destined by birth and by education in talmudic academies and a teachers seminary[46] to focus his fictive talents on oriental Jewry in the twilight of religious traditionalism and dissolution. And he became the painter in words of a whole gallery of Levantine epigones of a splendid civilization which had flourished during the Golden Age of Hebrew literature in Spain.

Isaac Shami (1889–1949), a younger friend of Burla and a student at the same teachers seminary, was also a native Palestinian and a scion of a Sephardic family in Hebron. He was barely twenty when he was discovered by Simhah Ben-Zion who published his first two stories, "The Barren Woman" and "Ransom."[47] The theme of "The Barren Woman" is an oriental wedding in which a second wife is added ceremonially to the first who is cursed with barrenness. When the father of the second wife tries to induce the first wife Flor to rejoice in the wedding and to sip some wine, she bangs the glass against the table with such vehemence that "the wine spills on his face, on her face. Then she flees in anger and shame." In "The Barren Woman" passions are uncontrolled; violence is a way of life. In "Father and Daughters" the protagonist spends time and effort to find suitable bridegrooms for his daughters. But the time and effort have been spent in vain: the daughters have prostituted themselves, aided and abetted by their cynical mother. Shami also excels in portraying the nobler characteristics of the Arab—his hospitality, his sense of dignity, his passionate piety. And he can penetrate into the soul of a simple Arab shepherd with all the empathy of a sophisticated writer. For he observes with love and understanding:

> Gumah knew his flock and his flock knew him. When he whistled or twittered the goats or the kids which were called by name would run to him in wild leaps . . . . He guessed their wishes from their lowing and bleating.[48]

Shami reached his apogee in "Ancestral Vengeance,"[49] a tale of two Arabized cities, Hebron and Shechem, a gory story of murder and repentance and revenge against a background of wild desert beauty and corruption. It was Shami's strength that he portrayed the Arab rather than the Jew with the greater tension and the greater realism. The compulsive but artistically inadequate drive to write about his own people rather than about the Arabs, who were more congenial to him, may have resulted in a meager output and the eventual desiccation of his creative resources. After his death Asher Barash found a revealing note in Shami's handwriting:

The spring of my creativity . . . was not . . . rich; it was a hard rock source, that did not pave a path toward the outer world; it raged within and, only at times, it moistened the smooth wall of the rock and returned to be swallowed within.[50]

During his lifetime Shami published a few stories. Posthumously, Barash collected his works of fiction in one volume. On the basis of that sparse output it can be said with certainty that he was not only the first Hebrew writer to penetrate the soul of the Arab with psychological acumen rather than with romanticized appreciation, but he also put his finger on one of the sources of enmity between Arab and Jew. It was the younger generation of Arabs which was affected by the religious laxity of the Jewish colonists; the older generation was frustrated, enraged, desperate.

While Burla and Shami delved into the ancestral resources of Sephardic Jewry in his last novels, their younger contemporaries with oriental background drew on the rich literature of their Arabic homeland. Simon Balas (1930-), a native of Baghdad who settled in Israel, paraphrased for children legends about Ashab of Baghdad, the prince of paupers[51] in the Abassid period. In his novel *Clarity*[52]—the story of a thirty-four year old engineer who sat out the Six-Day War in Tel Aviv on doctor's orders and against his own will—Balas sought and found integration with Israeli society. In that near-monolog the protagonist achieves clarity out of perplexity against the background of national anxiety and relief after the brief and victorious war.

Not only fiction but also scholarship was engaged in an exciting enterprise of discovery. Scholars connected with the Ben Zvi Institute, like Meir Benayahu, have uncovered manuscripts of considerable importance, largely in the realm of poetry and mysticism of Eastern Jewry. In the last few decades an entire literature of Kurdish Jewry has been brought to light, thanks to the labors of J. Mann and S. Assaf, Franz Rosenthal, J.J. Rivlin and A. Ben-Jacob: poetry in Hebrew as well as folk tales in Aramaic, mystic tracts, commentaries on biblical and post-biblical literature in a Judeo-Aramaic dialect—the so called neo-Aramaic or neo-Syriac.

19
The Totality of Jewry in the Works of Hayyim Hazaz

THE literary debut of the major Hebrew novelist, Hayyim Hazaz (1897–1973), is a tissue of unevenful and unexciting paradoxes. In a period of civil war which marked a new beginning for Russia and a beginning of the end for Russian Jewry, he published an innocuous sketch in prose "At Sunset" and an equally innocuous poem, "On Watch."[1] The sketch traced the encounter of a young man, "a Jew, most importantly a Jew," with a prostitute. It was suffused with a faint aroma of decadence and with literary reminders of Maupassant, Chekhov, and Gnessin,[2] the subtle master of the Hebrew short story. It even conveyed a delicate philosophical observation: "We are all of us together like one big irony on the surface of life's cadaver."

The poem had no relation to the cataclysmic events in Hazaz's native land. It was romantic in content, conservative in form; in five four-line stanzas it reiterated a nostalgic attitude to the Holy Land. Its military title—"On Watch"—suggested identification with Palestine, liberated from "the Philistines." This was a topical allusion to the victory over the Turks which General Edmund Henry Hynman Allenby had gained at Gaza and in the capture of Jerusalem on December 9, 1917. The periodical *Ha-Shiloah* which accepted the sketch and the poem for publication, from the year of its appearance in 1896 under the editorship of Ahad Haam, was the most important but also the most sedate literary monthly in the Hebrew language. Its title pointed to its preference for gradual progression in the inner development of the Jewish people. For Ha-Shiloah, the ancient brook to the south of Jerusalem, had already been invoked as the symbol of slow movement in biblical times.[3]

Hazaz published his two firstlings under the pseudonym H. Zevi. H. may have stood for the initial of his first name Hayyim. Zevi might

207

have had a number of possible connotations: as a symbol for Palestine which is called *Erez ha-Zevi*;[4] as the name of a false Messiah, Sabbatai Zevi; or, perhaps, as an ironic identification with Hakam Zevi (1660–1718), the rigorous and ascetic rabbi who never yielded to the rich and who defended the poor with extraordinary zeal. Of greater importance was the dedication of the poem to Saul Tschernichowsky who dared more than any other Hebrew poet before him to discard accepted techniques and traditional themes. A special jubilee issue of *Ha-Shiloah* had come out in his honor in August 1918. Significantly, but perhaps unconsciously, Tschernichowsky used the title "On Watch"[5] for a poem which reflected the anguish of the incipient civil war of 1936–1939 in mandatory Palestine.

Hazaz's first sketch and first poem were also his last. He never again published any sketches or poetry. The inner transformation—first into short-story writer, then into novelist—moved as rapidly as the revolutionary milieu which nurtured him in his youth. In the decade after the publication of his first pseudonymous juvenilia he became an acknowledged master of Hebrew prose. For his unique experiences and his unique endowments projected a startling and moving image of Jewry—startling in its novelty and moving by its contrasts.

Two contradictory forces shaped the life and work of Hazaz from 1897, the year of his birth, to 1921, the year of his emigration from Russia: the traditional and thorough Jewish education in his native Ukrainian village of Sidorovichi and the excesses of the Bolshevik Revolution with their attendant years of internecine fighting between Whites and Reds. The traditional education prevailed as the strongest force in his life: "I was opposed to communism from the start. I was revolted by the appearance of the pistol-bearing Communists in the streets of our town."[6] The later stages of Hazaz's life before his emigration to Palestine were equally decisive. The year and a half in Constantinople brought him face to face with an exotic community of Jewry; the ten difficult years in Paris, with brief intervals in Berlin, sharpened his literary longing for the lost past, particularly the pre-Revolutionary past of East European Jewry. After settling in mandatory Palestine in 1931, he consistently conquered new territory for his stories and novels. The three stories from the early period of communism in Russia—"On This Side and On That Side," "Revolutionary Chapters," "Shemuel Frankfurter"[7]—won him immediate acceptance. The vividness of portraiture, the situational irony, the originality of style justified the accolade. With deliberate intent Hazaz chose his theme—Russian Jewry in the throes of the Russian Revolution. Its freshness and newness startled, shocked, and seduced both readers and critics. There was, in these first three stories, a confrontation on many levels. The revolution forced and foisted attitudes of abysmal despair or enthusiastic acceptance on the younger and the older generations of Jews. It also generated transvaluations of traditional values.

What the ongoing revolution did to Russia—that may have been the business of writers like Alexander Blok, Vladimir Mayakovsky, and Maxim Gorki. What it did to the Jewish people—that was the special concern of Hazaz. For the Russian Revolution brought into focus for him and for his readers an ageless theme, an eternal craving of Jewry—redemption of mankind, justice for all, universal brotherhood. The three stories teem with characters who see their historic chance to create a new world. Only the old and the mature are stricken with a pathetic helplessness and an inability to adapt to changed conditions. The young are either mild and idealistic to the point of folly or ruthless and astute to the point of violence. They make speeches and they make love with the grim abandon of fanatic reformers, they deprecate the bourgeois—Jewish and Russian—and they destroy tradition with an unimaginable recklessness. But they hitch their thoughts to the star of redemption.

In his very first story, "On This Side and On That Side," Hazaz confronts Reb Nathan-Note, the representative of the bourgeoisie, with Motel Pyekelny, "the hellish one," the representative of the proletariat; the old with the new, the rooted with the militant, the traditionalist with the revolutionist. More subtly, he confronts the gentle son of Reb Nathan-Note, Henich, a complicated revolutionist, with the less refined Motel who marries Henich's sweetheart in his absence. Love which moves the sun and the other stars also dims and extinguishes life. Henich dies—victim of an illness aggravated by disappointed love. There are eulogies; there is the singing of the Internationale; and, above the din and the clamor of a revolutionary's funeral, the father's loud *Kaddish*, the traditional prayer for the dead.

The two other stories, "Revolutionary Chapters" and "Shemuel Frankfurter," are mere sequels. The chaotic times are sketched with bolder strokes, the revolutionary characters multiply: complicated comrade Soroka, "the Raven," ruthless comrade Polishuk, fire-eating Henia. The most ardent idealist and believer in the new gospel of redemption, Shemuel Frankfurter, draws his spiritual sustenance from the literature of social justice in the Bible and in post-biblical literature. And he is killed by the Whites—not only as a Communist, but also as a Jew. This is tragedy in a maddened world, in a satanized world: the revolutionary gospel brings the sad tidings of new martyr-dom for a martyred people.

More than thirty years elapsed before Hazaz decided to fuse the fragmentary stories of the Russian Revolution into a novel—*Doors of Brass*—which first appeared in 1956 and was revised in 1968.[8] The mature novelist recreated some of the characters from the stories and worked out their large destinies in the small community of Mokri Kut, Wet Corner. The unhappy love of Leytsah for Soroka, the anarchist, her helpless flirtations with Heshel Pribisker, a Hasid in his thirties, and Polishuk, the doctrinaire Communist, cast a murky shadow over the grim situation in Mokri Kut. The older and the younger generation meet head on—the younger with contempt for "the synagogue, the world to come, Paradise and all the rest of the fairy tales," the older with mortal fear of the immediate future, with bewilderment at the requisitions, expropriations, and destructions of property and life. The older generation realizes that it stands "before doors of brass and bars of iron," that the end of its world is imminent.

Soroka is a character of almost tragic dimensions in the novel: anarchist and revolutionary, anchored in tradition yet unattached to any ideal, he is condemned to grandiose dreams and ineffectual activities:

> "I am an anarchist. . . I love freedom and I hate slavery. . . . I despise deception everywhere and at all times, including political deception and party-line deception. I hate bolshevism which is nothing but wholesale murder, a regime of coercion and enslavement; I hate Marxism which is the lying law and the superstition of our generation."

This is Soroka's best self-characterization. And it is, to some extent, the characterization of a generation in search of an ideal. That ideal Soroka, with many of his contemporaries, strives to find in a fusion of revolutionary and nationalistic doctrines:

> "I search for revolution and I search for the people of Israel. I search for a revolution that fits all peoples, all human beings, all Jews. But this Bolshevik Revolution is a Russian Revolution . . . full of cruelty and lust for power. . ."

Soroka is a failure: he organizes communes in Russia and fails, he organizes anarchist groups and fails. And he comes to the bitter and sarcastic realization that Jews are an ineffectual people, "a nation of poets." The old are afraid of uncertainty and they trust in God, the young are cosmopolitan and they despise their fellow Jews or perse-cute them with savage self-hatred.

The stories of the revolution had a certain immediacy of feeling; they were written in the midst of the upheaval. The novel *Doors of Brass* boasts a larger perspective but also a more distant point of van-tage. In one generation the holocaust and the establishment of the State of Israel have turned Jewish history upside down: doors of brass have closed upon the tradition-centered world of Jewry.

Hazaz's novel is an epitaph for a community which is the epitome of the small town, the *shtetl*. It is still a fragment rather than a whole, a disjointed tissue of events rather than a carefully woven tapestry of an event. But it makes an important point with crystal-clear perception: "exile itself is in exile." Diaspora, the basic concept of Jewry which has needed urgent reinterpretation since the establishment of the State of Israel was already moribund on the eve of the Russian Revolution. No reader of Hazaz can avoid this inescapable fact of contemporary Jew-ish history.

The loss of tradition has been the primary theme of leading writers in the twentieth century. T. S. Eliot and James Joyce, Thomas Mann and Marcel Proust have written the great texts of man's alienation in the modern world. Hazaz depicted not only the destruction of religious values in a revolutionary milieu but also drew with ever increasing vigor the landscape of tradition in or out of the little town, the *shtetl*. In the very first novel, *Home in the Woods*,[9] he sounded the ominous note which was to be heard in his stories and novels in endless varia-tions: the slow dissolution of traditional Jewry. Like Tschernichowsky who discovered Jewry in the backwoods of Russia for Hebrew poetry, Hazaz portrayed a Jewish family in the forests of pre-revolutionary Russia during the first decade of the century. It was the last glimmer of the setting sun on Jewish life in Russia. The Russian lumberjacks, the Russian women, the Russian forest—these are evoked with an in-cipient mastery of style and characterization. In no other novel has Hazaz achieved such a plethora of gentile types in such persuasive por-traiture nor landscape vignettes in such plenty as in his first novel. The Jews—mainly members of one family—pale somewhat in the mi-lieu of stark gentile strength. They feel like strangers in the wild for-est but they hebraize "the green kingdom, the green vigor, the green brotherhood and friendship . . . the green inclination to evil . . ." That inclination to evil is, of course, one of the two instinctual powers—one for good, one for evil—which command our emotional life according to the talmudic sages. The Jews in the forest feel lonely and bored because they are not in Jewish company and because the children are unlike Jewish children in more familiar surroundings. The head of the family is still a traditionalist who enjoys the daily work and daily rest, food and drink, weekdays, holidays and Sabbaths. His wife is more complicated, better at repartee, but also lonelier. She suffers from quick alternation of moods: she is "a darkling cloud and a shining sun, a shining sun and a darkling cloud." The Jewish socialist teacher of the two boys in the family, Budnik, cuts a tragi-comic figure in his revolutionary zeal and in his subversive activities among the peasants. He is the eternal disciple of Marx and Plekhanov, the tireless talker, the dealer in abstract formulas, the uprooted among the rooted: "The whole world is his native land . . . the revolution is his native land . . . he is not a Jew." In his lonely forest walks he addresses himself in the third person and argues himself into untenable positions. He is a stranger to his charges and to the man and woman who hired him. The forest itself is uprooted. The novel begins with a massive destruction of trees against the historical background of the Russo-Japanese war and the first booming voices of the revolution. But it ends with a symbolic idyll: the family prepares the decorations and the food for *Shabu'ot*, the holiday which commemorates the gift of Torah to Jewry, the origin of Jewish tradition.

Home in the Woods is an important novel in spite of—perhaps even because of—its static environment. The characters are "worlds unto themselves," each shut in and off from the outside by his own loneliness. The revolutionary teacher who seeks contact with all, Jews and gentiles alike, is the loneliest of the protagonists in the novel which, in spite of its length, reads like a sequence of related lyrical passages.

Forest life versus urban life: this is an unusual set of options for a Jew. The choice is inevitable: urban life in spite of the green seductions of the forest. For a romantic American in the nineteenth century it was just as inevitable: forest life.

> To him who has once tasted the reckless independence, the haughty self-reliance, the sense of irresponsible freedom, which the forest life engenders, civilization thenceforth seems flat and stale.

Thus Francis Parkman (1823–1893) in the conclusion of the last volume of *The Conspiracy of the Pontiac*. Perhaps it is unfair to contrast the view of a historian and the insight of a novelist. But Parkman was a historian with a novelist's flair just as Hazaz is a novelist with a philosophical historian's penchant for valid generalization.

In Paris, far from the Jewish milieu which nurtured him, Hazaz recollected the past glories of his native environment with nostalgic fervor in the unforgettable beginning of his story "Former Generations":[10]

> I have a fondness for the small towns of the past . . . which have been vilified by generations of writers, undermined by poets and poetasters, mocked by fools and sages . . . till at last they came to nothing and passed out of the world. . . In mourning and in sorrow my thoughts cleave to them, to their pettiness and greatness . . . their longing and their despair; and their entire world which seems so calm and whole like a legend that has grown old in its passage down the corridors of generations.

Hazaz is unjust, of course, to generations of writers who have not vilified the *shtetl*. But he had in mind the young revolutionaries who, in word and in deed, undermined the values which gave the small towns their *raison d'être*. They certainly did not destroy the *shtetl*. It died in the flames of the Russian Revolution and in the Second World War. But in its heyday it monopolized Hebrew prose and, to a certain extent, Hebrew poetry. In a dialog with Ben-Gurion, Hazaz made some telling remarks about the *shtetl*:

> I know the *shtetl* of the past. I never looked upon it as the perfect specimen of a community. On the contrary, I thought of the *shtetl* as a place where life was drab and which was to be pitied. But it had some good in it; its life was enhanced by some of the finest qualities of our people. . . One of the distinguishing marks of *shtetl* culture is the book. In the small towns of Eastern Europe Jews studied the Torah, or discussed it, or read books. I am not speaking of mere mechanical reading or mere scholarship. It was reading and scholarship with a heart. That is a noble quality which uplifts the individual and the community.[11]

The town—like the Greek polis—was the center of Jewish life, communal, economical, social, religious, cultural. It lacked the political vigor and the artistic strength of the polis, but it compensated for this lack with a superabundance of religion and learning. Throughout the Middle Ages and modern times the town has grooved a path in the life of Jewry. Sura and Pumbeditha in Babylonia, Lucena and Toledo in Spain, Mayence and Worms in Germany, Lublin and Lemberg in Poland, Kiev and Odessa in Russia—these are centers of learning and literature which can be multiplied by the dozens and by the scores. *Shtetl* is a loving Yiddish diminutive for town, but the word can be applied to all the towns in all four corners of the globe. For the Jews transformed the *shtetl* with their deep probings into the arcane life of the spirit. "shtetlism" is their creation over a period of two thousand years.

"Former Generations" is the first story in a collection of short stories, *Broken Millstones* [12] and the first title issued by 'Am 'Obed, the important publishing house of the Labor Party. It stabilized Hazaz's precarious livelihood: a monthly allowance was assigned to him for life. Most of the stories in *Broken Millstones* are *shtetl* stories, some of the prerevolutionary, some of the revolutionary period. Only three of the nine stories in the book are Palestinian stories. But there are links which connect the *shtetl* of Russia and the *shtetl* of Palestine. In "Rahamim" Hazaz depicted a Jew from Kurdistan who is married to two wives and believes in matrimony with the simple faith of the illiterate: "No mountain without a peak, no belly without a navel, no man without a wife."[13]

Broken Millstones is a catalog of the main motifs of Hazaz—the little town, the revolution, the pre-revolutionary life of Jewry in Russia, the oriental and nonoriental Jew in the Land of Israel. It is also indicative of his style—a rich, racy idiom, which was fashioned out of the immense resources of a 3500-year-old language and out of a prodigious lingual sensitivity. Mapu's style was pseudo-biblical, Mendele's pseudo-rabbinical, Agnon's eclectic in the best sense of the word. Hazaz's style was Hazaz's—unmannered, unembellished unrestrained. An abundance of words and idioms cascades over his pages with pristine freshness, with springlike limpidity. His characters may have come from many linguistic areas and/or they may have reflected the vernaculars of their fellow-Jews: Yiddish, Judeo-Arabian, Ladino. Their Hebrew is both natural, in the sense that it would have been theirs had they spoken it, and artistic, in the sense that it is theirs by virtue of the author's "sleight-of-soul." Only Faulkner in American literature has that lush wealth of vocabulary which is a corollary to the passionate violence of his characters. Most of Hazaz's characters also move in a milieu of violence. But they don't create it; they are its victims.

It was on the ship carrying Hazaz from Sebastopol to Constantinople that he encountered a Yemenite Jew with whom he conversed in Hebrew. In Constantinople he was confronted with an exotic segment of Jewry which had previously been totally unknown to him.

I had thought that the Jewish people consisted of Russian, Lithuanian, Ukrainian and Polish Jewries—that these were the nation which was engaged in creating Jewish culture. Western European Jewry was marginal to me, and I placed oriental Jewry somewhere in the middle ages. In Constantinople it dawned on me that the Jewish people is not only "us," that there is somebody else, too. This was a great revelation to me.[14]

Under the influence of his experience in Constantinople Hazaz wrote his story "Rich and Poor Meet."[15] And he was the first Hebrew writer who dared to write a novel on the Yemenites. Even Berl Katzenelson, director of 'Am 'Obed which published it and leader of the Labor Party in mandatory Palestine, was shocked by the novelty of the theme. Play, poem or story: these genres had been regarded as suitable forms for exotic content. But an entire novel—that was a novelty. Hazaz had lived among the Yemenites in Jerusalem and observed them closely. The result was the first Yemenite novel in Hebrew literature, *She Who Dwells in the Gardens*.[16] Rashi had commented: "The Holy one, blessed be He, says to the congregation of Israel: 'You who are scattered in exile—you feed in the gardens of others and you sit in synagogues and houses of study.' " This is a capsuled characterization of the diaspora: economic parasitism and intellectual isolation. But since the locale of the novel is Palestine, Hazaz seems to impart ironic overtones to Rashi's comment. The twin theme of the novel is adumbrated in the title: economic dependence and spiritual independence. Mori Said and his disciple Mori Alfekah represent the Yemenites of an older generation that was nurtured by Messianic yearnings. For them reality and dream are interchangeable. The master is a man of faith, mystic and diviner, sage and scholar; the disciple is a rascal who exploits credulity for material purposes. The master is a dreamer of dreams: he consorts with Moses and Aaron in Paradise and gathers authentic information about the imminence of redemption. The disciple uses the esoteric knowledge for mundane goals and personal gain.

Toward the end of the novel, and his own end, Mori Said is aflame with redemption:

I asked a dream question: When will redemption come? They told me: A day of vengeance is in my heart, my year of redemption is come.[17] I said: When? What year? What month? They answered me: I will hasten it in its time.[18] But when? They answered me: I will love you freely. . . [19] It means now, in this generation because it is a guilty generation;[20] the Holy One blessed be he, will redeem us even if we are guilty. I was not satisfied with the answer and asked again: When? And again they answered me: For the day of vengeance is in my heart, my year of redemption is come. It means this year, this very year.[21]

A second generation of Yemenites is represented by Mori Said's son, Zion—a gross, rude and immoral character. Zion's daughter, Rumyeh, who represents the third generation, settles in a kibbutz and effects a total break with tradition. They all seem to belong to an age of innocence. Even their evil inclinations and acts are touched by childishness. The interplay of vision and reality has been achieved in the novel in a manner that is entirely believable—as if the twentieth century and all its sophistication had never existed at all. *Mori Said* is the saga of three generations of Yemenites in Palestine, a miniature Hebrew counterpart of the massive novels of Galsworthy and Thomas Mann, *The Forsyte Saga* and *Buddenbrooks*.

Hazaz's discovery of the Yemenites was more than an accident of fate; it was a psychological necessity. For the world of Eastern Jewry was merely a facsimile—on a more naive and more exotic plane—of other Jewries in the disintegrating molds of tradition. Only the speech of the characters was punctuated by Arabic instead of Russian phrases; and the milieu was Palestine in the comparatively tame process òf change into a Jewish homeland, instead of Russia in the agony of revolution.

Yemenites were not only a special species of Jews in their own eyes; they very nearly came to be regarded as a special Jewry by Hazaz. In the excellent beginning of the novel, the novelist characterized—with tongue-in-cheek—the numerous Jewries in Jerusalem: the Ashkenazim, the Sephardim, the Kurds, the Persians, the Bukharans, the Syrians, the Anatolians, the Moroccans. But the "select of the select are Yemenites, well-defined, sharply distinguished. You can never confuse them with any other Jewry. They are lively and keen-minded, salted and peppered. They are sinew and bone, with no flesh at all—as though they had eliminated the nonessentials and preserved the essentials."[22]

Hazaz did not exhaust his love and his knowledge of Yemenites in

Mori Said. It was an inner compulsion for him to write another novel about his favorite Jewry.

While *Mori Said* is a novel about Yemenites in Jerusalem, *Yaish*[23] is a novel about Yemenites in Yemen. The first volume appeared in installments in the periodical *Moznayim* under the pseudonym Zechariah Uzali. There was a Yemenite tradition that the capital of their country, Sana, was biblical Uzal.[24] And so authentic was the novel that Yemenites suspected one of their own as the author. *Yaish* is Hazaz's lengthiest but not most important work. It lacks the grand design and coherence of the massive novels of a Tolstoy or even a Roger Martin du Gard. And Hazaz deserves to be compared to the masters of world literature because of his encompassing celebration of the uniqueness of an entire people. *Yaish* attempts to recreate through its hero Yaish the life of an exotic community which is proud of its ancient lineage and which carries the burden of poverty with a mixture of royal disdain and Messianic hope. Not only is the hero not an ascetic; he is lusty and passionate—a younger and more complicated edition of Mori Said, a euphoric optimist and, above all, unbelievably religious: "From the hour he put on his phylacteries, he changed and became a new sort of man." He is also the man of righteousness who lives by faith. His name is an Arabic allusion to the verse of the prophet: And the righteous *lives* by his faith.[25] Adverse environmental forces steel his resolve— the tricky brother, the plain wife, the grass-widowed mother. His success as a silversmith only enhances his moral stance. He becomes the most esoteric Kabbalist; he is even convinced that his sudden blindness is the result of an angel's touch. A man like Yaish must settle in the Land of Israel:

> Its earth is pure gold, almost-almost pure, its stones are precious stones and pearls, its houses are built of jewels; its fruits are like the fruits of Paradise . . . a cluster of grapes is bigger than an average man.

It is easy for Yaish to turn the Holy Land into a legend because he is constantly living the legendary life. He visits the higher reaches of heaven in his imagination rather than in spacecraft, and seeks out his great heroes, the Yemenite mystic Shalom Shabbazi, Maimonides, spiritual hero of the Yemenites, and Isaac Luria, the saintly Kabbalist of sixteenth century Safed.

Yaish's inevitable emigration to Palestine is not only a change of locale; it is a complete transformation. Rooted in the soil of the Holy

Land, he abandons his heavenly excursions: "Heaven was closed to him and did not open to him any more—ever." This is the last sentence of the novel, nonmystical, nonesoteric, nonlegendary. Yaish, in Israel, has at last become a man whose legendary life has changed into a realistic life. But the change in the story is too abrupt—a *deus ex machina* solution to a complicated psychological problem. The end is good propaganda for Israel—but is it art? It is difficult enough to believe in Yaish's mysticism; it is almost impossible to understand his realism. The end of the novel and its occasional longueurs are not the only flaws. The many Arabisms and Judeo-Arabisms,[26] the excessive and refined punning aided, in Hebrew, by such devices as severance of words and combinations of half-words, creation of new words out of initials of two or more words; the wealth of citations from the Bible; the allusions to the Talmud and the Zohar and even to Yemenite literature—all these place heavy burdens on the reader's patience and tend to distract his attention from the story and his empathy from its protagonist.

Hazaz himself drew an excellent comparison between the two chief characters of his two Yemenite novels:

> Mori Said is a dreamer and a denizen of Jerusalem. Yaish is a visionary living in the diaspora, although he finally comes to Erez Yisrael. Mori Said is a redemption-obsessed rebel. Yaish is lost in many problems: life and death, sin and punishment, holiness and the Tempter, human existence generally . . . Mori Said is an idealist; Yaish, for all his visions . . . is a realist . . . Mori Said is tragic; Yaish is epic. . .[27]

The fascination with oriental Jews is a new dimension in modern Hebrew literature. Writers before Hazaz had introduced them into their work: Shimoni into poetry, Burla into prose. But Hazaz from the thirties on devoted his major artistic energies to them, especially to the Yemenites. Even in his novel *Chained Together*[28] the two protagonists who share one prison cell for armed resistance to Britain in mandatory Palestine are representatives of two Jewries: Eastern and Western. And their reactions under duress are as dissimilar as their fates are similar. Eliyyahu Mizrahi—the family name means oriental—is of Iraqi stock, poor, untutored, unsophisticated, partly artisan, partly factory hand by occupation. Menahem Halpern, a former Yeshivah student who also enjoyed a secular education, is an Irgunist, a member of a military underground organization, while Eliyyahu Mizrahi is a Sternist, a member of an extremist underground organization. Their different educational backgrounds account, of course, for their different affiliations and attitudes. But, on the whole, Eliyyahu is the more determined, Menahem the more hesitant, and the more reflective individual. This confrontation of oriental and occidental Jewry is also a major theme of the two fragmented stories with Rabbi Phinehas as hero. In "Rich and Poor Meet" Hazaz juxtaposes his Ashkenazic sage, rich in knowledge and poor in material goods, with inferior types of oriental Jewry in Istanbul. Hazaz's sympathies seem to veer naturally to the occidental type, but in the course of years he developed a great love for oriental Jewry, especially for the Yemenites.

In *Chained Together*, as in many previous works, Hazaz maintained his passionate concern with history. In an interview he remarked without pride but with conscious knowledge of his own worth:

I would like my books to be in every Jewish home. . . For my books are a cross-section of the life of Jewry in our generation—not only the biography of the Jewish people but the biography of each Jew.[29]

Hazaz acquired the authoritative right to make such a demand—both because of his endowments and because of his sacrifices: his only son, the very talented watercolorist Zuzik Nahum Hazaz (1928–1948), was a victim of the War of Independence.[30]

It should be said more precisely what Hazaz's modesty may not have allowed him to say: that his has been the most original evaluation of Jewish history. His "Sermon"[31] is justly famous as a crucial historiosophical story. The chief character, Yudkah, is an unlearned and inarticulate member of a cooperative. But he manages, in an unintentional sermon, to articulate his disenchantment with Jewish history. Like the preacher in Vermont who was against sin, according to the immortal remark by Calvin Coolidge, Yudkah is against Jewish history because

We have no history at all . . . we have not made our history. The Gentiles made it for us . . . we would have made it different . . . What is its content? Evil edicts, defamations, persecutions and martyrdom. Again and again and more and more—endlessly . . . From the day we were exiled from our land we were a people without history . . . We are subject to a special psychology, perverse, fantastic . . . nightlike . . . Exile, martyrdom, Messiah. These are three which are one. Exile . . . Holy, beloved, intimate, close to the heart, closer than Jerusalem, more Jewish than Jerusalem, more rooted, more spiritual . . . Exile is our pyramid. The base-martyrdom, the apex-Messiah . . . We began building that pyramid in ancient times, during the Second Commonwealth . . . What a terrible, what a marvelous nation . . . Belief in the coming of Messiah: this is the typical Jewish illusion . . . Commanded, Jews are commanded to stay in exile till they will be redeemed by Heaven . . . miraculously. They do nothing . . . no effort . . . nothing, nothing. They sit and wait. . . They believe. with perfect faith . . . and yet, in their heart of hearts . . . they don't believe a little bit. . . This is also a Jewish trait . . . to believe with perfect faith . . . and yet not to believe a little bit . . . Redemption is their chief desire . . . but at the same time they have bound themselves . . . not to be redeemed for ever and ever . . . Because they don't want to be redeemed . . . they don't ever   want   to   return   to   the   Land   of   their Fathers . . . This is not deceit . . . this is not duplicity at all. . . . Zionism and Judaism are not the same . . . Zionism is not continuation . . . it is the opposite of what has been . . . it is, with a handful of people at its head, the seed of a different people . . . the Land of Israel—it is already not Judaism. . . .

This text is one of the major documents of modern Hebrew literature. Paradoxically, it is the eloquent plea of a semi-literate worker for a new philosophy of Jewish history. Though his ideas gush with passionate logic, they do not cohere or coalesce or arrange themselves in the neat form of an essay. They are lived and experienced by a character in a story that develops from a banal, everyday incident into a climactic affirmation of a new view of Jewish history. It is a futile exercise in sterile academicism to determine whether these ideas are his or Hazaz's. They are there in their naked splendor to contemplate, to absorb, to live by. And they play havoc with accepted notions of Jewish history.

Yudkah reappears in another story, "The Corpse."[32] He follows the funeral procession of a man who was apparently killed by government forces and who was not well-known to him; he philosophizes about the other participants who were either indifferent or only superficially acquainted with the deceased. They are Jews; they make no wars, they gain no victories and suffer no defeats. They are the people whose dead are victims and whose living are victimized to such an extent that they have become living martyrs. Their communities are not only holy communities but martyred communities.

The tone is not defiant; it is sad, passive, in harmony with the tragic event. But within one generation this attitude to the Jews has become obsolete for they have demonstrated—in four wars—an ability to fight and to win victories; and they have given the lie to the accepted thesis of their martial impotence—even in the Yom Kippur War of 1973. Hazaz himself said at an assembly of writers after the Six-Day War in 1967:

> Jewry has changed. The war revolutionized our history and created a different reality and a different essence, not a repetition but a line drawn toward eternity.

But, in the forties, Hazaz was depressed by the course of cataclysmic events in Jewish history. In one of his stories he confronted a German Jew with a Russian Jew in Palestine. It is the Russian Jew, Moroshka, who makes keen observations and presents daring arguments. In his view German Jews in Israel are "the prayers deleted by the Reformers from the prayer books . . . the prayers about the belief in the coming of the Redeemer, the return to Zion, the Ingathering of Exiles . . ."[33] They are, in the words of Hazaz, "a spiritual incrustation." They are mending what the Reformers—"those history-conscious and spiritual salesmen"—have damaged. But they have not changed, really. First, they wanted to be like gentiles everywhere; a century later they wanted to be like Jews everywhere. Börne, Heine, Marx—they left the Jewish community in order to become Germans. A century later their coreligionists left the German community in order to become Jews—not out of choice but out of necessity. As for the Aryans, they are not free, they are bound by Jewish chains. Hitler's racialism is Ezra's racialism in new garb: no mixed marriages—that is a Jewish invention. Jews have created the forms for "this world which is ours, our doing, the spiritual child of the Jewish people." Europe itself is a Jewish creation and Philo the Alexandrian is the first European.

> More than all the peoples of the world we are rooted in Europe. . . We have choked the Roman eagle in his nest, not the barbarians . . . we have destroyed in the past the ancient world just as we are now destroying the old world for the sake of the future Europe. We will destroy and we will build. They will be of no avail,

the tyrants of the right and the tyrants of the left and all the Aryan foxes . . . [34]

The Jews in Israel are the little remnant of Europe in the Land of Israel, "in the laboratory of the world's creation and the world's improvement." Something stirs in the Land of Israel, something powerful, something decisive for the fate of humanity.

These are the arguments of Moroshka. He and Yudkah represent the Janus-like attitude to Jewish history: one, the negative caricature, the other, the positive caricature. Yudkah disdains exile, Moroshka praises it. Gentiles have requisitioned all spiritual goods from Jews except one: exile. Sinai, Land of Israel, exile—this is Moroshka's countertrinity to Yudkah's trinity of exile, martyrdom, and Messiah. And Moroshka's argument is carried to unprecedented hubris; without exile Jews would have been like gentiles—mere provincials who never left their original habitat and who never enjoyed the discovery of wider horizons. It follows with inexorable logic that what gentiles need is

> Exile which would refine them and purify them and teach them to see and understand what the world is all about and what man is all about . . . and love for fellow-men and pity and truth and justice and honesty. . . A nation, endowed with holiness, goes into exile at the end. For the spirit of holiness brings about exile, and exile brings about a spirit of holiness.[35]

Moroshka reappears in a third story, "Drabkin." Here the Zionist of means and influence who settles in Israel and becomes thoroughly disillusioned with the land and its inhabitants, carries the brunt of the historical argument:

> We have mistaken time for place, the whole for one little lowly detail, the world of the spirit for foul matter. . . Hence the danger to Jewry, the danger of decline, decadence. . . . There [in the diaspora] we were above place, in the depth of time . . . in everlasting life . . . a block of eternity in this passing ephemeral world . . . not of this world, different from all the evil nations . . . like a rose among the thorns . . . like the Bible among the classics of the gentiles, among lewd novels of debauchery and tales of nonsense, full of sadness and sorrow like the Bible, full of flaming faith and sanctity. Here [in Israel] we are like the gentiles, like hideous Europe and its evil culture. . . Here there are Zion-

ists without Zionism and Jews without Judaism . . . a world of lawlessness. All possessions are annulled, all values are abandoned, all fences are breached. . . A state of apostates . . . or of self-made, ignorant converts.[36]

The heated argument is carried on in another novella, *Expanded Horizon*.[37] The disputants have changed names. It is Benjamin Oppenheim, the American Jew who maintains that

> We are the milestone of the world. From the very first generations we are the milestone of the world. Abraham our Forefather, Moses our Master, the prophets, the Nazarene and his disciples, Marx . . . even exile is a milestone. All the desires and all the efforts of the prophets of Israel are enshrined in exile, the mystery of the redemption of humanity, the mystery of eschatology. Exile is a sign and a model for the peoples of the world to do as we do.

This is essentially what Moroshka says in "Muddy Barrel." But there are variations of this argument. If the peoples of the world were to imitate the Jews, there would be no wars, no hatred, no envy. Millennium. But the State of Israel changed all that. It diminished the stature of Jewry. To have suffered two thousand years and to have returned to the Land of Israel after all the trials and tribulations: this is a letdown. Hazaz expresses the idea in a beautiful and daring simile: it is as if Jesus, after the crucifixion, had been resurrected and gone back to Nazareth and engaged in carpentry. Hazaz was careful to indicate in an interview that he did not identify with Yudkah and Moroshka. "I described people in a certain setting . . . the historiosophical problems arose after the characters had been fashioned."[38]

Even Hazaz's last novel, *Chained Together*, is a discourse on history in the form of fiction. The determined protagonist, Eliyyahu, reaches an antihistorical conclusion: the history of the Jews is to be understood as a myth. The hero of mankind—the hero of the mythological past and present—is the Jewish people fighting the powers of evil from generation to generation. Salvation of the world means annihilation of the satanic forces through the mediacy of the Jewish people.

Thus, brick by brick, the protagonists of Hazaz's stories and novels erected a new edifice of Jewish history. Soroka, Yudkah, Moroshka, Benjamin Oppenheim, Mori Said, Yaish, Halpern—they all struggle by word and deed to prepare the way and the day for a new society. They are reformers and saviors, not philosophers. And they draw sustenance from the wellsprings of Jewish tradition and Jewish ethics. Though their ideas—often felt and imagined rather than clearly stated—can be reduced to a set of premises, these premises are inseparable from their conscious and unconscious lives as individuals and as members of a shattered social structure. For the sake of clarity they should be stated with cold precision. First premise: Jews have no history, for history has been made for them. Second premise: exile is a pyramid with martyrdom as base and Messiah as apex. Third premise: exile is the value of values; it could and should be exported for it is the school for the perfectibility of mankind. Fourth premise: statehood, in the larger context of Jewish history, is a descent from spiritual magnificence to mundane reality. Fifth premise: Jewish history is mythology with Jewry as its hero. Present-day Jewry, no less than past Jewry, is "the avant-garde of redemption. All past generations have deposited the fate of the nation in our hands."

No writer in our generation has submitted diaspora and Israel to an evaluation of such poetic depth as Hazaz. One has to go back to the second chapter of Judah Halevi's *Kuzari* to find words of similar strength and relevance about the position of the Jews in the world. The historiosophical texts of Yudkah in "The Sermon," Moroshka in "Muddy Barrel" and "Drabkin," Benjamin Oppenheim in "Expanded Horizon," Menahem and Eliyyahu in *Chained Together*, Yuspa in *At the End of Days*—these are guidelines of transcendent importance for our generation. And Mori Said as well as Yaish are the embodiments of the redemptive urge in a period of urgency for mankind.

In a dialog with Ben-Gurion which took place in Jerusalem on May 16, 1962 Hazaz chided the statesman for his addiction to the Bible as a literature "which is capable of maintaining the Jews as a people." He pleaded for larger cultural horizons beyond the Bible and the Talmud and emphasized the enormous values of modern Hebrew literature, ignored because people ignore books:

> Nowadays, the book has become unimportant and is ignored; spiritual life is gone from our midst; we have no outstanding moral leaders. We do not possess the moral and spiritual forces which are required for absorbing into our midst the many settlers who come from so many different cultures, to absorb them in a way which will raise them up or make of them a people in accordance with the great responsibility which history placed upon our generation.[39]

Most contemporary Hebrew writers in Israel write about Israelis but Hazaz is concerned with the totality of Jewry, Ashkenazic, Sephardic, Yemenite. Only the great Jewry of America is missing from his work; the hero of "Expanded Horizon" is an American Jew who settles in Israel. Hazaz's interest in the past was not obliterated by his concern with the present fate of Jewry especially that of the prerevolutionary Jewry of Russia in its transformation during the White and Red terror and contemporary Israeli and oriental Jewry. But it has been sporadic and fitful and peripheral in his oeuvre. A solitary drama against the background of seventeenth century Germany and a solitary story against the background of the earliest history of Jewry in the desert— these are his two past-oriented thrusts. As for the unfinished novel *Jesus of Nazareth*, it is a fragment on the apocalyptic struggle of Jews and gentiles[40] and it traces the growth of Jesus in spiritual strength against the background of his times. *At the End of Days*[41] suffers from two themes which clash but do not fuse the private conflict of the protagonist and the destiny of the Jewish people during the messianic turmoil. The problem of the diaspora reappears in the play but it adds no new dimension to Hazaz's previous concern with its complexities. The unconvincing call for the liquidation of the diaspora reaches a climax in the dialog between the chief protagonist of the play, Yuspa, and the Rabbi. The Rabbi represents the rationalist affirmation of Judaism and the patient expectation of the Redeemer. And he regards Yuspa and his followers as enemies of Jewry:

> You are worse for Jews than non-Jews . . . for they only have power over our bodies, but you take our soul. You seek our soul! You have monopolized redemption and you have lost your holiness. There is no Messiah without Providence and there is no redemption without faith. . . This redemption which you vaunt is an alien fire. . . You will repeat the deed of Korah who split Jewry . . .

Yuspa yearns for the end of exile and a world free from the oppressive laws of rabbinic Judaism:

> Exile is in exile. There is no exile in Messianic times. These absurd, worthless men you spoke of, Korah and his entire assemblage of people, will not merit redemption. They will remain in exile. You will be their rabbi.

The old and the new cannot unite. Exile is the reality, redemption is the dream. And this is the polarity of tension as it has been for the past two millennia in Jewish history. It is also a polarity which dominates the entire oeuvre of Hazaz. In an interview Hazaz was careful to point out that he was not one of the negators of the diaspora and that "burning the exile is not an idea and not a solution to our national problem."

Hazaz's lone play is matched by a unique story: "The Bridegroom of Blood,"[42] based on three verses in Exodus 4:24-26:

> At a night encampment on the way, the Lord encountered him and sought to kill him. So Zipporah took a flint and cut off her son's foreskin, and touched his legs with it, saying: You are truly a bridegroom of blood to me. And when she left him alone, she added: A bridegroom of blood because of the circumcision.

The locale of the story is the desert, the heroine Zipporah, the plot her interior monolog. More poem than story, "The Bridegroom of Blood" reads like a parallel to Molly Bloom's monolog at the end of Ulysses. Both women—the primitive and the modern who is essentially primitive—are driven by the instinctive forces of their biological needs. Both suffer from husbands who, in their estimation, have not fulfilled the marital ideal of bodily togetherness. Both—Zipporah even more than Molly—suffer from an exaggerated conception of their beauty:

> There had been no beauty like hers since the days of Naamah, sister of Tubal-Cain, and those beautiful girls whom the sons of God had married.

Like Molly Bloom, Zipporah is a deeply troubled woman. Her immense monolog is a mixture of tribal reminiscences, discomforts in the desert, worry about her son and, most importantly, dream-like reveries about Moses and God. In her vacillation and confusion she imagines God as a lover, Moses as the object of his envy. And, in a propitiatory gesture, "she smote the boy to the ground, seized the flint in her hand, jumped on him like a lioness on his prey and cut off the foreskin."

This is Hazaz's mysterious statement of a very mysterious text. The story is not crucial, not central to the oeuvre of Hazaz. But the marginal is as revelatory, if not more so, than the central in the work of a great artist. "The Bridegroom of Blood" is a masterpiece of small perfection. In virtuosity of language and in virtuosity of character delineation it is one of the most poetic stories in modern Hebrew literature.

A perceptive Hebrew critic, Abraham Kariv, has compared the work of Hazaz with Balzac's *Comédie Humaine*. Both share a romantic exuberance in language and in character delineation, both have the ambition to encompass a world in their writings. For Balzac it is the world of nineteenth-century France as a paradigm of humanity; for Hazaz, the world of Jewry as a model of mankind. But they part ways in one important attitude: Hazaz aims, over and above his art as teller of tales, at a historiosophy of Jewry, Balzac never shoots beyond the artistic mark. Within his works the drama of human existence is played out by people who have no message except their existential message. Hazaz's characters in his *"Comédie Juive"* are value-conscious, history-conscious, philosophically oriented even when they perform the common tasks of daily living. And his inestimable contribution to modern Hebrew literature, besides his lingual enrichment of Hebrew prose, is a deeply felt and deeply imagined reorientation of the contemporary Jew. Between the two world wars and in the three subsequent decades, the most seminal figure in Hebrew literature is Hayyim Hazaz.

20
The Historical Novel

AT the end of the third decade of the nineteenth century, Prosper
Mérimée published *A Chronicle of Charles IX.*[1] It was a historical
novel, "a bastard genre" in his view, but a genre that reached unprecedented popularity in the works of a contemporary, Sir Walter Scott,
and has continued to enjoy the favor of European and American readers up to our own time. The secret of its perennial bloom is in its two-
pronged thrust of fact and fiction. History records, the novel interprets;
history aspires to be science, the novel lies in the realm of art. It is true
that "we cannot reproduce with any accuracy what no longer exists."[2]
It is also true that historical writing involves sins of omission and commission which are constantly revised by each generation and within
each generation. So the Aristotelian dictum—"the historian describes
what has been"[3]—must be taken *cum grano salis,* with a grain of salt.

The historical novel, like life itself with its perverse contradictions,
has existed from time immemorial. Its illustrious roster of authors includes Tolstoy and Dickens, Defoe and Mark Twain, Stendhal and
Thomas Mann and, more recently, Solzhenitsyn and Yukio Mishima.
Except for novels which project the future—the utopias, the prophetic
visions in prose like Wells' *War of the Worlds*—all novels are historical
to a certain extent, for they embrace time past or Proustian recapture
of time past. Homer's "novels-in-poetry," the Iliad and the Odyssey,
which head the list of great imaginative works in the ancient world,
are the first historical novels in world literature. In a larger sense the
Pentateuch—with the exception of Leviticus—with the books of Joshua, Judges, Samuel, and Kings forms a historical novel on the origins of humanity in general and Jewry in particular.

In the strict sense of the word the historical novel depends on chro-
nology and past circumstance, on recorded events and spiritual adequacy. This limitation is not necessarily a disadvantage. It may induce
the novelist—as the tyranny of rhyme forces the poet—to exercise his

228

faculties of inventiveness within a prescribed framework. A fusion of fact and fiction, in appropriate dosage, in instinctive rightness, is the highest achievement of the historical novelist.[4] But he must not be a collector of lingual or ethnic curios; he must not be a slave of ingrained, immovable notions, an antiquated antiquary, an exploiter of "the fair license due to the author of a fictitious composition."[5] He must constantly prove his imagination at the cost of his erudition, he must evoke the image of an age and make the past contemporaneous with the present. Granted that such a novel is *voulu*—artificial and effortful. But it satisfies two simultaneous urges: a thirst for knowledge and a longing for the past. In a historical novel concupiscent curiosity is wedded to romantic regret.

In its earliest manifestations the modern novel in Hebrew literature dealt with historical themes. Abraham Mapu, the first major Hebrew novelist in the nineteenth century, was a historical novelist. With the exception of one contemporary novel, *The Hypocrite*, he established his fame with two historical novels, *The Love of Zion* and *The Guilt of Samaria*. He was compulsive in his need to mine the biblical past for fictive works. For the Bible was the object of his immense admiration as well as of the adulation of his contemporaries. Biblical diction was the paradigm for his style, the biblical past was invested with the aura of freedom which had been lost and redemption which had been craved for eighteen hundred years. The idyllic romanticization of the remote era served to underscore—by implication—the miserable reality of the Jewish people in the present.[6]

The search for Jewish rootedness in the Bible continued during the next century. Jacob Hurgin ventured into medieval times with stories like "An Ancient Chronicle"[7] and "Only a Jest"[8] but he chose sturdy female protagonists in "The Midianite"[9] and in "Yael, Wife of Heber the Kenite"[10] to highlight the first stirrings of ancient Jewish nationhood in quasi-biblical style. Asher Barash and Moshe Shamir drew on the period of Jewish kingship for their work. The former wrote one his best stories on the first king of Jewry: "Saul and the Asses";[11] the latter, a novella *The Poor Man's Lamb*[12] which depicts the Davidic period as well as a novel on Alexander Yannai.[13] The story about Saul missed being a masterpiece. From its beginning with the richly construed background of Saul's parents, Kish and Shelomot, to Saul's meeting with Samuel, it moves with patriarchal dignity. The aging father is a character almost wholly invented by Barash. And so is the young mother. Their idyllic love, the confrontation of youth and age, wealth and poverty, in a static society—these are ageless problems which Barash manages with superior *savoir-faire*. But after Saul's meeting with Samuel, Barash resorts to an unworthy stratagem: "All that is written in the Book of Samuel has come about fully to Saul King of Israel."[14] Then, in five short pages, Barash retells the story of Saul's reign. Perhaps he felt that he could not outdo the Bible in the complicated portrayal of the relationship between Saul and David, David and Jonathan. But the story's end—a *deus ex machina* end—is an artistic blemish on a miniature work of art.

Historical fiction in Hebrew literature—from Mapu through Barash to Shamir—is primarily concerned with the theme of redemption. The biblical, the rabbinic, the medieval, the hasidic age—they are all mined by Hebrew writers for redemptive material. Martyrdom—another major theme in historical fiction in Hebrew literature—is merely an adjunct of redemption and, in the eye of the orthodox, a condition of redemption whenever and wherever that condition is imposed on the prospective sufferer. The only possible exception is the novel *History of Gemini* by Benjamin Galai.[15] But even in this ironic mockery at Catholic excesses in the Middle Ages, the prime interest of Jews in esoteric speculation about eschatological justice for all mankind plays a marginal role. It was Asher Barash who created the outstanding novella of martyrdom, *Facing the Gate of Heaven*.[16] Set in the period of the pogroms perpetrated by the hordes of Chmielnicki in 1648–49, it projected in the person of the lowly beadle at the synagogue, Israel Mihal, the high qualities of ethical determination which characterized the best exemplars of Jewry throughout the ages. Alone the protagonist has decided to defend the synagogue against the onslaught of the Cossacks. He has collected in the attic two hundred heavy stones which were heaped in the courtyard for the repair of the House of Prayer and, when the enemy comes and charges with a hundred horses, he wounds and kills as many as he can with the only weapon he has: stones. Then the inevitable happens: he dies a slow death by Cossack lashings. The killer does his work with such merciless cruelty that he almost drops dead himself. The victim, in an unbelievable attempt at mercy for the victimizer, urges him in his agony to "rest . . . rest a while . . . rest";[17] it will relieve the superhuman exertion of his sadistic enterprise. Barash was determined to show, in an extraordinary finale of the story, that the God of Israel, the God of mercy and forgiveness, had won again. It was a victory which exacted the price of a life. But in the grim confrontation of Jew and gentile, it was a victory of gentle humanity over inhuman cruelty. That, in essence, was vintage Barash, an autobiographical projection of the humane author onto the plane of martyrdom in slow, almost idyllic patterns of rhythm.

Even in a story like "Down to the Foundation,"[18] with its background of blood and destruction in the last days of independence and the first days of subjection by the Romans, the author created the portrait of John of Giscala with almost idyllic reticence. A feminine aura suffuses the personality of the warrior-scholar who has renounced love to regain it amidst ruins. Even the desperate choice of preserving or destroying meaningless life, to paraphrase the words of the author,[19] seems somehow less desperate in his calm phrasing. And so is the choice between "endless faith and endless heresy."[20]

This yea-saying to life is also characteristic of Barash's "Last in Toledo."[21] The obstinate protagonist Don José refuses to die but decides to live in spite of the anticipated inquisitorial tortures. So he stays on in Toledo—the last remnant of a powerful Jewry, shadow of his former self, the crazed, quaint sojourner in the streets of his beloved town where, as a wealthy dealer in manuscripts, he owned a palace and reared a happy, though small, family. When he meets his death accidentally under the hoofs of the Infante's horse, he still clings to his psalmodic decision: "I shall not die, I shall live."[22] But the Infante also succumbs to the shock. "An evil spirit" tormented him all his life and, "when he died, it became the heritage of Spaniards to this very day."[23] This is the last sentence of the story, this is the curse of Jewry on Spain.

Both Asher Barash and Judah Leb Gordon in an earlier generation drew their literary material from two tragic events in Jewish history—the second destruction of Jerusalem in 70 C.E. and the expulsion from Spain in 1492.[24] Both concentrated on the heroes of the rebellion, Gordon on Simeon Bar Giyora, Barash on John of Giscala. Gordon depicted a representative type of the national tragedy; Barash drew the subtle portrait of the individual hero. Both were, however, motivated by an infinite love for their people and faith in ultimate redemption. Gordon may have riled and scoffed at the Deity; he may have vaunted his heretic strength; he may have stressed the didactic conclusion—less faith and spirituality, more realism and more practicality. But he was deeply concerned with the salvation of his people. And so was Barash, in a humbler but subtler aim, to evoke and to project the past for the present. And that's why he could afford, unlike Gordon, not to indulge in a repetitive accusation of the Deity, but in an affirmation of life through an implied didactism. The enemy of Israel is the enemy of mankind.

This persistence of Jewry, this insistence on life in closest proximity to death, exercised Barash's imagination. But it was and remained the *mysterium tremendum,* with no solution. Barash summoned arguments of Saadia and Halevi, Abraham Ibn Ezra and Maimonides to help him solve or resolve the arcane problem. He even invited Erasmus to a dialog with a learned Jew in his historical tale "In an Inn."[25] But for the sage of Rotterdam—as for all good Christians—Christianization of Jewry is the solution. Against the excessive spirituality of the Jewish people he advises with Ecclesiastes: "A little folly outweighs wisdom and honor."[26]

It is good advice from the author of *In Praise of Folly,* but it solves nothing. "In an Inn" is not one of Barash's better stories. Its structure is poor: the two separate stories, the dialog between Erasmus and the German humanist Willibald Pirkheimer (1470–1530) and the dialog between Erasmus and the Jews, do not mesh. But even this story is ingeniously plotted. In the summer of 1529 two Jewish students are sent out by the head of the rabbinical academy in Strasbourg to recover from a Christian friend in Regensburg some manuscripts which have been entrusted to his care when the Jews were expelled from the city. Their eventful journey on the dangerous roads of Germany at the beginning of the sixteenth century is rich in historical expertise and in a pervasive calm which animates Barash's work even in the gorier incidents. The characters, both the historical and the fictitious, are drawn with believable verisimilitude.

In the last two stories, "The Bones of Rabbi Shapiro,"[27] and "In Marburg,"[28] Barash approaches modern times. In the former he sketches the past glories of the town of Brody with sympathy and empathy. But he fails as an artist to convey the horrors of Nazism in this story. "In Marburg" is not a historical story. And it is too thin in content to be a story at all. The milieu is too exacting for the gentle pen of a Barash.

Obsession with history on the part of modern Hebrew writers is a recent phenomenon. Moshe Shamir (1921—) spoke for most of them when he declared that history has usurped the place of religion in Jewish life at the present time. In a deeper sense he stressed an inherent and essential trait of Judaism, for "the Jewish religion has been from the very beginning . . . an *historical* religion."[29]And that is why, deeply committed though he is to contemporary Israel, his imagination roams freely over the periods of the first and second commonwealth. He is particularly fascinated by two royal figures, David and Alexander Yannai (103–76 B.C.E.). Both had the passion associated with empire builders, both widened the boundaries of the Land of Israel. While David, the alleged author of Psalms, the "sweet singer of Israel,"[30] became the prototype of the ideal king and redeemer and, through the alleged descent of Jesus from his stock, the central figure in Christian Messianism; Alexander Yannai was mainly noted for his aggressive political policies which widened the boundaries of the Land of Israel at the cost of inner strife and religious dissension. Shamir seized on the dramatic element of guilt in both kings: the personal guilt of David in his attitude to Uriah the Hittite and the political guilt of Alexander Yannai in his attitude to the people. The clash of personal conscience with political sensitivity on the part of both monarchs: that was the tension which the author traced with sympathetic insight. In his conception—and in its execution—both kings are deeply aware of their momentous reach. And both are victors who are defeated by their victories. David satisfies a personal urge by marrying Bathsheba, the wife of Uriah, whom he sends to certain death; Alexander Yannai, the would-be hero of his people, becomes a target for violence and an object for revolt.

Both novels presented the author with difficulties which had to be overcome with artistic astuteness. For the first novel, *The Lamb of the Poor*,[31] Shamir invented a useful device; he made Uriah his own memoirist and protagonist in the bulk of the book.[32] But David hovers eagle-like over his life. In six chapters—five nights and a day—Uriah tells or rather writes the story of his life in a monolog in his native Hittite language. The final chapter is a postscript of Uriah's friend who gains possession of "Uriah's scrolls" and pens a sort of finale, also in monolog form, thirty years after his death. It is also Uriah's friend who draws the moral from reading the scrolls:

> Perhaps the sin of David against Uriah has not ended. Perhaps it is a mere deceptive delusion that the deed is contained in Solomon's crown and in the blessing of all those who know him. Perhaps, in the depth of depths, the curse of the man who has suffered treachery seethes continuously, perhaps the poisonous sin flows in the blood of future generations, perhaps the great and terrible punishment will come without delay.[33]

In *The King of Flesh and Blood*[34] Shamir invented another storytelling device. For the sake of authenticity he imitated the language of the period—the post-biblical idiom—with considerable skill.[35] But contrived structure vitiates the novel. The five chapters are not night stories as were the chapters in *The Lamb of the Poor*. They are "gate" stories: the Gate of Jerusalem, the Gate of Acco, the Gate of Modin, the

Gate of Bethshan, the Gate of Gaza. And they symbolize the main stages of the king's conquest. The book is more ambitious than *The Lamb of the Poor*. Though Yannai dominates the scene, sages and scholars, politicians and soldiers, Hellenizers and Hellenists, crowd the pages. As in the entire post-biblical literature the problem of Judaism is central to the book. It is the subject of a dialog between the Jewish sage, Simeon ben Shetah, and Absalom, the brother of the king. This dialog follows the receipt from Alexandria by Absalom of the *Scroll of the Maccabees* which, since it is written in Greek, serves as a pretext for the author's ideas on Hellenism and Judaism.

"Most Greek books, Simeon, especially the works of Homer and Plato, praise the good qualities in man. They tend to diminish the importance of deeds."

"How?"

"Look and see. What are these books about? They are full of beautiful words. Do gentiles do what these books say? . . They are not intended to be commandments but legendary stuff, parables, delights for the soul. These books are made for the leisured people. A man has a bit of time, looks at them, sees something similar in the theatre, discusses them. If he has no time, he does not bother about them. . . Are their artisans, laborers or slaves busy with the books and theories of their great leaders? This is not the case with our holy books for all Jews are commanded to study them; and they delve in them by day and by night as it is commanded in the Bible.[36]. . . Would the world be the loser if Greek books were forgotten? And, at the same time, would the world last one day if the books of our Torah were forgotten, God forbid?"[37]

This is chauvinism pushed to the extreme. And if it is intended as a sweeping evaluation of Judaism and Hellenism, it diminishes the statures of Absalom, the bibliophile and Simeon ben Shetah, the Jewish sage. For Homer and Plato, symbols of Hellenism at its most sublime imaginative insights and its most refined philosophical perceptions, are more than mere collections of beautiful phrases. They cannot be argued away in sweeping condemnation. Still, the fictitious dialog contains the germs of an incipient argument which has exercised the West for more than two millennia.

In *The King of Flesh and Blood* Judaism is subjected to antithetical comparisons with Hellenism; it also emerges as a self-renewing entity in its internecine disquisitions and triumphs, in its abhorrence of blood and in its reemphasis on biblical ethics in post-biblical garb. But the moral purpose of the novel has not led to any emasculation of the leading characters. The king, the queen, the king's brother, Absalom, and the queen's brother, Simeon ben Shetah, are characters of flesh and blood. Violent clashes of temper and temperament rather than constrictive laws of history govern their actions. It is fictive strength rather than wooden obeisance to a predetermined plot that has put Shamir's book *The King of Flesh and Blood* in the forefront of contemporary historical novels.

The dramatic version *War of the Sons of Light*[38] is, like most of Shamir's plays, a story in multilog form. For the author is a born story teller rather than a dramatist. His first novel, *He Walked in the Fields*,[39] was dramatized under the same title and performed by the Cameri theater. In that play and in the other plays tension of plot is more dominant than tension of character, but divine sanction dominates the action:

> All who want to walk in the middle must in the end succumb to the ways of evil characters, all who want to prevent sacrifice, must in the end bring their brothers as sacrifice on the altar of killers, all who want to preserve their purity, must in the end pollute the palms of their hands with blood. . . Redemption comes to the world by the strength of people who deliver it; redemption will be in their image and in their likeness. All are worthy of redemption, each generation is worthy of the Davidic Messiah. All are worthy of redemption, each one with his sins and defilements. . . Redemption is built of the stuff of which human lives are built. . . [40]

It is not an accident that these words are uttered in the play by Simeon ben Shetah. He is the spokesman of the people; he is also the spokesman of a grim theory of salvation authored by Shamir. Other writers, like Joseph Dolgin (1907–), better known by his pseudonym Arika, and Ari Ibn Zahav followed the tradition established by Mapu and dedicated considerable efforts to biblical themes. Thus Arika again went over the ground of his Lithuanian predecessor in *Sennacherib in Judah*,[41] if not in *The King's Scribe*[42] and in the historical play *Facing the Sword*.[43]

The personality of David fascinated Ari Ibn Zahav throughout his life. For hundreds of years Hebrew writers had celebrated the multitudinous aspects of his character in song and story, in juvenile novels and legends, in ambitious epics and plays. Poets were especially partial to the poet-king: Shalom Cohen and Judah Leb Gordon in the nineteenth century, Jacob Cahan and Jacob Fichmann in the twentieth century. In our time novelists mined biblical and extra-biblical sources for old-new material on David. Kabak wrote a dramatic *Midrash* on David,[44] Shamir evoked the image of David indirectly in *The Lamb of the Poor,* Ari Ibn Zahav directly in *David and Bathsheba.*[45] The latter novel is a monolog of the aging king who recalls the decisive stages of his life in the presence of his secretary, the scribe Seraiah. The device has its advantages: it romanticizes the past. But it also suffers from a disadvantage: it destroys the immediacy of events and actions. There are mainly two fresh emphases in Ari Ibn Zahav's novel: David the lover and David the poet are illumined with a vigor which few novelists have achieved when they chose David as protagonist. The genesis and the gestation of poignant psalms are interpreted with psychological acumen. The first day after the conquest of Jerusalem the king is overcome at dawn with its beauty and composes the lovely lines of the psalm:

> I lift my eyes unto the mountains. Whence shall my help come? My help comes from the Lord, the maker of heaven and earth. Those who trust in the Lord are like Mount Zion which cannot be moved but abides forever. As the mountains are round about Jerusalem, so the Lord is round about his people now and forever.

By a skillful combination of the first two verses from *Psalm 121* and the first two verses of *Psalm 125* Ari Ibn Zahav fashioned, as it were, a new poem on trust and humility. The landscape of Jerusalem is no mere background of the poem; it is foreground. The mountains surround the city, the Deity surrounds the people: the harmony between land and God and people is perfect. The protective landscape and the protective God are the guardians who have imprisoned the people in the everlasting vise of love.

For the genesis of David's love for Bathsheba Ari Ibn Zahav invented an imaginative setting. It is not David the King who suddenly sets his eyes upon the wife of Uriah the Hittite and experiences an insatiable feeling of lust; it is a young shepherd of fifteen—sheltered, pampered, inexperienced—who meets the thirteen year old Bathsheba somewhere in the fields of Bethlehem and falls so deeply in love with her that neither affairs of state nor affairs of the heart can drive her image from his heart. She is the beloved, she is also, in a certain sense, the mother substitute, the eternally feminine. The last words of the king—and the novel—are a fitting epitome of Eros: "There is nothing better for man than to know life with the woman he loves."[46] Love is the *spiritus rector* of the book, the Dantesque leitmotif. It is less ambitious than *The Divine Comedy*, but no less suffused with the spirit of love.

The figure of David has also a Messianic dimension in Judaism and Christianity. The historical king was emasculated throughout the ages, spiritualized into the national and global redeemer. That process began as early as the eighth century:

There shall come forth a shoot from the stump of Jesse,
And a branch shall grow out of his roots.
And the spirit of the Lord shall rest upon him,
The spirit of wisdom and understanding,
The spirit of counsel and might,
The spirit of knowledge and the fear of the Lord.[47]

This wise monarch was to usher in the ideal age of harmony between man and man, man and beast; he of "the root of Jesse shall stand as an ensign to the peoples; him shall the nations seek. . . ."[48]

In the person of Jesus Jewish Messianism reached a crucial stage. As the alleged descendant of David[49] the unintentional founder of a new religion, Christianity, became the redeemer for the Christian world. But Judaism which envisioned the Messiah and the Messianic age in a remote future, "at the end of days," persisted in the ideal of perfectibility rather than perfection symbolized by the figure of Jesus in Christianity.

Only in recent times did three Hebrew writers dare to deal with Jesus in their literary works: Shoham, Hazaz and Kabak (1883–1944). Shoham's play on Jesus was lost to posterity,[50] Hazaz's fragments of an unfinished novel on Jesus have been scattered in periodicals and failed to be included in the collected edition of his works. Kabak is still the only Hebrew novelist to have written a full-fledged novel on Jesus: *The Narrow Path*.[51] It was one of his last works, a mature novel which was preceded by another novel, a trilogy in fact, on the problem of the Messiah and Messianism, *Solomon Molko*.[52] Both are represented as the Jewish personifications of redemption, both achieve martyrdom, one on the cross which became the symbol of the new faith, one at the stake which the new faith invented for its heretics. Furthermore, both serve as paradigms of men who wish to travel the narrow path of redemption through ecstasy with its gift of unity between the human and the divine.[53] That Kabak depicted Jesus in merely human terms might be offensive to a Christian; as a Jew he could not do otherwise. In truth to history and the art of fiction he had to draw his character against the Galilean background of his formative years and the Judean background of his final years. And he succeeded in elevating him, by dint of his humanity, to superhuman stature—such was the strength of his spiritual heritage, such was the power of his personal transformation of that spiritual heritage. In the crucible of individual and national rebellion against the oppressive might of Rome a greater might was born. Kabak reconstructed that birth through beautiful juxtapositions of tranquil landscapes and seething people. In the deceptive calm of Nazareth and amidst the intolerable burdens imposed by the enemy, a new faith made its debut on the stage of history:

> Nazareth was like an ant hill. Everyone was diligent and industrious, and travellers who chanced to pass through the town rested their eyes upon the verdant oasis lying among the hills. The standing corn rustled in the upland fields, and fruit trees swayed under their burdens on the hillside terraces—olives, plums, quinces, cherries, and, in the vineyards, succulent grapes. . .
> But he who walked through its [Nazareth's] streets and stared into the faces of its inhabitants saw a different picture . . . Plots and intrigues . . . sprang up endlessly. Many people, unable to endure the terror . . . went out of their minds. Faith, confidence and the love of life were extinguished. . . The tributes and levies were inexorably heavy . . . yet . . . a mighty . . . beacon was flaring and inspiring its clandestine beholders—the faith that the days of the Messiah, the Anointed One, were imminent, of the Son of Man who was destined to come . . . [54]

Perhaps both novels were to be parts of a Jewish *Comédie Humaine,* for, like Balzac, who projected one hundred and thirty-seven novels and actually achieved eighty-five in print, the Hebrew novelist, more modestly, but almost as monomaniacally, intended to write eight novels on Jewish life under a serial title: *The Annals of One Family.*[55] It was to embrace Hasidism and enlightenment, religious reform and nationalism in sturdy portrayals of Jewish life in Eastern Europe and in the Land of Israel and, above all, redemption which exercised Kabak's imagination from the earliest days of his creativity in the very first novel *Alone.*[56] The two historical novels *Solomon Molko* and *The*

Narrow Path must be seen as introductory bases for a great monument in prose, a monument which has only recently received a thorough evaluation at the hands of an American scholar.[57]

Even writers who were not directly concerned with the figure of the Messiah or the problem of Messianism managed to weave redemptive threads into the tapestry of their historic novels. If Uriel Acosta, in the most ambitious historical novel of Yohanan Twersky, rises from religious doubts about Christianity, the religion of his childhood and youth, to religious security in Judaism, the religion of his maturer years, it is because he achieves personal salvation at the risk of estrangement from the Jewish community. In other novels, in *Rashi, Dreyfus, Ahad-Haam,* as well as in his hasidic oeuvre and in historical character sketches of Saadia and Spinoza, Leone Modena and Moses Hayyim Luzzatto, Mordecai Emanuel Noah and Theodor Herzl the author inevitably touches upon the theme of redemption.[58] His older contemporary, Harry Sackler, explored the vast panorama of Jewish history in incalculable depth. Hebrew literature owes to him character portrayals from biblical and talmudic, hasidic and Eastern European periods of Jewish history. A thorough reading of his work throws a strong light on the main concern of Jewry—redemption through the humanization and spiritualization of humanity.[59] Similarly, Yehoshua Bar-Yosef explores the older type of immigrant to the Land of Israel in *Enchanted City,*[60] a trilogy set in Safed and concerned with the changing fortunes of the Katz family over a period of one hundred years. The novel adheres to the tradition of the great family chronicles cultivated in European literature by Martin du Gard, Thomas Mann and John Galsworthy but it is poorer in character delineation and stronger on didacticism.

Two books follow the trilogy: *Sword of Salvation*[61] and *Between Safed and Jerusalem.*[62] The first, a novel, complements the trilogy; the second, an autobiography, sheds a personal light upon the author's birthplace. The novel revolves around Safed and its two thousand Jewish inhabitants during the War of Independence. The heroism, the poverty, and the despair before and after the demise of the mandatory power are the central realities of a stark work which describes Safed's "finest hour."[63] Personal observations and remote and recent history such as the massacre of 1929 add a dimension of intimacy and tension. The savage bombardment of the city, the bloody rhythm of the attack and the defense: these have been described with greater mastery than the individual protagonists. As in so much of Israeli literature till 1948 the collective rather than the individual is the hero. The vested belief in the expected redeemer—even with an ironic twist—exercises the people's minds.

—And the Messiah has not come yet?

—When he comes, we will let you know.[64]

This bit of dialog toward the end of the novel can serve as the motto of the Land of Israel for the past one hundred years and for many centuries before. In the autobiography which embraces the author's first thirty years, Safed, study in Transylvania and the return to Israel are depicted in plain, unadorned prose. It forms an interesting addition to the memoiristic genre which is underdeveloped in Hebrew literature. The deeply religious education of the boy and the young man in and out of Israel reads like an additional chapter to Lilienblum's *Sins of Youth.*[65] Only in his transition from a believer to a "heretic against his will," in his first attempts at literary composition in a changed environment, and in his decision to devote his life to literature does Yehoshua Bar-Yosef differ from Lilienblum. In one of the unforgettable incidents of the book he recalls a visit by the young author-to-be to Bialik and the trembling recital of a long poem which he inflicted on the older poet a year or two before the latter's death. It received a rather lukewarm reception in stark contrast to Sadan's warm encouragement.

With his autobiography Yehoshua Bar-Yosef reaches into the present, a present which, like most authors of historical novels, he keeps as conscious or unconscious foil and balance to the past. When Zevi Lieberman presents his readership with a novel like Nehemiah in 1950 he is obviously as concerned with the present and with the reestablishment of the two-year-old state of Israel as Nehemiah was concerned with the rebuilding of tiny Judea in the fifth century B.C.E. Unfortunately, the author delineates in predictable idealization not only his protagonist but also the protagonist's wife, Milkah, and his friend Ezra who preceded Nehemiah and laid the foundation of rabbinic Judaism. Lieberman develops his plot and characters with disarming simplicity and touching naiveté. The wiles of Sanballat the Samaritan and Tobiah the Ammonite and Geshem the Arab, the evils of the priests and princes, the rich and the very rich, the plots against Nehemiah as alleged rebel against the Persian sovereign: these facts and fancies, partly based on the biblical narrative partly invented by the author's imagination, are presented in a simple style and in a simplistic grid of events, too simple and too simplistic to be believed by a sophisticated reader of the twentieth century. Here is a sample of a characteristic passage in the words of Milkah in the presence of her husband and his friend Ezra:

> In Persia I imagined Jerusalem as a city of priests and sages; the brimming courtyard'of the Sanctuary, the sacrifices, the prayers, the immersion in words of law and vision and wisdom, tranquil and peaceful Sabbaths. Work ceases, the nation celebrates the Sabbath in freedom and rest; people visit friends and talk and greet one another.[66]

In the stilted, ordinary but idealized idiom of a plain imagination the wife of a Nehemiah presents herself as a model of conventionality. And when, in her eagerness to dispel the worries of her husband and her guests, she performs her duties as hostess and pours the cold pomegranate juice from a pitcher into silver goblets, she receives the traditional praise from Ezra:

> You are a woman of valor, Milkah. The smartest of all women. Anxiety and painful talk is forbidden on the Sabbath. But this is a time of misery for our people and saving of lives defers the Sabbath.[67]

Ezra speaks like the proverbial Jewish sage: he produces an effect of learning by combining a biblical phrase[68] with a talmudic adage.[69]

The book, which begins with a note of despair, ends on a note of hope. Jerusalem has been rebuilt and refortified, the Sanctuary has again become the center of Jewish life, the Sabbath is being observed with all the biblical rigor, the mixed marriages have been dissolved. Nehemiah has accomplished his work and writes his memoirs. The book ends with the famous quotation: "The Glory of Israel will not lie or repent."[70]

21
Contemporary Israel in Contemporary Fiction and Poetry: Jew and Rural Renascence; Peasant and Poet

THE Land of Israel, Jews and Arabs, confrontations of the individual with urban and rural society, industry and agriculture: these are the themes which dominate Hebrew literature in Palestine till the Second World War; the holocaust, the establishment of the State and the four wars—these are the *thèmes maitresses* from 1945 on. In the last decade of the nineteenth century literature was mainly an artifact of immigrants; within fifty years it became a literature of natives. Interestingly, the contemporary novel made a greater impact on the development of Hebrew letters than the historical novel. Not *The Narrow Path* by Kabak or *The King of Flesh and Blood* by Shamir, but the massive work of Yizhar on the War of Independence, *Days of Ziklag,* Yehudah Yaari's *Like the Light That Shines, Chained Together* by Hayyim Hazaz, and *Yesterday, Day Before Yesterday* by Samuel Joseph Agnon belong among the masterpieces of contemporary literature.

The first two waves of immigration—from the Biluim to those who came to settle before the First World War—were dominated by a few literary figures who set the tone for the future: Pines and Smilansky, Yellin and Eliezer Ben-Yehudah, Shimoni and Fichmann, Brenner and Agnon. They discovered the landscape and the Arab neighbor, agriculture and the delight in the establishment of new norms for a new society; they also created the first native newspapers and periodicals.

An important document of the reflection of the first decade of the twentieth century in Hebrew literature is Solomon Zemah's *First Year*[1]—an autobiographical account of the author's first year in the

242

Holy Land. Though written almost fifty years after the event, it does not sentimentalize the country and its inhabitants. On the contrary, it castigates the Jewish farmers who came with idealistic intentions, turned into pleasure-seeking materialists who lived parasitically on cheap Arab labor and sent their daughters to Paris to idle away their youth. It was this state of affairs which resulted in insistence on Jewish labor, on intense cultivation of the land, and on the Hebrew language.[2] In his stories that were published between the two world wars, Zemah could afford to describe a different milieu, a greater rootedness, a love for the soil and for domestic animals. These stories he balanced with a novel *Elijah Margalit* that is essentially the story of bohemian Paris in the early years of the century, and, more particularly, the history of a non-hero who lives amidst European decadence and dreams about the Hebrew renaissance.

Simultaneously with Solomon Zemah, Aaron Reuveni (1886-1971) was one of the first writers in the Land of Israel to devote his considerable narrative and poetic talents to his new homeland. While some of his contemporaries continued to weave their literary artifacts mainly around their experiences in Eastern Europe, Reuveni sporadically transmitted his experiences in Russia and the U.S. to his work. But his main effort was the trilogy, *To Jerusalem*,[3] projected against the background of the first year of the First World War. He wrote about his beloved city and the characters in his novel from a historical perspective, as it were,[4] with the responsibility of an artist who portrays an entire era: hence the profusion of characters with a keen sensitivity to the historical events of their times and to the chief protagonists, the accountant Zifrovich in the first part, the author Berentshuk in the second part, and the carpenter Funk in the third part of the trilogy. These main characters share several characteristics: they have immigrated from Russia in the early years of the century and they have been radicalized by revolutionary movements in Russia. At the same time they all have a deep need for rootedness in Jerusalem.

What is also original about Reuveni: more than any of his contemporaries he is possessed of a sympathetic feeling for the vegetative and animal world surrounding his protagonists. Even of greater importance is the first phase of confrontation between Arabs and Jews. Zifrovich and Mania walk in the Valley of Hinnom in the vicinity of Jerusalem at the beginning of the First World War. An Arab horseman had uttered a few Arabic words for the benefit of the young woman. The couple freeze in terrorized apprehension after his disappearance:

They heard his guttural, screeching voice, words which they could not comprehend; they saw the galloping horse in a whirl of dust—symbol of freedom and courage—and a feeling of strangeness overcame them.

Here is a paradox: the Jew in search of an old-new homeland is not only terrorized by the indigenous inhabitant, he is given a feeling of utter alienation at "home" or what is to become his ardently desired home. In Reuveni's novel *Shammot* the Algerian Haj had raped a mute girl. This act of moral turpitude becomes a symbol of ancient and modern Jerusalem—the chief protagonist of Reuveni's trilogy. Other novels, especially *Sadness*[5] written in 1915 and published in 1930, the story "By the Wall"[6] which analyzes the lonely thoughts of a guard, the poetry which is Victorian, and the essays subtract rather than add to his stature.

In his critical work Reuveni occasionally stumbles on just observations. He castigates Hazaz for lack of restraint in the use of language. And he reduces Shlonsky to barren narcissism though he appreciates his linguistic talents and poetic technique. But to burden Theodore Dreiser and Sinclair Lewis with Proustian ancestry is to carry critical irresponsibility too far. In his appraisal of contemporary culture in Israel, Reuveni emphasizes a fundamental fault—casuistry instead of thought, phrase mongering instead of poetry, interminable argumentation instead of instant acts.

The central fact of the new life in Palestine—and to a certain extent in contemporary Israel—was the rural cooperative, the kibbutz, which dates back to the first decade of the twentieth century. It has come to be regarded as the new form of socialism, the implementor of secular Messianism and guarantor of productive in lieu of parasitic existence in the diaspora—symbol of regeneration and redemption.

Literature echoed this attitude in a sort of reversed medievalism: it became the handmaiden of sociology, just as philosophy served as handmaiden of theology a thousand years ago. In the first crude novels of the kibbutz—*The Wooden Hut*[7] of Ever Hadani in the thirties and such stories of the sixties as Alizah Amir's *Like Green Marble*[8]—the revolutionary form of Jewish settlement fueled a literary conservatism which was not equal to the innovations on the social and individual plane.

Like Ever Hadani who knew life in the cooperative from direct experience, Yehudah Yaari (1901–), originally Wald, built roads, dried swamps, and founded, together with other immigrants after the First World War, Bet Alpha where he worked as farmer and shepherd. *Like the Light That Shines*[9] is the novel of the third wave of immigration. The horrors of the First World War in Europe and the pioneering in nascent Israel are the basic motifs of the four-part book. The first part depicts the horrors of a boy—not yet teenaged—who witnesses the hanging of his grandfather, the mutilation of people, the sadism of conquerors; the second part concentrates on the slaughters of Petlura; the third part reflects the struggles of pioneers in Palestine; the fourth part shifts to Jerusalem where the hero is helped to health and sanity by the efforts of a Yemenite, Maari Saadia. The novel breathes "beloved affliction."[10] And this, perhaps, is its moral: *amor fati,* love of fate no matter how hard the fate. After all, there are moments of exaltation such as the arrival in the Land of Israel:

> Our feet stood on its soil. The air about us was that of the homeland, the people waving to us were our brothers. We were happy.[11]

Tel Aviv was still an unassuming town of sunbathed houses "on the seashore among burning sand dunes." But the dreadful work in the malarial swamps is far from the idyllic ideal which brought the workers to the Land of Israel:

> Work in the swamp was difficult, standing barebacked in this mouldy, danky marsh, feeling the cold touch of the frogs on the naked body and, still worse, the maddening stings of the flies and mosquitoes. The flies were fat, multicolored, their sting was as painful as the prick of a needle. . . . The mosquitoes were slender, bluish like little ravens. Their sting was ticklish, almost unfelt but it planted the disease of the swamps in the body—the dreadful malarial disease.[12]

The anguish and the exaltation which accompanied the pioneers of the third wave of immigration after their arrival in the Land of Israel, the experience and memory of war before their arrival: these are the points and counterpoints of Yaari's novel which has enshrined the faith and the disillusion of a former generation. Two volumes of stories by Yaari read like altered or improved editions of the novel *Like the Light That Shines.* Again the author confronts his readers with youthful types who prepare in Eastern Europe for agricultural or mechanical work in the Land of Israel, as in the story "Ways of Man" or "The Hero."[13] In their acquired homeland they build and settle the *Emek*, the ancient valley of Esdrelon.

Yaari showed gentle sympathy with suffering humanity and special empathy for the plight of women in his second novel *Root Upon the Waters*.[14] This is, perhaps, his outstanding characteristic: in spite of the waves of violence which threatened to engulf him from his teenage years on he preserved a humane, almost feminine, delicacy of feeling toward all those who have not been favored by luck or fortune. In *Root Upon the Waters* this attitude reaches its full maturity. For the gentle story of deaf Sarah, who grows into youth and recovers her sense of hearing through a successful operation differs from other stories of Yaari *toto caelo*. Her infirmity leads to inwardness; removal of the infirmity after sixteen years of deafness leaves a deep scar. Such a situation strains Yaari's simple style honed for expressing the cooperative means of enterprise and not for describing the lonely life. The writer's honesty assumes the form of an apology for artistic inadequacy in terms congenial to him:

> When I speak of Sarah . . . I can't help remembering the deaf beggar in the "Story of Seven Beggars." Sarah is like that deaf beggar: her sense of hearing is more powerful than that of a hearing individual. Since the voices she heard did not enter her ears from the outside . . . they were all perfect. . . That's why it's impossible to translate into our mode of expression the melodies Sarah heard in every phenomenon and in every movement . . . [15]

Yaari has found fulfilment as a man and an artist in this combination of the Hasidic heritage wedded to the double experience of Galicia, his birthland and Israel, the native land of his spirit. The Hasidic heritage accompanied him unconsciously throughout his formative years and consciously in recent years when he devoted his talents to a reinterpretation—through a retelling—of the stories of Rabbi Nahman of Bratzlav.

Like Yehudah Yaari, Yizhak Shenhar (1902–1957), originally Schönberg, is also a scion of a Hasidic family, a descendant of the famed Rabbi Levi Isaac of Berditchev. When he settled in mandatory Palestine in 1924, he worked in the building trade, on a farm, and even as a railroad official. After a stint in the thirties at the University of Brussels where he studied sociology, he devoted himself to literature and translation. Works of Kafka and Steinbeck, Villon and Rilke, Leskov and Gogol, Balzac and Tolstoy owe their Hebrew versions to him. For *Dead Souls* he received the Tschernichowsky Prize in 1948.

But his forte was the short story: three volumes of sixty-five stories attest to the dedication of the author to that genre. In an idiomatic, lyrical style, he tended to concentrate on passions of deracinated youth— lust, envy, treachery—but not with impassioned vehemence. On the contrary: his stories move in a slow, almost elegant tempo. And they seem to be designed by a craftsman dedicated to his craft rather than to the exploration of humanity. A book that earned him wide readership, *On Seven Roads*,[16] embraces vignettes of life in France and Belgium, in Scandinavia and Latin America, in Germany and in Russia. As for the kibbutz, it is not so much the new life as the old relationships in a new milieu that interest Yizhak Shenhar. For the mere vicinity of a cooperative can elicit a salutary response from young lovers, bringing them closer together, removing doubts, firming up, perhaps, the decision to emulate that productive life as they touch in the cool night and listen to the spontaneous singing of old and young:

All of them sang, some with heads raised upward, some with heads bent to the ground. It was singing for the sake of singing, without a leader, as the cricket chirps, as the bird twitters . . . [17]

The Arab is not an enemy but a good neighbor who approves the energy and perseverance and self-reliance of Jews; the author apostrophizes his milieu in quasi-poetic tones:

Rise, man, sing a song to the desert and praise it in poetic metaphor. Rise and praise the expanses of sand, the golden dust spread out in the sun, the sweet silence at night.[18]

Imperceptibly Shenhar resorts to prose and probes the soul of the Arab station-master though he can't ever reach the simple, unsymbolic self of the Bedouin in their tents or the Bedouin girl, Azizah, the inevitable brothers, and the father eager to sell her to the rich, elderly Sheikh who wishes to divorce one of his two wives in exchange for the younger, prettier Azizah.

Arab, Jew, Frenchman, South American: Shenhar is eager to explore their humanity. And he seems to succeed—though with less than clearly focused vision.

It was S. Yizhar (1916–), a nephew of Moshe Smilansky, who became the chief exponent of a new trend in Hebrew literature. In numerous stories and in the bulky novel *Days of Ziklag*[19] he highlights the language of the worker and the soldier, the sympathy with the alleged enemy, the Arab, and the alienation from the gore and violence that destoy the equilibrium of the individual. The depths of the individual Jew and Arab who may have been harmed by the vicissitudes of war: those elusive recesses of the self are his main concern. As an Israeli, born in Israel, he has lived on a single cultural and political plane—unlike older authors like Barash or Brenner who expressed the polarity and tension of living on two planes: the diaspora and the Land of Israel. And he not only absorbed the native milieu—the cruel landscape, the besieged mentality—in all its aspects; he also fashioned it to a certain extent. This fierce concentration on Israel with its concomitant narrowness of scope has had one salutary effect: it gained depth where it lost breadth, it became Israeli where it lost much of its Jewishness and much of its universality.

Interiorization of the monolog—a form of the "stream of consciousness" technique—characterizes Yizhar's short stories and his single novel. This is a remarkable paradox in view of the fact that many of his best stories like "Before Departure" or "Midnight Convoy"[20] embrace shared experiences. "Before Departure" depicts a group in a cooperative settlement, assembled in the dining hall on the eve of an attack by the underground in the months which preceded the establishment of the state. The tension is immediate and absolute. "This time," says one "it's bound to be." "Yes," says another, "too late to change." And from the beginning of the story the young men hardly speak to each other though they are united by an inexorable fate. Instead they meditate, they are ravaged by the contradictory moods of sadness and gaiety, they ogle the beautiful girl in the dining room. And then: no rhetoric, no fireworks, no heroics. A whistle. And the young men are off on a dangerous mission. "What a beautiful night, eh?" "Bewitching." And they leave and they don't know whether "something has ended . . . or something has begun." That's the end of the story which was written at the beginning of 1948. Another story against the background of the War of Independence, "The Prisoner," portrays man's inhumanity to man—Jewish inhumanity to an Arab. The cruelty can be understood, but it cannot be justified by war, by violence, by self-defense. The fact is that an ignorant Arab shepherd is caught, taken prisoner, beaten in order to elicit information from him. Yizhar is not an eighteen-karat patriot; he is human, humane, conscience-riddled. And he voices his humanity through the mouth of the guard who drives the prisoner in his jeep to an interrogation center:

This man who sits here at your feet, his life, his security, his home . . . they have been delivered somehow into your hand as if you were a little God sitting in a jeep.[21]

Another story "The Tale of Hirbet Hizah"[22] deepens the conflict between conscience and contingency. It is also justice which is being sacrificed on the altar of expediency. Arabs suffer the fate which has so often dogged the life of the Jews in the diaspora: they are driven from a village because military necessity prescribes expulsion. And the individual soldiers who wish to act ethically are too weak to follow the small, silent voice within.

Indecision is the mark of Yizhar's heroes. Most of them are young men with the impulses of youth. Most of them have reached their maturity in the crucible of hard work or hard war. What enhances the value of Yizhar's stories is his very original style. In a mixture of slang and classical Hebrew he has evolved a language which is, perhaps, the first successful attempt at native Hebrew after a hiatus of almost two thousand years. The superb command of the author over his own dense diction and the skein of problems which runs through his better stories come to the fore in *Days of Ziklag,* his most ambitious work to date and one of the most ambitious novels of contemporary Israel. Its forbidding length—fifty-five chapters in one thousand one hundred and forty-three pages—places it alongside the novels of Thomas Mann or James Joyce in length and *For Whom The Bell Tolls* in content. Since the whole action is concentrated in one week's time—a few days preceeding and a few days succeeding the Jewish New Year of 5709 (1948) in Ziklag in the southern part of Israel[23] during the War of Independence—the novel gains in intensity. The young soldiers, the protagonists of the novel, rail against war but they are impotent to halt its inexorability; they rail against their elders but they are impotent to create a new style of life. And so they fulfill their duties with grim heroism in the hope that somehow, somewhere life will take a humane course. Meanwhile they talk to themselves and to each other between the battles, and they reminisce. The New Year, *Rosh ha-Shanah 5709,* is like any other day: discourse, meditation, fear, battle, fatigue, "what bitchy fatigue. Fatigue from nothing. Overwhelming fatigue. You are engulfed by fatigue . . ."[24] And all this malaise occurs mainly at night, at some impossibly beautiful night in the Negev, "a Mozartian night."[25] Nothing is certain, not even the place. "This ain't Ziklag . . ." "Why not Ziklag?" "Because Ziklag ain't here." "And what's here?" "Hill 244.2."[26] Monolog and dialog punctured by battle day and night, relieved by the immense beauty of the Palestinian landscape—such is the novel *Days of Ziklag*, a monument of indecision but also a monument of young humanity struggling for decision. Hemingway's heroes of the Spanish war fight and suffer; Yizhar's heroes fight with the ancestral compulsion of the ethical imperative. They bear the burden of their selfhood as "a crown and a cross."[27]

The intensity of Yizhar's soldierly world is relieved to a certain extent by his pedagogical interests. As a teacher in a secondary school of his native Rehovot and as a student of educational theory[28] he sought to come to grips with the world of the child and the teenager. As a writer he found release for this special interest in stories for the young which were illustrated by his wife Naomi.[29] They are carefree and exuberant, a complete antithesis to his other works of fiction.

There have been attempts to classify Arab-Jewish relationships in chronological sequence.[30] First, there was the supposedly ideological attitude of the Jew to the Arab. It found its poignant expression in the stories and novels of Yizhar and Orpaz and Shamir, Mati and Aaron Megged and Tammuz. Then, there was the period of desperation when naive ideology gave place to existentialist sobriety in the works of fiction of Amos Oz, A. B. Yehoshua, Dalia Rabikowitz, and the later oeuvre of Shamir, especially *The Border*. Finally, there is the extreme nationalist position that the Arabs are the permanent nightmare in the reality and vision of the Israeli.

For the first period S. Yizhar's story "The Prisoner" and Isaac Orpaz's story "On the Tip of a Bullet"[31] convey characteristic attitudes. Both writers and their protagonists suffer from the amorality of war and they cannot reconcile themselves to bloodshed. They hate war although they make war. In unmistakable terms Yizhar identifies with the soldiers whose physical and spiritual lives were not a preparation for slaughter.

Shamir's contemporaneous stories and novels and even his considerable work as a journalist move in one direction and pursue one goal: the direction—the destiny of his people; the goal—the form which that destiny must assume. As a former member of the kibbutz Mishmar ha-'Emek[32] and the Palmah, as editor of the underground weekly *Ba-Mahneh* which represented the views of illegal Jewish organizations for the country's defense, *(Haganah)*,[33] during the last years of mandatory Palestine, he was not only witness to historic events; he had a hand in shaping and directing them. The fierce struggle for independence before the establishment of Israel, the fanatic concern with Israel's existence immediately after the proclamation of independence, disasters like the holocaust and internal clashes between secularizing and traditional tendencies in the land of his birth—these were and are the themes which exercised his imagination and which evolved the heroic and unbending characters from the first novel *He Walked in the Fields* to *The Border*[34] which depicted Israel in the sixties. Even innocent stories like *The Fifth Wheel*[35] meant for juvenile consumption and written with consummate skill confronted the reader with a deeper realization of Israeli individuals and Israeli society. And, though Shamir was the spokesman of a Greater Israel after the Six-Day War—together with other eminent literati like Hazaz and Alterman—he strove for peace:

> . . . all my articles and speeches and words . . . are nothing but a common network of intrigue for the speedy attainment of peace for all the people of Israel and for all the peoples of the region . . . [36]

This is not the pious declaration of a politician; this is the ardent wish of a man whose brother fell in the War of Independence in 1948, whose uncle fell at the gates of Warsaw as a hero of the Red Army in 1920, whose grandfather's brother was murdered by Ukrainian peasants in 1891.[37] It is also the realization of a realist who knows the millennial history of his people before and after settling in the land:

> There has never been peace in this country . . . the first settlement was the beginning of a history of about seven hundred years for a nation living in its own country; the second settlement ushered in a period of . . . five hundred years . . . the third settlement . . . is destined to last for hundreds of years. If possible in peace. If not, without peace.[38]

This determination, bred by sacrifice, is an assurance of continuity for the State of Israel, for its literature, for its cultural eminence.

Mati Megged also sympathizes with the Arabs. In his story "The Bitter End of D.,"[39] he depicts the gradual deterioration of an Israeli officer—the military governor of a township in the Gaza Strip. Power corrupts his personal mores and destroys him gradually with mounting inevitability. Contempt is his attitude and that of his underlings to his Arab charges. The town, the streets, the inhabitants—they all stink. At the end of the story D. is knifed to death by his Arab mistress. And his death is probably a release from pangs of conscience and from ethical immaturity.

As in the case of the brothers Mann, Thomas and Heinrich, so with the brothers Megged, one overshadows the other. Aaron Megged (1920–) is better-known, both as story-writer and playwright; Mati Megged (1923–   ) earned a greater reputation as a critic of modern drama and fiction than as a narrative writer. Aaron Megged, born in Poland, is almost a native Israeli. At the age of six he came to the Land of Israel. The cooperative near ancient Caesarea, Sedot Yam, claimed his allegiance, the port of Haifa employed him as a worker. Since 1950 he has led an urban life, first in Tel Aviv as editor of *Massa*,[40] then as cultural attaché in London. These experiences were transformed into stories and novels. Thus, his life in the cooperative Sedot Yam was reflected in his first book of stories, *Sea Wind*,[41] in his first novel *Hedvah and I*,[42] and in his play *Hannah Szenes*[43] whose protagonist was also a member of the cooperative Sedot Yam. The negative aspects of the cooperatives are the main concern of Aaron Megged: he castigates the moral bankruptcy of Israeli society in his stories and novels.

> There is no greater pain for a member of a cooperative than aloneness. He resembles the Hasid in a strange environment; he cannot pray with the congregation on ordinary days; it is even worse on Sabbath eves when the goodness of togetherness is doubly good.[44]

Megged is not only disturbed by the vice of rural gregariousness; he is also exercised by the generational gap. In a beautiful story like "The Name"[45] he creates a dramatic confrontation which revolves around the naming of a child. The grandfather of the young parents suggests Mendele—a beloved, never-to-be-forgotten grandson who was killed at the age of twelve. Since that is not acceptable to the young couple, "a ghetto name, ugly, horrible," the mother's mother suggests "Menahem." But that name—a happy and acceptable compromise to the grandfather, a Hebrew name usually associated with Mendel—does not please the young couple either: "It's not an Israeli name . . . it's from the *Golah*." They call him Ehud, after a heroic figure in the period of Judges.[46] But for the grandfather the preservation of the name is fraught with deep symbolism:

> You are ashamed to give your son the name Mendele lest it remind you that there were Jews who were called by that name. You be-

lieve that his name should be wiped off the face of the earth. That not a trace of it should remain. . . You're finishing off the work which the enemies of Israel began. They took the bodies away from the world, and you—the name and the memory. . . No continuation, no evidence, no memorial and no name.

For the grandfather Mendele is not only an individual name; it is the totality of Israel as it was and as it will never be again.

"The Name" is a characteristic story of Megged; *Living on the Dead*[47] is a characteristic novel—or, to be more precise the first novel in a trilogy.[48] What the three novels have in common is the problem of literary creativity as it is refracted in the person of the *littérateur*. The ancillary problem—the writer vis-à-vis society—is no less prominent. As a matter of fact, the social and the individual problems mesh so intimately that they may be said to form one problem.

The protagonist of *Living on the Dead*, Jonas Rabinowitch ,shares certain traits with Jonah the prophet: he endeavors, vainly of course, to flee the burden of responsibility; he is the bearer of a message which, perhaps, it is "death to hide" and death to utter. As he goes about his arduous biographical task—he is writing a documentary history of Abraham Davidov, hero of the resistance in mandatory Palestine—he uncovers a complicated human being and, at the same time, he bares his own private life. Thus he composes a "parallel life" in the Plutarchian manner. But the matter is more complicated: the life of Davidov never gets written, the life of Jonas never gets lived. For the life of Abraham Davidov is image and reality: the image of a heroic figure, admired by "thousands of people," and the reality of a womanizing bohemian who neglected wife and child, who seduced, among many others, a fifteen year old girl, and exposed her to pregnancy and abortion. The life of Jonas Rabinowitch is imagination and realism; imagination which weaves strands of emotion into delicate patterns of literary symmetry and realism as an incompatible plane with the life of imagination. Almost at the beginning of the novel the protagonist divorces his wife Ahuva who is "the beloved," as her name indicates:

On May 5, a little more than two years ago, I went to the memorial ceremony at Davidov's grave. On June 7 in the same year I was divorced from Ahuva.

That's what happened as far as I remember. One evening, between the aforementioned two dates, as I sat at my desk, while Ahuva was ensconced behind me in an armchair in the corner of the room, calm, sure of her husband, cutting out paper letters for her kindergarten class, I said casually, without turning my head to her: It's time to separate, isn't it?[49]

This failure at marriage parallels the failure at literature. And over the two failures hovers the trial: "D. Karpinowitch Publishers Limited versus Mr. Jonah Rabinowitch, known as Jonas."[50] While the two failures move in unreal reality, in a Kafkaesque syndrome, the trial unlike Kafka's Trial is real. The counsel for Jonas assures his client that legal postponements can stretch the case into infinity. "That fool does not understand that, as long as this trial hangs over me, I can't begin anything new."[51]

This last sentence of the book points to an imprisonment which is the result of willed impotence, of escape from the creative imperative. Perhaps this is what the novel, what the dominant theme of Megged and his generation has been: the failure of the creative imperative.

In the second novel of the trilogy, *The Short Life*,[52] a writer is again the center of the plot, a woman writer who is also lecturer at the University of Tel Aviv, Dr. Elisheva Tal-Blumfeld. The literary and non-literary life presents an opportunity for a two-level novel. The unhappy marriage to an insurance agent, the mutual infidelities and disloyalties are lived on a realistic plane and are also transmuted into a novel which she composes in her mind though she cannot decide even on the opening sentence. She is sure that a realistic approach à la Madame Bovary or Anna Karenina would be fatal: it would fail to transmit the delicate shades of subconscious drives and conscious meditations. Besides life is short. And, within a framework of brevity, a questioning alternative to psychological complications beckons to husband and wife—hedonism.

The *Notebooks of Evyatar*[53] imitate, in theme at least, *Living On the Dead*. Both novels attempt a biography of a dead protagonist. As in the sophisticated structure of the *Notebooks of Evyatar* the dead writes about the dead. Dr. Azaryahu Wolfson, editor of the projected edition of the collected works of Joseph Richter, is eager to produce a solid piece of research. He turns to the proofreader Evyatar Levitin but gets scant cooperation. An automobile accident puts an end to Levitin's life, and his notebooks fall into the learned hands of Dr. Wolfson who furnishes an *apparatus criticus*: introduction and notes.

The notebooks unfold a strange love affair with the Hebrew language and its literature. Both Richter, the writer, and Levitin, the proofreader, are the lovers. But Richter gets the plaudits, Levitin suf-

fers neglect; Richter has the talent, Levitin possesses knowledge of mi-
nutiae which improve Richter's work and other writers. Levitin's work
is done in the recesses of the printing shop and the editorial rooms. His
disappointments and frustrations are entrusted to the notebooks
which glow with real talent. But they are not destined for posterity.
They are an accident. An erotic relationship for the Hebrew letters
animates Levitin. He feels that only a proofreader can experience their
charm and magic. Yet he serves them as a eunuch while the writers delight in their intercourse with language. Levitin is lonely, forgotten,
unsuccessful; Richter, tall and handsome and successful. Yet Richter
who emerges from Levitin's pen as a parasite and ingrate, as a super-
cilious cheat and arrogant miser, can portray paradigms of moral in-
corruptibility. This talented crook—a paradox which Levitin fails to
fathom—is forgiven by everybody because his work is a contribution to
humanity:

> Only we, the weak ones, we are slaves of ethics. The strong govern
> morality. Even their sins assume a certain nobility. We are not for-
> given for lies, treachery . . . exploitation.[54]

This is a dilemma, as old as literature. Evyatar Levitin is impaled on
its horns. The problem of criticism interests Richter who is moved by
intellect rather than emotion, cold-blooded analysis rather than insight, critical appraisal rather than creativity. In a sense the whole
novel is a critique of criticism, the whole trilogy an inquiry into the art
of literature, more suitable for a philosophic discourse of a Leavis or a
Frye than the novelistic dissection of a Megged.

Introspection as a corollary to alienation seems to be the dominant
preoccupaton of Megged in search of a holy prop in the midst of the unsatisfying desanctification of modern life. Perhaps it is not without
significance that the first story in the anthology of his writings is entitled "Sabbath,"[55] and the last story "A Jew"[56]—dedicated to the memory of this father—ends with the words "the great Sabbath."

The viability of Israeli society—its inherited ethos projected against
a difficult reality—permeates the work of Nathan Shaham (1925-   ).
A son of Eliezer Steinman, the prolific novelist and journalist and pop-
ularizer of Hasidism, he has less in common with his father than, say,
Micah Joseph Lebensohn with his parent.[57] A native Israeli, a farmer
in the cooperative Bet Alfa and a soldier in the War of Liberation, he
was totally dedicated to the contemporary scene in nascent Israel and
Israel after 1948. In a steady output of stories, novels, and plays he

made a realistic assessment of Israeli society in the cooperative and in war. Problems like German reparations to surviving victims of the Nazi terror excited his imagination in the novel *First Person Plural*.[58] But even these problems are posed and lived in the setting of a rural cooperative where private income from any source—even "defiled money"[59]—must be used for the benefit of all *in loco*. And, in a sense, these are also problems connected with war—the most terrible war for survival the Jews have had to wage since their emergence on the stage of history. The cruelty and the inhumanity of friend to friend, friend to enemy in battle, obsessed Shaham with particular force. In one of his most gripping stories "They Were Seven"[60] he described the terror that overwhelmed a company of forty-five on a hill where seven mines had been sown and the map of their location had been burnt. That meant certain death for any one who might tread on a mine inadvertently. When the first man fell, the rest ceased to be a company. The tension, the suspicion, the hunger—these created an atmosphere of intolerable discord. To add to all the misery, the hill stank because they threw their excrements out the window out of fear: they were afraid to move. The useless, undramatic deaths which happened with the inevitability of tragedy are described in deliberate, singularly charged cadences.

There and Back[61] is a novel of the rural cooperative. The protagonist, a girl from a cooperative, decides to become a person like any person in London where "birds chirp in English."[62] In vain: she is for the stranger abroad a symbol of Israel. And she has to explain her brand of socialism and Zionism to friends and foes, to defend her views even to potential lovers. Return to Israel becomes more and more a decision, a necessity, a reality and a realization. What happened in London was "an adventure in a foreign milieu." But it is important to lead "an ordered life, governed by common sense, a life built slowly, a family life, a home, children, a homeland and values called by proper names."[63]

The negativist criticism of the kibbutz reaches apogees of sarcasm in the satires of Reuben Miran, especially in "Each Sabbath, After Breakfast,"[64] where the sadism of children against a helpless child is tolerated without punitive consequences for the guilty. In the sarcastic story of Amos Rodner, a native of a kibbutz, the establishment and disappearance of the kibbutz "Hill of Goats"[65] is depicted with grim humor. After a brief life the village becomes a place of sojourn for goats. The founders have built nothing.

Early idealization of the kibbutz between the two World Wars gradually gave way to realism. In 1945 David Maletz uncovered with minatory fervor shortcomings in the idealized villages and farms.[66] Almost fifteen years later he again castigated the inhospitality of the communal society: the closed ranks, the xenophobic stance. Even the title of his accusing novel bore ominous undertones: *The Gate is Closed.*[67] Hanok Bartov also criticized the kibbutz and bared its unidealistic attitude to the sick in general and to a sick member in its midst in particular. A healthy group, an unhealthy individual—they don't mesh. A cooperative of six hundred and fifty souls does not behave like a welfare organization, its ideals wither in the midst of grim realities; individual idleness—even enforced idleness—cannot be tolerated with composure if it involves a protracted period of seventeen years. The end of the protagonist is as inconvenient as his life: he dies amidst preparations for a Purim party and manages somewhat to dim the infectious hilarity. As an alert, vivid observer Bartov has few equals among his confrères. His journalistic activities have taught him to use his pen with pungent accuracy in reportage and in fiction. In a novel[68] with a collective hero—the Jewish Brigade of the British Army in the Second World War—he sketched a portrait of a Jewish soldier, Elisha Kruk, in confrontation with the strange and estranged victims of the holocaust on the one hand and the victimizers on the other. That soldier on the European continent remained an outsider, unable to achieve selfhood, not satisfied, not integrated—"not with our dead, not with their living."[69] David Shahar also boasted cynical atitudes to the sanctity of work,[70] to Jewish nationalism, to the entire idea of kibbutzism which, in the language of one of its members, resembled barracks militarism. Little wonder that the love life of Shahar's antiheroes is a trip from bed to bed. But as a fifth-generation native of the Land of Israel he is more rooted than his fellow writers in the soil of Israel, in its multiple ethnicity and the sounds and sights of its ancient cities. Few modern writers have had his ability to capture the shouts of the evocative vendors of Jerusalem in that variety of languages—Yiddish and Ladino, Hebrew and Arabic—which is at once the charm and the curse of that unimaginable city.[71] And even fewer writers have been able to depict with such adroitness as he has used in "The Dagger of Ali Ibn Masrur"[72] types of the haute bourgeoisie and their close associations with the less fortunate who shared with them the mystique of the Holy City.

Yigal Mossinsohn (1917–), originally a farmer, is a web of incongruous complications. His formal education was meager, his informal education rich. As a native Israeli and a member of kibbutz Naan (1938–1950) he shunned no manual labor and worked at various trades. Builder of homes, paver of roads, shepherd, guard, police officer as well as member of the Haganah and Israeli Army of Defense: all these occupations hardened his resolve and his character. Six years (1959—1965), spent in the United States, deepened his interest in the visual media of communication.

In time, writing became his exclusive activity. Stories, novels, books for children, plays for adults poured in a steady stream from his pen. Barely twenty-nine when he published his first collection of stories *Gray as A Sack*[73] and only thirty-one when his first play *In the Plains of the Negev*[74] was staged by Habimah, he enjoyed an instant success. The stories were tales of adventure, especially in erotic exploits, and the play celebrated the quiet heroism of a small village against the Egyptian army during the War of Independence. Even the juvenile thrillers *Hasambah*[75] which have appeared steadily since 1950 earned him a quick reputation. For in these three genres, fiction, drama, juvenile literature, Mossinsohn captivated his audiences with a realistic stance which was based on deep knowledge of plain folk, youth, the rural milieu and the shady aspects of the city. Sometimes his realism degenerated into sensationalism as in the novel *The Way of a Man*[76] or in the stories for children, but at his best he produced memorable vignettes of life in Israel. A story like "Yoreh," autumn rain, reproduced the landscape at the end of summer with a master's knowledge. And, within that framework, he fitted the simple characters of two generations: the elderly couples and their offspring on their marriage day, divided by age, united by common aspiration.

As a police officer Mossinsohn observed the youthful criminal with dedicated interest. The result was *Eldorado* in its various metamorphoses: play, film, story. The crooked streets of Jaffa instead of the blooming fields of Esdrelon, the shifty young criminals and prostitutes instead of idealistic workers in rural landscapes, guilt instead of innocence: the provocative contrasts were only seemingly antithetical. The young criminal in *Eldorado* was a Jewish criminal with an unsated yearning for the good and clean life. And this conflict between criminality and the desperate will to escape the gambling dens, the billiard dives, the drugs, the prostituting females, became, in spite of the heady brew of sensationalism, a landmark in Hebrew literature. *Eldorado* dared to depict the immoral Israeli with refreshing realism and turn the gilded goal of romantic yearnings since the sixteenth century into a café where murder was committed and a young man, innocent of the act but burdened with a prison record, almost paid with his life for a murder that he did not commit. Even the sadism of the police received its proper evaluation from Mossinsohn. And the police station itself became a symbol to the young criminal: "white on the outside, soiled on the inside."[77] There is no doubt that the work of Mossinsohn is a primer of information on the social structure of Israel after the establishment of the State. The analysis of this structure has the advantage over a sociological study: it uncovers unsuspected fissures in the flinty substratum of life in Israel.

Benjamin Tammuz (1919-   )[78] who arrived in mandatory Palestine in 1924 has inhabited two worlds of art, sculpture and fiction. In both media he strives for the unusual effect: he often invents contrived situations which fail to convince or impress. But in some stories and novels he makes up with an exciting sensationalism for the loss in intensity. Early association with the radical Sternist Fighters for Freedom of Israel and the Canaanite movement parallels his later extremism in art. That the experience of uncompromising ruthlessness was never lost on the writer can be easily demonstrated from a passage in his novel *Jacob*. In describing the clandestine struggle with the British before the Second World War the author makes this pregnant observation:

Not one of the people of the underground was born here. But all of them believed that they rid themselves of their native inheritance and they had become Hebrews in all matters. Whenever one of them failed with the typical clumsiness of a diaspora Jew, it was proof of the self-evident truth: you cannot rely on an immigrant. Respect him and suspect him—that's the rule.[79]

This typical "Canaanite" attitude to the non-native in the Land of Israel and the concomitant absurdity of hatred for Zionism,[80] this radical division of Jewry into right and wrong Jews, played its role in realms of purely human concern—in the dichotomy of flesh and spirit, for instance, which haunts the work of Tammuz. An obsession with physical desire does not justify the dictum that "only the flesh can lead to the spirit:" it may but it may not, as in the notorious case of Rasputin or, to use one of Tammuz's examples of concupiscence in *Castle in Spain*[81] in the case of Elly, the twenty-nine-year-old Israeli, obsessed by Nora, a forty-four-year-old secretary at a Scandinavian embassy. In Spain both protagonists achieve an unconvincing fulfillment: Nora sates her nostalgia with romantic illusions, Elly, who wanted to forget his Jewishness, regains his commitment to Judaism on foreign soil after an unsuccessful attempt at total assimilation.

In *Orchard*[82] the central character Luna leads a somnambulistic ex-

istence—in conformity with her name—and indulges in sexual relationships with two brothers and with her own son. Is she old, is she
young, "is it at all possible to know her age and measure it by the yard-
stick of years? Perhaps she is not a creature born of woman . . . "[83]
And, perhaps, the added symbolism of the orchard is a mere caricature
of the garden of esoteric wisdom which aroused the intellectual curiosity of Ben Azzai, Ben Zoma, Aher and Rabbi Akiba.[84] For the orchard
belongs to the Turk Mahmed Effendi. And Daniel, son of a Jew from
Russia, who buys the "sick" orchard, develops it into an exemplary plot
of land with modern machinery and modern methods of horticulture.
The allegory is obvious: the orchard is Israel, the former neglectful
owner, the Turk, adoptive father of Luna. And Luna bears a son—
either by Daniel or by his half-brother Ovadiah—who eventually becomes his mother's incestuous paramour. This son is apparently the
"healthy" Jew, emancipated from tradition and its ethical stance as
contrasted with the "sick" Jew chained to tradition and morality.

Times change. The "healthy" Jew as conceived by a Ratosh or a Tammuz may, perhaps, in the future reacquire some of the "unhealthy"
characteristics of former generations. Who knows, he may even be better off than the superman stripped of essential humanity.

Not unlike Jacob Horowitz, who preceded him, Tammuz hovers over
the vagaries of expressionism. Somewhat closer to the realism of his
contemporaries who arrived in mandatory Palestine with the third
wave of immigration—Yaari and Shenhar—he also indulges in technical excesses which are designed to capture attention by "sleight-of-
mind." This is also the case of Yoram Kaniuk (1930-), the incurable romantic in love with absurdity projected by bizarre characters. From
the adored master William Faulkner he inherited an addiction to excess in portraiture, in plot, in style. From his bifurcated life in Israel
and in the United States he drew the raw material—wild and chaotic—
for his fictive work in the earliest stories and in his last novella with
the uncommon name *The Story About Aunt Shelomzion the Large*.[85] A
native of the Land of Israel, he participated in the paramilitary exploits of the Haganah and the military action in the War of Independence, and spent eleven formative years—from 1950 to 1961—in the
United States. The double perspective set him apart from most Israeli
writers and sharpened his artistic vision and nostalgic love for Tel
Aviv where houses rise with dizzying speed, where Jewish children
grow up with an almost gentile insouciance and speak a disgraceful
Hebrew—sometimes to spite their elders, sometimes out of mere ignorance.[86] And when the age of Bar Mizvah arrives, they don't want a

Bar Mizvah celebration, the gifts of fountain pens or the *Complete Works of Ber Borohov* or the poems of Bialik or even the poems of Shlonsky. Is this young Jew a *persona desiderata*? Such moral questions may not be the concern of art. But they insist on being asked even at the risk of disdainful answers from the apologists of the new Jew in the new Land.

The love for Tel Aviv is balanced by the perennial attachment to Jerusalem which dominates even such rebellious writers as Kaniuk. In *Himmo, King of Jerusalem*[87] the writer translated his experience in the battle for Old Jerusalem during the War of Independence into a weird tale of torture. But even in that taut novel the nurse Hamutal is a Telavivian who falls in love with Himmo, an eyeless stump without arms and legs, a mere fragment of a man whose handsome looks had earned him once the sobriquet "King of Jerusalem." The maternal instinct in its supreme triumph—that is the impossible feat of evocative strength in the novel of Kaniuk. And it is written with imaginative vigor but without sentimentality.

Before he published in Hebrew, Kaniuk made his literary debut in English with a collection of stories and a novel *The Acrophile*.[88] Both in the stories and in the novel he showed a vivacity, a sense of humor, a wild associative power which immediately drew attention to his work. In the story which gave its title to the book an itinerant actress plays the role of an old flower vendor—a symbol of death.

> She played death and she had to live it with great fidelity. She was sad to die each night in a different city. . . . One day she died in Cincinnati and ate breakfast in Akron, Ohio, in order to die there at night . . .[89]

Her suitor is introduced to her parents who "examined and surveyed" him thoroughly and only then gave their assent, but not "with enthusiasm."[90]

It is his exotic behavior, his strange talk which raises people's eyebrows:

> Every miserable flea can fly: I can't. He can reach any destination: a king's nose, a thumb of your enemy. A small insect can bite the ass of any woman.[91]

In *The Acrophile* Kaniuk presents monologs, jokes, dreams, fantasies. The novel has no beginning, no middle, no end. Its title is provocative: it may mean lover of heights rather than lover of citadels. This is only proper for a novel which tells the incoherent story of a young man in Manhattan, the city of stony heights. Soaring verbal acrobatics mock the serious, the pretentious, the unctuous. Man may not fly like the flea in Kaniuk's story, but his words have wings—in *The Acrophile* and, especially, in *Adam Resurrected*.[92] Ostensibly, this novel tells the story of an impossible former clown Adam Stein, survivor of Auschwitz by dint of his funny feats and his quick wit, and inmate, at last, of Mrs. Seizling's Institute for Rehabilitation and Therapy at Arad in Israel where he imagines himself to be a dog. Cured and released he does not enjoy sanity; it diminishes man's stature: "It lacks greatness, it lacks true joy as well as the awful sorrow which slashes the heart."[93] In the perusal of such a book the reader has a right to ask: is this madness or sophistication, symbol of alienation or discovery of a true identity? The answer is in the question.

The worker as poet who does not cease to be a worker is a new and rare phenomenon in modern Hebrew poetry, the cooperative farm which is his home is his main theme. Hence the adulatory sympathy with Rabinov and Basok and Tene, Fania Bergstein, Zerubavel Gilead and, especially, Levi Ben-Amittai (1901–   ), the poletarian poet of Deganyah Bet.[94] The bed and the furrow, the flower and the grass, the ploughing and the weeding—they sing in his lyrical poetry which is drenched with the scent of the open spaces of upper Galilee. As for man and woman:

> We are the stalks of the field. When the time comes
> God stoops down as we do.
> Stoops down and gathers with his own hands
> Unto himself in infinite mercy
> The harvest of the generation.[95]

The worker-poet borrowed metaphorical strength from the humble tasks of the peasant and, without blasphemous intent, turned God into a peasant. For himself and his contemporaries he wrested a sense of piety out of the soil of Deganyah with the tenacity and obstinacy of a man whose horizon is bound by the area of his native village. And if poetry is indicative of the future trends of a nation or an aggregate of nations, then it may be said with some measure of certainty that a deep sense of religiosity permeates cooperative villages of Israel and spreads imperceptibly to the whole country. This may be a startling statement—tales of religious indifference in the kibbutz are common among superficial observers. But it is enough to read the poems of Levi Ben-Amittai on the Sabbath and, especially, "Sabbath in the Cooperative," to realize at once what a deep-seated urge for the ancient ceremonial of religion informs the members of the kibbutz:

> Mother Sabbath! Listen to the yearning hearts
> And the silent speech to-night on Jordan's banks.
> Spread your hands on our bread
> And bless our peace.
>
> Bless the loyal ones, the ones who sow the light in the field.
> May deep joy rule the heart that longs for brotherhood.
> All will come one day to celebrate
> The Sabbath of peace.[96]

This artless poetry is an indicator of reviving religiosity in the communal settlements of Israel. It is no accident that, like Shamir, Levi Ben-Amittai was drawn to the austere simplicity of the Essenes. In the ancient sect he discovered a milieu which must have reminded him of Deganyah Bet where he has spent most of the years of his life. And a book of poems, *A Gift Out of the Wilderness*,[97] is entirely devoted to the places and personages connected with their lives. But even more than the evocation of a remote past *A Gift Out of the Wilderness* often resembles a gift out of Deganyah Bet:

> An Essene came at dawn
> With humble step
> In whitest garb.
>
> From tent and hut—
> The Essenes' homes
> Which know no lord no master—
>
> They gather in their hall.
> They talk no profane talk
> Before sunrise.[98]

Except for the special indications of the Essenes—the white garment, the abstention from profane talk before sunrise—these people could have been transported to a cooperative in modern Galilee without loss of identity.

Poets like Levi Ben-Amitai need not go too far in search of poetry; it beckons to them on their doorstep:

> At the door of your house
> Trees bloom
> And trees wither.
> Don't search for your poem
> Too far.
> Turn hither.[99]

Levi Ben-Amittai belongs to the family of poets who, like Francis Jammes, find no happiness in the metropolitan civilization of their times. The touch of the earth precipitates idyllic naiveté into their verse and into their environment.

Earnest modesty informs the poetry of Zerubavel Gilead (1912–   ) who, like Levi Ben-Amittai, combines the avocation of poetry with the vocation of a farmer. The field in his poems is a real field and not the fanciful vision of a city-dweller. The poet not only does not shy away from the "odor of dung"; he balances it with the "scent of grass."[100] His hands touch wheat, his feet walk the paths between the waving seas of wheat. At dawn he burrows in the furrows and observes the bluish mists. With buoyant and original sensitivity he endows the wind with tender fingers, the ears of corn with mysterious whispers, the sun with the power to pattern braids of light and shadow on the earth.

For Zerubavel Gilead the Land of Israel is the axis upon which his whole life turns in happy contentment. Conversely, in his travels he has acquired deep distrust of the diaspora and its exposed and un-defended position in the world: foreign springs reverberate with echos of the scaffold. But above and beyond the landscape of the Promised Land the inevitable promise of the end makes surprising appearances in the verse of Zerubavel Gilead.

> Soon the strong-toothed harvesters will burst into the corn.
> Can you hear the music of the scythe of time around us?[101]

There is a breath of death in these verses. Yet Gilead is essentially a happy poet. Against death he poses love as the antidote, love as escape and lullaby for the mature man.

> Let us be good to each other
> Tonight.
> Around us is nothing but shadow and dark

And sorrow that's sown and sadness that's grown
And the open abyss without saving support.[102]

This is the sadness of a man who believes in the joy of love, spread like the veil of Maya over the unreal world.

Ogen (1909–   ), loyal to his Polish homeland, sought to strike roots in Israel. His adoration of the peasant and worker reached almost religious dimensions:

And I suppose that God comes from on high
And walks among the conquerors of soil
In working clothes and turns the clods in toil
And prays for rain with child and beast and rye

And speaks the heavy Hebrew words and when
They tremble for their goods, he trembles too,
And when they pave the ways, he paves them too,
And when they long, he longs like one of them

And is a man, a tree upheld by loving hand,
And brings forth seed to pass to future men
His fire, and is a worker on the land

And falls in weariness upon the glen
When evening comes, and loves the orphaned seers
And dreams with them the dreams of brighter years.[103]

In this sonnet Ogen places the Deity itself among the conquerors of the soil and, by inference, the destiny of the land in their hands.[104]

Of the various strands which made up the unfinished pattern of his poetical quilt, redemption, nature and woman seem to be preeminent. To short lyrics, sonnets and narrative poems he entrusts the pessimistic outpourings of a reflective introvert. From the first to his tenth collection of poems—significantly entitled *Poems to the End of Hope*[105]—there is hardly a change in technique or content. The poet moves along his paths of life with calm non-assurance.

While Levi Ben-Amittai and Zerubavel Gilead and Ogen struck roots in the Palestinian soil, Mordecai (1909–   ) remained an alien in his new homeland. The city of his longing and love is the city immortalized by Shneour: Vilna. In Israel he never experienced the joy of integration.

> The sun, the heart of dawn, trembles on my arms.
> How shall I, a stranger and a guest,
> Carry it into the festive day
> Of bloom with zest?[106]

These verses might have been written by Shlonsky. Both in imagery and content they resemble his acrobatics. A line like "our eyes do not know how to bloom" also seems to be inspired by Shlonsky. Sometimes Mordecai projects a vague mysticism into his poems.

> There is someone here, I own,
> There is someone here, I know,
> Who prays for every seed that's sown
> And every hand that works with the hoe.[107]

Like most Hebrew poets Mordecai reacted to the misfortunes of mandated Palestine and the diaspora before the outbreak of the Second World War. And like most of them he did not find the proper expression for the tremendous events of the times. Bialik who was shaken to the depths of his soul by the pogrom of Kishenev in 1903 created a new genre of penitential psalms in the long poem "In the City of Slaughter." But the far more tragic events of the next few decades rarely found such poets as Tschernichowsky who protested with the defiant sonnets "On the Blood" against the Ukrainian massacres of 1919 or Gruenberg who hurled his quasi-prophetic *Book of Accusation and Faith* at Jew and gentile alike. Mordecai lacked tragic perceptivity. Only in his love poetry did he show originality:

> On the fire of your hair we burn and die,
> The sunset and I.[108]

This is a startling metaphor, a contribution to figurative speech in Hebrew lyrical poetry, a fruit from the tree of the lost Eden the poet mourned in a collection of lyrics.[109]

Mordecai has become more ambitious with the passing of years. Beyond the brief lyric he discovered the longer poem in the form of a series of lyrical poems bound by thematic unity as in *The Giants Were on the Earth*. [110] It is one of those cosmic attempts of man as superman challenging fate, of Jew as super-Jew asserting his eternality against all odds. But the lyric expression is not strong enough to infuse new life into the old idea—except, perhaps, in the poetic rendition of the interrupted sacrifice of Isaac. For it is not God tempting Abraham, but

Abraham tempting God to take his son, his only one, and guard
him in the desert like a palm:

> For his heart is aflame, his hand is afire.
> And he goes to the mountain of sorrows
> To exalt your name and to sanctify
> The name of all the tomorrows.[111]

These memorable lines are, perhaps, more powerful than any in all
the six books of his verse.[112]

Benjamin Tene (1914–   ), originally Tennenbaum, romanticizes the
ancestral and personal past. In his biblical poem "Miriam"[113] he veers
to the ballad:

> When the waters stood like walls
>   The deep welled up in Miriam's heart:
> Arise O tree, arise O rock,
>   Dance together, hills, and part.
> Women, let us sing, rejoice
>   And dance the dances of the heart.
>
> Out they went in Miriam's wake
>   With dance and drum and singing hands.
> The east winds laughed with their sweet laugh,
>   The heavens kissed the face of sands,
> The bramble sang a lusty song,
>   The bramble's leaves bloomed out in strands . . .
>
> Out they went in Miriam's wake
>   To dance in fury, dance in sound.
> They danced and whirled, they danced and whirled,
>   And fell exhausted on the ground.
> But Miriam danced like birds in flight
>   With burning body round and round.

In "Miriam" Tene reached maturity of expression: he conquered an ancient theme with lyric strength. A simpler conquest—also in the form
of a ballad—was the story-in-verse of a desolate piece of land in the
mountains of Ephraim and the will to convert it to productive cultivation:

When we went up to Giara on high,
We were met by dry fields, by a burning sky.
But we knew the desert would end our quest,
Would be shelter and mother and breast.

It is "work that hides the seed and hopes for golden bread"[114] that attracts Tene with irresistible fascination, and work, especially in the kibbutz, is his favorite theme. The best sonnets in the series of seventy sonnets[115] proclaim the virtues of the fields and the flowers, the trees and the seasons of the year. In his "Yesterdays on the Threshold" Tene romanticizes Warsaw in pedestrian, narrative verse: the Jewish ghetto with its noisy streets, the "educational" institutions, the communal buildings, and the final revolt against the tyranny of the Nazis. But he is at his best when he describes, in simple and effective verse, the conquest of ancestral land by pioneers who are not Messiahs but simple farmers and the chief contributors to the sanation of the Jewish people.

Quiescence rather than acquiescence is characteristic of Tene's "Vision in Galilee."[116] This series of poems reads like a long poem about the experiences of the poet in northern Israel: work, love for wife, care for child, deep concern with the fate of the land in the years which preceded the Second World War. Like Landan's *Massadah*, this autobiographical mélange by a worker-poet stresses the inevitability of Israel for Israel: nowhere to go in an inimical world.

The unaffected poetry of Fania Bergstein (1908–1950), who published her first poem "My Dream" in Warsaw,[117] derives spiritual sustenance from the soil. A farmer-poet like Gilead, Levi Ben-Amittai, and Tene, she revels in rural glory. The seed that is sown, the plant that is planted, the fruit that is gathered—this is the simple stuff of her poetry.

I have sown and hidden deep
The golden seed in furrowed land,
I looked seaward, I prayed windward,
I prayed for the cloud from heaven.
I watched for the autumn rains,
I stooped to every living bud,
I cheered my soul with sprouting green.
I counted days, I counted nights.
I grew together with the air,
And when it filled with golden seed,
My soul filled with the seeds of hope.[118]

Her volumes of verse *Vintage* and *Passing Clouds*, collected in *Autumn*, are scented with the scent of the earth, with the life of the peasant, with the revolving seasons of the year. And so are her children's songs in the book of poems for children *I Hid a Seed* and children's stories with an incongruous title *Red Verses*.[119] Fields and vineyards, poplars and palms, are as common in her lines as in rural landscapes.

22
Jew and Arab

IN a world of annihilated distances exclusivism is dead, nationalism is deader, hatred is deadest. Utopianism in the form of one world where each human unit—familial, tribal, national—plays its lonely instrument, yet harmonizes with the others in a symphony of humanity: that is the coming reality. The alternative is the suicide of the human race. For war is a device of impotence. When man fails to convince man with his humanity, with reason, he resorts to his animality, to war. It has been argued by a brilliant Harvard critic that Thomas Mann's oeuvre forms a dialectical pattern of *Künstler* versus *Bürger*, artist versus citizen. Similarly, Hebrew literature is essentially an Israel-Arab syndrome.

In his book *The Land of the Hart*,[1] Aryeh Lova Eliav revives the idea of a world federation of states, a sort of United States of the World, and sees such a conglomeration as the only hope for mankind. He also postulates a humane and democratic socialism as the form of government for the United States of the World and, naturally, embraces the idea of "two peoples, two states" in present-day Israel.[2] From that view—the long-range view of the *Kulturhistoriker*—both Jews and Arabs with their extremist insistence on political monopoly of the present area of Israel—are engaged in a recidivist struggle.

Political figures fan the fires of discontent or keep them at a low glow. But they don't extinguish them. On the contrary, at the Festival of Unity which occurred on February 22, 1965, the charismatic Arab leader, Gamal Abdel Nasser, said openly: "Arab unity means the liquidation of Israel . . ."[3] Such dangerous generalizations of statesmen are paralleled by harmless disquisitions on such impossible themes as *The Zionist Mind, The Arab Mind* and *Understanding the Arab Mind*

270

which are supposed to hand over the golden key to the door of a great people's inner sanctum or *Love-Hate Relations* which purport to analyze the perennial problem of English and American sensibilities. Authors of such books—Alan R. Taylor in the first instance, Raphael Patai and Fayez E. Sayegh in the second instance, Stephen Spender in the third instance, are doomed to failure. For the Zionist mind or the Arab mind or the English mind are nonexistent categories. Individual minds in ethnic context may crank up some similarities but their machinery often creaks in the effort. Literature yields a more fruitful approach to the individual mentality of an alien. Unfortunately, Jews made little effort to explore and exploit the writings of Arabs in the last century. Yehudah Burla, a native of Jerusalem, was the first Hebrew novelist who attempted to assess Arab literature in Egypt and Syria in the twenties of this century.[4] With all his efforts at fairness, he delivered a devastating critique: Arab literature was mediocre at best, usually poor in quality, lyrical and emotional to the point of pathos. Burla's translations of a few fragments of prose and a few poems presented to the Hebrew reader the first meager insights into the literature of his Arab neighbor. More than three decades later a first-rate Arabist assessed the Arabic literature in mandatory Palestine and also came to very negative conclusions:

> During the thirty years of the mandatory administration of Palestine, Arab creative writing was undistinguished, lacking originality and depth, and concentrating almost entirely upon topical, political themes.[5]

Even in the fifties "standards of Arabic literature . . . reflected the youth, immaturity and inexperience of the writers."[6] A perceptible change can be detected in the collections *Palestinian Stories* and *Arabic Stories*.[7] In an enlightening introduction on Arabic literature in Palestine and present-day Israel the Hebrew writer Simon Balas strives to assess sympathetically the imaginative work of young Arabs. Though it suffers in comparison with Arabic literature in Egypt, it does reflect the poignancy of their special situation. In spite of its propagandistic ingredients—sometimes mere lipservice to prevailing pan-Arabic slogans, sometimes political conviction—it struggles to win imaginative perspectives which were unthinkable a generation ago. This is especially true of Samira Azam (1924–1967) who produced a commendable body of short stories during her short life.

Arabs showed even less interest in the writings of Jews than the

Jews in the writings of Arabs. Had the Jews delved in Arab writings, they would have been startled by the rash generalizations of a Muhammad Jamil Baihum: "The Jews," he says, "wrote their scriptures, their psalms, and their Talmud by the hand of their rabbis; they wrote their history with the ink of their spirit, which is impregnated with selfishness and arrogance."[8] Such revelations about the authorship of the Bible and the Talmud—the Psalms, apparently, being considered a third branch of Jewish learning—were propagated in all seriousness. And, in a brilliant *non sequitur*, the Jews were portrayed as selfish and arrogant. Elsewhere, they were simply "the scum of the earth."[9] Not so the Arabs, who are in possession of the glorious Koran[10] and an exemplar of peacefulness and good neighborliness.[11] Such naive propaganda was matched by an adoration of the rhetoric of Gamal Abdel Nasser whose political dicta were inflammatory and whose excursions into philosophical thought, hollow. In his view, "history is . . . charged with great heroic roles which do not find actors. . ."[12] This unfortunate attitude or non-attitude on the part of two related ethnic groups was merely a conspicuous symbol of mutual distrust and neglect.

In an article which echoed and reechoed in the contemporary press in the first decade of the twentieth century, a Hebrew essayist named J. Epstein made the sound observation: "While we feel passionate love for the land of our fathers, we forget that the people who live there now also have a feeling heart and a loving soul. The Arab, like all men, is tied to his birthland with strong ties."[13] The ties are agricultural and religious: the Arab peasant is attached to his land and to the graves of his ancestors on the land. No matter how much money is given to him for the few dunams he sells sometimes from economic necessity, he resents the loss. And Epstein foresaw—rightly—that the Arabs "will finally awaken to restore by might what was taken from them for gold." Though no national Arab movement" existed at the time in the Land of Israel, Epstein thought that "that people needs no movement": it is strong physically, it is part and parcel of a great nation in Syria, Mesopotamia, Arabia, and Egypt. In his view, "we will sin to our people and to its future if we will throw away lightheartedly our choicest weapon: the justice of our enterprises and the purity of our ways." It is true that the segment of the Middle East which we now call Israel took a giant stride into the twentieth century because of the Jewish settlement. And out of the millions of dollars that Jews spent on the vineyards, Arabs received the greatest share—for their labor, for the transport of grapes, for fertilizer. But—as Americans have learned since the Second World War—"it is difficult to buy lovers" and it is "easy . . . to create enemies." Therefore Epstein counsels that when Jews come to the Land of Israel, they should take what others have not taken, they should settle in places where others have not yet settled, they should open up—for their own good and for the happiness of all—the riches in the dormant layers of the soil. And since the area of untilled land exceeded the area of tilled land, the problem of Jewish settlement could be solved. Wherever tilled land could be acquired justly, the original settlers should not be disinherited; they should be taught to improve their lot and convert their extensive methods of tillage to intensive methods. Similarly, the urban Arab could be helped—in education, in commerce, in industry. As long as two criteria were followed, an ideal development might result: one, the Jews, who were the first to give humanity ideas of justice, equality and brotherhood, must honor the rights of every individual, every tribe, every nation; two, the Jews, who aspire to freedom in their land are brothers to all nations who aspire to freedom and to the development of their national consciousness.

Somewhat naively, Epstein thought that it was for the good of the Arab to encourage Jews in their immigration: both peoples have much in common, they need each other, they can help each other. And he bolsters his arguments with a biblical quotation toward the end of his article:

> And it shall come to pass, that you shall divide it [the land] by lot for an inheritance to you and to the strangers that sojourn among you . . . and they shall be to you as the homeborn among the children of Israel. They shall have inheritance with you among the tribes of Israel.[14]

The voice of Epstein was not heeded. When tiny Jewish settlements began to dot the landscape of the Land of Israel a hundred years ago, little account was taken of the indigenous population. Moshe Smilansky, the philarabic writer, was dismayed by the lack of mutual understanding between Arabs and Jews and wrote in 1914:

> From the inception of the Zionist idea Zionist propaganda described the land . . . as a wasteland . . . waiting for its redeemers with longing eyes. All these redeemers had to do was to immigrate and settle and remove its veil of widowhood. Thus in the first years of Zionism we developed this certainty: the Land of Israel is virgin soil. On the basis of that certainty all Zionist systems were

built . . . they lacked one thing: attention to those people who have settled in our land before us.[15]

That was the fatal mistake. Ignorance bred contempt, contempt bred enmity. Lonely voices preaching rapprochement with Arabs were heard from the beginning of the Zionist movement. Smilansky, Ahad Haam and Brenner regarded fraternization as a natural bond between the two ethnic groups. With simplistic naiveté Ahad Haam assumed that, as long as Jews were economically useful to the Arabs, they would tolerate them.[16] Brenner counseled contact with Arabs without any *arrière pensée*[17] and regretted his ignorance of Arabic.

Practical steps at implementation of a good neighbor policy were taken in the preceding century. Arabic was taught in some settlements: in Petah Tikvah in the nineties, in Rehovot since 1900/1901. And when the Federation of Teachers was founded in Zikhron Yaakov in 1903, one of the members, Eliyyahu Sapir, demanded that Arabic be taught in Hebrew schools not as an elective but as an obligatory subject.[18] A few decades later the novelist Moshe Shamir ridiculed his socialist comrades who preached brotherly love but neglected to learn the brotherly language.

There were also cases of Arabs learning Hebrew—not officially, not in schools, but from their Jewish neighbors. In his *Galilean Diary* S. Shalom noted that Arab girls who served Jewish farmers spoke Hebrew.[19] In the "Figseller"[20]—a story written in the first decade of the century—the wife of Ben-Yehudah, Hemdah, commends Hassan, a simple Arab peddler from Bethlehem, for his attachment to Jewish children. But the ruralization of Jewish immigrants caused consternation among Arabs and inaugurated a campaign of hatred in the Christian and Moslem press of Syria and Palestine. Venomous diatribes compared the new Jewish settlers with armed robbers who steal the soil from the legitimate workers; at best they were strangers who strove to establish their own state. Plans for peaceful coexistence remained in the planning stage. One of the first to call for cooperation between Arab and Jew was Isaac Ben Zvi, the future president of Israel. In an article, published at the end of 1911, he advocated escalatory education among the Arab masses in the spirit of democracy and international peace, and enlightened dialog with the Arab intelligentsia. And he thought that the best forum for such a plan would be a pro-Jewish Arab newspaper.[21] But the idea was not implemented. Only after the establishment of the State of Israel was an Arab daily, *al-Yawm*, published jointly by the Labor Party, *Mapai*, and its organizational arm, the *Histadrut*. It lasted twenty years, from 1948 to 1968, and it contained contributions by Israeli, Druze, Christian, and Moslem Arabs.

Neither Smilansky nor Brenner, neither Ahad Haam nor Ben Zvi prevailed with their simplistic solution to a problem which required more than idealistic vision. The hard realities of economic rivalry frustrated their ineffectual attempts at fraternization. The conquest of work meant rivalry with Arab labor. But "the conquerors of work," the pioneers, came to be regarded by a large segment of the Jewish population in Ottoman Palestine as the true liberators of the land:

> They were the ones who restored to the people the primary loss after the loss of the land: the power of work, the will to work and the pleasure of work. They assured the people . . . economic independence.[22]

Economic friction was the added reason for the exacerbation of relations between Jew and Arab. Polarization was inevitable: the builders of the third Jewish commonwealth clashed with the indigenous population which had also deep religious and chthonic roots in the land.

The Jews who came in the thirteenth century before the Christian era, the Arabs who came in the seventh after the Christian era: these were two seminal events in the life of the Land of Israel.[23] The two peoples avoided cultural interpenetration and, as contacts between them multiplied at the end of the nineteenth century, Arabs showed increasing hostility to the West in general and to Jews in particular.[24] But Jewish writers became increasingly interested in their Arab neighbors. Jacob Steinberg recollects in one of his poems[25] an Arab's lonely song at an ancient Palestine crossroad with disarming charm. For the song—"nameless pain, sadness without bitterness"—merges in complete harmony with the silent landscape at night. Steinberg's poem is a typical *fin de siècle* effusion: romantic and nostalgic and spiced with a dash of exoticism. But it is also the response of a Hebrew poet to an Arab neighbor, an unconscious wish, perhaps, for a bond of friendship, for a renewal of friendship. For Steinberg probably shared the myth of his contemporaries that Arabs were Jews who converted to Islam in times of stress and persecution.

Yehudah Yaari, a contemporary of Jacob Steinberg, enshrined an Arab-Jewish friendship on an individual basis in his story "A Bird's Nest."[26] A warm, human relationship develops between two young men, Mishka and Saad, who work in a quarry in Galilee. The shared toil and admiration for each other's skills matures into a bond which even death does not sever. The first of May, the socialist holiday, assumes symbolic significance when Mishka dies on that day. "The First of May"—says the Arab when asked about the significance of the day by his colleagues—"is the day when Nabi Musa died." Thus the Arab, almost lightheartedly, adds another saint's day and another Musa to the Arabic calendar. It is the Jew's quest for native skills which brings Jew and Arab together in "A Bird's Nest" and in "The Shepherd and his Dog"[27] in which the purchase of a flock of sheep is consummated in an atmosphere of biblical hospitality. But the utilitarian purpose often develops into a humanitarian and human togetherness. In "The Sun Also Rises and the Sun Sets[28] the need for a native shepherd cements a friendship between Solomon and Hassan, who gets the job amidst the general rejoicing of the kibbutz. It is not only the Jew who is satisfied; the Arab is deeply impressed with the creative tempo on the Jewish farm in contrast with the lethargic somnolence in his native village.

In an anthology *Hebrew Stories From the Life of Arabs*[29] a roster of forty-two writers has been selected from many more who could have been included as the articulate spokesmen for the Arabs in Hebrew literature. Some of them were its prime movers: Burla and Hazaz, Agnon and Brenner, Jacob Steinberg and I.D. Berkowitz, S. Yizhar and Aaron Megged, Benjamin Tammuz and Nathan Shaham. The editor, Joseph Arika, was right when he characterized his work as an "anthology of the Hebrew story . . . In depicting the life of the Arabs the story also portrays, indirectly, the development of the Hebrew community . . . till the achievement of independence and the establishment of the State."[30] In earlier stories Arabs are portrayed in their humanity, dignity, simplicity. It is not so much the relationship between the Jews and the Arabs that is important to writers like Shami and Smilansky, Burla and Reuveni. The Arab as an individual in an Arabic milieu, his donkey and his mule and his camel: they claim attention and excitement. In his memoirs Burla describes a four-day journey from Karak—ancient Kir Moab in Jordan—to Hebron as a disguised Arab in the company of Arabs. It affords a glimpse into the primitive landscape and the simple mores of Arabs in the second decade of the century.[31] At the same time, the first contacts between Arab and Jew are explored. The problem of cheap Arab labor that competed with not so cheap Jewish labor disturbed Agnon, Zemah and other writers as is evident in the former's novel *Yesterday, Day Before Yesterday* and in the latter's novel *First Year*.[32] In the face of that problem Zemah's protagonists and, especially, Agnon's protagonists Isaac Kummer and Jedediah Rabinowitz cease to be individuals; they are Jews competing with gentiles not only for the sake of a livelihood, but also for the possession of the Land.

Socialist complications exercised the mind of Shamir who sympathized with the exploited Jew and Arab. For him the exploiters were the Jewish gentlemen-farmers who owned a great deal of acreage and a great labor force. In a passage of the novel *Under the Sun* he characterizes them in the vocabulary borrowed from extreme Arab nationalists:

> These lords will bring destruction to the Land of Israel . . . If they [the Arabs] come to them and slaughter them, we are not obliged to lift a finger . . . These are not brothers.[33]

Writers like Hayyim Hazaz and Aaron Megged evaded this perverse ideology. The former depicted in his novel *In One Yoke*[34] an individual Arab, Abu Yusef—a peasant turned prison guard—as an admirer of Jewish courage. The latter told the poignant story of an Arab who had to abandon his home, and noted that Arab's self-abasement in face of Israeli tenacity and perseverance.

> Israel—good. . . Good that they came here. We are dung, we Arabs. Not worth even the dung of the camel. Not even the dung of the donkey. May it be wiped out—the name and the memory of the entire Arab legion . . . and the King Abdallah and the King Farouk and that one—I forgot his name—from Syria and the one from Lebanon . . .[35]

The traditional impossibility for the Jew of adjusting to a world where people kill and are killed—this is the burden of the message from the mouth of the protagonist Absalom in Phinehas Sadeh's novel *On Man's Condition*.[36] The radicalism of Absalom stems from two unusual acts: one dictated by necessity, one dictated by choice. He kills an Arab soldier in a retaliatory raid against Jordan and lives through a crisis which dogs his life: he leaves the army, he isolates himself in Jerusalem, he is reunited with his sister Abigail after a separation of many years, and he commits incest. The mystic justification for the state of sin is an esoteric tradition: the Messianic world is a world without sin. But while the Pharaohs indulged in breaking an almost universal taboo, the young Jew who attempts to live beyond good and evil, achieves doom rather than redemption. In his search for renewed and meaningful relationships with the Deity he loses contact with society. But, in a strange poem, Sadeh encounters the false Messiah, Jacob Frank, who tells him that "the trouble of the Jews stems from their faith in a male Messiah and the peace of mind of the Edomites stems from their faith in a female Messiah."

For she is the true Messiah. Guide and redemptress.
Happy he who will come before her and kiss the soles of her feet.
Happy he who will say to her: Sister, and she will say to him:
Brother.[37]

Strange lines these, strange conclusions. That a Hebrew poet of the twentieth century should need to have recourse to one of the most vulgar representatives of Messianism of almost two hundred years ago—Frank died in 1791—is a disturbing indication of a deep malaise among the younger writers of Israel.

It is also a disturbing phenomenon that Sadeh was not the only one who chooses suicide for his protagonist as a way out of a dilemma. In Yariv Ben-Aharon's novel *The Battle*[38] the protagonist commits suicide after his stint in the Sinai War. Suicide is also the solution of the young woman who becomes involved with an Arab and cannot endure her pregnancy.[39] In Ehud Ben-Ezer's novel *Nor the Battle to the Strong*[40] the chief character, a university student, cannot reconcile his passion for a private life with his public obligation, specifically, his service in the army. He also commits suicide, in effect, by exposing his body to bullets.

Poignant expression was given to the general frustration by the poet Meir Wieselthier, who deplored with bitter irony the unity of the Mediterranean landscape on the one hand, the disunity of its peoples on the other:

All of us travel by trains of reflection.
Winter and frost have gone, spring with shoot upon shoot
Is here. Away with acrimony, hurray for lucidity.
We shall never get from Lod to Beirut.[41]

And in the gripping story "The White City"[42] an Israeli soldier faces the great moment of truth in his life: "One murder will lead to another and one humiliation will lead to another and there'll never be an end to it. . . . When I kill others, my life loses its integrity."

In the "Story of an Olive Tree"[43] Benjamin Tammuz also sympathizes with the Arab and takes an antagonistic view of his countrymen. An olive tree—symbol of earthliness and rootedness and object of Mahmud Tawil's love—is uprooted when the Arab and his family abandon the farm. The biblical attachment to the soil is romanticized at the expense of the rootless Jewish settler from Europe. In another story "Swimming Contest"[44] an Arab who, as a young man, excelled in the aquatic sport, is killed in the War of Independence and mourned by his Israeli friend. And the loss—keenly felt and keenly articulated—becomes a symbol of defeat in victory: "I was defeated. We all were defeated." In "Meeting at Al Abridge"[45] Ode, son of a Bedouin sheikh, and a Jew fall into each other's arms after an interval of twenty-six years.

The Israeli stories of the Megged brothers, Yizhar, Shamir, and Orpaz suffer artistically from comparison with the stories of Amos Oz and the fictive and dramatic work of A.B. Yehoshua whose subtlety of portraiture and semi-surrealist style place them in the forefront of modern Israeli literature. The difference in their attitude toward the Arab is this: for Yizhar and his generation the Arab presents a problem in the realm of ethics; for Oz and Yehoshua and their generation the Arab presents an evil menace, an enemy who is as ruthless as the desert sun. The first collection of stories by Amos Oz (1939–   ) bears a symbolic title: *The Lands of the Jackal*.[46] The howling, wailing animal and the ever-present dispenser of death are common occurrences:

> Suddenly, with numbing swiftness, you are surrounded by them, besieged and petrified. Their eyes burn with eternal hatred. Their opened mouths breathe heavily, their crooked knives glisten in their hands. They curse you with abrupt sounds, with sounds choked with anger. Their stinking rotten teeth are bared against you with beastly threat. Their dirtied hands delve in your flesh with fevered anger . . .[47]

The inimical landscape is paralleled by the inimical man who threatens life in city and village. The rural cooperative is especially sensitive to this enmity. For the landscape breathes peace but man disturbs its hallowed air. In Oz's novel *My Michael*[48] a girl falls in love and marries. She and her husband and their child live an ordinary life, yet she loses her sanity. The Arab twins, Aziz and Halil, who were her playmates, become death-dealing guerrillas in her hallucinatory imagination.

In his novel, *Another Place*,[49] Amos Oz juxtaposed the holocaust and the kibbutz, Israelism and Arabism. In a sense he offered a parallel to the hammer and anvil. Eva Harish, the German Jewess married to a Hebrew poet in a Galilean kibbutz *Mezudat Ram*, returns to Munich in Germany after the holocaust. There, together with her new husband, Isaac Hamburger, she opens a nightclub. The partner, Zechariah Siegfried Berger, is a demoralized victim of the holocaust. In time he comes as an emissary to the kibbutz with an unholy mission—to seduce Eva's daughter away from her Israeli roots. He fails. Idealism wins. This is one confrontation: the bloody European heritage that almost extinguished Jewry, and the attempt to reconstruct an independent life in Israel. There is also a second confrontation. The new Israelism is impeded by rising Arabism. The kibbutz in the verdant valley, three kilometers from the boundary, symbolizes Israel. The raw mountains of the Golan: they are the threat posed by Syria. A retired colonel who visits the kibbutz as a tourist observes to his Israeli guide that from the military point of view the situation is hopeless. The Israeli guide is unperturbed: "different laws of gravity"[50] govern the country. There is a disparity between the geological and geopolitical facts."[51] The impossible reality, the reality of the impossible: this seems to be the message of Jewish history, this seems to be the intent of the novel. Siegfried is cast as spokesman of the impossible reality: "it seems that Jewish fate pursues Jews everywhere."[52] In the kibbutz, the nightly prayer of perseverance, the reality of the impossible must win: "Would that the night would end without the transfer of children to shelters."[53] Besides the prayer, the historic consciousness, the pride of achievement is transmitted in a lesson from teacher to pupils:

A generation ago this valley was desolate, wild waters engulfed it and spread contagious diseases, thorn and thistle grew here, foxes and evil jackals wailed at night, owls hooted among the ruins. Do you see the bald mountains there? That's how this valley was in those days. Your fathers and mothers did not come here with intent of war, they did not teach their hands to strike with the fist. But a destructive, threatening force endangers our work. . . . There is no hatred in our heart. . . They, over there, on the mountain, they are blind, they don't know what they do . . . not the Arabs are our enemy, but hatred. Let us guard against the contagion of hatred.[54]

It is the poet Reuben Harish—plain and pithy—who characterizes the Arab-Israeli syndrome in no uncertain terms.

This war cannot possibly end at all. It is the war of light and darkness, the desert and the town, the mountain and the valley . . . an eternal war.[55]

This is a stark and sincere and simplified statement, a repetition of the final days of the second commonwealth, Essene asceticism and gentile profligacy as described in The Scroll of the Sons of Light and the Sons of Darkness. The Arabs have become a symbol, a paradigm of enmity. Thus a soldier, mad at another man, thinks: "Such people must be broken. Like Arabs."[56] But there are gentler voices and opinions. Arab and Jew claim the land: "Each one says that his ancestors lived in the land and each one is absolutely right."[57] The dénouement of the novel is surprisingly melodramatic: the battle over a few acres of land, ridiculed by Voltaire in Candide, reaches a climax of fire and crossfire in the novel Another Place. People are killed, people die, the shelling exacts its toll. Nogah marries Rami, a member of the kibbutz. The corrupt stranger, Siegfried from Germany, is asked to leave the kibbutz which went through its ordeal of fire "to call this last occurrence by the name of love."[59]
by the name of love."[59]
In his latest novel Touch the Water, Touch the Wind[60] Amos Oz has executed a tour de force. The central character Elisha Pomeranz—a teacher in a gymnasium—experiences the horrors of the holocaust. He had been hiding in the Polish woods and emigrated to Israel ten years after his weird progress through the stations of his personal cross. There he first settled in an abandoned Arab house by the Sea of Galilee—

To live there and to create there the pure life, the free life. There all hopes will materialize, deeds will silence thoughts.[61]

Perhaps the protagonist feigns naiveté. For he is also a philosopher who pursues his researches somewhere in the twilight regions between pure mathematics and theoretical physics. In parallel chapters to the story of Elisha Pomeranz, the story of beautiful Stefa, his former wife, is told with obvious relish: her marriage to a spy with a promising career, the hanging of the spy and her inheritance of the spy's post, her rise to power, her meeting with almighty Stalin. This woman of valor rejoins her husband. Both had accomplished impossible feats. She had achieved political power, he had achieved global fame with the solution of the mathematical riddle of infinity. But the greatness of the unbelievable pair is related rather than realized. And the novel is saved from artistic disaster by the graceful manipulation of plot and character, style and mood.

A.B. Yehoshua (1936–   ) is a visionary in a writer's garb. In the play *Night in May*[62] he confronts the fates of individuals with the fate of the nation on the eve of the Six-Day War. But the fate of the individual—in a situation which partakes of the absurdities of Ionesco and the grimness of Beckett—is his real concern. In an interesting story, "In the Beginning of the Summer of '70,"[63] A.B. Yehoshua has chosen, as the title indicates, the War of Attrition as his theme. It is refracted through many characters, chiefly through the mind of an old Bible teacher who reconstructs in a monolog the alleged death and resurrection of his son. In form and format it resembles the monolog of Camus in *The Stranger*; in content it abounds in thanatic tensions created by the erroneous information about the death of a son; in course of time, it changes into uncertainty and, finally, into certainty of the son's survival. At the same time the story is more than the tragedy occasioned by the Jewish-Arab war. It is, primarily, the tragedy of father and son, teacher and student. The generational gap is most apparent in the attitude to tradition. The older generation is driven by the dream of regeneration on the basis of old Messianic promises; the younger generation is sacrificed on the altar of that dream without knowing or appreciating its cogency. In that sense, Yehoshua's story is a modern version of the intended sacrifice of Isaac by his father Abraham. The sacral Messianism of the father is superseded by the profane Messianism of the son. Too much identity, too little practicality: that is the older generation. Too little identity, too serious a proclivity for dying in the defense of the country: that is the paradox of the younger generation.

"In the Beginning of the Summer of '70" is a powerful story, stark in its realism and in its implications. In another story "Facing the Forests" an Israeli student, engaged in historical research, becomes a temporary fire watcher in a forest. His function: to prevent fires. His performance: responsibility for the setting of a fire by his friendly enemy, the mute Arab, who was the original inhabitant of the Arab village that was supplanted by the forest. The orchestration of the crusade motif and the modern Israeli peace-in-war motif in the story is one of the highlights of contemporary Hebrew literature. The compulsive awareness of the crusades engulfs the student's thoughts and feelings. A group of tourists in the forest is likened to "a caravan of crusaders." Even the mute Arab is given a history lesson on the crusading times by the fire watcher:

> He tells him about the enthusiasm, the cruelty, the Jews who commit suicide, the Children's Crusade; things he culled superficially from books, his own unsubstantiated theories. His voice is full of tenderness, overflowing with imagination. The Arab listens— absorbed, deeply tensed. He is filled with hate.[64]

This crusading motif also dominates Isaac Shalev's book *The Story of Gabriel Tirosh*.[65] The protagonist, who is a teacher, uses the crusaders as an analog of our times. They were qualitatively superior, but quantitatively inferior to the indigenous population. They failed. But the Jews of the present must learn from their mistakes. They must not fail; they must not become—as the crusaders did—a passing episode in the East.

In poetry, the crusading theme had reached its apogee in the extremist work of Gruenberg and Ratosh. It reappeared in a poem by Dalia Rabikowitz. With undeniable poetic vigor she described a gorgeous company of crusaders—kings and commoners—who sailed away in golden ships in the twelfth century:

> Twin-necked ships sailed to Egypt.
> Beautiful armies—electrified—besieged Acre.
> They were all swift knights with the bishop's blessing upon them.
> A big herd of wolves.
> How their blue eyes gleamed
> At the sight of the palm in the wind . . .
> They built many forts,
> Snipers' towers and basalt walls . . .[66]

Then the inevitable happened. Saladin, "the dog, the heretic," came from the East and destroyed the crusaders' kingdom. In Dalia Rabikowitz's poem there is a faint possibility of a masochistic identification with the crusaders. And this is irony carried to extremes. The crusader, enemy of the Jew, becomes a Jew in an imaginative leap of an Israeli poet.

In a novella on the crusaders—without overt allusions to the Arab-Israeli conflict—Amos Oz delves into the Jewish-Christian conflict with surprising originality. For his protagonist, Count Guillaume of Touron who begins his crusading adventure with a motley band of peasants, serfs, and outlaws, continues on the usual road of cruelty in 1096: robbery, torture, liquidation of individual Jews. But the Count is a bit of an introvert:

> His heart told him . . . that even Jerusalem was not the goal of his journey . . . and perhaps Andrés [the piper] is the hidden Jew, or perhaps not Andrés but he himself.[67]

This is the point of the story: the Jew is evil incarnate, subtly insinuating himself into Christian society to such an extent that the true Christian, like the crusading Count, begins to doubt his identity and conceives the possibility that the Christian is the Jew. The enemy as the self: here is a new dimension of a historical conflict that is not without possible overtones of the present conflict.

But new voices are heard in the land: the voice of an Eliav, the dovish Israeli, the voice of the writer Rachel Ambar. That the latter, a native of Tiberias, could write a poignant story or rather novella of one hundred and thirty-four pages on Arab-Israeli symbiosis: that, too, is a miracle of renascent Jewry in the Holy Land. The patriarchal setting of *House in the Street of the Messiah*[68] is inadvertently symbolic. Since, according to legend, the Messiah will come out of Tiberias, the city fathers have given the name of Messiah to one of its streets. And in that city, in that street, a Jewish family lives its uneventful life in mandatory Palestine with an Arab shepherd Halil who tends the sheep and with his wife Amane who tends to the household with the loyalty of a faithful servant. But the peaceful atmosphere is threatened when Mahmoud, a bloodthirsty scoundrel, incites a mob to bloodshed in a "Day of Long Knives." The scheme is frustrated but the reality of the experience cannot be easily extinguished.

That it was possible, on neutral ground in America, for an Israeli author named Amos Elon and an Egyptian named Sana Hassan, daughter of Mahmoud Hassan Pasha, former ambassador of Egypt to the U.S. and the U.N., to collaborate on a book, *Between Enemies*,[69] is the guarantee of coexistence and cooperation. Not the fire-eating speeches of politicians on both sides of the fence, but the gentle and sensitive voices of the intellectuals and the artists will win, the voice of the Israeli who senses "a persistent predilection for self-censure" in Israeli literature and the voice of the Arab who feels that the work of some Arab writers, a Naguib Mahfuz or a Tewfik al Hakim, points to "another morality, utter repugnance of all war and of the suffering it inflicts, and which it will continue to inflict mercilessly if the differences are not peacefully resolved."[70] Theirs is the future.

23
Children's Paradise[1]

A TWO-PRONGED concern with children appears in Hebrew literature from its earliest beginnings. On the one hand parents and teachers and elderly folk are admonished to treat their charges with efficient adequacy; on the other hand the very young are provided with literary materials which are meant to serve their intellectual needs. A biblical example of advice on child education—much as it disturbs modern sensibilities—has been quoted throughout the ages as a pedagogical principle of incalculable value: "He who spares the rod hates his son."[2] Another biblical proverb which has met with approval by amateurish and professional psychologists exhorts the educator to "educate a child according to his way and when he is old he will not depart from it."[3] In rabbinic times parents were warned against favoritism such as Jacob displayed in his attitude to Joseph,[4] and against unfulfilled promises to children.[5]

In the first centuries of the current era attempts were made to deal with the child on his own terms. Alphabetical ditties and mnemotechnical devices—jointly or separately—have been devised to lure and inure the child's mind to learning. This alphabetizing propensity continued into the present and found its classic expression in the Yiddish song by Mark Markovich Warshawski (1848–1907) which was on everybody's lips at the turn of the century:

> Little fire on the hearth,
> Much warmth in the room.
> Teacher teaches little ones
> The alphabet's loom.[6]

This song was part of an oral tradition of poems, lullabies, and stories committed to print decades and even centuries after wide dissemination among the people. It is not without interest that the first play in modern Hebrew literature—*Comedy on Marriage* by Leone da Sommo[7]—contains two prose dialogs with a child's participation. In the eighteenth century the first serious attempts were made to produce books for children. Abraham Cohen in his *Beginners' Hebrew for Children*[8] presented his young readers with easy legends and parables. And Judah Lev Ben-Zeev, grammarian and lexicographer, devoted his considerable pedagogical skills to children. His reader, in two parts,[9] includes songs for children such as "We Are Children"[10] which achieved and held their popularity for more than a century. And David Samość, poet and teacher in the early years of the enlightenment, devoted his literary work primarily to children. As the author of the first Hebrew play for children he endeavored to develop their moral traits through didactic dialogs.[11] As the author of the first biblical history for children[12] he fostered knowledge of the past and pride in Jewish achievements. He also adapted Joachim Heinrich Campe's adaptation of Daniel Defoe's *Robinson Crusoe*[13] and his *Discovery of America*;[14] he even adapted a biblical divertissment on the childhood of Moses by Stéphanie Félicité du Crest de Saint-Aubin, Countess of Genlis (1746–1830).[15]

By the middle of the century Hebrew readers for governmental Jewish schools in Russia were being published in an ever increasing tempo. Hebrew writers began to devote some of their efforts to pedagogical literature. Mapu, as is well known, composed three readers for children and teenagers: *Teach the Lad, Amon Pedagog* and *Der Hausfranzose*.[16] The most popular text, *Amon Pedagog*, was designed for Jewish youth just as *Teach the Lad* was aimed at children of seven and eight years of age. The latter was a primer, the former, a combination of grammar and reader. It hoped "to teach Jewish youth impeccable Hebrew" and it proudly announced that goal on the title page. Mapu also stressed moral values in its lingual exercises which were published with excisions as a continuous narrative under the title *The House of Hanan*[17] by Joseph Klausner. *Der Hausfranzose*—a French textbook as the title indicates—was probably to be followed by textbooks for Russian and German.[18] The three textbooks were not only exercises in pedagogy: they were extensions of Mapu's literary works and they shared the author's predilections for purism in style and naiveté in characterization, especially in *The House of Hanan*. In a certain sense they marked an advance over his novels: they used rabbinic Hebrew more generously. By the end of the century the first periodicals for children appeared in Jerusalem and in Lyck: *'Olam Katan*[19] in 1893 under the editorship of Eliezer Ben-Yehudah, Yehudah Grasovski-Gur

(1862–1950) and David Idelovitch (1863–1943); *Gan Sha'ashuim* in 1899 under the editorship of Abraham Mordecai Piórko (1853–1933) who devoted his main literary efforts to children. The first was too short-lived to exercise any influence, the second—unlike the editor's name—was neither light, nor limpid, nor "feathery." Its didactic stance, its mournful note, its hackneyed nationalism was ubiquitous.

While Piórko was busy with the compilation and publication of children's books in the diaspora at the turn of the century, Ben-Yehudah, Gur, and Idelovitch issued textbooks, stories, and fables for children. Gur probably played the same role in the Land of Israel which Ben-Avigdor carved out for himself in the diaspora: an incessant stream of textbooks and readers, translations and original works emerged from his pen or under his imprimatur. Somewhat later Leon Kipnis (1894–   ) created children's works with exclusive fervor for more than fifty years. He rendered their imaginative world and their rich experiences in an idiom that won him their love and admiration. There was hardly a holiday or national event which did not summon his obedient muse; there was hardly a theatrical performance for children that did not utilize his plays.[20]

Another periodical named *'Olam Katan* appeared in Warsaw between 1901 and 1905 under the joint editorship of Abraham Leb Shalkovich, better known under his pseudonym Ben-Avigdor (1860–1921),[21] and Samuel Leb Gordon (1865–1933). But the gaiety and insouciance associated with children was as nonexistent in *'Olam Katan* as in the life of Jewry. Microcosm paralleled macrocosm in tone and tenor. Only later, periodicals for children between the two world wars, especially *Ha-Kokab* and *Ben-Kokab* under the editorship of Aaron Luboshitzki (1874–1942), the monthly *'Eden* under the editorship of Daniel Persky (1887–1962), *Ha-Doar la-No'ar* under the joint editorship of Persky and Simhah Rubenstein (1889–   ) in New York, and *Davar li-Yeladim* which began to appear in 1936 and maintained an enviable longevity—it still continues its publication today—achieved maturity and correctness of expression.

On the threshold of the twentieth century the three great stars of the modern renaissance in Hebrew literature—Bialik, Tschernichowsky and Shneour—revitalized poetry and prose for children. Bialik created a wealth of imagery, fun, and humor for the little ones. He drew on the rich resources of midrashic and folkloric literature, translated and paraphrased from the Yiddish, invented imaginative entertainment. As a matter of fact his first contribution to children's literature was a Yiddish poem that became popular immediately after its

publication,"Under the Green Little Trees."[22] His two great collections
of children's poems[23] were illustrated by Nahum Gutman. His rhymed
tale *Knight of Onions and Knight of Garlic*[24] still delights readers
with its expansive exuberance. It has been stated with ample justification that his entire oeuvre may be characterized as *la recherche du
temps d'enfance*.[25]

Saul Tschernichowsky was also aware of a deep kinship with the
world of children; one of his collections of children's poetry also was illustrated by Nahum Gutman.[26] In his thirty-fourth year he published
his first collection of *Poems for Jewish Children*.[27] And throughout his
life an abundance of prose and poetry for children characterized his
creativity. It was Jewish to the core. It not only celebrated Judaism in
its festive and daily garb, it judaized nature. If Tschernichowsky's
tales—with the solitary exception of the verse-tale "Story of a Wolf,
Son of a Wolf"[28]—are less poignant than his poems, it is because his
prose never equaled his poetry.[29] But he had a firm belief that the
world exists everywhere and always "by virtue of the virtues of the
little ones."[30]

Shneour began his literary career in the periodical *'Olam Katan*
which was especially designed for children, and he was barely twenty
when he published two collections of children's songs.[31] Throughout
his life he wrote poetry which was designed to stimulate the senses and
the sensitivity of the little ones. His prose for children was equally
abundant: legends, tales, and even an epic of the forest flowed from his
pen incessantly. The poet of plenty cannot be accused of unconcern for
children.

Other poets of stature, Fichmann, Hameiri, Cahan, Katzenelson, Judah Steinberg, I.D. Berkowitz, Frischmann and Berdyczewski, wrote
for children with a zest not common among serious writers who aspire
to solid fame. Fichmann must be singled out as a pedagogic force *par
excellence*: his numerous anthologies for the young, his numerous poems and stories for children and, especially, his biographical stories of
writers and sages, statesmen and heroes, were designed to stimulate
latent estheticism and a spirit of emulation among the very young.

Avigdor Hameiri used his innovative élan in his work for children.
He not only taught them "the wisdom of animals;" he directed their attention to the stars and other astronomical phenomena, to the extrava-
gances of Karl Friedrich Hieronymus, Freiherr von Münchhausen
(1720–1797) and to the delicate tales of Andersen. A Hungarian by
birth he was in a position to translate the immensely popular *Csibi* by
Béla Szenes, father of the paratrooper and poet and martyr, Hannah

Szenes. The book, written with tongue in cheek, depicts the story of a poor child who manages to get an education in a private school for the rich where everyone is judged according to his clothes and social position.

Another poet of note, Jacob Cahan, deserves a special accolade as a writer for children: he emphasized joy rather than the despair that was the common note of Hebrew poetry for centuries. And one of his better poems discloses a bright, sunny temperament—a rarity in Hebrew literature.[32]

Isaac Katzenelson, light and graceful and childlike by temperament, lived in a world peopled by innocent dreams of childhood. In Lodz where he spent many years of his life, he organized a drama circle for children and fed it with his own plays and playlets which breathed an uncommon *joie de vivre*, a reckless humor, an almost destructive delight in the misery of his people's enemies such as *Stupid King Ahasverus* or *Purim Merry Makers*.[33] So enamored was he of children that he wrote more than two dozen books of verse and tales for them. But his abundance was surpassed by that of Judah Steinberg who was nicknamed "the Hebrew Andersen." This was an inaccurate sobriquet: he lacked the perceptive and reflective qualities which characterized the Danish author. But in the parable and the fable that were the favorite vehicles for his brief children's tales, he achieved mastery of style and grace in content. If he emphasized Jewish history, Jewish law, and Jewish lore, it was because this conceptual trinity appealed to him and to his potential readers.

Isaac Dov Berkowitz, who excelled in translations of Shalom Aleyhem, did not exclude the children's stories of the Yiddish humorist: "Motl Pesi the Cantor's Son" or "The Penknife." But the scathing critic, David Frischmann, was more aware than his fellow writers of the need for children's books. To return to children the childhood which was rooted out of Jewish children for many centuries: that was his plea and his goal. Though his quantitave output for children was meager, he managed to convey to them the stories of Herzl and Nordau in splendid paraphrase. Quest for quality impelled him also to translate tales of Grimm. While he drew upon his vast knowledge of the literatures of the world, Micah Joseph Berdyczewski concentrated on Jewish tales exclusively. More than a thousand of them were collected posthumously by his widow and his son, the critic Immanuel ben Gorion, in six volumes under the title *From the Source of Jewry*.[34] And he also adapted tales and legends for youthful readers in less forbidding quantities.[35]

Contemporary poets and novelists devoted their considerable talents to children. Abraham Shlonsky, in imitation of the American cartoon world, hebraized Mickey Mouse and transformed him into Miki Mahu. From that name he extracted endless rhyming possibilities for his lingual wizardry. A disciple of Shlonsky, Solomon Tanny, delighted children with fantasies of laughing houses and doves fluttering in and out of dreams in his prose and poetry. Another disciple of Shlonsky, Aaron Amir, translated Andersen's tales for children.[36] And a sensitive poet like Aaron Zeev (1900-1968) achieved almost complete identification with the world of the child. The inquisitive innocence, the startling observation, the unconscious depth of the little world—they are mirrored with imaginative precision in his books. *White Doves* and *Wild Flowers*:[37] these are the appropriate symbols which pervaded his poetry. The very popular poet, Nathan Alterman, managed to transmit to children his love for the circus: the clowns, the acrobats, the trained animals. And he gave his unstinting efforts to the translation of Winnie-the-Pooh by Alan Alexander Milne (1882-1956). Yehuda Amichai, with his penchant for adventure, transplanted an Israeli child of "more than five and not yet six," Ronny, to New York and dispatched him back—unscathed by the American adventure—to Israel. In the story-in-verse the child protagonist is exposed to American baseball and football, automats and skyscrapers, subways and escalators: a wonder-world seen with wondering, eager eyes.[38] And the poet O. Hillel tells the story-in-verse of an Israeli child's reflections on a queer uncle.[39] Even American Hebrew poets—Moses Feinstein for instance—contributed children's poems to Hebrew literature.[40]

Of contemporary novelists, Yigal Mossinsohn achieved enormous successes with adventure stories for children in Israel. He charmed them with his tales of *Hasambah*[41] which depicted young heroism in victorious fight with ubiquitous enemies in and outside the Land of Israel. War or near-war in mandatory Palestine and in the battles which followed independence and statehood—these were also the burdens of Nathan Shaham's stories for children under the collective title: *One Can Reveal Already*.[42] In another work *That's Because*[43] he repeated the theme with humorous variations and added adventure stories which reflected the early years of the century in Turkish Palestine.

When women emerged as writers in substantial numbers, they concentrated on the prime concern of their lives: children. A few devoted all their efforts to them. Thus Miriam Yalan-Stekelis drew her inspiration from a source hallowed by Bialik: folklore. The kid and the dove, the doll and the bunny, the teddy bear and the bad, bad wolf—they populate her world in musical cadences. She richly deserved the Israel Prize for Children's Poetry in 1957 because she shared the blessed innocence of the very young. Another writer for children, Yemimah Avidar Tchernowitz, published legends for children since her twelfth year. Her vivid style and her narrative ability delighted the very young; the drawings of Nahum Gutman enhanced some of her many volumes and presented an additional attraction. But it was adventurism in her stories which captivated "the little world." Her book *Eight in Pursuit of One*[44]—the story of a group of children in pursuit of a German spy—was not only the delight of children in the Land of Israel; it was translated into English, it was made into a moving picture and it was presented on the stage. Serious poets like Anda Pinkerfeld-Amir and Leah Goldberg, both city-bred and sophisticated, and Fania Bergstein, member of a cooperative, have written books for children which expanded their horizons and brought them nearer to the experience of rural and urban landscapes. In many instances their poems have been the first literary experiences of children in modern Israel and sources of gay enrichment. If they can be faulted at times, it is because they make too easy transitions from frivolity to triviality, from playfulness to superficiality.

24
Neglected Areas in Hebrew Literature: Drama; Humor; Criticism

Drama

In his essay "On Polarity: Dialogue After the Theater" Buber made some sage remarks about drama:

> All poetry tends toward drama. Every lyric work is a dialogue the partner of which speaks in a superhuman language . . . Every epic work is a dialogue in which the Fates speak along with the poet . . . The drama is pure dialogue; all feeling and all happening has in it become dialogue.

Buber could have gone one step farther to say that dialog is essentially a monolog of self with self. But that would have meant modification of a position which he achieved in *I and Thou* after considerable soul-searching.

Drama is probably as old as the earliest literary remains of mankind. For it is based on the ritual and the myth of seasonal death and rebirth. It appears in rudimentary or fragmentary lines of Egyptian and Hittite, Babylonian and Hebrew and Canaanite peoples. Since the Egyptian is the oldest extant literature of the Ancient Near East, it is not surprising to find there the oldest vestiges of drama: a papyrus, written in the time of Sesostris I (c. 1970 B.C.E.) where material from the time of the first dynasty (c. 3300 B.C.E.) was undoubtedly repro-

293

duced.[1] Greece, which is generally accepted as the birthplace of drama, must now be regarded as a comparative latecomer in the development of the dramatic genre.

That the Jews created an embryonic dramatic literature before the Greeks must come as a shock to people who have been educated in the universities of the West and who have been taught that drama is a monopoly of the Hellenic genius. Yet the weight of evidence seems to point to pre-Hellenic developments of the drama. The Hebrews, along with their Semitic and non-Semitic neighbors, cultivated the form of the dialog to the accompaniment of dance and song and music which are essential to early forms of drama and which are recorded in Biblical literature.[2]

Some of the biblical psalms were more than individual expressions of piety. They possessed a liturgical function and were recited at the recurrent New Year festival in symbolic enthronement ceremonials of the Deity. In them God has been depicted as acquiring kingship after the destruction of his enemies—the Sea or the Dragon—and establishing order, restoring fertility to the land.[3]

The Song of Songs has also been regarded as a dramatic composition. It was no less a man than Ernest Renan who endeavored to straitjacket those charming poems of love into a drama in five acts and an epilog.[4] He justified his daring in a lengthy and learned introduction and arrived at the conclusion that the Song of Songs can be regarded as something between a true drama and a pastoral in dialog.[5] Renan was followed by many scholars and writers. In our own day Max Brod, the sensitive novelist and editor of Kafka, used considerable ingenuity in dramatizing the story of Esther.[6]

The friend of John Chrysostom, the Cilician bishop Theodore of Mopsuestia (c. 350-428),[7] already regarded Job as a dramatic composition. He propounded the theory that Job was patterned after Greek dramas and that its author was familiar with Greek literature. Ever since that time numerous scholars and writers persuaded themselves and others that Job was a drama. In the aftermath of the renaissance, Theodore Beza (1519-1605), the brilliant friend, biographer, and successor of Calvin, considered the book of Job a tragedy.[8] In our own century, Horace Kallen insisted—and he was taken seriously by as seminal a scholar as George Foote Moore—that Job was a Greek tragedy.[9] Charmed by the philosophical impasse of the hero, he regarded the biblical book as a Euripidean tragedy and its author as one acquainted with Euripidean form but "un-Greek in his emulation of it."[10] Like a Euripidean tragedy, the book of Job relates in a prolog the preliminary version of the legend; the drama itself imitates the Euripidean *agon* in argumentative and emotional verse.

Kallen is perhaps the most daring of Job's exegetes. While a Goethe had drawn inspiration for his Faust from Job and, in our own time, Archibald MacLeish constructed a play *J.B.* and Robert Frost *A Masque of Reason* in imitation of the biblical Job, Kallen read a new Job into the biblical Job without substantial changes in the text. And even the daring hypothesis of Kallen was preceded by that of Karl Fries who detected Euripidean elements in the Book of Job[11] though he classified it categorically as a "philosophical dialog;"[12] and the Isaianic chapters, depicting the suffering "Servant of God," have been rearranged by Julian Morgenstern as a drama "patterned unmistakably after the classic Greek drama"[13] with chorus and two principal speakers: God and the Servant. It is possible, according to that erudite scholar, to arrange the drama into three acts "after the modern manner:"[14] the call of the Servant and the inauguration of his mission; the progress of the mission; the death of the Servant and the accomplishment of the mission. Morgenstern bolstered his daring hypothesis with the fact that in the middle of the fifth pre-Christian century the city of Dor, south of Mt. Carmel, was garrisoned by Athenian troops. The drama of the Suffering Servant, he argues, could have been composed by someone in the vicinity of Dor in the middle of the fifth century. And it may even have been influenced by "Greek drama which thrived so favorably in the Periclean age."[15] The chronological difficulty was solved ingeniously by Morgenstern. Since the drama must have been composed in the middle of the fifth, and Deutero-Isaiah lived in the middle of the sixth century, the latter could not have authored it. The anonymous playwright whose style resembled the style of Deutero-Isaiah was simply incorporated into the Book of Isaiah.

We have, then, many dramatic remains of various length in the Bible: The Song of Miriam, some Psalms, the Servant of God chapters,[16] the Song of Songs, the Book of Job. There is undoubtedly a great deal of arbitrariness in all the assumptions which pretend to find dramas in unexpected and unsuspected places. If every dialog in the Bible were to be regarded as rudimentary drama, then the genre would be abundantly represented in ancient Hebrew literature. Even Leviticus could be arranged in dramatic form with Moses and God as chief interlocutors, but this would be carrying the matter *ad absurdum*. Between informal dialog and formal drama there is an immense distance. The Greeks covered it, the Jews and their neighbors did not quite achieve that feat. Only toward the end of the biblical era and under the impact of the

Hellenistic environment, did the Jews produce tragedies which resembled the Greek models. They are all lost with the exception of 269 verses of a tragedy called *Exodus, Exagoge* in Greek. The name of the author, Ezekiel of Alexandria, has not been challenged, but the place of his birth and activity, the age in which he flourished, even his Jewish provenance—all these have been questioned by scholars. That he was not a Christian, that he was not living in Samaria, and that he probably flourished in the time of Ptolemy Euergetes (246-222) or a little later has been established with a fair degree of certainty.[17] It was in Alexandria that Ptolemy Philadelphus (285-247) fostered dramatic competitions, it was there that the Jews lived in the thousands, it was there that the Pentateuch was translated into Greek in the middle of the third century before the common era.

Exagoge is the only tragedy which survives—in fragmentary form. Other tragedies of Ezekiel, though attested to by Eusebius of Caesarea, Clement of Alexandria and Alexander Polyhistor, have been lost to posterity. *Exagoge* is an undoubted work of art though the verses in iambic trimeter are somewhat "less elegant"[18] than their Attic paradigms, especially Euripidean paradigms beloved by the author who based his play on Exodus but did not follow the Bible slavishly. Erroneously, he placed Midian in Libya; happily, he invented scenes like the dream of Moses about a man sitting on a throne reaching up to heaven and presenting him with the diadem and scepter. Ezekiel also inserted a description of a phoenix, a bird of extraordinary beauty, into his play.[19] But he was not lavish in the construction of the plot and, like his classic predecessors, kept the number of protagonists at a minimum. In a long monolog he had Moses relate the flight from Egypt to Midian, the fortunes or rather misfortunes of the Jews in Egypt from the arrival of Jacob and Jacob's issue, biographical incidents such as the killing of the Egyptian. The tragedy really begins with the encounter with Zipporah, the description of the dream and Reuel's interpretation as an indication of leadership on the part of Moses. It continues with the burning bush episode, the dialog between God and Moses, the description of the plagues, the promise of delivery, the Passover. A messenger describes the miraculous victory, the passage of the Red Sea, the wonderful oasis "where there were twelve springs of water and seventy palm trees."[20]

It was Emil Schürer who made the acute observation that the aim of Ezekiel's play was identical with the scriptural plays and the passion plays in the Christian Middle Ages: "to make the people . . . better acquainted with sacred history . . . and chiefly, to supplant—*oust* is the better verb for the German *verdrängen*—as far as possible profane and heathen pleasures . . ."[21] Wieneke argued that the play was probably meant to be read rather than produced.[22]

The search for drama in intervening centuries between the pre-Christian era and the renaissance yielded little or nothing—unless allegorical dialogs in verse of both a sacral and secular character, and satirical dialogs of an Abraham Ibn Ezra or Immanuel Frances—can be called drama. The attitude of the sages to theatrical performances was understandably inimical; the theater had obvious connections with levity and idolatry.[23] In disdainful remarks they juxtaposed "theaters and circuses" and "houses of learning and houses of prayer." And they hoped that, one day, theaters and circuses would be converted to places where Torah would be taught.[24]

The Hebrew theater was born in the first decade of the twentieth century when Nahum Zemah organized an itinerant troupe in Bialystok before the First World War. In 1917 he opened a Hebrew studio in Moscow and, after it received the status of a State Studio, he appealed to Stanislavsky for assistance. Thus it happened that on the advice of the latter, an Armenian, Vakhtangov, became the artistic *régisseur* of the Hebrew theater, Habimah, a post he held until his death in 1922. In 1926, during an artistic tour in Europe, the Hebrew theater severed its ties with Russia and, eventually, settled in Tel Aviv where it finally became the State Theater of Israel.[25] But the Hebrew drama still leads a meager existence as it has in the last four hundred years. Giuseppe Gallo's adaptation of *The Celestina,* Leone da Sommo's *Comedy on Marriage,* Moses Zacuto's mystery play *Hell Set* and dramatic poem *Foundation of the World* and Joseph Penço de la Vega's *Prisoners of Hope*—these few plays almost exhaust the Hebrew repertoire in the sixteenth and seventeenth centuries. In the eighteenth century Hisquiau David Franco Hofshi Mendes and Moses Hayyim Luzzatto delighted their few readers with biblical or allegorical plays,[26] two genres that were well represented in the last two hundred years.[27]

The historical play—that of Jacob Cahan, Harry Sackler, Mattathias Shoham—has the strongest claim to dramatic maturity in our century.[28] The plays of Aaron Megged and Aaron Ashman and Yehuda Amichai concentrate on biblical themes—from Adam and Eve through the dynastic entanglements of Saul to the prophets. Thus Megged uses the biblical material on the first man and woman as a paradigm of relationships between man and woman; Ashman explores the intricacies of *Michal, Saul's Daughter*[29] in a play of that name, and the timely analog of Nehemiah in his play *The Walls of Jerusalem.*[30] A.A. Kabak and Jacob Shabtai, Benjamin Galai and Israel Eliraz probe the depths of the human rather than the heroic stature of king David. Like Moshe Shamir, Benjamin Galai delves into the dramatic possibilities of the idealized king from Uriah's vantage point[31] and the period of the second commonwealth from Herodian rather than Yannaic perspectives.[32] With a theatrical imagination as supple as an acrobat's leap he conjures up relevances of distant pasts to the distracting present. Under the influence of Hazaz's "The Bridegroom of Blood" Eliraz dramatized an embittered Zipporah.[33] And Yehuda Amichai focused his attention on Jonah.

The post-biblical play is well represented by Moshe Shamir, Jacob Cahan, Nathan Agmon [Bistritski], S. Shalom and the single plays of Tschernichowsky and Hazaz. Both Hazaz and Agmon interested themselves in the period of Sabbatai Zevi in their plays; and both—Agmon in the play *Judas Iscariot*[34] and Hazaz in the unfinished novel on Jesus—attempted to wrestle with the theme of Christianity.

The contemporary plays of Shaham, Yehoshua Bar-Yosef and especially Nissim Aloni tend to entertain rather than to lay serious claim to critical consideration. The last named is hailed as "Israel's most original dramatist."[35] But he is merely a faint echo of the Theater of the Absurd, especially that of Samuel Beckett which he studied and absorbed in Paris. In his adaptation of Dudley Fitts's rendition of *Lysistrata* and in his version of O'Casey's *Purple Dust* he has missed the high poetry of the Greek master of comedy and the subtle poetry of the Irish playwright; and though he succeeded in having *The American Princess* staged in Oslo and *The Bride and the Butterfly Hunter* adapted for television in Israel, his artistic laurels have yet to be won.[36]

Even the very popular dramatization of a novel on the kibbutz—*He Walked in The Fields*—by Moshe Shamir, and a play on the War of Independence, *In the Plains of the Negev*,[37] by Yigal Mossinsohn—verge on the melodramatic. And the plays on the holocaust by Leah Goldberg and Ben-Zion Tomer also tend to melodrama. Only the realistic plays of Berkowitz and Shenhar, which owe much to Ibsen and Chekhov, and the modernistic plays of Alterman and A.B. Yehoshua stand out as harbingers of fruitful developments for the future.

Critics who tried to justify the dramatic deficiency of Jews were often led to absurd statements. Dov Sadan argued that a nation which produced the theatrical and dramatical ceremony of a Passover Seder or a Yom Kippur eve and day "needs no other drama and no other theater"; the need for dramatic performance among Jews grew in proportion to the erosion of traditionalism, which lacked no dramatic or theatrical elements in the worship in the synagogue, in the study of the rabbinic academy, in the courtyards of the Hasidim and at their festive tables. In brief, the Sabbath, the holidays, the customs, and the ceremonies make the theater superfluous.[38] What Sadan neglects to see is that an event may be dramatic and/or theatrical in the highest degree without being either drama or theater until it is articulated in monolog, dialog and multilog.

Humor

Incongruity which provokes or evokes risibility: this is humor. Sophisticated speech in the mouth of a rustic, frivolities or innuendoes on a solemn occasion such as a funeral or a wedding ceremony, solemnity on a trivial occasion, self-esteem in lieu of self-abasement, pride in lieu of modesty—these are occasions and situations which give rise to laughter. The literatures of all nations teem with examples. Ring Lardner (1885-1933), the American humorist, produces in "*I Gaspiri*" a bit of dialog which is the soul of incongruity:

> First Stranger: Where was you born?
> Second Stranger: Out of wedlock.
> First Stranger: That's a mighty pretty country around there.[39]

Another example: somebody declares, "If I do not praise myself, nobody else will." The sophisticated listener will savor the perversion of a well-known adage, "Let the stranger praise you, and not your own mouth."[40] In shifting the punctuation mark you can pervert the adage: "Let the stranger praise you. If not [if he neglects to do it] let your own mouth do it." The story of the Messiah of Chelm mixes fact and fancy in incongruous measure. Messiah—as far as Jews are concerned—has not come, but he may come unexpectedly any day, any minute. Though the simple and the simpletons believe in the immediacy of Messianic times, the millennium is millennia away. The Jews of Chelm—a favorite butt of ridicule—feared that they would miss the Messiah when he came: their town in Eastern Europe was isolated by mountains. So they built a tower on a mountaintop and hired a man to watch and alert everybody to the arrival of the Messiah. The pay was poor; the watchman complained to the city elders. But they thought they had a legitimate reason for their niggardliness: "The pay is low but the work is steady."

The golden future was a foil for the miserable present. Incongruity fed on self-laceration, self-laceration reverted to incongruity:

—Are you ever so happy that you have to cry?
—No. But sometimes I feel so wretched that I have to laugh.

Spontaneous dialog in daily social intercourse was the rich source of oral humor. But the humorists who invented it in the solitude of their study were few and far between. Shalom Aleyhem was the first and last Jewish humorist to achieve an international reputation. In the sixty years that have elapsed since his death a number of humorists have plied the sad art of satire but none has reached his exalted heights.

While Shalom Aleyhem laughed good-humoredly at his miserable, all too human types in the *shtetl*, the emergent homeland created its first major institutions and its first minor humorists. When the Jewish welfare board of Germany, the so-called *Hilfsverein der deutschen Juden* founded in 1901, began to build the embryonic School of Technology, the Technion, in Haifa, it insisted on German as the language of instruction. The battle of languages in 1913—German versus Hebrew— ended in defeat for German. And one of the protagonists in the fierce combat was a journalist who published at irregular intervals satiric newspapers like *La-Yehudim* (1909-1927) and *Aspeklariyyah* (1920), and authored textbooks and books for children: Kadish Yehuda Leb Silman (1880-1937). In two treatises, written in the ponderous talmudic form in the beginning of the second decade of the century, he carried the banner of the Hebrew language to victory.[41] These parodies belonged to a beloved, popular form of satire. Gershon Rosenzweig in America had used it in his *Yankee Talmud*[42] and, after the establishment of the State of Israel, Bar-On satirized Israeli society in his *Treatise on Holidays*.[43] During the mandatory period satiric theaters, broadsides, and invectives flourished in profusion. The political regime—perfidious Albion—was castigated mercilessly by a columnist who wrote under the *nom de plume Afarkeset*. In the style of the Passover Haggadah[44] he ridiculed the mandatory government. Here is a bit of dialog from its title page:

Herzl (to Balfour who had just arrived in Paradise):
   Welcome, Reb Balfour. Why were you in such a hurry
   to leave the world? What's new about the Balfour
   Declaration?
Balfour (sadly): I saw the new interpretation of the
   Balfour Declaration by the Commission of Inquiry.
   In a little while nothing will be left of my

Declaration. So I said to myself: if it's a matter of survival for
Balfour without a declaration, it is better that
the Declaration remain without Balfour.

In autonomous Israel—in spite of the constant crises—satire has
continued its lively existence. Among the outstanding humorists in
present-day Israel Kishon is the most popular, Talmi the most talented
of the lot. Both are entertainers rather than literary figures. Kishon
concentrates on the typical and topical—together or separately. The
social and political arena are the preferred butts of his satirical barbs.
But Kishon also dispenses fun for sheer exhilaration of fun. No wonder
he is one of the most translated authors of Israel.[45] Kishon neglects no
device of language which can serve his purpose: pun, hyperbole, under-
statement, symbolism, and family names. In his vocabulary Hansel
and Gretel become a grim fairy tale; the orthodox rabbi hears a reform
service and exclaims "Yecch;" the author claims authorship of an encyclopedia in twenty-four volumes.

It is a known fact that terrorist organizations are not squeamish:
they use violence to achieve their goals. But if the expected effect is reversed, a funny reaction is achieved. Thus, the exploits of Al Fatah become, in a sense, mere innocent love stories; the purpose of Al Fatah is
described as destruction of imperialist Israel and, after its eradication,
the substitution of a democratic, binational state where "Arabs and
Jews would live and die—in just that order."[46] Such a reversal of an
expected effect is the substitution of the phrase "Woe to the Victors"—a title of one of Kishon's books—for the Roman *Vae Victis*,
"Woe to the Vanquished." Zungspitz, Wasserperl, Frisch—the German
names—vie with Boulanger and Fromage—the French names. And, of
course, Zungspitz is a mere bookkeeper, Wasserperl, a leisurely craftsman, a fancy leather-goods maker who never delivers an ordered brief-
case; Mrs. Frisch, a storekeeper, who sells colored pictures to be glued
in an album by kids who love to leave the glue on the carpet; Boulanger, the dramatic casting director; Fromage, a representative of the
majesty of the International Red Cross. Kishon's characters surprise
the reader, tragic events yield a laugh, comic situations—confrontations of Israeli tourists with foreign peoples and lands as depicted in
The Seasick Whale—yield hilarious gaucheries and achieve their goals
of harmless entertainment. Effortlessly, exaggeratedly, vulgarly, or
urbanely Ephraim Kishon delights Israel and audiences outside Israel
with genuine humor in sketches and essays, in films, on television and
in comic plays—especially one-acters.[47]

Talmi, more restricted in scope, manages to shock his audience. The world of Oriental Jews and their violent behavior is his happy hunting ground. And out of this world, he chooses the gangsters, the thieves, the robbers, the jailbirds. Also the lowly characters: the servant girls, the chauffeurs, the street vendors who fill the pages in the collection of sketches *When Man Was Man*.[48] What Talmi loses in his peculiar selectivity, he gains in concentration on a tiny, nontypical segment of outlaws and outcasts and paupers in Israeli society. Their behavior is crude; their language cruder than their behavior; their attitude to the Occidental Jew—the Ashkenazi—a mixture of envy and contempt.

The relationship of the two communities in Israel worries politicians and statesmen, the popular media and the nonpopular literature. The Orientals are the disadvantaged:

—Beethoven, did you ever hear of him?
—Never. Who is he? . . .
—One with hair like Ben-Gurion, writes music—something terrific. For Ashkenazim. Go, see for yourself what it's like. I went. Hall of Culture. A few thousand Ashkenazim sitting well behaved. On the stage some hundred musicians with all kinds of instruments.
Silence. The conductor came in a black suit like the waiters in the Hilton. They all clapped bravo. He said "Thank you very much" and perched on a small box. In his hand a small stick. His function: to see everybody and prevent them from shirking their duty. In the beginning everybody looks at him . . . everybody fears him like Satan. If he tells them to jump on their head, they'll jump. But no sooner do they begin to play, you see immediately that you are dealing with smart cookies. That conductor turns his head right, the whole gang on the left stops playing. He looks at them again, they pick up their instruments and play like mad. But then all those on the right stop playing—one by one.[49]

This is probably exaggerated ignorance. But Talmi succeeds in telling Israel that between the crude and the sophisticated there is an almost unbridgeable chasm.

Talmi is the creator of the language of the Jewish underworld, the idiom of the lowest stratum of society. Its grammar is no grammar, its Arabisms consist mainly of curses and obscenities. But this dark world which Jews lacked for two millennia is a discovery of Talmi. And with that discovery he achieved a unique place.

In a generation which lacked genius in humor, collections of witticisms by previous masters served as good substitutes. The four outstanding collectors of humor—Druyanov, Olsvanger, Lipson, Sadan—contributed each in his own way to the growth of humorous literature.

As an intelligent critic of Zionism, as editor of the Zionist weekly *Ha-'Olam* from 1909 to 1914, as editor of six volumes of folklore between 1918 and 1936[50] and especially as editor of a documentary history of early Zionism,[51] Alter Druyanov (1870-1938)—he derived his name from Druya in Lithuania—was regarded as an important figure in Hebrew literature in the early decades of the century. But his magnum opus was the *Book of Wit*,[52] an anthology of three thousand one hundred seventy humorous stories, parables, and adages. In his introduction to the work, Druyanov utilized the seminal studies of Freud on *Wit*[53] and Bergson on *Laughter*[54]—studies which emphasized the origin of laughter in instinctual drives, in a feeling of superiority toward an inferior creature, or in a mask hiding defeat, or as illusory means of keeping away what is not wanted.[55] Druyanov also utilized literary works, scientific tracts, and opinions of the sages on laughter.[56] By his appreciation of humor, by his researches into humor and by his Hebrew adaptations of Yiddish humor he established for himself a permanent niche in Hebrew literature.

Immanuel Olsvanger (1888-1961), the fastidious translator into Hebrew of Dante's *Divine Comedy* and Boccaccio's *Decameron*, transliterated Yiddish wit and humor into Roman characters.[57] The popular collections won him large audiences among nostalgic lovers of audial Yiddish who were no longer able to read the Hebrew script. Similarly, but not as squeamishly as Olsvanger, Mordecai Lipson (1885-1958) anthologized Jewish humor in Yiddish and Hebrew. And Dov Sadan who enriched the study of Yiddish and Hebrew on the literary, historical, and philological plane, was an ardent collector of wit throughout his mature life. With the scientific curiosity of a surgeon and with the enthusiasm of a poet he dissected witticisms and adages into their component parts, traced their origins and restored their meaning to new glory. Hundreds of folk proverbs, biblical and rabbinical apophthegms, medieval and modern synonyms and homonyms owe new illumination to him.[58] For generations to come his three main collections of jokes and witticisms—*Plate of Raisins, Plate of Nuts, Fair of Delights*[59]—will delight the reader with their keen insight into the Jewish psyche and with their idiomatic style.

In the many fields of cultural endeavor, journalism, folklore, literary history, literary portraiture, translation, Hebrew and Yiddish language, Sadan scattered witticisms with ample generosity. As the most prolific Hebrew writer in the twentieth century he is probably exceeded only by Joseph Klausner in the volume of his written output. But as an oral seducer of audiences, as an analytical dissector of locutions and adages, witticisms and obscure vocables and, finally as an essayist of taste and elegance, he has no equal in modern Hebrew literature.

Criticism

It is a remarkable fact that, in an age of criticism—as our age has been called—few Hebrew critics of distinction responded to the critical urges in the West and the critical necessities in their new homeland. Was the new milieu—away from the familiar centers of Eastern Europe—so busy creating a new literature that it had no time to subject it to penetrating analyses and syntheses? Was the land so small that personal acquaintance between critic and author prevented a just evaluation out of excessive squeamishness or sheer inability to hurt, or worse, out of vengeful slight or slur? The fact remains that no major critic arose in the last fifty years—not even one with the authority of a Frischmann or a Fichmann. Only in the field of monographic studies on the major figures of Hebrew literature—on Bialik and Tschernichowsky, Ahad Haam and Berdyczewski, Agnon and Jacob Steinberg—did contemporary literature surpass previous ages. Certainly Lachower's *Bialik* and Lichtenbaum's *Tschernichowsky,* Simon and Heller's study of Ahad Haam and Keshet's work on Berdyczewski, Tochner's study of Agnon and Adir Cohen's study of Jacob Steinberg enriched our knowledge of modern Hebrew classics with detailed documentation. And so did the penetrating analyses of Perl by Samuel Werses, Gnessin and Shalom Aleyhem by Dan Miron.

Close interpretation of texts—individual stories and novels, plays and poems—also surpassed that of previous ages which had been inclined to generalize rather than analyze, to impress by impressionistic conclusions rather than with textual analyses. Dissections of individual pieces of literature were especially common in the literary periodical *Molad* under the editorship of Ephraim Broide, who translated several of the plays and all the sonnets of Shakespeare, and in *Ha-Sifrut* which boasted of academic orthodoxy under the editorship of Hrushovski.

Dov Sadan's outstanding contribution to the literary essay is one of the most refreshing phenomena in modern Hebrew criticism. Mounds of exegesis have been built by his agile pen. A native of Brody, he was the last of the many writers and scholars who graced that city for two hundred years. In a few pithy sentences he characterized it as a place of learning and piety, wisdom and enlightenment, poetry and song, business and wealth.[60] It was in Brody that he laid the foundation of his dazzling erudition which often clarified what was befogged, obfuscated, uneven or uncertain. His wit, urbanity and irony set him apart from the host of journalists and book reviewers who sometimes pose as literary critics. In his autobiography[61] he communicated to his readers the sunny temperament of his childhood which developed into sunny manhood. His enormous output commenced at the age of twelve and flowed in a stream of poems and translations, stories and, above all, literary essays. In 1921 he published his first slight book of poems in Przemysl—of all places— and called it *Sounds*.[62] The title emphasizes an important aspect of his sensitivity—audial receptivity. The other— the visual—was its comlementary aspect. Together they gave him superb tools for judging himself and others.

Baruch Kurzweil was the very opposite of Sadan. Though he dominated literary criticism in the fifties and sixties, he was too arrogant to gain authority, too cumbersome to please with a Germanic quasi-philosophical style, too rigid in his theses. To regard modern Hebrew literature—and that was the literature of the last two hundred years from his conservative point of view—as discontinuity, as a break with the past was patently absurd. For this view assumed the sacral character of Hebrew literature prior to the enlightenment and its secular character after the enlightenment. This dichotomy never existed except in the heated brain of a Kurzweil and his able disciple Zevi Luz;[63] and it was demolished by Sadan, who pleaded for continuity and for a return to traditionalism. In his sage and temperate way he urged "neither continuity nor revolution but transition."[64] For, in spite of the plethora of problems which faced contemporary Judaism, or "Judaisms" in his view, in a period which he characterized as "an era . . . of disorientation," he was certain that deracination would give way to racination.[65]

Kariv lacked the supple subtlety which enables a critic to achieve authority. His rigidity in the valuation of dominant figures militated against his critical acumen. There is no denying the importance of his reassessments of Mendele and Brenner. Mendele's contempt or Brenner's disdain for Jewry have jarred on the sensibilities of readers and critics. And Kariv treated their harsh animadversions with harsh denunciation.[66] Though he tended to see Mendele and Brenner as masters of self-hatred and diminishers of Jewish stature, he had a salutary influence on Hebrew criticism. For Mendele and Brenner did exaggerate the people's faults and minimize the people's virtues. Against these detractors Kariv assumed the role of a people's tribune:

> In the cellars of Spain and Portugal, in the ghettos of Germany and the Netherlands, in the alleys of Poland and Lithuania there lived the most remarkable people in Europe, the people of the noble and the humbled, the giants of faith and saintliness. . . They formed the stubborn opposition to the rulers of the world, the silent and eternal protest against human evil, human impurity. . . From their lowly estate they looked on high—above the dark deeds that are perpetrated under the sun . . . that was the caravan of the Messiah.[67]

In four negations Kariv poses his positive ideal: "There is no earth without heaven, there is no time without eternity, there is no generation without a chain of generations, there is no people of Israel without the chosen people of Israel."[68] As far as Kariv was concerned, Zionism meant a triple transformation for Jewry. It called for a change from civilized Europe to underdeveloped Asia, from city life to country life at a time when country life was being abandoned for city life, from internationalism to nationalism at a time when internationalism was the fashion. Hence Kariv's complete antagonism to the so-called normalization of Jewish life in Israel, his contempt for a state which will be like any other state: "The vision of normality is an empty vision . . ."[69] A new link must be forged in the chain of generation longing for redemption. Significantly, Kariv called his polemic tract *Let Us Brace the Chain.*

The revisionist views of Kariv were accepted with mixed feelings by Israeli critics. Israel Cohen (1905-) opposed them and preferred to judge the writer not on ideological grounds but on the quality of his equipment in his creative work. Benjamin Isaac Mikhaly tended to evaluate works and individual authors according to ideological idiosyncrasies. And so did Israel Cohen and Israel Zemorah, S.Y. Penueli and Shalom Streit, Solomon Kramer and David Aryeh Friedmann.[70] Hayyim Toren, a sensitive short-story writer, wrote with fine insight on contemporary writers and on poets of previous generations such as

Mordecai Zevi Mane. And his three-volume anthology of modern Hebrew literature—with carefully selected samples of authors and intro-
ductions to their works—reflected his preferences and became a popular object of study in American and Israeli institutions of learning. Az-
riel Ukmani, on the other hand, applied ideological criteria to literary
artifacts. From his point of vantage—socialist realism—the poetry of
Shneour and Gruenberg, for instance, was less than poetry because of
its reactionary stance.

No major theorists of criticism accompanied the creative work of Hebrew writers. Zevi Woislavsky endeavored to place selected writers of
the twentieth century in a sociological framework[71] and Solomon Zemah showed an interest in esthetics in his book *On the Beautiful*.[72] But
he did not contribute new insights; he was satisfied with a discussion of
theories from Kant to Freud. Only in the last chapter of the book did
he adumbrate a skeletal theory of creativity in a series of disjointed or
loosely connected notes. In his view the artist, in conquest of inner re-
straints, experiences the pleasure that finds relief in work. In general
the will to do seeks an outlet in triple form: work, play and art. And art
is essentially a transfer: the existence of things becomes the existence
of the images of things.[73] In his book *In Lands of Exile*[74] Zemah collected his essays on Hebrew and non-Hebrew writers. In a short-lived
quarterly *Behinot* he welcomed critics who aspired to reinterpret literature. But he was at his best in random remarks, sage observations,
critical flashes, and diaristic notations which graced his book *Pages
from a Notebook*.[75]

Neither Zemah nor Woislavsky can measure up to the best theorists
of our time. They lack the intelligence, the inventiveness, the acuity
and the erudition of a Frye or a Foucault, a Kenneth Burke or a
Cleanth Brooks, a Bowra and a Wellek, a Leavis and a Richards, a
Ransom and a Tate, a Wilson and a Matthiessen.

Our age has been rich not only in massive literary histories by
Klausner, Lachower, Zinberg, Schapiro and Shaanan, [76] but also in the
efflorescence of biblical and post-biblical studies in the Hebrew language. Critical insights into the Bible by Fichmann and Kariv and Jacob Steinberg, though not buttressed by rigorous erudition in the field
of Semitic studies, can be neglected by scholars only at the risk of diminished appreciation of the Book of Books. For the Bible is literature,
and its evaluation by literary men must not be regarded by scholars as
a harmless pastime or worse, as an unwarranted intrusion by untrained specialists. The knowledge of the writing craft that a creative

author of our time brings to the study of an ancient text produced by a creative author of the past can serve as valuable supplementation and even as directive guidance to the scholar. For his philological and cultural knowledge of the ancient Near East may well be coupled with as great an ignorance of literary values as the writer's knowledge of literary values in the Bible is often coupled with ignorance of Semitic philology and other cultural interrelationships of the peoples in the Near East. This is not to detract from the massive work in the field of biblical research by Moses Goshen-Gottstein, the important contributions of Zeev Ben-Hayyim to the study of the Samaritan texts, and the valuable studies of the Dead Sea Scrolls by Shemaryahu Talmon.

Poets and novelists have not invaded the field of Hellenistic and rabbinic studies. The preeminence of Saul Liebermann in these contiguous disciplines is as firmly established as the primacy of Sholem and Tishbi in the study of the Kabbalah; Klausner and Baer in the study of history; Ezekiel Kaufmann, in the study of Jewish faith; Jacob Nahum Epstein, Ephraim E. Urbach, Shraga Abramson, Hanoch Albeck and Benjamin M. Lewin in rabbinic studies; Goitein and Ashtor in the study of medieval society; Yellin and Schirmann in the study of medieval poetry; Mazar and Yadin in the study of archaeology; Habermann, Yarden, Aloni, Naphtali Ben-Menahem and Meir Benayahu in critical editions of texts; Shunami and Kressel in the study of bibliography. The massive researches of Jewish scholars in America—Baron in Jewish history, H.L. Ginsberg in Bible, Wolfson in Jewish philosophy— have been translated to a limited extent into Hebrew.

Medieval studies have especially profited from the critical acumen of writers. Dan Pagis, poet in his own right, has mastered the tools of textual criticism and applied them with salutary results to medieval poetry. And so did Mirsky, who has a slim body of poems to his credit.

Modern Jewish philosophy has had a checkered career in Israel where Samuel Hugo Bergman and Martin Buber and even Julius Guttman eventually switched to Hebrew, while Leon Roth and Nathan Rotenstreich enriched the study of general and Jewish philosophy. Since all of them—with the exception of Leon Roth—were strongly influenced by German philosophy, it was only natural for them to cultivate Kantian studies. This was especially true of Bergman and Rotenstreich. Some literary critics, especially Baruch Kurzweil and Eliezer Schweid, combined an interest in philosophy with their primary taste for literature. But the specialist journal, *Iyyun,* which has served philosophical writers as an organ of publication and translation for many years, has not radiated its influence into nonspecialist circles. And its intellectual fare may have delighted the producers of ideas: it has had almost no influence on the consumers.

25
Hebrew Literature as Source of Untapped Values

IN our sloganized society value itself has become a slogan. In education, the slogan for the past few years was, and still is, "excellence." John W. Gardner, former Secretary of Health, Education and Welfare, has written an excellent book on *Excellence*. Even violence on campus is alleged to be a precondition for excellence. "Value" is also in the running—a close second. The late Clyde Kluckhohn, Professor of Anthropology at Harvard University, properly diagnosed the weakness of our civilization when he said that "in the long run the Achilles heel of the West is in the realm of ideas and values. . . We lack a system of general ideas and values to give meaning to human life in the mid-twentieth century."[1] Perhaps these two slogans, excellence and value, should be married and appear under the joint name: valuable excellence or excellent value. The adjective component will naturally play the humbler, qualifying role as all good adjectives should. Or should one say like all good adjectives should?

The word "value" is Rome's gift to the English language. Derived from a root *valere* which means to be strong (hence valiant), to be of worth, it has invaded many branches of science and invested them with multiple meaning. In economics it is identical with price, in music it points out the duration of a note (thus a quarter note has the value of two eighth notes), in daily use it is equal, roughly, to importance. The late Professor Horace Kallen has underlined the essential qualities of value: they usually point to someone or something—to a person or an item—"about whose prosperous survival and growth we are actively concerned."[2] This is the dynamic aspect of values—it demands a constant vigil about them, otherwise they may be attenuated or they may deteriorate altogether. Sociologists like Alfred McClung Lee speak of "multivalent man," i.e., man belonging to many groups—family, professional association, club—and adjusting his values to a particular group at a particular time and place.

To isolate value out of a mass of literary artifacts and to place it in the context of modern civilization is our task, a task undertaken by Leo Baeck in his *Essence of Judaism*[3] and, in recent times, by the controversial English rabbi, Dr. Louis Jacobs. Baeck dwelt on the essence of Judaism as the faith without an intermediary between man and God, as "the faith that confronts man continually and directly with the moral decision, with God's mystery . . ."[4] as the great chain of tradition in which each generation confronts tradition . . ."[5] Jacobs, who published his book on *Jewish Values* more than a half-century after Baeck, constructed a decalog of his own: 1. Study; 2. Love and fear of God; 3. Sanctification of the Name; 4. Trust in God; 5. Holiness; 6. Humility; 7. Love of neighbor; 8. Compassion; 9. Truth; 10. Peace.[6]

Both Baeck and Jacobs formed their sets of values on the basis of classical Judaism, that is Judaism as it existed prior to the American and French Revolutions; Baeck from a neo-liberal point of view, Jacobs from a neo-orthodox vantage point. Others, like Professor André Neher[7] reemphasize religion as the preservative factor of Judaism. Still others try to reinterpret aspects of Judaism—Joseph Weiss,[8] mysticism; Jacob Taubes,[9] beliefs and opinions in nineteenth-century theology; Nathan Rotenstreich,[10] neo-nationalism. This frantic search for values—and it is not only a Jewish, but a worldwide search—may be merely an infinite regret for the loss of an Infinite Being. In one of his rare excursions into our age, the late Professor Harry A. Wolfson warned against "the gentle art of devising deities." And he mentions, among some current substitutions, "man's aspiration for ideal values."[11] This is more than a *caveat*; it is an indictment couched in a memorable phrase. For, especially in America, there is a brisk and frantic trade in panaceas which last a day and give way to others. The authorized and the unauthorized, the educated and the half-educated shout their new values, even new religions: psychoanalytic modernizations of the Nietzschean "death of God," existentialist theology, death of secularism, ecstatic theology.

Contemporary Hebrew literature emphasizes values that differ from those of Baeck and Jacobs, Neher and Weiss, Taubes and Rotenstreich. As an integral part of world literature it shares some of the current values of the literatures of the world, but it contributes its own coloration to them and it offers some values which are peculiar to its people. Like all major contemporaneous literatures of the West, Hebrew literature is a literature of alienation.[12] This theme was, for centuries, a *Jewish* theme. *Golah*—exile—was alienation. And when Ezekiel Kaufmann, the sociologist and biblical scholar, joined these two concepts in a multivolume work *Golah we-Nekar, Exile and Alienation*,[13] he seemed to allude to a tautological entity. For the concept of exile symbolized the unassimilated and unassimilable life of the Jew, ethnical alienation par excellence. With the establishment of the State of Israel the concept of alienation assumed new significance for Jews. It was no longer a sociological designation for the situation of an entire people; it was a name for the isolation of the individual in a faceless, technological society. At that point it intersected with alienation which, for peoples and literatures of the West, was a forgotten phenomenon.[14] And at that point poets like Yehiel Mar and Wystan Hugh Auden and Allen Ginsberg meet; Mar in his frantic search for "the other"—any other, any thou; Auden in his capitulation to technology; Ginsberg in his cult of the bizarre ego. All three abandon traditional poetics for new devices in form and format, in theme and content. Consciously or unconsciously they intimate or indicate that the driving force of our civilization, technology, is also the major cause of our dehumanization, alienation, decline.[15] And Heinrich Böll, the German laureate, indicated in an address to the congress of PEN in Jerusalem in 1974 that ours was a "century of exiles."

Hebrew poets of former generations built on biblical or rabbinic associations: knowledge of the source texts, the Bible and Talmud, was taken for granted. Modern poets still weave biblical and talmudic phrases into the texture of their poetry with exemplary skill. Both they and the writers of prose are specially concerned with modern youth which drifts in an uncharted sea void of values. In the United States, they were the beat generation, the beatniks in the previous decade; they are the alienated or the hippies or the SDS in this decade; they march, riot, picket, parade, participate in antisegregation sit-ins, teach-ins, love-ins, be-ins, mill-ins. And they include the usual repertoire of beatniks: coffee-shops, sex, marijuana, LSD (lysergic acid diethylamide), long hair, eccentric or extravagant forms of dress or rather undress. Lest it be thought that this is an indigenous phenomenon exclusive to America with a celebrated habitat in the Haight Ashbury section of San Francisco,[16] it should be immediately stressed that a few years ago "city authorities of Elat in southern Israel ousted a colony of 200 beatniks by burning the wooden shacks they had set up on the beach."[17] And even in Japan the so-called *futenzoku*, the crazy tribe, have occupied a tiny park near the railroad station at Shinjuku, the Tokyo equivalent of Greenwich Village, to the annoyance of the police and the established social order. A new international set has come into being: it cherishes identical nonvalues.

But—a very important qualification—contemporary Hebrew poets and novelists draw some positive values out of their alienated selves: intense identification with Israel and with the landscape of Israel. To put it tersely: alienation is an ancient concept but identification with his own native land and landscape as a sequel of alienation is a new concept with the Jew. The reverse is true of the non-Jew.

The logical culmination of the Jew's identification with his land and the landscape was the establishment of the State of Israel which had been preceded by the most painful experience of Jewry: the holocaust. The link between the two dominant events of contemporary Jewry is obvious to all trained and untrained observers. What is not obvious is the climate of cultural decay which preceded the holocaust in German-speaking countries, in Germany and in Austria, and the impact of the holocaust on Hebrew literature. It was Friedrich Nietzsche who advocated a dangerous transvaluation of all Judaeo-Christian values at the end of the nineteenth century. The lesser-known Max Scheler observed the dissolution of traditional values and, already in 1915, published the first edition of his essays, *The Subversion of Values*.[18] German and Austrian writers of the first decades of this century—Hofmannsthal, Kafka, Karl Kraus, Musil, Brecht, and Broch—are full of apocalyptic intimations. They anticipated a private rather than objective corrosion as the correlative of the erosion of human rights in the totalitarian state. They are the prophets of despair. But if civilization means anything at all, it is primarily freedom from violence. The holocaust is a long lapse from civilization into barbarity. And a catastrophe of such dimensions cannot possibly be converted into an immediate literary masterpiece. It is *sui generis,* it postulates an attitude to life which is perhaps adumbrated in the words of Rabbi Isaac Nussenbaum in the Warsaw ghetto:

> This is the time of *Kiddush ha-Hayyim,* sanctification of life, and not for *Kiddush ha-Shem,* the holiness of martyrdom. Previously the Jewish enemy sought his soul, and the Jew sacrificed his body. . . Now the oppressor demands the Jew's body and the Jew is obliged therefore to defend it, to preserve his life.[19]

The holocaust is an apocalyptic event in Jewish history, holocaustism is a tragic value of the modern Jew. The last years of the mandatory government, the establishment of the State of Israel, the ingathering of the exiles from the West and especially from the East, enriched our concept of the totality of Israel; Jewish interdependence and inter-relationship became a matter of existent actuality rather than a matter of romantic aspiration. This totalism is a new, a third value, in addition to alienism and holocaustism.

It is taken for granted that oriental Jewry, more primitive and more naive than Ashkenazic Jewry, is also more religious. While the older generation of oriental Jews is rigidly orthodox, the younger generation is almost as lax in observance as the younger generation of European, American and Israeli Jews. The Jewish crisis of religion is merely a link in the chain of the world-wide crisis which dates back to the days of the high renaissance. It was toward the end of the fifteenth century that an emergent anthropocentrism dislodged an entrenched theocentrism, that, to put it simply, a passionate concern with man replaced a fanatic pursuit of God. Jews were not unaffected by the critical attitude of the Italian renaissance to matters of religion. But amidst prevalent doubt and confusion they clung, on the whole, to ancestral ways. Even in this century of cynicism and extreme sophistication and bizarre alienation a truly religious vein runs through contemporary Hebrew literature. This is the notable paradox of secularized Jewish life and letters. The Hebrew language itself, like all ancient languages, is not only rich in religious idioms; it is textually and texturally religious. And the world expects from that language and that people a religious revival. It is a justified expectation. Hasidism, for instance, was not only the great efflorescence of religion among Jews two hundred years ago; it proved to be—through the interpretative genius of a Buber—a message of faith to the gentiles.

The revival of Hasidism is not the only religious contribution of contemporary Hebrew literature. Saul Tschernichowsky and Zalman Shneour sought to achieve a religious stance with a daring leap into Jewish history, a sort of pre-Israelism or proto-Israelism.[20] It was the loss of traditional ways which prompted a feverish search for religious substitutes: neo-Hasidism and proto-Israelism. Both concepts share a taste for history. They are imbued with a quality which might best be characterized as unconscious historicism. And this is a fourth value in addition to alienism, holocaustism, and totalism.

Conscious historicism in contemporary Hebrew literature is almost purely secular. In one of the few idyllic sections in that grim book on the holocaust, *Rehobot ha-Nahar,* its author identifies with a boy in the reign of the Hasmonean warrior-king, Alexander Yannai (103-76). Together with his father he watches the splendid procession of the sovereign and the nobles and the peasants into the Sanctuary. Con-

trasting the subsequent miseries and contemporary woes with the ancient glory, he allows himself to be seduced into hope that the people
will turn their ploughshares into swords and inaugurate a robust dawn
for themselves. This idealization of a virile king who fought constant
battles of conquest and violent civil wars could not but lead to a complete reversal of the Isaianic dream. It is perhaps more than a literary
coincidence that Moshe Shamir has published a historical novel and a
play about Alexander Yannai. Interest in Jewish history verges on
fetishism in Shamir's *Weltanschauung*:

> The bridge which the younger literature seeks to build between
> ourselves and our great past does not resemble bridges of yore. We
> lost the religious, physical ties with the heritage of our people. In-
> stead we raise historic ties. All those wonderful things which our
> predecessors regarded as slices of life, essential experiences, eter-
> nal principles—the prayer book, the traditional holidays, the typi-
> cal modes of thought, the world of the Halakah, the customs—all
> these are history as far as we are concerned, and their value is only
> the value of a historical heritage.[21]

Not only Shamir but writers who recreated other epochs in Jewish
history, novelists like Twersky and Hurgin, playwrights like Sackler
and Shoham, sought out the great religious periods of Jewry. They
may have felt that lasting works must indicate ways of spiritual transformation to individuals and peoples, that history and religion complement each other in Hebrew literature.

A final word about a final value—Hebrew. Unlike modern languages, it is veined with religious associations. Two examples will
suffice. Science is a secular word in English; *Madda'*, its Hebrew equivalent, is a deeply theological expression as well. When Maimonides
called the introductory book to his great code *Sefer ha-Madda'*, he did
not mean the Book of Science but the Book of Knowledge [of God].
Another example from everyday speech:"welcome" is a secular expression; the Hebrew equivalent *Baruk ha-Ba,* "Blessed be he who
comes," is part of a biblical verse.[22] These examples can be expanded
into a book; they make the point: Hebrew is a religious language.
When the Communist regime began to liquidate Hebrew as a reactionary, anti-revolutionary language—and that meant a religious language—it was right in its reasoning though wrong in its anti-civiliza-
tional, anti-humanistic drive.

Even the secularization of modern life did not affect the essential character of the Hebrew language. Between Anglo-Saxon and English there is a chasm; between the language of Isaiah and the language of Bialik there is a strong bond in grammar and in idiom. Only the vocabulary is quantitatively larger than it was twenty-six centuries ago. If proof were needed for the essential unity of the Hebrew language, it was given by the pioneer of spoken Hebrew, Eliezer Ben-Yehudah. The monumental Hebrew dictionary in sixteen volumes, initiated by him and completed by Professor N. H. Tur-Sinai [Torczyner], testifies on every page to the marvelous continuity of the language. Almost eighty years elapsed from the initial labors of Ben-Yehudah on the dictionary to its completion by Tur-Sinai. But they gave the Hebrew language its most important chronicle of words from their emergence in pre-biblical times to their resurrection and continuation in our time.

It is in the realm of neologisms and new, startling word combinations that the modern Hebrew writer made his most lasting contributions. He was, of course, not the only architect of language. The people in the cities and on the farms fashioned new expressions for new needs. Children at play coined words. From 1890 on, a Committee on Language, *Va'ad ha-Lashon,* functioned in Palestine both as watchdog over evolving Hebrew in spoken form and as creator of words in new and old fields of human endeavor. The Committee evolved into the Academy of Hebrew Language which has performed and is still performing a valuable service to the people with the publication of an academic periodical and a popular series of brochures on lingual problems.[23] The historical dictionary in preparation will probably be its crowning achievement.[24]

But the most important single factor in the development of the Hebrew language was—and still is—the Hebrew writer. It is he who has adapted Hebrew to modern use and has recreated it as a tool of infinite suppleness and subtlety. It is he who has enriched its vocabulary to such an extent that it has become a modern language with an infinite variety of expression. It is he who has made the common and the uncommon words which are on everybody's lips today. Thus no less a person than Bialik created the words for import, *Yebu,* and export, *Yezu.* And Tschernichowsky was responsible for hundreds of terms in medicine, botany, and zoology. Shlonsky, the poet who made his debut in the twenties, was so inventive in new coinages and in new word-combinations that Shneour called him facetiously *Lashonsky,* Mr. Language,[25] a sobriquet he well deserved. For like Hebrew writers in Eastern Europe a century ago he had an almost compulsive attitude to the Hebrew language. But he was infinitely more inventive and imaginative in his translations and in his original poetry. In an interview, occasioned by his new version of Alexander Pushkin's *Yevgeni Onegin*, he paid a handsome compliment to the hidden resources of Hebrew:

> I like to struggle with the language, with the sentence, with the word. And when I am victorious and when I feel that I have found the proper expression, I smile and say to myself: Shlonsky, it is not you. It's she—it's the Hebrew language which is victorious.[26]

The language is female in Hebrew. And this fact accounts for the endearment lavished on her beauty by Hebrew writers who, until recent times, were ninety-nine percent and some fraction, male. A responsible appreciation of the Hebrew language for this generation was made by the novelist Amos Oz:

> You compose a Hebrew sentence, combine a few Hebrew words: a palaceful of echoes and secondary echoes answers you. . . I and people like me stand before a difficult experience with no similarity in the entire history of Hebrew literature. We have to write in a language which, on the one hand, belongs to us more than to former generations and, on the other hand, belongs to us less than to former generations because its treasures were opened before them day by day in an ever-living reality.[27]

What Amos Oz is saying amounts to a sound appreciation of the language situation vis-a-vis the creator of language: the untutored Hebrew writer is at a disadvantage, the learned Hebrew writer is overwhelmed by the associational wealth of the Hebrew language. Still, it is no exaggerated claim that the Hebrew writer has converted a sacral language into the secular language of a modern state. It is still a powerful link between the ethnic groupings of Jewry: a *lingua franca*, an international medium of expression that binds the Jew from Bokhara and the Jew from Warsaw into a fraternal community. It has also become an academic discipline, taught in the universities of Europe and America as a modern language. Now that it is a living language again, it is right to remember that the Hebrew writer is not only one of the architects of the State of Israel; he is also the creator of its modernized language—a value of unimaginable spiritual significance for modern Jewry. Unfortunately, the untutored immigrants from the West and the East have carried the secularization and vulgarization of the language to extremes. Younger writers—either to curry favor with the populace or in blissful ignorance of the sources and resources of language—have aided and abetted the process of barbarization. But foreign words like *normali* and *offiziali* and *instrumentali, dominanti* and *relevanti* and *pikanti, konotaziah* and *variaziah* and *indikaziah, institut* and *consensus,*[28] *model* and *amplifier*, which have good equivalents in Hebrew, mar the language. The anglicized aroma of the Latin words has successfully banished the Hebrew vocable.[29] More offensive than the unnecessary neologisms is the sloppy and shoddy syntax or the unidiomatic translation of phrases from the English into Hebrew without regard to the niceties of Hebrew. Here is a veritable anglicization of Hebrew.[30] And the careful Hebraist is branded either as a flowery phrasemonger or as an unrealistic speaker of Sabbath Hebrew.[31] But this phase in the Hebrew language is, hopefully, a passing phase. In the first blush of restitution and restoration after the destruction of Jewish independence in 586 B.C.E. Nehemiah, the great architect of the second commonwealth, was dismayed by the lack of Hebraic knowledge and called the corrupt language of the Jews "the speech of Ashdod."[32] But the Hebrew language became a vehicle of great elegance in its Mishnaic repository and, in the commentaries of Rashi and in the Code of Maimonides, it reached an unprecedented refinement, precision and concision. That it can again revive in new splendor is not an unreasonable assumption. Greater erudition and greater sensitivity to lingual structures: these are the guarantees of refinement in the development of the Hebrew language.

Postlude

HUNDRED years of creative effort in the Land of Israel have produced a literature which reflects with increasing adequacy but with a dearth of brilliance or genius the great events of the century—discovery of the neighboring Arab and the Arabized Jewry of the orient; reorientalization of Hebrew literature; genuine and sham socialism in the rural cooperative; tension between the collective and individual will on the collective farm and in the non-collective urban milieu; the battles and the wars with Turks, British and Arabs; the involuntary militarization of the country's population; the holocaust, the liberation of the Middle East, the reestablishment of a Jewish State; and last, but not least, detheologization of the land and landscape in the Land of Israel.

Not a single novelist of the stature of a Kafka, Mann, or Proust, not a poet of emotional and intellectual sublimity like Rilke, Yeats or Valéry and not an inventive dramatist of new techniques and scopes like Strindberg, Beckett or Brecht graces the hundred-year-old literature in the Land of Israel. The eternal themes of life and death, love and hate, peace and war, nature and man, man and God in their intricate inter-relationship have not been invested with articulation that has a ring of the eternal. The exhilarating reconquest of the Palestinian landscape in all its rich variety instead of the monotonous repetition of biblical place-names, the building of a socialist milieu in the form of rural cooperatives, the bitter strife against the indigenous Arab— these major themes were reflected and refracted by men of talent in the novel and in the poetry of Israel. But genius, the liberating power of genius is missing. Like the era of the enlightenment, the era of pre-independence and independence was greater than the men who moved in its dizzying orbit. Even the single Nobel Prize laureate lacked the charisma of literary leadership. A new Torah has not yet come out of Zion.

319

1   Notes to Hebrew Literature
in its Ancestral Home

1   The phrase—a paraphrase of a Russian radical—is Sir Isaiah Berlin's. It reads in full: "A Russian radical of the last century once observed that his country, compared to the West, had a great deal of geography but little history. It might be said that with Jews the opposite pertains: more than enough history, too little geography. . ." See Isaiah Berlin, "Weizmann as Exilarch" in *Chaim Weizmann as Leader* (Jerusalem, 1970), p. 13.

2   Ben Zion Dinur, *Israel and Diaspora* (Philadelphia, 1969), p. 90.

3   A. B. Rivlin, *Yerushalayim* (Tel Aviv, 1965/66), p. 32.

4   In Hebrew: *Hazon Zion.* "Return to Zion"—*Shivat Zion*—was the contemplated name, but it met with the Gaon's disfavor because of its political implications and the possible negative repercussions among gentiles. So *Hazon Zion* was chosen; it had the advantage, in the Gaon's opinion, that its numerical value equaled *Berakhah,* "blessing." See *Hazon Zion,* ed. H. H. Rivlin (Tel Aviv, 1964/65), p. 6.

5   The hyperbolic statement was made in a lecture at *Mikveh Yisrael*: "The State of Israel was not founded in 1948 . . . the origin of the State is here . . ." *The Alliance Review XXIII* (Spring, 1969), p. 32.

6   The Society *Nahalat Shiv'ah* was founded in 1866/67. It was named for the seven partners who acquired the property—approximately 14,500 square meters at a cost of 170 Turkish pounds—and organized themselves into a cooperative: Joseph Rivlin, Bainish Salant, Leib Horowitz, Hayyim Halevi Kovner, Michael Cohen, Yoel Moshe Solomon, Yehoshua Yellin. On Joseph Rivlin, whose great-grandfather, Hillel Rivlin came to the Holy Land with the disciples of the Gaon of Vilna in 1809, see the interesting article of Rabbi Aaron M. Wise, "The Man Who Breached the Walls of Jerusalem," *Conservative Judaism* (Winter, 1970), pp. 76–85. In the first years *Nahalat Shiv'ah* was called derisively, in Yiddish, *"Reb Yoshe's Derfl"* ("Joe's Village") because Joseph Rivlin has planted trees and a garden to adorn the house. Some called it "Joseph's Dream." See Joseph Joel Rivlin, *Reshit ha-Yishuv mi-Huz le-Homat Yerushalayim* (Jerusalem, 1939), p. 36. The late Professor Joseph Joel Rivlin

(1889–1971), a descendant of Joseph Rivlin, was an authority on Arabic literature and the translator of the Koran into Hebrew.

7   In 1856/57, the first building outside Jerusalem, Judah Touro's Court, had already been erected by Sir Moses Montefiore with money from the estate of an American philanthropist, Judah Touro. See Joseph Joel Rivlin, op.cit., p. 5. But old Jerusalem was not abandoned; Ezra Hamenahem described its rich, pulsating life in the first two decades in *Sippure ha-'Ir ha-'Attikah* (Tel Aviv, 1968). And so did Aaron Reuveni.

8   The words are taken from Genesis 26:12. They have nothing to do with gates—as is popularly assumed.

9   Bilu is an acronym based on Isaiah 2:5: *Bet Ya'akob Leku we-Nelekhah*, "House of Jacob, come, let us go." For a portrait of a Biluist, Jacob Solomon Hazanov, see *Kitbe Moshe Smilansky VIII* (Tel Aviv, 1934/35), pp. 234–38. On Hazanov (1861–1922), see *Enziklopediyyah La-Haluze ha-Yishuv u-Bonav II*, ed. David Tidhar (Tel Aviv, 1947), p. 736.

10   Melford E. Spiro, *Kibbutz: Venture in Utopia* (New York, 1963), p. 11.

11   Since the kibbutz makes fascinating history, historians are busy chronicling its achievements and failures. Harry Viteles, managing director of the Central Bank of Cooperative Institutions during the British Mandate, published a source book in seven volumes: *A History of the Cooperative Movement in Israel* (London, 1966–70).

12   See Eliyahu Kanovsky's introduction to his book, *The Economy of the Israeli Kibbutz* (Cambridge, Mass., 1968), p. 3. On the difference between the Jewish cooperative, the kibbutz, and the Russian cooperative, the kolkhoz, see ibid., pp. 3–4.

13   Walter Rothschild (1868–1937), zoologist and Fellow of the Royal Society, became a peer of the realm in 1915. His interest in Zionism moved him to become its spokesman. On July 18, 1917, he sent Arthur James Balfour a draft declaration of what eventually, in an amended version, became the Balfour Declaration. In an accompanying letter he expressed his willingness to serve in a mediative capacity between the British Government and the Zionist Federation. The so-called Balfour Declaration was Balfour's delayed answer "on behalf of His Majesty's Government" to Rothschild's letter. The selection of Weizmann, a British subject, or Sokolow, a foreigner who outranked Weizmann in the Zionist hierarchy, would have presented certain embarrassments. See Leonard Stein, *The Balfour Declaration* (London, 1961), pp. 470, 548–49.

14   The text of the Balfour Declaration: "His Majesty's Government view with favor the establishment in Palestine of a national home for the Jewish people, and will use their best endeavours to facilitate the achievement of their object, it being clearly understood that nothing shall be done which may prejudice the civil and religious rights of existing non-Jewish communities in Palestine, or the rights and political status enjoyed by Jews in any other country." In extenuation of its shabby style it should be stated that Leopold Amory, secretary to the British government in 1917, put the final hurried touches to a draft by Lord Milner on the back of a discarded memo (Leopold Stein, op. cit.,

p. 521). France and Italy approved the policy of the British Government as it was set forth in the Balfour Declaration (Stein, op. cit., p. 588). At San Remo the Allied Supreme Council agreed on April 25, 1920, to insert a declaration into the Turkish Treaty which envisioned Great Britain as the mandatory power for Palestine. The Council of the League of Nations approved it in 1922 (Stein, op. cit., pp. 661–62). In the same year the United States—through a joint resolution of both Houses of Congress-approved the Balfour Declaration (Stein, op. cit., p. 598).

15   See Balfour's introduction to Nahum Sokolow, *The History of Zionism* I (London, 1919), p. xxix–xxx. In a letter to the classicist Alfred Zimmern,who was connected with the Political Intelligence Section of the Foreign Office during the First World War and who read the draft of his introduction, Balfour stated: "The eventual Jewish State . . . is what I should like to see." "Documents—Lord Balfour's Personal Position on the Balfour Declaration," *The Middle East Journal* XXII[3] (Summer, 1968), p. 342.

16   Leonard Stein, op. cit., p. 641. The agreement was a document which provided mutual help: Zionists undertook to support the future Arab State, Faisal on behalf of the Arabs conceded in effect "Palestine, unencumbered by any Arab claim," to the Jews (ibid., p. 642). There were Arab retrenchments and subsequently reaffirmations of the agreement. In a letter to Felix Frankfurter on March 1, 1919, Faisal wrote: "I look forward, and my people with me look forward, to a future in which we will help you and you will help us, so that the countries in which we are mutually interested may once again take their place in the community of civilised peoples of the world." Ibid., pp. 643–44.

17   In his article "Ra'ayon Shibat Yisrael ba-Mahshabah ha-Protestantit be-Angliyyah be-Shanim 1790-1840" Meir Vereté has skillfully traced the genesis of the Return to the new interpretation of Scripture in the era of the Reformation. In his historical analysis he pointed up four components of the idea of Return: the physical return, the problem of the lost ten tribes, conversion, and England's role in the Return. See *Ziyyon* XXXIII[3-4] (1968), pp. 156–79.

18   On the Jewish Legions, see the memoirs of a participant who became the second President of the State of Israel: Isaac Ben-Zvi, *Zikronot u-Reshumot me-ha-Ne'urim 'Ad 1920* (Jerusalem, 1965/66, pp. 237–42, 253–88. Also his book *Ha-Gedudim ha-'Ibriyyim; Iggarot*, ed. David Benvenisti (Jerusalem, 1968).

19   Documentary evidence supports the contention that Lloyd George and his cabinet—in contradistinction to his predecessor Herbert Henry Asquith—gradually veered to sympathy with Zionist aspirations. See D. Barzilai, "Le-Toledot Hazharat Balfour," *Ziyyon* XXXIII[3-4] (1968), pp. 194–202.

20   Isaiah Berlin, *Chaim Weizmann* (New York, 1958), p. 11.

21   In Hebrew: *Sefer ha-Koah* (Warsaw, 1897). It is based on the researches of the Scottish physicist, Balfour Stewart (1828-1887) and it is written in easy Hebrew. Pines provided his book with a list of scientific terms which have been largely superseded. The historian of the Hebrew language will be amused by such terms as *semarmoret* for electricity and *'onah* for minute.

22   In Hebrew: *Torat Mishpete Togarmah* (Jerusalem, 1886/87).

23   In Hebrew: *Yalde Ruhi* (Mainz, 1872).

24   *Kitbe Yehiel Michael Pines* II, ed. David Yellin and Joseph Meyuhas (Tel Aviv, 1938), p. 213.

25   Ibid., p. 214.

26   Ibid., p. 236.

27   Golda Pines, sister of Yehiel Michael Pines, was Jawitz's second wife. His first wife died a year after their marriage when he was nineteen. See Klar's introduction to Zev Jawitz, *Leket Ketabim* (Jerusalem, 1943), p. 7.

28   Ibid., p. 43.

29   The day—winter in northern countries—is the New Year for Trees. See *Rosh ha-Shanah* 1:1. It was designated as an informal religious festival because it was held that sap began to rise in the fruit trees on that day. It was—and still is—customary to eat fruit from the Holy Land on that day: almonds, carobs, figs, nuts, pomegranates. See Theodor H. Gaster, *Festivals of the Jewish Year* (New York, 1955), p. 255.

30   *Rosh ha-Shanah le-Ilanot*, op. cit., pp. 51–52.

31   In Hebrew: *Toledot Yisrael*. The history begins with the patriarchal age and ends with Hibbat Zion. Of the fourteen volumes, the first six are devoted to Jewry in Israel from legendary beginnings to the end of the tannaitic period; the last eight to Jewry in the Diaspora.

32   R. Benjamin, *Keneset Hakamim* (Jerusalem, 1960), p. 264.

33   In Hebrew: *Sheelah Nikbadah, Ha-Shahar* (1879).

34   Zemah who arrived in Ottoman Palestine in the beginning of November, 1904—according to his own testimony—observed that members of Eliezer Ben-Yehudah's family spoke among themselves not only Hebrew but also Russian and French. See Solomon Zemah, *Dappe Pinkas* (Jerusalem, 1972), p. 132.

35   Itamar Ben-Avi coined thousands of Hebrew words—more than any Hebrew writer in the past hundred years. See Isaac Avineri, *"Ha-Yeled ha-Gadol," Maʿariv* (April 20, 1973), p. 34.

36   Hebrew title: *Netivot Ziyyon wi-Yerushalayim*. It was first published in Jerusalem in 1876. An excellent edition of the selected writings of Luncz with a substantial introduction and brief notes in *Netivot Ziyyon wi-Yerushalayim*, ed. G. Kressel (Jerusalem, 1970). In spite of total blindness after his twenty-fifth year, Luncz enriched Hebrew letters with his comprehensive knowledge of Jerusalem. His twelve volumes of *Yerushalayim* (1881/82–1916) and his *Almanacs* of the Land of Israel under the title *Luah Eretz Yisrael* (1895/96–1915) are a mine of information on the Land of Israel and a valuable source for the early history of the new Jerusalem.

37   He settled in Palestine in 1887 and not in 1877 according to R. Benjamin's conjecture (see R. Benjamin, op. cit., p. 42).

38   See his article " 'Ibrit be-'Ibrit," *Ha-Shiloah* IV (November, 1898), pp. 385–96.

39   In Hebrew *'Ad Ematai Dibru 'Ibrit* (New York, 1919). An extended version appears in the introductory volume of Ben-Yehudah's *Dictionary* (Jerusalem, 1948), pp. 83–254.

40   One of the volunteers in the Jewish Legions was Moshe Smilansky, at age forty-four. See *Kitbe Moshe Smilansky* I (Tel Aviv, 1933/4), p. 11. He utilized his experiences as a soldier in two stories "Mi-Sippure ha-Gedud," *Kitbe Moshe Smilansky* IV, pp. 19–48.

41   The first volumes appeared in 1908; the last—the sixteenth volume edited by Professor N. H. Tur-Sinai—in 1959.

42   Original title of the Society for the Advancement of Hebrew: *Va'ad ha-Lashon*. Its purpose was to enable Hebrew to become a spoken language; "to preserve the oriental character of the language . . . in the pronunciation of the consonants . . . to superimpose the kind of elasticity which is necessary for the expression of human thought in its entirety in our time." See *Zikronot Va'ad ha-Lashon ha-'Ibrit bi-Yerushalayim* (Jerusalem, 1912), pp. 11–12. In 1953 the Society became an Academy: *Ha-Akademiyyah la-Lashon ha-'Ibrit*.

43   The founders were the first intellectuals of Jerusalem who used Hebrew in daily conversation. It should be noted that *Va'ad ha-Lashon* was originally "a sort of branch of *Safah Berurah* which was founded at that time" [1890]. Ibid., p. 2.

44   Robert St. John has devoted a book to the life and work of Eliezer Ben-Yehudah, *Tongue of the Prophets*. It is also available as a Dolphin Book in paperback (Garden City, New York, 1952). But, since it is based on second-hand knowledge of Hebraic sources, it teems with well-intentioned inaccuracies and incorrect points of view.

45   N. Sokolow, *Ishim* (Jerusalem, 1958), p. 199.

46   Dov Sadan, *Polemos u-Sheve Polemos* (Jerusalem, 1972), pp. 215–16.

47   In Hebrew: *Ba'al Leshon ha-Kodesh*. See *Hazon Zion*, p. 140.

48   *Kitbe Moshe Smilansky* VI, p. 1.

49   Ibid., V, VI, VII (Tel Aviv, 1933/34). Palestinian Arabs were less alert to processes of modernization and intellectualization in the pre-First-World-War period than Arabs in Cairo and Beirut, Damascus and Baghdad. See Hisham Sharabi, *Arab Intellectuals and the West: The Formative Years, 1875–1914* (Baltimore and London, 1970), p. 5.

50   For the play, see op. cit., IV, pp. 155–92.

51   From an article, written in the first decade of the century, under the title *"Ha-Hityashvut be-Eretz Yisrael,"* op. cit., XI (Tel Aviv, 1936–37), p. 85.

52   See "Yom 'Avodati ha-Rishon," *Kitbe Moshe Smilansky* VIII (Tel Aviv, 1934/35), p. 81.

53   David Ben Gurion, *Zikronot* I (Tel Aviv, 1971), pp. 22-23; for the English version of the passage, see *Memoirs* compiled by Thomas R. Bransten (New York and Cleveland, 1970), p. 48; on the early days of Petah Tikvah, see "Yeme Petah-Tikvah ha-Rishonim," *Kitbe Moshe Smilansky* VIII, pp. 206-12.

54   On *Ya-Hai-Li,* see the interesting mongraph by Manasseh Rabina, *Ya-Hai-Li, Li Hah 'Amali u-Mehabro Bar-Nash* (Tel Aviv, 1966). "The folksong" was written by one of the early settlers in Ottoman Palestine—an immigrant from Kishinev by the name of Noah Schapira; *nom de plume: Bar-Nash.* The second half of the pen name is an acronym of Noah Schapira. The song was written in 1895 and the melody, westernized, was originally borrowed from the Arabic. For a facsimile of the poem, ibid., p. 24. On "Sadness and Happiness," in Hebrew: "Yagon wa-Osher," see A. R. Malachi, "Hebrat Yishuv Eretz ha-Kodesh," *Horeb XIV-XV* (New York, 1959/60), pp. 235-36.

55   See the lovely story "Sultana" in *Kitbe Yehoshua Barzilai.* English translation by Minna Givton in *Israel Argosy* 6, pp. 26-32.

56   On the repudiation of the West by Arab intellectuals see Hisham Sharabi, op. cit., pp. 133-36.

57   Brenner also wrote under such pseudonyms as Bar-Yohai, B. Bezalel, H. F-n (Hayyim Feuerman) which, like Brenner, means "a man of fire." And Feuerman, the family name of the chief protagonist in *Ba-Horef,* shows a strong autobiographical strain in his first novel. Sometimes Brenner signed essays with his initials, H. J. B.

58   In the apt phrase of Hillel Zeitlin, Brenner's close friend during his formative years in Homel: "Ish Beli Hokmot." See *Joseph Hayyim Brenner—Mibhar Dibre Zikronot,* ed. Mordecai Kushnir-Shnir (Tel Aviv, 1971), p. 29; and in the beautiful summation by Agnon, who rarely ventured into the genre of the literary essay: Brenner sanctified his life by his death; he sanctified his death by his life (ibid., p. 119).

59   Brenner was also compared to Gorki at the outset of his literary career. See A. Simon, "J. Ch. Brenner—a Jewish Gorki," *Jewish Chronicle* (June 22, 1906).

60   A week before Brenner was murdered he is supposed to have said— and the saying has a ring of authenticity: "Each tanner, by himself, is weak, all tanners united are a force. Each writer, by himself, is a force, all writers—in an organization—are weak." Ibid., p. 330, n. 14.

61   Hebrew title: *Ba-Horef.* See *Kol Kitbe J. H. Brenner* (Israel, 1955), pp. 7-59. It was first published in *Ha-Shiloah* (March–December, 1903).

62   Hebrew title: *Me-'Eber li-Gebulin,* ibid., pp. 200-230. It was first published in *Ha-Me'orer* (1907).

63   Hebrew title: *Shekol we-Kishalon, Kol Kitbe J. H. Brenner* I, pp. 375–449. The novel, in an excellent translation by Hillel Halkin, was published by the Jewish Publication Society in Philadelphia in 1971. There is also a Yiddish translation by Peretz Opoczynski. On this victim of the Holocaust see *Yedi'ot Genazim—Soferim 'Ibrim she-Nispu ba-Shoah* (Tel-Aviv, 1973), pp. 314-18.

Had Brenner settled in New York before the First World War as he intended, we might have had an "American" novel from his pen. See his letter in Yiddish, dated September 8, 1911, to the Yiddish poet Abraham Reisen (1876-1953). The irony of the situation: the letter is an answer to the poet who had asked Brenner's advice whether he should come to Israel. The letter was published in *Kol Kitbe J. H. Brenner* II, p. 369. In a letter to Lisitzky, dated January 6, 1913, Brenner asks whether he could come to America for a year or two (ibid., p. 377).

64 *Kol Kitbe J. H. Brenner* III (1967), p. 37. Brenner admired Berdyczewski and regarded him as a man of primary importance in Hebrew literature. See J. H. Brenner, *Mibhar Zikronot,* pp. 293, 322.

65 Some writers were dissatisfied with the pretentious name: Schoffmann thought it was "loud," Berkowitz chided Brenner in gentler terms: "Let the name of your monthly be *"Ha-Me'orer"* [*The Wakener*] or *"Ha-Meyashen"* [*The One Who Puts to Sleep*]. What is important is this: to awaken writers to excellence." See manuscript letter of Schoffmann and Berkowitz to Brenner in *Genazim.* To awaken the Hebrew reader to deeper thought, to rob him of "placidity and self-deception"—this is how Brenner saw the aim of *Ha-Me'orer* in the second year of its publication.

66 Only eleven issues of the periodical appeared consecutively. The twelfth was published posthumously in 1923.

67 *Ha-Adamah* I (1919), p. 71. The article appeared under the pseudonym Bar-Yohai.

68 *Kol Kitbe J. H. Brenner* II (Tel Aviv, 1967), p. 481.

69 For an exhaustive list of Brenner's editorial ventures see *Kol Kitbe J. H. Brenner* III (Tel Aviv, 1967), p. 504.

70 It was called *Ha-Lebanon* and it published twelve issues in the first and only year of its existence. It was reestablished in the diaspora—first in Paris in 1865–1870, then in Mainz in 1870–1882. In 1854 there were already first faint stirrings of periodical publication in Jerusalem. See G. Kressel, *Toledot ha-'Ittonut ha-'Ibrit be-Eretz Yisrael* (Jerusalem, 1964), p. 22. Important periodicals after *Ha-Lebanon*: *Ha-Havazelet,* founded in 1863 by Israel Dov Frumkin; *Ha-Zevi,* founded in 1908 and edited by Ben-Yehudah; *Ha-'Omer* (1907–1909), founded by Simhah Ben-Zion and David Yellin; *Ha-Po'el ha-Zair,* the influential labor periodical, also founded in 1907. Important dailies: *Davar, Ha-Aretz, 'Al ha-Mishmar, Doar ha-Yom, Ma'ariv.*

71 Hebrew title: *Bat he-'Ashir.* It appeared in Warsaw in 1898/99.

72 Hebrew title: *Nedude 'Amasai ha-Shomer.* The name 'Amasai appears in the Bible as a Levite, as a priest in David's time, as a military prefect. 1 Chron. 6:10; 6:20; 2 Chron. 29:12. See also Mandelkern's *Concordance s.v.* Two volumes of critical essays resembling conversational pieces appeared posthumously: Jacob Rabinowitz, *Maslule Sifrut* (Jerusalem, 1971).

73 As for the adjective "Zionist" which is commonly attributed to Birnbaum in the nineties of the nineteenth century, it is most probable that Alfred Nos-

sig coined the term in Polish *syonski* in an almost forgotten tract which appeared in 1887 under the title *Attempt at a Solution of the Jewish Problem*. In the original Polish: *Proba rozwiązania kwestji żydowskiej*. See Dov Sadan, *Alufai u-Meyuda'ai* (Tel Aviv, 1972), p. 12.

2 Notes to Singer of the Desacralized Land: David Shimoni

1 In Hebrew: *Yeshimon* (Warsaw, 1911). Fichmann in an essay " 'Al ha-Lirikan" makes the following observation: "The name of the book is interesting . . . the desert, the dwelling-place of loneliness, the refuge of poetry and prayer. . . " See Jacob Fichmann, " 'Al ha-Lirikan" in *Davar Literary Supplement* (August 14, 1936), p. 3.

2 "Aharon" in Hebrew. *Shirim* I (Tel Aviv, 1953/54), pp. 21–22.

3 David Shimoni, *Yeshimon*, p. 20.

4 "Yardenit" in *Sefer ha-Idiliyyot*, pp. 3–16.

5 On regional differences in the talmudic period see *'Erubin* 53b.

6 "Milhemet Yehudah we-ha-Galil" in *Sefer ha-Idiliyyot*, pp. 33–43.

7 *Ketabim* II, p. 67.

8 "Ziyyonah," *Sefer ha-Idiliyyot*, pp. 189–242.

9 "Mazebah" (Tel Aviv, 1937). It had several editions. Also included in *Sefer ha-Idiliyyot*, pp. 242–86. The poet received a prize from the municipality of Tel Aviv for the idyll.

10 In Hebrew: *Resise Laylah.* Ibid., pp. 293–350.

11 In Hebrew: *Laylah be-Kerem, Ha-Shiloah* XXV (July, 1911), pp. 7–21. Ibid., (August, 1911), pp. 105–14.

12 In Hebrew: "Ha-To'eh bi-Zeman," *Ha-Shiloah* XXIX (1913), pp. 10–19, 107–20, 228–39.

13 See manuscript letter of February 18, 1911, from Shimoni to Klausner in the Manuscript Division of the National and University Library of Jerusalem. It was with apologetic hesitation that Shimoni sent his "Night in a Vineyard" to Klausner, the editor of *Ha-Shiloah;* but he decided that the combination of realism and symbolism in the depiction of the Palestinian milieu merit-

ed publication. After all it was not a drama but a fragment—as he declared in the interesting letter.

14   In Hebrew: "Ba-Ya'ar ba-Haderah." Ibid., pp. 17–29. Rabbi Phinehas, the ideal of idealists, who appears in several idylls of the poet, seems to have been modeled on the worker-philosopher, A.D. Gordon, who was Shimoni's friend.

15   In Hebrew: 'Obede Kokabim.

16   In Hebrew: "Eshet Iyov."

17   In Hebrew: "Halom Lel Horef."

18   Shimoni attributes to his father's influence his infatuation with Lermontov: "I cannot speak about my father without deep emotion. He was a scholar . . . a lover of modern Hebrew literature, and he knew long passages of Lermontov's poetry by heart." See "Sihah Im Ba'al ha-Yovel," in Ha-Aretz (August 7, 1936), p. 10. In 1954 Shimoni said: "I have returned to Lermontov. With all the change of fashion in poetry I remain loyal to him." And he praised "the sublime simplicity in Lermontov's style." See Abraham Braudes, "Pegishot u-Devarim," Moznayim 24 (Tevet, 5727-1966/67) p. 113.

19   In Hebrew: Moledet; the satires appeared in Bi-Shevile ha-Bevar, pp. 223–357.

20   In Hebrew: Ba-Hashai (Tel Aviv, 1954/55). In the preface the poet claims that the disjointed pieces were mainly diary jottings, "a diary of inner experiences." Hence the title.

21   Critical estimate on the poet has not crystallized. It ranges from very high to very low opinions: "He is the great poetical genius of the Yishuv." Thus Max Meir, "David Schimonowitz, " Davar Literary Supplement (August 14, 1936), p. 4. Isaac Shalev pays tribute to Shimoni's "living, blooming landscape of idylls." See Elohai ha-Noshek Lohamim (Jerusalem, 1957), p. 136. "Teaching and journalism are the usual occupations of the Hebrew writer. They are incidental as far as other writers are concerned . . . but essential characteristics as far as Schimonowitz is concerned. . . He is the journalist among poets." Thus A. Regelson, "Meshorer ha-Sharet" in Hadoar (November 20, 1936), p. 42.

3   Notes to Rediscovery of
Landscape: Jacob Fichmann

1   Jacob Fichmann, *Zelalim 'Al Sadot*, (Tel Aviv, 1935).

2   Ibid., p. 11.

3   The most controversial novel of the twentieth century, *Ulysses*, owes to Homer its title, its framework, and its wealth of associations, as does the massive and innovative epic by Nikos Kazantzakis, *The Odyssey*. Also the prose rendition of Thomas Edward Lawrence [Lawrence of Arabia] succeeded in boosting the vogue for Ulysses who, in his restless search and travel, may be regarded as the epitome of the generation which grew up after the First World War. It is not mere coincidence that Tschernichowsky translated the *Odyssey* into Hebrew between the two world wars and provided younger poets like Hayyim Guri with an identifiable hero. See Hayyim Guri, *Shoshannat ha-Ruhot* (Tel Aviv, 1966), p. 115; *idem, Tenu'ah le-Magga'* (Ramat Gan, 1967/68), pp. 10–11.

4   In Hebrew: "Yehudah," *Zelalim 'Al Sadot*, pp. 161–73.

5   For S.J. Kahn's sensitive, informal translation of two sonnets by Fichmann, "Hermon" and "The Valley of Sorek," see *Israel Argosy* 6, p. 60, 74.

6   See introduction to *Yeme Shemesh* (Tel Aviv, 1934), not reprinted in *Kitbe Ya'akob Fichmann* (Tel Aviv, 1959), pp. 7–9.

7   For a different point of view see Shalom Streit, *Pene ha-Safrut* II, (Tel Aviv, 1939), p. 103: "In the longer poems Fichmann reached the height of his power."

8   *Yeme Shemesh* conveniently reprinted in *Kitbe Ya'akov Fichmann*, pp. 98–167.

9   *Yeme Shemesh*, p. 7.

10   There are variants: Hazlelponi, Hazlelponit, Zelelponi.

11   Quoted by Fichmann from *Tanna de-Be Eliyyahu Rabba*.

12   In Hebrew: *Idiliyyot Yam*, op. cit., pp. 98-112.

13   This is also true of his translations and numerous educational ventures which include poems for children, juvenile stories and novels, and such popular textbooks for Hebrew schools as *Lashon wa-Sefer* in six parts.

14   See Fichmann's *Anshe Besorah* (Tel Aviv, 1938), pp. 71–196.

15   See Jacob Fichmann, "Musag ha-Lirizm" in *Sefer Klausner* (Tel Aviv, 1937), p. 427.

4   Notes to Poet in Prose:
Jacob Steinberg

1   *Kol Kitbe Ya'akob Steinberg* (Tel Aviv, 1957), p. 14.

2   Ibid., pp. 31–43.

3   The general atmosphere of the poem is influenced by Bialik while individual lines are borrowed from Cahan and Tschernichowsky. The verse "Yamim Baim, Yamim Holfim" (ibid., p. 34, 35, 36) reads like a transcription of the first line of a famous poem by Jacob Cahan: "Baim yamim, holfim yamim," *Kitbe Ya'akob Cahan* I (Tel Aviv, 1950), p. 172. "Ner ha-Hayyim Hu ha-Shemesh" *(Kol Kitbe Ya'akob Steinberg,* p. 36) is a paraphrase of a line by Tschernichowsky: *En ha-Shemesh Hem ha-Hayyim* (see Saul Tschernichowsky, *Shirim* (Jerusalem, 1953), p. 70.

4   *Kol Kitbe Ya'akob Steinberg,* p. 77.

5   On these plays, see the author's *From Renaissance to Renaissance* I (New York, 1973), pp. 11, 64–65, 112.

6   The three volumes—with addenda from the poet's estate—have been collected in a large, one-volume edition by Dvir. All quotations are from that edition.

7   Hebrew title: "Bat ha-Rav," Steinberg, op. cit., pp. 122–29.

8   In Hebrew: "'Al Gebul Ukraina," ibid., pp. 133–51.

9   In Hebrew: *Reshimot,* ibid., pp. 273–431.

10   Critics have noticed the glamorless sobriety of modern poetry. In the preface to *a New Anthology of Modern Verse* (New York, 1939), pp. 23–24, the editor Selden Rodman stresses "a few . . . characteristics of modernity . . . imagery patterned increasingly on everyday speech . . . emphasis on the ordinary . . . concern with the common man."

11   What loss of faith means to literature is best exemplified by the eloquent remarks of T. S. Eliot, *After Strange Gods* (New York, 1934), pp. 45–46: " . . . with the disappearance of the idea of Original Sin, with the disappear-

ance of the idea of intense moral struggle, the human beings presented to us both in poetry and in prose fiction today, and more patently among the serious writers than in the underworld of letters, tend to become less and less real. It is in fact in moments of moral and spiritual struggle depending upon spiritual sanctions . . . that men and women come nearest to being real. If you do away with this struggle, and maintain that by tolerance, benevolence, inoffensiveness and a redistribution or increase of purchasing power, combined with a devotion, on the part of an elite, to Art, the world will be as good as anyone could require, then you must expect human beings to become more and more vaporous."

5 Notes to The Avant-gardists:
Avigdor Hameiri, Uri Zevi Gruenberg, Jacob Horowitz

1 Madách's *Az ember tragediaja* was translated and appeared in book form under the title *Hazon ha-Adam* (Warsaw, 1924); translation of a selection of Petöfi's poetry also appeared in book form under the title *Mi-Shire Sándor Petöfi* (Tel Aviv, 1952), and Ady's poetry appeared under the title *Shire Endre Ady* (Tel Aviv, 1954).

2 The poem appeared in book form: Avigdor Hameiri, *Yosele Teglashi* (Ramat Gan, 1967).

3 "Shirat Shimshon ha-Aharonah" in Avigdor Hameiri, *Be-Livnat ha-Sappir* (Jerusalem, 1962), p. 153.

4 In his poem "Ba-Hekal," ibid., p. 36.

5 In Hebrew: *Ashre ha-Gafror* (Tel Aviv, 1958).

6 *Ha-Shiga'on ha-Gadol* (Tel Aviv, 1930). The book titled *The Great Madness* has been translated into English by Jacob Freedman and published by Vantage Press, Inc. (New York, 1952).

7 "Te'udat Mawet" in Avigdor Hameiri, *Sefer ha-Shirim* (Tel Aviv, 1933), p. 214.

8 See "Shelihah le-Immi" in *Be-Livnat ha-Sappir,* p. 66.

9 "Ziyyon ha-Niggelet," ibid., pp. 41–42.

10 *Sefer ha-Shirim,* p. 358.

11 "Halomot Shel Bet-Rabban" in *Be-Livnat ha-Sappir,* p. 77.

12 *Sefer ha-Shirim,* p. 223.

13 Teapot—Kumkum in Hebrew—was organized in 1927 and lasted almost a year. Broom—in Hebrew Matate—was organized by secessionists from Kumkum and lasted a quarter of a century. On these satirical cabarets, see Mendel Kohansky, *The Hebrew Theatre,* pref. Tyrone Guthrie (Jerusalem, 1969), pp. 107–11.

14   Other poets of note—Shlonsky and Alterman and Leah Goldberg—also lampooned social and political conditions of mandatory Palestine in light verse. See S. Dani, "Pizmonim Satiriyyim Shel Leah Goldberg," *M'ariv Literary Supplement* (8/29–30, 1974), p. 37.

15   "Shete Nishmotai" in *Be-Livnat ha-Sappir*, p. 7.

16   In his numerous manifestoes, especially in his *Manifesto tecnico della letteratura futurista* (1912) Marinetti postulated the destruction of the twin conceptions of Woman and Beauty in literature; the machine in prose and poetry was to be the substitute. Gruenberg adhered to the negative part of the program: he eschewed Woman and Beauty in the romanticized version of Victorian poets. He also adopted the typographic artifice and the cubistic incoherence of the French poet, Guillaume Apollinaire, born of a Polish mother and Italian father and named Wilhelm Apollinaris Albertus de Kostrowicki. Today Marinetti and Apollinaire are the happy hunting grounds of academic exegetes but not the living paradigms of durable poetry.

17   Half a century later a distinguished poet—W. H. Auden—characterized Dada and Surrealism as "asinine movements." See his review of *In The Twenties: The Diaries of Harry Kessler, The New York Review of Books,* (August 31, 1972), p. 4.

18   In Hebrew: *Emah Gedolah we-Yareah* (Tel Aviv, 1924).

19   Uri Zevi Gruenberg, *Kelape Tish'im we-Tish'ah* (Tel Aviv, 1928), p. 35.

20   *Emah Gedolah we-Yareah*, p. 50.

21   *Kelev Bayit* (Tel Aviv, 1929), p. 30.

22   In Hebrew: *Ezor Magen u-Neum Ben ha-Dam* (Jerusalem, 1929/30).

23   In Hebrew: *Sefer ha-Kitrug we-ha-Emunah* (Tel Aviv, 1937).

24   Ibid., p. 164.

25   For Klatzkin's use of the terms, see the author's *From Renaissance to Renaissance I*, pp. 170–71.

26   *Kelev Bayit*, pp. 15–16.

27   *Sefer ha-Kitrug we-ha-Emunah*, p. 64.

28   Baruch Spinoza, *Ethics III, Def. 2: Laetitia est hominis transitio a minore ad maiorem perfectionem.*

29   *Kelev Bayit*, p. 64. According to a talmudic legend, elaborated in later ages but based on a fanciful interpretation of Isaiah 30:18, thirty-six *Zaddikim* sustain the world in each generation. See *Sanhedrin* 97b.

30   *Ha-Gabrut ha-'Olah* (Tel Aviv, 1926), p. 31. Shlonsky compared the full moon to the golden phylactery on God's head in *Ba-Galgal*, p. 165. In another poem he posed the query: Who bound the sun-phylactery on dawn? See his *Ketabim* II (Merhavyah, 1969), p. 142.

31   *Sefer ha-Kitrug we-ha-Emunah*, p. 132.

32   *Kelape Tish'im we-Tish'ah,* p. 9.

33   Ibid., p. 34.

34   *Ha-Gabrut ha-'Olah,* p. 31.

35   Gen. 36:37; 1 Chron. 1:48. Another poet also used the place-name *Rehobot ha-Nahar* but in a non-pejorative sense. See Phinehas Sadeh, *Sefer ha-Shirim* (Jerusalem and Tel Aviv, 1970), p. 145.

36   Critics, unaware of the biblical *Rehobot ha-Nahar,* have recourse to fanciful theories about its interpretation and meaning. See, for instance, Sholom J. Kahn, "Uri Zevi Gruenberg—Poet of Kingship," *Ariel* 13 (1966), pp. 47–48.

37   The original in Uri Zevi Gruenberg, *Rehobot ha-Nahar* (Jerusalem and Tel Aviv, 1951) p. 347.

38   *Ha-Shiloah* **XXIX** (August, 1913), p. 149. Hebrew title of the poem: *'Im ha-Sheki'ah.*

39   In Hebrew: *Or Zarua'* (Tel Aviv, 1929).

40   Ps. 97:11.

41   Horowitz plays on lingual similarities in Hebrew: *Erez Ra'* and *Or Zarua'.*

42   In Hebrew: *Sha' are ha-Tumah* (Berlin, 1929/30).

43   In German: *Entartung* (Berlin, 1893).

44   In Hebrew: *'Olam She-Lo Neherav 'Adayin* (Tel Aviv, 1949/50).

45   Jacob Horowitz, *Ketabim* (Tel Aviv, 1965).

6   Notes to The Neo-liturgical Poets: Isaac Lamdan; Judah Karni; Joseph Zevi Rimmon; Jacob Rimmon

1   Isaac Lamdan, *Massadah* (Dvir le-'Am, Tel Aviv, 1952), p. 40; *Kol Shire Yizhak Lamdan* (Jerusalem, 1973), pp. 46–47.

2   See jacket of *Massada* by Yigael Yadin. The book, first published in London in 1966, was as successful as the author's lectures on Massadah which attracted thousands of people. See preface to Yigael Yadin, *Massada,* p. 8.

3.   The Hebrew title of stories by M. Siko—pseudonym for Meir Smilansky—is *Even Tiz'ak.* It is based on Hab. 2:11.

4   In Hebrew: *Ba-Ritmah ha-Meshulleshet,* (Tel Aviv, 1930); *Kol Shire Yizhak Lamdan,* pp. 77–171.

5   *Ba-Ritmah ha-Meshulleshet,* p. 44; *Kol Shire Yizhak Lamdan,* p. 102.

6   In his book on Isaac Lamdan, Leon I. Yudkin published the facsimile and translation of "the only love-poem that Lamdan ever wrote." See Leon I. Yudkin, *Isaac Lamdan: A study in Twentieth Century Hebrew Poetry* (Ithaca, New York, 1971), pp. 247–48.

7   In Hebrew: *Mi-Sefer ha-Yamim* (Tel Aviv, 1939/40); *Kol Shire Yizhak Lamdan,* pp. 299–329. In the edition of Lamdan's collected poems, *Mi-Sefer ha-Yamim* is included in *Be-Ma'aleh 'Akrabim.*

8   In Hebrew: *Be-Ma'aleh 'Akrabim* (Tel Aviv, 1944); *Kol Shire Yizhak Lamdan,* pp. 173–329. Like Gruenberg, Lamdan chose the name of a biblical locality 'Akrabim for the title of a book of poems. It is mentioned in Num. 34:4; *Jo. 15:3 Le-Ma'aleh 'Akrabim;* in Judg. 1:36: *Mi-Ma'aleh 'Akrabim.* The obvious symbolism of the name—the difficulty of ascent and the potential harm which scorpions inflict on daring climbers—exerted an irresistible attraction on Lamdan.

9   *Be-Ma'aleh'Akrabim,* p. 29; *Kol Shire Yizhak Lamdan,* p. 191.

10   Nathan Zach, *Kol ha-Halav we-ha-Devash* (Tel Aviv, 1966), pp. 42–43; 70.

11   See facsimile of Lamdan's lengthy letter to Shenhar [Schönberg] of July 19, 1935 in *Genazim* 68 (Tel Aviv, 1969/70), p. 508. The monthly may not have fulfilled the high aspirations of the founder. But it justified the investment of his endless labor in spite of material and intellectual disappointments which dogged its career from the beginning. Ibid., especially p. 509.

12   *Ba-Ritmah ha-Meshulleshet*, p. 149-50; *Kol Shire Yizhak Lamdan*, p. 156.

13   The one-volume edition of Lamdan's poetry which contains published and unpublished poems owes much to the combined labors of Yeroham Luria and Simon Halkin. The latter prefaced the edition. See "'Al Shirat Yizhak Lamdan" in *Kol Shire Yizhak Lamdan*, pp. 11-35.

14   In *Bi-She 'arayik, Yerushalayim* (Tel Aviv, 1934/35) Karni indicated that the volume was a collection of *Piyyutim*, liturgical poems rather than *Shirim*, mere poems.

15   Yehudah Karni, *She 'arim* (Jerusalem-Berlin, 1923), p. 6.

16   Yehudah Karni, *Shir we-Dema'* (Tel Aviv, 1944/45), p. 29.

17   Ibid., p. 219.

18   Karni's poems on Jerusalem, culled from his books, have been published under the title *Yerushalayim* (Tel Aviv, 1944).

19   *Bi-She'arayik, Yerushalayim*, p. 179.

20   J.Z. Rimmon, *Devir* (Jaffa, 1913), p. 27. Also J.Z. Rimmon, *Shirim*, (Givatayim-Ramat Gan, 1973), p. 58. *Devir* followed his first volume *Leket* (Jerusalem, 1910) which was not well received by Brenner. See *Kol Kitbe Brenner* II, p. 295. Brenner eventually became the poet's friend. See the introduction of the poet's son David Rimmon to his father's *Shirim*, p. 9.

21   *Mi-Shirot ha-Zeman*, p. 161; 111. Also Rimmon, *Shirim*, p. 128.

22   *Mi-Shirot ha-Zeman*, p. 79. Also Rimmon, *Shirim*, p. 122.

23   "Zimaon le-El Hai" in Hebrew. See Kook's *Orot* (Jerusalem, 1961), pp. 119-20.

24   Ibid., p. 63.

25   In *Ha-'Ivri*, a journal edited by Brainin in New York, Rimmon published an article on Kook: "Meshorer ha-Yahadut." It was republished in a pamphlet in Tel Aviv (1918/19) under the same name. After the First World War Rimmon published a pamphlet *R. Abraham ha-Kohen Kook we-Ra'ayon ha-Tehiyah*. When Phinehas Grayevski edited a pamphlet in honor of Rimmon, *Hoveret ha-Yovel li-Melot 'Esrim wa-Hamesh Shanim le-Shirato* (Jerusalem, 1931/32), he received a letter on the poet from R. Kook.

26   See Jacob Rimmon, *Demuyot Min he-'Avar* (Tel Aviv, 1972), p. 212. Joseph Zevi Rimmon dedicated a melancholy poem to A.Z. Rabinowttz. See his third volume of poems *Ba-Mahazeh* (Jaffa, 1915/16), pp. 23–25. The last and fourth volume *Ketarim* appeared in Tel Aviv, 1934/44. Rimmon's son David published a posthumous selection of his father's poetry which contains poems from

the preceding books and poems which had not appeared previously. See Joseph Zevi Rimmon, *Shirim,* p. 39. For a poem on his son's Bar Mizvah, ibid., p. 201.

27   See the introduction "Hayye Avi" by the poet's son David Rimmon to Joseph Zevi Rimmon, *Shirim* (Givatayim-Ramat Gan, 1973), p. 7.

28   In Hebrew: *'Aze Hayyim* (Jerusalem, 1945/46). The book *'Aze Hayyim* is about the great ones of Jewry, while his numerous commentaries on the Bible endeavor to penetrate into the spirit of prophets like Isaiah, Jeremiah and Ezekiel.

29   Ibid., p. 48.

30   Joseph Zevi Rimmon, *Shirim,* p. 182. The last line alludes to Genesis 8:21.

31   Ibid., p. 191.

32   In Hebrew: Jacob Rimmon, *Seneh* (Tel Aviv, 1945/46). The title alludes, of course, to Exod. 3:2.

33   Ibid., p. 10.

34   Jacob Rimmon's poem "Shaali Keneset Yisrael," ibid., pp. 31-32 is a modernized version of Judah Halevi's famous "Zionide."

35   Ibid., p. 94.

36   Ibid., p. 69.

37   Ibid., p. 81.

38   In Hebrew: *Ha-Shahar Ran* (Tel Aviv-Jerusalem, 1962/63).

39   In Hebrew: *Yeladim be-'Oni—Mi-Yomano Shel 'Oved Soziali,* (Tel Aviv, 1945/46).

40   Jacob Rimmon, *Demuyot Min he-'Avar* (Tel Aviv, 1972).

7   Notes to The Poets of Jerusalem:
Asaf Halevi, Jacob David Kamson,
Ari Ibn Zahav, Zerah Halevi, Isaac Shalev

1   Pindar, *Fragment 76.*

2   Pss. 48:3.

3   Isa. 52:1.

4   Zech. 8:3.

5   *Kiddushin 49b.*

6   The other three cities of paradise: Mecca, Medina, Damascus. See Herbert Busse, "The Sanctity of Jerusalem in Islam," *Judaism* XVII[4] (Fall, 1968), p. 464.

7   *Urbs Syon Aurea:* this is Bernard de Cluny's phrase in his poem *De contemptu mundi.* For Jewish sources of the sobriquet, see *Nedarim* 50a; *Shabbat* 59a.

8   See the introduction to an anthology of Hebrew stories in English translation titled *First Fruits* (Philadelphia, 1973), pp. xxiii–xxiv. The anthology is edited by James A. Michener.

9   The better known anthologies of Jerusalem in poetry and prose: *Yerushalayim be-Shir we-Hazon,* ed. Jacob Cahan (Tel Aviv, 1937); *Yerushalayim be-Yezirat ha-Dorot,* ed. Hayyim Toren (Tel Aviv, 1951); *Yerushalayim be-Shiratenu ha-Hadashah,* ed. Shalom ben Baruch [Schwartz] (Jerusalem, 1955); *Sefer Yerushalayim,* ed. Ephraim and Menahem Talmi (Tel Aviv, 1956). For a selection of prose and poetry on Jerusalem in French and English: *Centre du P.E.N. d'Israel—Bulletin 12,* May 1968 (Jerusalem, 1968).

10   Even the *Reader's Digest* took note of the poem. See Linda Gottlieb, "The Song That Took a City" (December, 1967), pp. 112–15.

11   Pss. 137:5. On a solemn occasion, when the honorary citizenship of Jerusalem was bestowed on Hayyim Hazaz, in 1969, the author made a few remarks which epitomize the Jewish attitude and love for the Holy City: "Jerusalem has been with me since childhood, Jerusalem was in our home; the climate of Jerusalem pervaded the Jewish ambience of our town. During festivals, on fast days, in the prayers, in grace after meals. Jerusalem was on the tongue of the infants, women and men alike. . . Today, too, Jerusalem is for me the city of the future . . . Jerusalem is destined to be a great light indeed." See "Hayyim Hazaz—Freeman of Jerusalem, City of the Future," *The Jerusalem Post* (October 6, 1969), pp. 13–14. Cities of the diaspora, renowned for Jewish learning, often earned the sobriquet "Jerusalem," e.g., Vilna, Jerusalem of Lithuania.

12   See the thin twenty-four page collection of poems by Dalia Ben-David, *Yerushalayim u-Malkut*. There is no mention of date or place of publication.

13   Asaf Halevi, *Megillat Kedem* (Jerusalem, 1919/20), p. 302.

14   Ibid., p. 117.

15   Ibid., p. 124.

16   Saul Tschernichowsky, *Shirim* (Tel Aviv, 1953), pp. 291–301. On the sonnets "To the Sun," see Eisig Silberschlag, *Saul Tschernichowsky: Poet of Revolt*, pp. 60–61.

17   Asaf Halevi, op. cit., p. 95.

18   Ibid. p. 309.

19   Ibid., pp. 311–18.

20   Ibid., p. 290.

21   Jacob David Kamson, *Yerushalayim* (Jerusalem, 1949/50), p. 15.

22   Ibid., p. 142.

23   Ibid., p. 129.

24   Ibid., p. 20.

25   Both novels appeared in an English translation. The former was rendered into English by I.M. Lask (New York, 1951), the latter by Julian Meltzer (New York, 1948). An early version of the novel *David and Bathsheba* was published in three volumes under the title *Yeme David* (Jerusalem 1928/29), a completely altered version in *Mibhar Ketabim* (Jerusalem, 1969).

26   In Hebrew: *Be-Tokeki Yerushalayim* (Jerusalem and Tel Aviv, 1927).

27   Ibid., p. 6.

28   Ari Ibn Zahav, *At Yerushalayim* (Jerusalem, 1939), p. 10. The book appeared in a de luxe edition with reproductions of the Israeli artist Jacob Steinhardt (1887–1968). Some poems from the book were reprinted in the selected writings of Ari Ibn Zahav under the title *Yerushalayim Shel Ma'alah* (Tel

Aviv, 1969). Jerusalem is also the subject of the author's brief oratorio, partly prose, partly poetry. See *Yom Yerushalayim* (Tel Aviv, 1937). Jerusalem also figures in the prose trilogy *Yerushalayim Shel Mattah* (Tel Aviv, 1969).

29 Ari Ibn Zahav, *At Yerushalayim,* p. 13.

30 Ibid. There are numerous allusions to the pillar of cloud and the pillar of fire in the Bible. See, for instance, Exod. 13:22.

31 Ibid., p. 17.

32 Ari Ibn Zahav, *Yerushalayim Shel Ma'alah,* p. 42.

33 The third line alludes to Pss. 42:7 and Isa. 14:14, the last line to Dan. 12:7.

34 Ari Ibn Zahav, *At Yerushalayim,* p. 30.

35 Ibid., introduction.

36 Zerah Halevi learned the trade from his father who was poor although his artistic accomplishment in all kinds of metal work attracted the attention of Professor Boris Schatz (1867–1932), the founder and first director of the Bezalel School of Art and Bezalel Museum in Jerusalem. See prose reminiscences of Zerah Halevi in *Shire Zerah Halevi* (Jerusalem, 1967), pp. 100–101.

37 Ibid., p. 5.

38 For the poem "Higgali Na le-Or ha-Shemesh," ibid., p. 50, Zerah Halevi published his own musical score, ibid., p. 86.

39 Ibid., pp. 69–83.

40 Ibid., pp. 12–13.

41 Ibid, p. 96.

42 Isaac Shalev, *Shire Yerushalyim* (Jerusalem, 1968), p. 13. The book is an assemblage of four volumes of Shalev's poems: *Ohezet 'Anaf Shaked, Kolot Enosh Tamim, Kol 'Anot, Elohai ha-Noshek Lohamim.*

43 Ibid., p. 27.

44 Ibid., p. 22.

45 Pss. 48:3.

46 *Shire Yerushalayim,* p. 43.

47 Ibid., p. 87.

48 Ibid., p. 89.

49 Hayyim Guri, *Dappim Yerushalmiyyim* (Tel Aviv, 1968), pp. 267–68.

50 Ibid., p. 282.

51 Ibid., p. 286.

52 Ezra Sussman in the poem "Shuv Har ha-Zetim" in *'Aze Tamid* (Tel Aviv, 1972), pp. 158–59.

8   Notes to The Revolutionizer of the Hebrew Language: Abraham Shlonsky

1   Abraham Shlonsky, *Devai* (Tel Aviv, 1924), p. 19. The poem is now available in the first volume of the ten volume edition of Shlonsky's poems and translations of poetic works from the literatures of the world: *Ketabim* I (Merhavyah, 1971), p. 105 ff. A posthumous volume-*Sefer ha-Sullamot* (Tel Aviv, 1973)-rounds out his oeuvre. Only one other Hebrew poet earned the distinction of a ten volume edition: Saul Tschernichowsky. On that edition, see Eisig Silberschlag, *Saul Tschernichowsky: Poet of Revolt,* p. 196.

2   Abraham Shlonsky, *Ba-Galgal* (Tel Aviv, 1927) p. 23.

3   *Ketabim* (1927–1935), *Turim* (1933–1934), *Orlogin* (1950–1957)—the three periodicals associated with the name of Shlonsky—were havens of avantgarde writers with leftist tendencies in the twenties, in the thirties and in the fifties.

4   Poems on pioneers in *Ketabim* IV, 149–53; on the holocaust, ibid., pp. 154–70.

5   Abraham Shlonsky, *Ketabim* III, pp. 182–83.

6   *Devai,* p. 48.

7   Since "Song for the Clatter Bones" is not well known, it is appropriate, perhaps, to quote the first stanza:

God rest that Jewy woman,
Queen Jezebel, the bitch
Who peeled her clothes from her shoulder-bones
Down to her spent teats
As she stretched out of the window
Among the geraniums, where
She chaffed and laughed like one half daft
Titivating her painted hair.

8   *Sefer Shirim* (Tel Aviv, 1933), p. 139. To put money on a deer's horn means, in rabbinic parlance, that one cannot reclaim the unauthorized expense. See,

for instance, *Ketubot* 13:2. There is an interesting parallel to Shlonsky's lines in Rabindranath Tagore's *The Gardener* (London, 1913), p. 119:

> I hunt the golden stag.
> You may smile, my friends, but I pursue the vision that eludes me.
> I run across hills and dales, I wander through nameless lands
> Because I am hunting the golden stag.

9   Abraham Shlonsky, *Ba-Galgal*, p. 18; *Ketabim* I, p. 27.

10   *Ketabim* II, pp. 128–38. Filial piety was a poetic fashion in the twenties. Many pioneers were overwhelmed by longing for their parents abroad. A typical instance: Dov Sadan, *A Bintel Briv fun a Halutz tzu Tate-Mame* (Lvov, 1925/26).

11   On translations from Mayakovsky and Yesenin, see Abraham Shlonsky, *Targume Shirah* I, pp. 144–95. Other Russian poets in that volume: Balmont, Blok, Akhmatova, Pasternak, Mandelshtam, Tsvetaeva and others.

9   Notes to In the Wake of Shlonsky:
Nathan Alterman; Raphael Eliaz; Abraham Halfi;
Joshua Tan-Pai; David Rokeah;
Solomon Tanny; Noah Peniel;
Jacob Orland; David Avidan;
Alexander Pen

1   In Hebrew *Ha-Tur ha-Shevi'i*. The first volume appeared in 1948, the second in 1954. The poems, collected in two volumes, were published originally in the seventh column of *Davar*, the daily of the Israeli Labor Party, Mapai; hence the title. The publication of the poems in the daily press began in 1943 and continued for twenty-two years. After the conclusion of the Second World War some poems were censored by the mandatory government. They appeared clandestinely and helped to increase the poet's popularity.

2   The articles, written between April, 1967, and February, 1970, for the eveing paper *Ma'ariv*, were collected and published in book form posthumously under the title *Ha-Hut ha-Meshullash* (Tel Aviv, 1971). The title of the book, based on Ecclesiastes 4:12, appeared in an article which was written immediately after the Six-Day War on June 16, 1967: "This is the meaning of our victory: it erased, for all practical purposes, the difference between the State of Israel and the Land of Israel. For the first time since the destruction of the Second Sanctuary the Land of Israel is in our hands. The state and the land are henceforth one entity that lacks Israel the people for historical association—Israel that will weave . . . the triple thread which will not snap." Ibid., p. 39.

3   Nathan Alterman, *Kokabim ba-Huz* (Tel Aviv, 1938), p. 19, *Shirim mi-she-Kevar* (Ramat Gan, 1970/71), p.19. The first volume of poetry, *Kokabim ba-Huz*, together with the two succeeding ones, *Simhat 'Aniyyim* and *Shire Makot Mizrayim* (Tel Aviv, 1944) appeared under a new title *Shirim mi-she-Kevar* under the auspices of the public committee for the publication of the collected works of Nathan Alterman. The notes are based on *Shirim mi-she-Kevar*.

4   Ibid., p.37.

5   Ibid., p. 32.

6   Ibid., p. 37.

7   Ibid., p. 84.

8   Ibid., p. 67.

9   Ibid., p. 99.

10   In addition to the Hebrew titles of the first books of poetry by Nathan Alterman (see note 3), the following are the respective Hebrew titles for *Summer Party*, *The Oppressing City* and *The Book of Riddles: Hagigat Kayiz* (Tel Aviv, 1965); *'Ir Ha-Yonah; Sefer ha-Hidot* (Tel Aviv, 1971). The title of *'Ir ha-Yonah* (Tel Aviv, 1957) is based on Zephaniah 3:1. For erroneous translations of the title—*City of the Dove* for example—see *Anthology of Modern Hebrew Poetry* II selected by S. Y. Penueli and A. Ukmani (Jerusalem, 1966), p. 387; *The Modern Hebrew Poem Itself*, ed. S. Burnshaw, T. Carmi, E. Spicehandler (New York, Chicago, San Francisco, 1965), p. 113. Same error in *Orot* II (Jerusalem, June, 1966), p. 7 and 77.

11   Nathan Alterman, *Sefer ha-Hidot*, p. 159. A later version: "For all practical purposes [man] is a riddle that bares new riddles."

12   Ibid., p. 122. The first line is taken from Joshua 6:1.

13   Ibid., p. 52.

14   In Hebrew: *Ha-Massekah ha-Aharonah* (Tel Aviv, 1968).

15   The title of the book: *Be-Ma'agal* (Israel, 1970/1).

16   *Ha-Tur ha-Shevi'i* II, p. 387.

17   In Hebrew: "Magash ha-Kesef," *Ha-Tur ha-Shevi'i*, I, pp. 366–67.

18   It appeared in *'Ir ha-Yonah* under the title "Shir 'Asarah Ahim," pp. 285–352 and in a special bibliophile edition in 1961. It is based on a popular Yiddish ballad which was sung throughout eastern Europe. The first verse in the original "Zehn Brider zenen mir geven."

19   In Hebrew: *Sefer ha-Tevah ha-Mezammeret* (Tel Aviv, 1958).

20   In Hebrew: *Mass'ot Binyamin mi-Tudela*. Ibid., pp. 7–11. The medieval traveler, Rabbi Benjamin of Tudela, published an account of his travels which was translated into English and edited by A. Asher (London, 1840).

21   The respective Hebrew titles: *Pundak ha-Ruhot* (Tel Aviv, 1962), *Kinneret, Kinneret*(Tel Aviv, 1962), *Mishpat Pythagoras* (Tel Aviv, 1965), *Esther ha-Malkah* (Tel Aviv, 1966).

22   *Mishpat Pythagoras*, pp. 131–51.

23   The first version, under the title *Shelomoh ha-Melek we-Shalmi ha-Sandlar* appeared in 1942; the later version in 1964; the latest version in 1975—five years after the poet's death.

24   See note 2.

25   Raphael Eliaz, *Shemesh ba-Derakim* (Tel Aviv, 1939), p. 7.

26   Ibid., p. 36.

27   Ibid., p. 25.

28   In Hebrew: "Hevel Mevakeh Et Kayin."

29   See the opening couplet of "Abel et Cain" in *Les Fleurs du Mal:*
Race d'Abel, dors, bois et mange;
Dieu te sourit complaisamment.

30   Raphael Eliaz, op. cit., p. 116.

31   Ibid., p. 54.

32   Ibid., p. 70.

33   Ibid., p. 94.

34   Raphael Eliaz, *Ahavah ba-Midbar* (Tel Aviv, 1946), p. 80.

35   In Hebrew: *Ha-Bubbah Zivah* (Tel Aviv, 1957).

36   Eliaz's translations of the Spanish poet in: Federico Garcia Lorca, *Mibhar Shirim* (Merhavyah, 1958).

37   The poet dedicated a poem to Shlonsky, "Song and the Shadow of Song," in *Mul Kokabim we-'Afar* (Ramat Gan, 1962), pp. 68–69; he also devoted a peculiar poem "To the Memory of Yesenin," ibid., pp. 32-33. In the body of that poem he twice quoted a couplet of the Russian poet in the original and rhymed the Russian word for smoke—*dim*—with the Hebrew words for friends—*Yedidim*—and lonely—*Bodedim*. Halfi seems to have suffered from dedicatory compulsions. Quite a few of his poems are inscribed to literary friends: to Eliaz, ibid., p. 56 , to Isaac Norman, ibid., p. 63, to Alterman, ibid., pp. 100-101.

38   Abraham Halfi, *Mi-Zavit El Zavit*(Tel Aviv, 1939), p. 78.

39   Abraham Halfi, *Enpanav ha-Holekim li-Kerati* (Tel Aviv, 1966), p. 9.

40   Abraham Halfi, *Mi-Zavit El Zavit*, p. 27.

41   See especially the poems "Be-Moti," "Mul Pene ha-Orlogin," "Efoh Yippol," "Ahare she-Matti" in Abraham Halfi, *Shirim* (Tel Aviv, 1968), pp. 8, 9, 30, 40.

42   Abraham Halfi, *Mi-Zavit El Zavit*, p. 65.

43   In Hebrew: "Shir 'Al ha-Tukki Yosi" in *Mul Kokabim we-'Afar*, pp. 24–25. The parrot is Halfi's favorite bird. One of the poems in the book—ibid., p. 125—begins with these lines:
    If,
    Like a green parrot,
    I were to search for joy in the prison of my being...
The parrot reappears in other poems. See pp. 79, 107, 186. Is there any connection between a parrot and a poet who is a professional actor?

44   Ibid., p. 29.

45   In Hebrew: *Mi-Zavit El Zavit.*

46   Abraham Halfi, *Be-Zel Kol Makom* (Tel Aviv, 1970), p. 53.

47   Abraham Halfi, *Me-Ashpot Yarim* (Ramat Gan, 1974), p. 36.

48   Joshua Tan-Pai, *Me-Alef 'Ad Tav* (Tel Aviv, 1937), pp. 11, 14, 31.

49   Ibid., p. 22.

50   Joshua Tan-Pai, *Shire ha-Heshek we-ha-Re'ut* (Tel Aviv, 1942), p. 16.

51   For the most representative collection of his poetry from 1937 to 1974, see Joshua Tan-Pai, *'Olam Ka-Zeh 'Olam Ka-Ba* (Jerusalem, 1975).

52   By 1973, Rokeah published nine volumes of poetry. The latest—*We-Lo Be-Yom Aher* appeared in 1969 and in a refurbished edition in 1973. Some of his poems have found their way into the *Times Literary Supplement* and numerous other publications. There is also a bilingual selection of his poetry—in Hebrew and German—with translations by Nelly Sachs, Hans Magnus Enzenberger, Friedrich Dürrenmatt, Paul Celan and others. See David Rokeah, *Poesie* (Frankfurt am Main, 1962).

53   For a different translation of the poem, see Ruth Finer Mintz, *Modern Hebrew Poetry* (Berkeley-Los Angeles, 1966), p. 279. For the original, David Rokeah, *'Ar'ar 'Ale Shaham* (Jerusalem, 1958), p. 83.

54   The poem was also translated by Erich Fried in the bilingual *Poesie*, p. 12.

55   David Rokeah, *Yamim 'Ashenim* (Jerusalem, 1941), p. 16.

56   Ibid, p. 41.

57   In Hebrew: "Me-'Ever la-Dimyon." For a different translation of the poem, see Ruth Finer Mintz, *Modern Hebrew Poetry*, p. 270.

58   David Rokeah, *'Enayim ba-Sela'* (Tel Aviv, 1967), p. 32.

59   Solomon Tanny, "To Learn to Part" in *Nihushim*, p. 28. *Till the Day Arrived* in Hebrew: *'Ad she-Higi'a ha-Yom* (Givatayim, Ramat Gan, 1967).

60   *Siah Meshorrim.* p. 25.

61   See Peniel's poem "Europa" in *Shirim* (Jerusalem, 1971), pp. 76-77.

62   Ibid., p. 87

63   Ibid., p. 166.

64   Ibid., p. 89.

65   See "Beki 'Al he-Harim," the last poem in *Shirim*, pp. 216–18. It was in this book, incidentally, that Peniel's new poems were published and previous collections of poetry were republished: *Shamayim Adummim, 'Al Pithe Tehom, Nofim Genuzim, Netiv Lavan, Siah le-'Et 'Erev.*

66   In Hebrew: *Ilan ba-Ruah* (Tel Aviv, 1939).

67   Ibid., p. 10.

68   In Hebrew: *Shirim me-Erez Uz* (Tel Aviv, 1963).

69   Ibid., p. 139.

70   Jacob Orland, *Ilan ba-Ruah*, p. 20.

71   Ibid., p. 45.

72   Jacob Orland, "Pinnat ha-Neviim" (*Ma'ariv*, May 15, 1975), p. 37. This is a fragment from his work-in-progress *Ariel, Yoman Yerushalmi be-Shishshah Perakim*. For his narrative technique in poetry, see his translation of a part of Chaucer's Prologue to the Canterbury Tales, *Musaf Ma'ariv Rosh-Hashanah 5736*, p. 20.

73   David Avidan, *Megaovertone* translated from the Hebrew by the poet, with translations and an introduction by Abraham Birman (London-Tel Aviv, 1966), pp. 93-94.

74   Even the translator, Abraham Birman, is affected by hyperbole: he regards Avidan as "the most controversial poet in Israel." See his *Introduction*, p. 9, note 1.

75   Ibid., pp. 17-18.

76   Ibid., p. 51.

77   Ibid., p. 50.

78   In Hebrew: "Be-'Inyan Ahavato ha-Umlalah Shel J. Alfred Prufrock" in David Avidan, *Mashehu Bishevil Mishehu-Mivhar Shirim 1952-1964* (Jerusalem and Tel Aviv, 1964), pp. 38-39.

79   *Megaovertone*, p. 81.

80   David Avidan, *Mashehu Bishevil Mishehu*, p. 176.

81   Ibid., p. 53.

82   Ibid., pp. 246, 248, 250, 252, 254.

83   In Hebrew: "Balladah Al Sheloshim wa-Hamishshah." It was written in 1948 and it is easily accessible in Yonah David, *Et Asher Baharti* (Tel Aviv, 1959), pp. 116–20.

10   Notes to The Canaanism of Ratosh

1   Jonathan Ratosh is the pseudonym for Uriel Shelah. Both words allude to violence: *ratosh* = dash; *shelah* = sword. In rabbinic parlance *ratosh* is "an emigrant or fugitive whose estate is abandoned." Marcus Jastrow, *A Dictionary of the Targumim, the Talmud Babli and Yerushalmi, and the Midrashic Literature*, s.v. The pre-Israel name of the family: Halperin.

2   *Alef*, of course, is the first letter of the Hebrew alphabet. It was chosen deliberately and presumably as an indication of a new era in Israel. But the periodical lasted only five years, 1948–1953. From 1948 till 1950 it was edited jointly by Jonathan Ratosh and his younger disciple Aaron Amir; then it was taken over by Aaron Amir who edits, at the present time, the avant-garde *Keshet*.

3   On the "Young Hebrews," see Eisig Silberschlag, *Saul Tschernichowsky: Poet of Revolt*, p. 38.

4   See "Yahadut Mahi—'Immut Ben ha-Rav Dr. Aharon Lichtenstein we-ha-Meshorer Yonatan Ratosh" in *Ma'ariv* (September 16, 1974), p. 19.

5   *Shire ha-Herev* (Tel Aviv, 1969).

6   *Huppah Shehorah* (Tel Aviv, 1941), p. 30. The poem reappeared in *Yohemed* (Tel Aviv, 1952), p. 36. On the history of *Huppah Shehorah*, see Jonathan Ratosh, "Sifri ha-Rishon," *Yokani* 5 (Tel Aviv, July1967), pp. 22–24.

7   *Shire Mammash* (Tel Aviv, 1964/65), p. 73. Other books by Ratosh: *Zel'a, Shire Heshbon, Shire Herev, Ha-Holeki ba-Hoshek*. Four volumes of his verse—*Huppah Shehorah, Be-Argaman, Yohemed, Zela'*—have appeared under the title *Shire Yonatan Ratosh* (Tel Aviv, 1974).

8   Ibid., p. 39

9   Ibid., p. 24.

10   Gen. 15:12.

11   *Shire Mammash*, p. 113.

12   Ibid., p. 21.

13   The first line is almost a quotation from Ps. 24:7; the second line is a lingual reminiscence of Num. 7:26; the third line is a quotation from the Song of Songs 7:2; and the rare word for "blossom" in the fourth line appears only three times in the Bible—always in the Song of Songs: 2:13, 2:15, 7:13.

14   Ratosh has been characterized as a lone wolf, a strange and distant figure, a nonconformist. See "Bi-Mehizatan Shel Muzot," *Ha-Arez Weekly Supplement* (February 28, 1975), p. 19.

352   EISIG SILBERSCHLAG

11   Notes to The Tranquil Poets: Temkim; Meitus; Wolfovsky; Keshet; Lichtenbaum; Lander; Bass; Kariv; Mohar; Rosen; Goldenberg; Solodar; Span; Homsky; Braudes; Benshalom

1   *Netafim* (Jerusalem, 1926/27); *Sefer ha-Shirim u-Tefillot* (Jerusalem, 1933/34); *Sefer ha-Shirim we-ha-Tefillot* (Tel Aviv, 1941/42); *Be-Elem Kol* (Jerusalem, 1956); *Eged Kat* (Tel Aviv, 1961); *Shire Yerushalayim* (Jerusalem, 1965).

2   From the poem beginning with the line "At Afurah we-Galmudah" in Mordecai Temkin, *Netafim*, p. 13.

3   In Hebrew: "Bi-Re'osh Markebot Nizzahon," ibid., pp. 78-81.

4   Mordecai Temkin, *Shirim u-Tefillot*, p. 43.

5   On the poet's relationship to the world, see Zevi Luz, "Shirat ha-Boded," *Moznayim* XXXIV[5-6] (1972), pp. 374–75.

6   From the poem *Ushsharti ha-'Erev* in Asher Barash, *Mibhar ha-Shirah ha-'Ibrit ha-Hadashah,* p. 395.

7   Eliyyahu Meitus, *Trioletim* (Tel Aviv, 1960/61). E.E. Lisitzky exceeded Meitus's record in triolets and published 370 of them. See his *Kokabim Nofelim* (Tel Aviv, 1963). Meitus is also one of the most prolific sonneteers in Hebrew. In his book *Bi-Kezeh ha-Gesher ha-Sheni* (Tel Aviv, 1967) he collected fifty-three sonnets.

8   Ibid., triolet 5.

9   Ibid., triolet 7.

10   Ibid., triolets 67 and 94.

11   Ibid., triolet 99.

12   Ibid., triolet 69.

13   Ibid., triolet 7.

14   In Hebrew: "Mi-Marot Yehezkel" in *Shirim u-Poemot* (Tel Aviv, 1953), pp. 43–48.

15   In Hebrew: *Yirmeyah u-Bet ha-Rekavim* (Tel Aviv, 1968).

16   In Hebrew: "Bi-Mezudah Aharonah" in *Shirim u-Poemot*, p. 168.

17   In Hebrew: *Sofe Shevilim* (Tel Aviv, 1927/28).

18   Keshet's line in his poem is conveniently available in Barash's anthology, *Mibhar ha-Shirah ba-'Ibrit ha-Hadashah* , p. 408.

19   Ibid., p. 257.

20   See Frischmann's *Miktavim 'Al Devar ha-Sifrut, Miklat* IV (New York, 1920), pp. 367–69.

21   In Hebrew: *Ben ha-'Armon we-ha-Lilak* (Tel Aviv, 1967). Significantly, the English title of the autobiography: *Charmed Youth* .

22   In Hebrew: *Keren Hazut* (Jerusalem, 1966).

23   See the essay "Yahadut he-'Atid," ibid., pp.123-31.

24   Mordecai Zev Feierberg, "Sifrutenu ha-Yafah we-Hobotehah" in *Kobez Sippurav we-Ketabav* (Cracow, 1904).

25   In Hebrew: Joseph Lichtenbaum, *Be-Zel ha-Sha'ot* (Jerusalem, 1927/28).

26   In German: Rainer Maria Rilke, *Das Stundenbuch.*It was written between 1899 and 1903.

27   Joseph Lichtenbaum, *Be-Zel ha-Sha'ot*, p. 11.

28   In German: Stefan George, *Das Jahr der Seele*. It was written in 1897.

29   Joseph Lichtenbaum, *Be-Zel ha-Sha'ot*, p. 64.

30   Samuel Bass, *Adam* (Tel Aviv, 1927), p. 36.

31   Samuel Bass, *Hofim* (Tel Aviv, 1933), p. 13.

32   S. Bass *'Ad Kezeh ha-Derek-Shirim u-Balladot* (Tel Aviv, 1969/70), pp. 144–47.

33   Ibid., p. 256.

34   Ibid., pp. 168-69.

35   Ibid., p. 324.

36   Ibid., p. 245.

37   For children's poetry of Bass see "Perihat ha-Shaked—Shire Yeladim" in *'Ad Kezeh ha-Derek*, pp. 387–415.

38   See the poem "Be-Nof Etmol" in S. Bass, *'Ad Kezeh ha-Derek*, pp. 192-193.

39   Abraham Isaac Kariv, "Yehudi we-Goy" in *Kol u-Bat Kol* (Tel Aviv, 1951/52), pp. 46-50.

40   See "Ha-Yehudi ha-Nizhi El Europa," ibid., pp. 54-65.

41   Ibid.

42   Meir Mohar, *Be-Heret Enosh* (Tel Aviv, 1959), p. 254 and the poem *Shiri* in his book of poems *'Ayin be-'Ayin* (Tel Aviv, 1950), p. 139.

43   See "Pirke Nof" in *Be-Heret Enosh*, pp. 63-127.

44   Meir Mohar, *Be-Heret Enosh*, p. 22.

45   In Hebrew: "Le-Nir Abot," the first six chapters of *Sheloshah ba-Moledet* (Tel Aviv, 1940/41), pp. 7-30.

46   In Hebrew: *Sheloshah ba-Moledet*, pp. 7-78.

47   Ibid., p. 43.

48   Abraham Rosen, *'Im Loven Derakim* (Jerusalem, 1933), p. 57.

49   Ezek. 3:15.

50   It seems that the poet had an unfavorable opinion of some—if not most—of his poems. See his introduction to *Reshafim ba-'Arabah* (Kishinev, 1939). A second edition appeared in Tel Aviv in 1945/46.

51   Abraham Solodar, "Galiliyyah" in *Shirim* (Chicago-New York, 1939), pp. 53-55.

52   In Hebrew: "Hevle Mashiah," ibid ., pp. 36-42.

53   Ibid., p. 28.

54   Solomon Span, *Shirim we-Sippurim* (Tel Aviv, 1964), p. 97.

55   For Span's essays, see his *Massot u-Mehkarim* (Tel Aviv, 1964).

56   Dov Homsky, *Zeharim la-Baot* (Tel Aviv, 1937), p. 9.

57   Dov Homsky, *Vilaot* (Jerusalem, 1940), p. 37.

58   Ibid., p. 57. Compare the forty-third sonnet from the second book of *Sonnets pour Hélène* in Ronsard, *Oeuvres Complétes* I *(Bibliothèque de La Pleiade*, Paris, 1950), which begins with the words "Quand vous serez bien vieille, au soir, a la chandelle" and Yeats's paraphrase, "When you are old" in *The Collected Poems of W.B. Yeats*, (New York, 1933), p. 46.

59   Dov Homsky, *Ezov ba-Even* pp. 115-22.

60   Dov Homsky, *Vilaot*, p. 31.

61   Dov Homsky, *Be-'Et u-be-'Onah* (Ramat Gan, 1969), p. 100.

62   Dov Homsky, *Ezov ba-Even*, p. 12.

63   Ibid., p. 254.

64   Dov Homsky, *Be-'Et u-be-'Onah*, p. 99.

65   Dov Homsky, *Avak Huzot* (Ramat Gan, 1972), p. 72.

66   Ibid., p. 108.

67   See the parody on Isaiah 4:1 in *Ezov ba-Even* , p. 244.

68   See the poem "Ani Mehager" in *Be-'Et u-be-'Onah* , p. 56.

69   In Hebrew: *Mahazevet* (Tel Aviv, 1965).

70   See especially the poem "Gam be-Arzi," ibid., p. 7.

71   See the poem "Ha-Mashiah Shelli," ibid., p. 99.

72   *El ha-Shahar ha-Ganuz* (Israel, 1961), p. 84.

73   One of Braudes's volumes of poetry is called *Shorashim ba-Sela'* (Tel Aviv, 1955).

74   Abraham Braudes, *Tahanah wa-Derek* (Tel Aviv, 1969/70), p. 28.

75   Ibid., p. 83.

76   Abraham Braudes, *Mi-Bayit* (Tel Aviv, 1935–36), p. 35.

77   In Hebrew: *Kol 'Od 'Odi* (Tel Aviv, 1974).

78   Ibid., p. 17.

79   Benzion Benshalom, *Sheki'ot Yerushalayim* (Tel Aviv, 1965), p. 128.

80   Ibid., pp. 131–35.

81   Ibid., pp. 7–15. See especially the section which gave the name to the entire book: Sheki'ot Yerushalayim.

12   Notes to Holocaust

1   In German *Todesfuge*. It appeared in the book by Paul Celan, *Mohn und Gedächtniss* (Stuttgart, 1952).

2   In German: *O die Schornsteine*. See the bilingual edition: Nelly Sachs, *O The Chimneys*, tr. Michael Hamburger, Christopher Holme, Ruth and Matthew Mead, Michael Roloff (New York, 1967).

3   In German: *Der Stellvertreter* (Hamburg, 1963). In English translation by Richard and Clara Winston and with a preface by Albert Schweitzer: *The Deputy* (New York, 1964).

4   In German: *Die Ermittlung, Oratorium in 11 Gesängen* (Frankfurt, 1965). In the English translation by Jon Swan and Ulu Grosbard: *The Investigation* (New York, 1966).

5   "Babii Yar" by Yevgeny Yevtushenko has been translated by several hands. For an excellent English version, see the bilingual edition of *The Poetry of Yevgeny Yevtushenko*, tr. and intr. George Reavey (New York, 1965). The poem, with its wide, almost global repercussions, first appeared in *Literaturnaya Gazeta* (Septmeber 19, 1961). The Russian composer Dmitri Shostakovich used the poem in the first movement of his thirteenth symphony.

6   In French: *La Danse de Gengis Cohn* . Translated into English by the author with assistance of Camilla Sykes and published in New York in 1968.

7   In French: André Schwarz-Bart, *Le Dernier des Justes* (Paris, 1959) tr. from the French by Stephen Becker (New York, 1960).

8   For a study of the holocaust in Western poetry, see Brian Murdoch's "Transformations of the Holocaust: Auschwitz in Modern Lyric Poetry," *Comparative Literature Studies* (June, 1974), pp. 123–50.

9   See Jacob Robinson, "Research on the Jewish Catastrophe," *The Jewish Journal of Sociology* VIII[2] (December, 1966), p. 201.

10   Professor Abraham I. Katsh discovered, translated and edited *Scroll of Agony: The Warsaw Diary of Chaim A. Kaplan* (New York, 1965). It was also translated into Hebrew and into several European languages: German,

French, Swedish, Portuguese. Additional chapters appeared in *Bitzaron* LIX[2] (November-December, 1968), pp. 61-68, ibid., (January-February, 1969), pp. 109-15 and ibid., (March, 1969), pp. 150-54.

11   On Katzenelson, see Eisig Silberschlag, *From Renaissance to Renaissance* I, pp. 213-16.

12   For an anthology of their work see Yonat and Alexander Sened, *Le-An u-me-Ayin* (Tel Aviv, 1974). It contains all of *Tandu* and chapters from *Ben ha-Metim u-ben ha-Hayyim, Ha-Nissayon ha-Nosaf, Adamah Le-lo Zel.*

13   In Hebrew: "Hishtannut."

14   In Hebrew: *Kefor 'Al ha-Arez* (Tel Aviv, 1966).

15   In Hebrew: *Ha-'Or we-ha-Kutonet* (Tel Aviv, 1971).

16   Ibid., p. 7.

17   See the story "Ha-'Ofot" in *Adne he-Nahar* (Tel Aviv, 1971), p. 77.

18   This is the beginning of the story "Lahashe ha-Kor," ibid., p. 133.

19   For a different translation of this fragment from Appelfeld's story "Shelo-shah" see *Orot* 15, ed. Adah Zemach (October, 1973), p. 47.

20   In Hebrew: "Sibir" in *Ba-Gai ha-Poreh* (Jerusalem and Tel Aviv, 1963), pp. 83-100.

21   *Adne ha-Nahar,* p. 183.

22   In Hebrew: *Ha-Nissayon ha-Nosaf.*

23   In Hebrew: *Dr. Barkal u-Beno Michael* (Tel Aviv, 1967).

24   In Hebrew: *Hayyale 'Oferet* (Tel Aviv, 1967).

25   In Hebrew: *'Ad Mahar* (Tel Aviv, 1959).

26   In Hebrew: *Pize' Bagrut* (Tel Aviv, 1965).

27   In Hebrew: *Yalde ha-Zel* (Tel Aviv, 1963).

28   The German initials K.Z., pronounced Ka-Tzet, stand for *Konzentration Zenter*, concentration center. Every inmate had his number branded on the left arm. The author's number was 135633.

29   See author's note in his *House of Love* (London and New York, 1971), p. V.

30   In Hebrew: *Ka-Hol me-Efer* (Tel Aviv, 1966). The title is based on Job 29:18 and on the legend about the phoenix in *Bereshit Rabbah* 19:5.

31   In Hebrew: *Ahoti Ketannah* (Ramat Gan, 1967). The title is based on the Song of Songs 8:8.

32   In Hebrew: *Panim El Panim* (Tel Aviv, 1955). The phrase is common in the Bible: Gen. 32:31; Exod. 33:11; Deut. 34:10; Judg. 6:22; Ezek. 20:35.

33   In Hebrew: *Peredah me-ha-Darom* (Tel Aviv, 1949).

34   Abba Kovner, *Ahoti Ketannah,* p. 40. For another translation see the rep-

resentative selection of his poetry in *A Canopy in the Desert—Selected Poems* by Abba Kovner, tr. from the Hebrew by Shirley Kaufman with Ruth Adler and Nurit Orchan (University of Pittsburgh Press, 1973), p. 18.

35   The phrase is lifted verbatim from the Song of Songs 8:8.

36   Abba Kovner, *Ahoti Ketannah*, p. 75. For a different translation, see *A Canopy in the Desert* , p. 59.

37   Abba Kovner, *Peredah me-ha-Darom* , p. 12.

38   Abba Kovner, *Panim El Panim* , p. 144.

39   In Hebrew: *Huppah ba-Midbar* (Ramat Gan, 1970).

40   Ibid., p. 53.

41   In Hebrew: *'Ad Lo Or* (Tel Aviv, 1947). The English translation of this title on the title page: *While* [!] *Still There is Night* .

42   Ibid., p. 17.

43   Ibid., pp. 147-48.

44   In Hebrew: *'Ad 'Alot ha-Shahar* (Tel Aviv, 1950). The title is based on Genesis 32:25.

45   "Milhemet Meat ha-Shanim" in Hebrew. See Hayyim Guri, *Dappim Yerushalmiyyim* (Tel Aviv, 1968), p. 166.

46   Ibid., pp. 264-86.

47   The quotation is from Guri's introduction to *'Ad 'Alot ha-Shahar* .

48   In Hebrew: *Kelulot* . It is the poetic part of *'Ad 'Alot ha-Shahar* .

49   The name appears in the Bible: Judg. 3:31; 5:6. In recent times Ugaritic texts have identified the goddess in some detail.

50   In Hebrew: *Shoshannat Ruhot* (Tel Aviv, 1966).

51   Ibid., p. 24. The poem is quoted *in toto*.

52   Ibid., p. 94. The poem is quoted *in toto*.

53   Ibid., p. 115.

54   *Tenu'ah le-Magga'* (Tel Aviv-Ramat Gan, 1968), pp. 10-11.

55   In Hebrew: *Mul Ta ha-Sekukit* (Tel Aviv, 1963).

56   In Hebrew: *'Iskat ha-Shokolad* (Tel Aviv, 1964/65).

57   The Hebrew term at the time: *'Aliyyah Bet* .

58   In Hebrew: *Ha-Sefer ha-Meshuga'* (Tel Aviv, 1971).

59   See Amir Gilboa's poem "Zakor" in his book *Kehullim wa-Adummim* (Tel Aviv, 1963), p. 311. For English translations of poems from *Kehullim wa-Adummim* and *Raziti li-Ketov Sifte Yeshenim* (Tel Aviv, 1968), see *Ariel 33–34* (Jerusalem, 1973), pp. 4–13. For other poems of Gilboa in English translation,

see *Ariel 29* .

60   There are two poems on Isaac, ibid., p. 213; pp. 312–13.

61   Gilboa's first poem "Ki Az Ezak" was published in 1941 in *Dappim le-Sifrut* under the editorship of Abraham Shlonsky. Gilboa also received the Shlonsky Prize in 1961. Ten years later he also received the prestigious Bialik Prize.

62   Amir Gilboa, *Sheva' Reshuyyot* (Tel Aviv, 1949), p. 11.

63   Ibid., p. 98; reprinted in *Kehullim wa-Adummim* , p. 103.

64   *Kehullim wa-Adummim,* p. 288.

65   *Shirim ba-Boker ba-Boker* , p. 18. The generous critic can read mysterious meanings into repetitions and read them doubly—in their syntactic logic and in their typographical logic. See the interesting analysis of "We-ka-Asher Yagorti" in *Raziti li-Ketov Sifte Yeshenim* , p. 20 by Mati Megged, "Dovev Sifte Yeshenim" in Amir Gilboa, *Mibhar Maamare Bikkoret 'Al Yezirato,* ed. Abraham Balaban (Tel Aviv, 1972), pp. 161–62. As for the title *Sifte Yeshenim*: this was the first Hebrew bibliography. The author: Sabbatai Meshorer Bass (Bassista); the place of publication: Amsterdam, 1680. Several works are titled *Sifte Yeshenim* . See H.B. Friedberg, *Bet 'Eked ha-Sefarim* III² (Tel Aviv, 1954), p. 1042.

66   Ibid.,p. 287.

67   *Sheva' Reshuyyot,* p. 13. The poem is quoted in full.

68   Ibid., p. 72.

69   Amir Gilboa, *Raziti li-Ketov Sifte Yeshenim* , p. 21.

70   *Kehullim wa-Adummim,* p. 42.

71   Ibid., p. 54.

72   Ben Zion Tomer, *'Al Kav ha-Mashveh* (Ramat Gan, 1968/9), p. 32.

73   In Hebrew: "Asham."

74   In Hebrew: "Shir Ahavah," ibid., p. 46.

75   See *Nahar Hozer* (Tel Aviv, 1958/59), p. 27.

76   Ibid., p. 49.

77   The representative selection of Nelly Sachs's poems in English is entitled: *O The Chimneys* (Philadelphia, 1968). The name of the book is based on a poem by Nelly Sachs: "O The Chimneys," ibid., p. 3. Interestingly, Yaoz-Kest entitled one of his volumes of poetry: *Landscape in Smoke.* In Hebrew: *Nof be-'Ashan-Pirke Bergen-Belsen* (Tel Aviv, 1961).

78   Yaoz-Kest, *Shirim* (Tel Aviv, 1966), p. 95.

79   In Hebrew: "Gidre Laylah," ibid., unpaginated.

80   In Hebrew: *Yerushat 'Enayim* (Tel Aviv, 1965).

81   In Hebrew: *Or ha-Nehshak* (Tel Aviv, 1963).

82   In Hebrew: *Avi-ha-Shoresh,* a series of poems in *Yerushat 'Enayim,* un-paginated.

83   Yaoz-Kest, *Le-Morad Betah* (Tel Aviv, 1969).

84   In Hebrew: *Ha-Kav ha-Zarhani* (Tel Aviv, 1972).

85   In Hebrew: "Balladah 'Al Delet Ne 'ulah" in *Kayiz Shel Viyolah* (Tel Aviv, 1973), unpaginated.

86   *Siah Meshorerim 'Al Azmam we-'Al Ketivatam,* ed. Jacob Besser (Tel Aviv, 1971), pp. 117–18.

87   Ibid., p. 121.

88   *Yerushat 'Enayim,* unpaginated.

89   In Hebrew: *Ba-Halon ha-Bayit ha-Nose'a* (Tel Aviv, 1970).

90   In Hebrew: *Zel ha-Zippor* (Tel Aviv, 1971).

91   Yaoz-Kest, *Shirim* (Tel Aviv, 1966).

13   Notes to Dissociation and Discontinuity in Contemporary Hebrew Literature: Yehuda Amichai

1   In Hebrew: *'Akshav ba-Ra'ash* (Tel Aviv, 1968).

2   In Hebrew: *Lo me-'Akshav, Lo mi-Kan* (Tel Aviv, 1963). A section of Amichai's book *Shirim* (Tel Aviv, 1962), pp. 9–59 is entitled *'Akshav u-ba-Yamim ha-Aherim.*

3   See Yehuda Amichai, *Shirim*, pp. 163–64.

4   *Sanhedrin* 91b.

5   *'Akshav ba-Ra'ash*, p. 17. For another translation, Harold Schimmel, "Homage to Jerusalem" by Yehuda Amichai, *Midstream* (March, 1971), p. 5.

6   *Poems* by Yehuda Amichai from the Hebrew by Assia Gutmann; introduction by Michael Hamburger (New York and Evanston, 1968). For a smaller English edition by the same translator, see Yehuda Amichai, *Selected Poems* (London, 1968). For a representative selection of Amichai's poems in Harold Schimmel's translation, see *Orot* (August, 1970), pp. 70-85. Amichai has not only been translated extensively but he has also been invited to read from his works at the Festival of Poetry at Festival Hall in London in 1967 and at Spoleto, Italy.

7   Introduction to *Poems* by Yehuda Amichai, p. VIII. Paul Celan, an avantgardist who wrote the moving poem on the holocaust *Todesfuge [Fugue of Death]*; Erich Fried, a poet with political overtones, translator of Eliot, Synge, and Dylan Thomas into German. Some of Amichai's contemporaries of German provenance—M. Winkler, T. Rübner, Ozer Rabin—deserve a specialized study, as do the poets who came from an Anglo-American milieu: T. Carmi, Reuben Ben-Yosef, Reuben Avinoam.

8   See *'Akshav ba-Ra'ash*, pp. 171–72.

9   *Poems* by Yehuda Amichai, p. 49. *'Akshav ba-Ra'ash*, p. 145.

10   Ibid., p. 16. *Shirim*, p. 126.

11   Ibid., pp. 2–3. *Shirim*, pp. 103–104.

12   Ibid., p. 5. *Shirim*, pp. 152–53.

13   Ibid., pp. 33–34. 'Akshav ba-Ra'ash, p. 42.

14   Ibid., p. 8. 'Akshav ba-Ra'ash, p. 27.

15   Ibid., p. 38. 'Akshav ba-Ra'ash, p. 59.

16   Yehuda Amichai, 'Akshav ba-Ra'ash, p. 125. Incidentally, Amichai regards the poem as the best he has even written. See Siah Meshorerim, p. 54. Benjamin of Tudela, the medieval traveller, was also a favorite of Nathan Alterman (see p. 77).

17   Poems by Yehuda Amichai, p. 31; 'Akshav ba-Ra'ash, p. 94.

18   Yehuda Amichai, Shirim, p. 69. For a different translation by Abraham Birman see Orot 2 (June, 1966), p. 39.

19   Ibid., pp. 70–71.

20   Yehuda Amichai, Shirim, p. 81.

21   Ibid., p. 80.

22   Ibid., p. 120.

23   In Hebrew: Ba-Ruah ha-Noraah ha-Zot (Tel Aviv, 1961).

24   Not of This Time, Not of This Place, p. 344.

25   Ibid., p. 308. For the identical thought in the poem "Sof Elul," see note 17.

26   The translation by Shlomo Katz is a condensed version of the original. It was published by Harper & Row (New York and Evanston, 1968).

27   William Shakespeare, As You Like It, Act II, Scene VII. The metaphor was brilliantly developed into a scientific theory by the Dutch historian Johan Huizinga who viewed culture sub specie ludi and man as homo ludens: "You can deny, if you like, nearly all abstractions: justice, beauty, truth, goodness, mind, God. You can deny seriousness but not play." See J. Huizinga, Homo Ludens—A Study of the Play Element in Culture (Boston, 1955), p. 3.

28   In Hebrew: Mi Yitneni Malon (Tel Aviv, 1971). The title is based on Jeremiah 9:1.

29   Massa' le-Nineveh in the collection of dramatic sketches and plays Pa'amonim we-Rakkavot (Tel Aviv, 1968).

30   Ibid., p. 31–50. The play was translated into English by Noam Flinker and Burton Raffel, Midstream (October, 1970), pp. 20–31.

31   Ibid., pp. 51–81. Hebrew title: Shetah Shel Hefker.

32   Ibid., pp. 7–30. The play was translated by Aubrey Hodes, Midstream (October, 1966), pp. 55–66. Hebrew title: Pa'amonim we-Rakkavot.

14   Notes to Disengaged Poetry: Carmi; Mar; Zach; Rübner; Pagis; O. Hillel

1   For the different translation by Dom Moraes, see *Anthology of Modern Hebrew Poetry,* ed. Abraham Birman (London, New York, and Toronto, 1968), p. 217.

2   T. Carmi, *En Perahim Shehorim* (Tel Aviv, 1952/53), p. 20.

3   The Hebrew title of the poem: "Kammah Yamim, Kammah Shanim." See Carmi, *Ha-Yam ha-Aharon* (Tel Aviv, 1958), p. 31.

4   T. Carmi, *Davar Aher—Mibhar Shirim* (Tel Aviv, 1970), p. 15.

5   T. Carmi, *Davar Aher,* p. 182–85.

6   The incantation *Shariri, Beriri, Riri, Yeri, Ri* is in *'Abodah Zarah* 12b, the poem in T. Carmi, *Davar Aher,* pp. 128–29.

7   T. Carmi, *Davar Aher,* p. 98.

8   Song of Songs 5:2.

9   Name of the film, which is in reality a sequence of short lyrical poems: *Zemer Derek ba-Midbar.* Hebrew text and English translation by S.J. Kahn in *Israel Argosy* 6, pp. 94–109.

10   For the translations, see T. Carmi, *Davar Aher,* pp. 205–25. Carmi based his translation of Sophocles's *Antigone* mainly on the version of Dudley Fitts and Robert Fitzgerald. His translation of *Midsummer Night's Dream* appeared in 1964.

11   Hebrew title of the poem: "Ma'avar." See Carmi's *Ha-Unicorn Mistakel ba-Marah* (Jerusalem, 1967), p. 10. For another translation see T. Carmi, "Five Poems" in *Orot* 12 (December, 1971), p. 33.

12   Song of Songs 1:6

13   T. Carmi, *Tevi'ah* (Jerusalem, 1967), unpaginated. This poem—"The Claim"—appeared in an album-sized edition of three hundred and eighteen copies with etchings by Tamara Rikman.

14   *Siah Meshorerim 'Al 'Azmam we-'Al Ketivatam*, p. 7.

15   *Mi-Lev wa-Nof* (Tel Aviv, 1951).

16   This is the title of Yehiel Mar's book of poems: *Melo Hofnayim Ruah* (Tel Aviv, 1962).

17   Ibid., p. 143. For a different translation, see Ruth Finer Mintz, *Modern Hebrew Poetry*, p. 346.

18   Yehiel Mar, "Kayiz 1966" in *Panim le-Kan* (Tel Aviv, 1968), p. 14. For a different translation, see Ruth Finer Mintz, "Handfuls of Wind" in *Poems From the Hebrew* selected by Robert Mezey (New York, 1973), p. 126.

19   Yehiel Mar, *Shirim Hadashim* (Tel Aviv, 1965), p. 14. Mar plays frequently with inversions from classical quotations. Thus, the important adage of Rabbi Akiba "Everything is predestined, but free will is given" (*Abot* 3:24) is converted into: "The angle is given, but everything is predestined." Ibid., p. 52. Sometimes Mar builds a whole poem from a recollection of a single adage in *Abot* and a single phrase in the Bible:

> If we take into account the fact that now there are no
> Prophets . . .
> And no king castigates
> And no whip strikes . . .
> Is it not a wonder, gentlemen, is it not a wonder
> That no man does yet
> What is right in his eyes
> At this time
> In these days.   Ibid., p. 44.

Mar even changes clichés into new clichés: "He who says A, is not obliged to say B." Ibid., p. 57. The well-known adage *Male Mizvot ke-Rimmon* becomes in the grotesque paraphrase of the poet: *Attah Male Teshuvot Ke-Limon*. And this phrase is addressed to the poet by an anonymous interlocutor in mock chastisement.

20   These are the three ingredients of a good poem from Mar's point of view. See *Siah Meshorerim 'Al 'Azmam we-'Al Ketivatam*, p. 12.

21   In Hebrew: "Adam." *Shirim Hadashim* (Tel Aviv, 1965), p. 13.

22   Yehiel Mar, *Panim le-Kan*, p. 11.

23   See the posthumous poem "We-Hu she-Leka" in the facsimile of his own handwriting in the miscellany *Sefer 'Alim* (Ramat ha-Sharon, 1970/71) which Mar's friends published in his memory.

24   *Kol he-Halav we-ha-Devash* (Tel Aviv, 1966), pp. 42–43; 70.

25   Nathan Zach, *Shirim Shonim* (Merhavyah, 1974), p. 86.

26   Nathan Zach, ibid., p. 55.

27   Nathan Zach, *Kol he-Halav we-ha-Devash*, p. 28.

28 Ibid., p. 8.

29 For samples of Zach's criticism: *Zeman we-Ritmus Ezel Bergson u-ba-Shirah ha-Modernit* (Tel Aviv, 1966); "'Al ha-Bayit ha-Boded we-'Al Ketav Yado Shel Ha-Meshorer," *Yokani* 5 (Tel Aviv, 1967), pp. 29-45.

30 For translations from Arab folksongs—Palestinian and Syrian and Lebanese—see *Dekalim u-Temarim* (Tel Aviv, 1967).

31 An example of a disjointure of words: *ha*—at the end of a line, then *'Enayim* in the next line. See *En le-Hashiv* (Ramat Gan, 1971), p. 5; ibid., p. 18. An example of a pair of far-fetched neologisms: *ofhi* and *ofhu, she-fowl* and *he-fowl*. The title of the book is a *non-sequitur: Unreturnable.* As a matter-of-fact everything in the book is arbitrary and returnable.

32 In Hebrew: "Holek ba-Rehov," ibid, p. 23.

33 In Hebrew: *She 'on ha-Zel* (Merhavyah, 1959); *Shahut Meuheret* (Tel Aviv, 1964); *Gilgul* (Ramat gan, 1970).

34 *Shahut Meuheret,* p. 7.

35 Ibid., p. 44.

36 In Hebrew: "Ha-Mahazor" in *Shahut Meuheret,* p. 39. For a translation of "The Cycle," see Dan Pagis, *Selected Poems* tr. from the Hebrew by Stephen Mitchell (Oxford, 1972), p. 57.

37 See *Shahut Meuheret,* p. 8.

38 For the translation of the poem on the field-mouse under the title of "Harvests," see Dan Pagis, *Selected Poems,* p. 58; also *Ariel* 31 (Jerusalem, 1972), p. 73.

39 Op. cit., p. 10.

40 Proverbs 6:6-11.

41 O. Hillel, *Tarof Toraf* (Tel Aviv, 1964), pp. 64–65.

42 Ibid., p. 66.

15   Notes to Mysticism in Poetry: S. Shalom

1   S. Shalom, *Sefer ha-Shirim we-ha-Sonetot* (Tel Aviv, 1940), p. 7; idem, *Ketabim* I (Tel Aviv, 1966), p. 9.

2   The quotation is from "Megillat Elifele" in S. Shalom, *Ketabim* III (Tel Aviv, 1966) p. 257. The poem with its numerous allusions to Ecclesiastes reads like a mystical paraphrase of the book.

3   S. Shalom, *Sefer ha-Shirim we-ha-Sonetot*, p. 9; *Ketabim* I, p. 10. The ladder is Shalom's favorite metaphor: "if poetry means climbing the ladder of selfhood . . . I am a poet." From a letter to Bialik, written in 1928, in *Ketabim* X (Tel Aviv, 1973), p. 13.

4   Ibid., p. 25. My translation appeared in *S. Shalom—The Poet and His Work* (New York, 1950), p. 10. The booklet was prepared and edited by Gabriel Preil and Jacob Kabakoff.

5   *Ha-Yoman in Meassef le-Divre Sifrut, Bikkoret we-Hagut* V-VI, ed. Benzion Benshalom and Israel Cohen (Tel Aviv, 1966), pp. 37–62.

6   Deut. 21:1–9.

7   Lev. 16:5–28.

8   S. Shalom, *Sefer ha-Shirim we-ha-Sonetot*, p. 127; *Ketabim* I, p. 90.

9   S. Shalom, *Sefer ha-Shirim we-ha-Sonetot*, p. 188. *Ketabim* I, p. 195. My translation appeared in the booklet mentioned in note 4.

10   In Hebrew: *Mi-Tok ha-Lehavot* (Tel Aviv, 1935/36).

11   *On Ben Pele* in *Ketabim* III, pp. 7–62.

12   In Hebrew: *Yeriyyot El ha-Kibbutz*. In a new edition of the play was called *Dan ha-Shomer* in *Ketabim* VII (Tel Aviv, 1967), pp. 145–197. It was produced as an opera with a libretto by Max Brod.

13   Song of Songs 2:1.

14   *Ketabim* III, p. 10. Shalom also reproduced incidents from his early life in prose. See especially "Pirke 'Aliyyah" in *Ketabim* VII, pp. 7–55.

15   A.E., *Song and Its Fountains* (London, 1932), pp. 13–14.

16   In Hebrew: *Shabbat ha-'Olam* in *Ketabim* III, pp. 85–169.

17   Betar: the fortress associated with Bar Kohba's initial victory over the Romans in the unsuccessful revolt which lasted from 132 to 135 C.E.

18   In Hebrew: *Ma'arat Yosef, Ketabim* III, pp. 171–253.

19   *Sifrut Ze'irah* (Jerusalem, March 16, 1939), p. 3.

20   Max Brod, "Sheloshah Miktabim le-S. Shalom," *Moznayim* (January, 1969), p. 101.

21   In Hebrew: *Yoman ba-Galil, Ketabim* VI (Tel Aviv, 1967), pp. 7–69.

22   First published under the title *Ba-Metah ha-Gavoah* (Jerusalem, 1956).

23   S. Shalom, *Yoman ba-Galil,* p. 51. For a different translation, see S. Shalom, *Storm Over Galilee* tr. from the Hebrew by Batya Rabin (London, 1967), pp. 74–75.

24   Shalom also reproduced incidents from his early life in prose. See especially *Pirke 'Aliyyah* in *Ketabim* VII (Tel Aviv, 1967), pp. 7–55. Bialik made the keen observation: "There are some whose world is open and clear but they complicate it in expressing it; Shalom's world is mysterious and complicated but he simplifies it in expressing it." See *Ketabim* X, p. 20.

16   Notes to Poetry and Prose of Women: Rahel; Bat Miriam; Amir; Goldberg; Raab; Rabikowitz; Zeldah; Tur Malka; Baron; Hendel; Karmon.

1   Judg. 5.

2   Her fame is attested by such authorities as Longinus and by such poets as Alcaeus who adored her and Catullus who paid her the supreme compliment of translation. Her poetry, with the exception of the hymn to Aphrodite and an almost complete love poem, is too fragmentary to accord her the greatness which the ancients attributed to her on the basis of her nine books. See Denys Page, *Sappho and Alcaeus* (Oxford, 1955), pp. 110–12.

3   *Sotah* 3:4.

4   *Shirat Rahel*[2] (Tel Aviv, 1939). The title is a misnomer: the book contains the poetry of Rahel that appeared originally in three little books—*Safiah, Mi-Neged, Nebo*—and selections from her prose. Its popularity is attested to by the fact that it went through several editions. By 1971—eighty years after her birth, forty years after her death—more than twenty editions, more than 100,0000 copies of her collected poems had been published. Some of her poems have been translated into as many as thirteen languages. Several composers— Yehudah Sharet, Abraham Sharon, Ephraim ben-Hayyim, Judah Engel—set her poems to music. See *Rahel we-Shiratah*, ed. Mordecai Snir and Shimon Kushnir (Tel Aviv, 1971), p. 10 and especially, p. 305.

5   Rahel's first published poem in *Ha-Shiloah* was dedicated to A.D. Gordon. See *Rahel we-Shiratah*, p. 307.

6   See Zalman Shazar's essay "Orah ha-Zarua'" in *Shire Rahel u-Miktavehah bi-Ketav Yadah*, pp. 8–9.

7   See her early impression of the Sea of Galilee in the prose description 'Al Sefat ha-Kinneret in *Shirat Rahel*, p. 196.

8   "'Im Zav ha-Goral." The grave of Rahel has become a mecca for pilgrims, an object of contemplation by poets. See the poem "Mazzevet Rahel" in Levi Ben-Amittai, *Kinnrot* (Merhavyah, 1970/71), p. 66 and the poem "'Al Kivrah Shel

Rahel be-Kinneret" in Solomon Tanny's *Nihushim* (Ramat Gan, 1972), p. 34.

9   *Shirat Rahel,* p. 88. Rahel's nephew, Uri Milstein, was named after the poem. And since Berl Katzenelson was called Uri by her, it is possible that the poem was dedicated to him. See *Rahel we-Shiratah,* pp. 79–80.

10   Ibid., p. 109.

11   Job 5:18.

12   *Shirat Rahel,* p. 160.

13   *Rahel we-Shiratah,* p. 91. A variant on the ephithet, "Miriam's Choir," ibid. Bialik placed Rahel's poetry alongside her romantic predecessors: Micah Joseph Lebensohn, Mordecai Zevi Maneh, Uri Zevi Gnessin. Ibid.

14   The "myth of femininity" can be usefully traced in male writers. As a matter of fact a recent study explores it in the work of Henry James, Robert Musil and Marcel Proust. See Lisa Appignanesi, *Femininity and the Creative Imagination* (London, 1973).

15   For the adoration of Elisheva, see the three brief essays collected in a pamphlet, *Elischewa. Drei Aufsätze zur Charakteristik der Dichterin* (Tel Aviv, 1928). Also Dr. Max Raisin, *Dappim Mi-Pinkaso Shel Rabbi* (Brooklyn, 1941), pp. 254–55. There was no actual conversion—as many friends and acquaintances asserted.

16   Her essays on Blok in *Ha-Tekufah* 21–22 and in the literary supplement to *Davar* (Elul, 1926) were reprinted in a special·edition under the title *Meshorer we-Adam* (Tel Aviv, 1928/29).

17   Elisheva, *Kos Ketannah* (Tel Aviv, 1926), p. 36.

18   In German: "Ein Fichtenbaum." It is one of the better-known poems from Heine's *Lyrisches Intermezzo* (1822–1823).

19   Elisheva, *Kos Ketannah,* p. 24.

20   A translation of Charles van Lerberghe's poem by Rahel appeared as early as 1922 in the periodical *Hedim.*

21   A sympathetic critic, Jacob Fichmann, characterized her poetry as art "on the boundary of prose." See his "Le-Yovelah Shel Meshoreret" *Moznayim* 8 (1939), p. 499. At that time such a characterization was not a compliment. See Elisheva's letter of June 15, 1919 to M. Niviazeski, *Genazim* I (Tel Aviv, 1961), p. 152.

22   In her tiny sixteen-page volume of Russian poetry, *Tayniya Pyesni* (Moscow, 1919), p. 3, Elisheva prefaces her first poem with the quotation from Ruth 1:16: Your people shall be my people, and your God my God.

23   In Hebrew: "Nerot Shel Shabbat" in *Sippurim* (Tel Aviv, 1927/28), pp. 71–98.

24   In Hebrew: "Malkah la-'Ivrim," ibid., pp. 17–46.

25   In Hebrew: *Mikreh Tafel* (Tel Aviv, 1928/29).

370   EISIG SILBERSCHLAG

26   In Hebrew: *Simtaot* (Tel Aviv, 1929).

27   Yoheved Bat-Miriam, *Shirim* (Merhavyah, 1963), p. 30.

28   Ibid., p. 19.

29   Bat-Miriam, *Me-Rahok* (Tel Aviv, 1932), p. 99.

30   See Bat-Miriam's poem on Tel Aviv—one in a series of poems on five cities, St. Petersburg [Leningrad], Kiev, Paris, Tel Aviv, Jerusalem—in *Demuyot me-Ofek* (Tel Aviv, 1941), pp. 27–47.

31   Bat-Miriam, *Me-Rahok*, p. 164.

32   Bat-Miriam, *Shirim*, pp. 295–307.

33   Ibid., p. 301.

34   Bat-Miriam, *Erez Yisrael* (Tel Aviv, 1937), p. 7.

35   Ibid., p. 10.

36   Anda Pinkerfeld-Amir, *Yuval* (Tel Aviv, 1932), p. 81.

37   Amir, *Tehiyot* (Tel Aviv, 1967), p. 24.

38   Amir, *Yuval*, p. 12; *Gadish wa-'Omer*, p. 16.

39   Amir, *Yuval*, p. 51; *Gadish wa-'Omer*, p. 170.

40   In Hebrew: *Geisha Lian Tang Sharah* (Tel Aviv, 1934). It appeared in a mock-Japanese booklet form and was reprinted in *Gadish wa-'Omer*, pp. 97–107.

41   This is the first poem in the Japanese cycle: *Gadish wa-'Omer*, p. 97.

42   *Tehiyot*, p. 14.

43   In Hebrew: *Kokabim ba-Deli* (Tel Aviv, 1956/57).

44   In Hebrew: *Ani Ohev li-Sherok ba-Rehov* (Ramat Gan, 1967).

45   In Hebrew: *Harpatkah ba-Midbar* (Tel Aviv, 1966).

46   In Hebrew: *Gan ha-Hayyot* (Tel Aviv, 1941, 1970).

47   See her *Sheloshah Sippurim* (Tel Aviv, 1970) and *Yedidai me-Rehov Arnon* (Tel Aviv, 1967).

48   Leah Goldberg, *Shibbolet Yerokat ha-'Ayin* (Tel Aviv, 1939), pp. 49–50.

49   See S. Dani, "Pizmonim Satiriyyim Shel Leah Goldberg," Ma'ariv Literary Supplement (8/29–30, 1974), p. 37.

50   From a different vantage point, Professor Robert Alter argued brilliantly about the virtues and limitations of Leah Goldberg's conversational technique in her criticism and poetry. See his article "On Leah Goldberg and S.Y. Agnon," *Commentary*, (May, 1970), pp. 84–85.

51   In Hebrew: *Sheerit ha-Hayyim* (Ramat Gan, 1971).

52   Ibid., p. 7.

53 Ibid., p. 62.

54 Leah Goldberg was dramatic critic of *Davar* (1943–1945) and *Mishmar* (1943–1954). She published a book on the art of the short story *Omanut ha-Sippur* (Tel Aviv, 1963).

55 In Hebrew: *Ha-Sifrut ha-Rusit ba-Meah ha-Tesha' 'Esreh* (Tel Aviv, 1968).

56 See Leah Goldberg, *Pegishah 'Im Meshorer* (Tel Aviv, 1952). The family name of the poet was Sonne. Leah Goldberg also dedicated nine poems to him and painted his portrait in verse (ibid., p. 7). See *'Al ha-Perihah,* pp. 16–24; also *Mukdam u-Meuhar,* pp. 93–97.

57 See the beautiful poem "Ashre ha-Zore 'im we-Lo Yikzoru," Abraham Ben Yizhak, *Shirim* (Jerusalem, 1967), p. 22. This little book contains the eleven poems which were published during his lifetime and twelve previously unpublished poems: the whole poetical output of Abraham Ben Yizhak. A poem called "La-Zore'a" which suffered from editorial changes was not acknowledged as his own though it was published under his name when he was alive. The bilingual edition of his poetry with translations by I.M. Lask, a biographical note and an essay by Benzion Benshalom, was followed by a fuller edition a year later: it contained the posthumous fragments, a biographical note in Hebrew and Benzion Benshalom's essay in the original Hebrew. See Abraham Ben Yizhak, *Shirim* (Jerusalem, 1968).

58 Esther Raab, *Tefillah Aharonah* (Tel Aviv, 1972), p. 72.

59 *Shire Esther Raab* (Ramat Gan, 1963).

60 In Hebrew: "Shu 'alah," ibid., p. 87.

61 See *Moznayim* (1934), pp. 27–31.

62 Dalia Rabikowitz, *Horef Kasheh* (Tel Aviv, 1967), p. 44.

63 Dalia Rabikowitz, *Ha-Sefer ha-Shelishi,* p. 63.

64 *Horef Kasheh,* p. 14. For another version by A.C. Jacobs, see *Ariel* 36 (Jerusalem, 1974), p. 53.

65 *Ha-Sefer ha-Shelishi,* p. 28.

66 Ibid., pp. 44–45.

67 *Horef Kasheh,* p. 26. Keshet characterizes Rabikowitz's poetry as "love for the wondrous" in "Shire Dalia Rabikowitz," *Moznayim* (June, 1968), p. 49.

68 Mahlon and Chilion: Ruth 1:2.

69 See Ps. 118:6. Zeldah quotes the verse as a characterization of an elderly person. But it applies to her with equal strength. See *Penai* (Ramat Gan, 1967), p. 20.

70 Zeldah devoted two poems to her grandfather, ibid., p. 24–26. And she remembered him in her poem on "The Bad Neighbor," ibid., p. 44.

71 Ibid., p. 29. In a tiny, eighty-one page book of lyrical poems, Zeldah devot-

ed three poems to the Sabbath. Ibid., pp. 29–34.

72   Ibid., p. 70. The allusion: Isaiah 2:4.

73   Ibid., p. 60.

74   Ibid., p. 51.

75   The last line alludes to the 310 worlds. Ibid., pp. 36–37.

76   Ibid., p. 80.

77   In Hebrew: *Ha-Carmel ha-I-Nireh* (Tel Aviv, 1972).

78   Ayin Tur-Malka, *Shirat ha-Beerot* (Jerusalem, 1971), p. 9.

79   Ibid., p. 15.

80   In Hebrew: "Mebassre Yerushalayim ha-Hadashah," ibid., p. 93.

81   Ibid., p. 51.

82   In Hebrew: *Ha-Golim* (Tel Aviv, 1970).

83   See the brief snapshots of the bakers Layzer and Meir—father and son—in the story "Family" in the collection of stories by Deborah Baron, *The Thorny Path*, tr. Joseph Schachter and ed. Itzhak Hanoch (Jerusalem, 1969), p. 2.

84   See the story, "Trifles," ibid., pp. 38–39.

85   See "A Day in Rami's Life," ibid., pp. 66–76. In the original: "Yom Ehad Shel Rami" in Deborah Baron's book, *Be-Lev ha-Kerak* (Tel Aviv, 1948/49)—part of her book *Shavririm* (Tel Aviv, 1948/49).

86   For the character of Mina, see the story "What Has Been," ibid., pp. 77–153; for Zivah, the story that bears her name, ibid., pp. 174–207; for Nehamah and Naomi, the story "In the Bond of Life," ibid., pp. 253–268.

87   *Hebrew Short Stories* I selected by S. Y. Penueli and A. Ukmani (Tel Aviv, 1965), pp. 169–81. Shulamit Schwartz-Nardy's translation, a combination of aptness and empathy, adds a dimension of strength to the story "Fradel" in Deborah Baron's book *Shavririm,* pp. 37–61.

88   Deborah Baron, *The Thorny Path*, pp. 174–207.

89   In Hebrew: *Rehov ha-Madregot* (Tel Aviv, 1956).

90   See the beautiful story—one of Hendel's best—"Zili wi-Yedidi Shaul" in *Anashim Aherim Hem* (Merhavyah, 1950), pp. 69–89. For an English translation of Miriam Shimoni, see "Zili and My Friend Shaul" in *The New Israeli Writers,* ed. Dalia Rabikowitz (New York, 1969), pp. 61–76.

91   See the story "Almanato Shel Eliezer," ibid., pp. 93–148.

92   Amalia Kahana-Karmon, *Bi-Kefifah Ahat* (Tel Aviv, 1966), p. 309.

93   In Hebrew: "Lev ha-Kayiz, Lev ha-Or," ibid., pp. 235–300.

94   In Hebrew: "Ne'imah Sason Kotevet Shirim," ibid., pp. 191–207.

95   In Hebrew: "Muskalot Rishonim," ibid., pp. 301–311.

96 In Hebrew: "Ani Zame le-Memayik Yerushalayim," ibid., pp. 135–68. It was Y. Razaby who identified the quotation for her. Ibid., p. 7.

97 Ibid., p. 9.

98 Ibid., p. 86.

99 Ibid., p. 115.

100 In Hebrew: "Beersheba Birat ha-Negev," pp. 59–67.

101 Ibid., p. 306.

17   Notes to Antecedents and Contemporaries of Agnon: Samuel Joseph Agnon; Hasidism in Hebrew Poetry; Seminal Impact of Hasidism

1   In Hebrew: *Shalom 'Al Yisrael.* A new, abbreviated edition: Eliezer Zevi ha-Kohen Zweifel, *Shalom 'Al Yisrael* (Jerusalem, 1972/73) Even before Hess and Zweifel we meet with a rare instance of interest in Hasidic proverbs. The editor of *Kerem Hemed* quotes with approval six proverbs of the Maggid of Dubno. See Eisig Silberschlag, "Para-poetic Attitudes and Values in Early Nineteenth Century Hebrew Poetry," in *Studies in Nineteenth Century Jewish Intellectual History,* ed. Alexander Altmann (Cambridge, Mass., 1964), p. 137, n. 90. Jacob Samuel Byk (1784–1831), a well-known *Maskil,* also sympathized with Hasidism. See Isaac Barzilay, *Shlomo Yehudah Rapoport* (Ramat Gan, 1969), p. 76.

2   There is no doubt that Peretz was born in 1851, in spite of his official birth certificate which was deposited in the archives of the municipality of Zamość—his birthplace—and which listed May 18, 1852 as his birthday. There was no precision in those days, either on the part of the parents or on the part of Russian officials. The jubilee of Peretz was celebrated in 1901. See N. Meisel, *Sefer Judah Leb Peretz* (Merhavyah, 1960), pp. 432–34.

3   See his poem "Ha-Shutafut" in *Ha-Shahar* (Vienna 1874-75), pp. 551–52.

4   See Judah Leb Peretz, *My Memoirs,* tr. from the Yiddish by Fred Goldberg (New York, 1964), p. 75.

5   "If Not Higher," in *Peretz,* tr. and ed. Saul Liptzin, *Yivo Bilingual Series* (New York, 1947), pp. 180–81. My translations differ from Liptzin's.

6   *Peretz,* p. 214.

7   Ibid., p. 222.

8   *Hurban Bet ha-Zaddik* in *Kol Kitbe J.L. Peretz* II (Dvir, 1961/62), pp. 175–212.

9   Harry Sackler, *The Seer Looks At His Bride* (Boston, 1932), p. 12.

10   *Kelape Mizrah* in Sackler, *Sefer ha-Mahazot* (New York, 1943), p. 405–16.

11   *Nesi'at ha-Zaddik* in Sackler, *Sefer ha-Mahazot*, pp. 199–268. Sackler has not achieved recognition on a scale commensurate with his talents. For an appreciation of his dramatic oeuvre, see Eisig Silberschlag, "Zevi Sackler," *Bizaron* (1944), pp. 252–54. Recently G. Shaked, *Ha-Mahazeh ha-'Ibri ha-Histori bi-Tekufat ha-Tehiyyah—Noseim we-Zurot* (Jerusalem, 1970), pp. 148–50, 183–84, 218–21.

12   Dybbuk means "cleaver," usually the soul of a dead person that enters the body of another. For a convenient English summary of the play, see Mendel Kohansky, *The Hebrew Theater—Its First Fifty Years* (Jerusalem, 1969), pp. 34–36. For the theory of the Zaddik's descent as a necessary condition of ascent, see the important article of Joseph Weiss, "Reshit Zemihatah Shel ha-Derek ha-Hasidit" in *Ziyyon*, 16 (1950–51), pp. 82–88.

13   On Vakhtangov and his role in the production of *The Dybbuk*, see Mendel Kohansky, *The Hebrew Theater*, pp. 34–43.

14   Berdyczewski's first article on Hasidism was entitled "Mishnat Hasidim," see *Kol Maamare Micah Joseph Berdyczewski* (Tel Aviv, 1951–52), pp. 3–5. Under that title it appeared in 1899. See Meisel, op.cit., p. 379. Interestingly, Peretz's first Hasidic story is also known as "Mishnat Hasidim." See *Kol Kitbe J.L. Peretz* II (Tel Aviv, 1961/62), pp. 56–62. Berdyczewski changed his favorable attitude to Peretz in later years. Ibid., pp. 382–86. On Peretz's attitude to Berdyczewski see now Jeshurun Keshet, *Micah Joseph Berdyczewski [Ben-Gurion]-Hayyav u-Poalo* (Jerusalem, 1958), pp. 90–92. It is interesting to learn from Immanuel Ben-Gurion, Berdyczewski's son, that in his teens his father wrote a tract under the title *Korot ha-Hasidut we-Rodefehah*. It has not been preserved for posterity. Ibid., p. 281.

15   *Kol Kitbe Yehudah Steinberg* IV, pp. 11–14.

16   Ibid., pp. 143–46. These two brothers are real personages, disciples of Dov Ber of Mezritch: Meshullam Zusya (Zishe in Yiddish) of Hanipol (Annopol), who died in 1800, and his younger brother Elimelek of Lizensk, who died in 1809. On the parables of the two brothers, see Martin Buber, *Tales of the Hasidim—The Early Masters* (New York, 1947), pp. 235–64; also Jiri Langer, *Nine Gates*, pp. 115–37.

17   Ibid., pp. 150–54.

18   For novels on Hasidism, see Eisig Silberschlag, *From Renaissance to Renaissance*, pp. 199; 298–99; 319–21.

19   On the town—the locale of numerous stories—see Agnon's posthumous work *'Ir u-Meloah* (Jerusalem and Tel Aviv, 1973).

20   Russian Jews are apt to call Galician Jews: *Geshtrofte*, the punished. Perhaps it is jealousy, perhaps it is envy, perhaps mere sport of name-calling.

21   Agnon who had a first-rate knowledge of Jewish sources may have been attracted to the Aramaic interpretation of Isaiah 24:22 which yields a closer sound to Agnon than 'Agunot. Though " 'Agunot" is the first story to appear under the name of Agnon, it is not the author's first prose tale. As a matter of fact—in view of Agnon's hazy recollection of his own beginnings—it is still a

moot problem whether he began his literary career in Yiddish or in Hebrew. On the difficulties in dating the literary origins of Agnon in print, see Dov Sadan 'Al Shai Agnon (Tel Aviv, 1967), pp. 125–27.

22   In Hebrew: We-Haya he-'Akov le-Mishor.

23   In Hebrew: Oreah Natah la-Lun. The title is based on Jer. 14:8.

24   In Hebrew: Temol Shilshom. The title—like many titles of Agnon's stories and novels—is based on a biblical locution.

25   Shirah (Jerusalem-Tel Aviv, 1971).

26   Agnon emphasized the visual power in literary art in no uncertain terms: "The main trouble in modern Hebrew literature is the precedence of feeling over seeing." From the Agnon Archive in the National and University Library of Jerusalem; quoted by Gershon Shaked, Omanut ha-Sippur Shel Agnon (Merhavyah and Tel Aviv, 1973), p. 13; see also the discussion of the phrase, ibid., pp. 26–29.

27   In Hebrew: Haknasat Kallah. English translation by I.M. Lask (New York, 1937); republished by Schocken Books in 1967.

28   On the concept of man as wayfarer, see Gerhart B. Ladner, "Homo Viator: Medieval Ideas on Alienation and Order," Speculum XLII² (April, 1967), p. 256.

29   The source for the sobriquet: an incorrect translation of Exodus 20:3: Lo Yiheyh Leka Elohim Aherim 'Al Panai; Elohim Aherim is rendered deos alienos.

30   These are the first two words of the formula which is recited by the bridegroom under the bridal canopy: Hare At Mekuddeshet Li be-Taba'at Zo ke-Dat Moshe we-Yisrael.

31   In Hebrew: Ketubbah.

32   Mazal Tov: "Good Luck."

33   Even a casual look at Agnon's manuscripts in the Agnon Archive—Yad Agnon—which, incidentally, contains almost one thousand manuscripts and twenty thousand letters, proves with the impact of immediacy that the author spared neither labor nor effort to produce the desired effect in a word, a phrase, a sentence. The deletions and additions are endless. A good example is the seventeenth chapter of The Bridal Canopy. The first few lines on the transition from winter to spring are shorter in the printed version than in the manuscript version. And so is Reb Yudel's reaction to the changing landscape.

34   In Hebrew: Sippur Pashut.

35   In Hebrew: Shevu'at Emunim.

36   "Edo and Enam" made its first appearance in Luah ha-Arez (1970/71) Agnon inscribed the first edition with a dedicatory poem for the author; it was published in Hadoar (May 24, 1974), p. 472. In the third line of the poem read Af instead of Sof and delete period at the end of the line.

37   *Shirah* and *Ba-Hanuto Shel Mar Lublin* are the two novels of Agnon which were published posthumously. On the latter novel, see the article of Agnon's daughter Emunah Yaron, "Kak Hutkan ha-Sefer," *Ha-Arez* (February 21, 1975), p. 18.

38   Agnon maintained that he was totally ignorant of Kafka and that his wife did not succeed in reading to him any one of Kafka's stories (*Ma'ariv,* March 9, 1973), p. 39. He emphatically denied, in conversations with the author, any knowledge of Kafka. The question of Kafka's influence on Agnon must, therefore, be relegated to the myths of modern Hebrew literature. This does not prevent critics like Edmund Wilson and Baruch Kurzweil from searching for parallel perceptions of and sensitivities to the malaise of our time in the works of Agnon and Kafka. There is even a comparatist study on the disparate pair of writers by Hillel Barzel, *Ben Agnon le-Kafka* (Ramat Gan, 1972).

39   In Hebrew: *Yamim Noraim* (Jerusalem, 1937).

40   In Hebrew: *Atem Reitem* (Tel Aviv, 1958/59).

41   In Hebrew: *Sefer, Sofer, Sippur* (Jerusalem, 1937).

42   See Agnon's speech of acceptance in *Nobel Lectures Including Presentation Speeches and Laureates' Biographies—Literature 1901-1967,* ed. Horst Frenz. Published for the Nobel Foundation (Amsterdam, London, New York, 1969), p. 616. For a variant, see Agnon's speech on the occasion of his seventieth birthday, published in a brief, unpaginated brochure *Li-Kevod 'Azmi-Devarim she-Higadti be-Sifriyyat Schocken be-Or le-Yom Dalet Parashat wa-Ethanan Tav Shin Yod Het.* There he said—among other things: "He whom God favored with a writer's pen has to write about God's works and his miraculous ways with men. And if he writes about himself, he should write only as part of Israel, His people."

43   In Hebrew: *Balladot Agnoniyyot.* The ballads form the second part of Bertini's book of poems: *Mahshakim u-Derakim* (Jerusalem, 1974).

44   See E.E. Lisitzky, *Be-Ohale Kush* (Jerusalem, 1953), p. 3.

45   See Abraham Regelson, *Hakukot Otiyotayik* (Tel Aviv, 1964), p. 220.

46   In Hebrew: *Kedushat Levi.* It first appeared in Slavita in 1797/98.

47   Uri Zevi Gruenberg, *Anacreon 'Al Koteb ha-'Izzabon* (Tel Aviv, 1928), p. 71.

48   Idem, *Kelape Tish'im we-Tish'ah* (Tel Aviv, 1928),p. 35.

49   Samson Meltzer, *Shirim u-Balladot,* (Tel Aviv, 1953), p. 36. The tenth edition—for students—appeared in Tel Aviv in 1974.

50   On Rabbi Zusya and Rabbi Elimelech, see n. 16.

51   The translator has remarked that *I and Thou* is indeed a poem. See the introduction to Martin Buber, *I and Thou,* by Ronald Rego Smith (New York, 1958), p. XI.

52   In recognition of his services to Hasidism and as a mark of personal

friendship Agnon dedicated seven paraphrases of Baal Shem Tov's stories to Buber; they appeared under the title *Sippurim Naim Shel R. Yisrael Ba'al Shem Tov, Molad 144–145* (1960), pp. 357–364.

53   Martin Buber, *Hasidism*, tr. Maurice Friedman (New York, 1949), p. 18. A contemporary mystic, Rabbi Abraham Isaac Kook (1885–1935), regarded the early Hasidic rabbis as intermediaries of divine light between the Deity and the people. But later hasidic rabbis and Hasidim degenerated—like rabbinic Judaism—into ordinary establishmentarianism. This deterioration must have been extremely painful to a man whose work is regarded as "a veritable *theologia mystica* of Judaism equally distinguished by its originality and the richness of its author's mind." See Gershom G. Scholem, *Major Trends in Jewish Mysticism*, p. 354, n. 17.

54   Paul Arthur Schilpp, ed., *The Philosophy of Martin Buber* (La Salle, Illinois, 1967), p. 731.

55   Martin Buber, *I and Thou*, pp. 82–83.

56   E. William Rollins and Harry Zohn, ed., *Men of Dialogue: Martin Buber and Albrecht Goes* (New York, 1969), pp. 204–205.

57   *The Philosophy of Martin Buber*, pp. 742–743.

58   Martin Buber, *I and Thou*, p. 4.

59   Preface by Martin Buber to *Ten Rungs: Hasidic Sayings* tr. Olga Marx (New York, 1973), p. 7.

18   Notes to The Rediscovery of Oriental Jewry in Hebrew Literature: Tabib; Burla; Shami

1   *From the Land of Sheba: Tales of the Jews of Yemen* collected and edited by S.D. Goitein (New York, 1947), p. 9. New and revised edition: (New York, 1973). It contains a new preface, an introductory essay "About the Jews of Yemen" and an updated bibliography. The documents are identical in both editions.

2   Himyar is the name for Yemen in the pre-Islamic era.

3   In Hebrew: *Iggeret Teman*. A pseudo-Messianic impostor in the nineteenth century provoked Jacob Halevi Saphir to publish his *Iggeret Teman ha-Shenit* (Vilna, 1873). For an excerpt from *Iggeret Teman ha-Shenit* in English, see S.D. Goitein's *From the Land of Sheba*, pp. 119–21. New edition, pp. 137–38.

4   In Hebrew: *Sefer ha-Musar—Mahberot R. Zachariah al-Dahiri*, ed. Yehudah Razaby (Jerusalem, 1955). For an analysis of four stories in the book, see Hayyim Schwartzbaum, "Le-Heker Arba'ah Sippure 'Am be-Sefer ha-Musar le-Rabbi Zechariah al-Dahiri" in *Boi Teman—Mehkarim u-Te'udot Yehude Teman*, ed. Yehudah Razaby (Tel Aviv, 1967).

5   In Hebrew: *Sefer ha-Mahashavah.*

6   Adani's commentary is known by its Hebrew title *Meleket Shelomoh.*

7   His chronicle, under the title *Dofi ha-Zeman*, was published in *Sefunot* 1 (Jerusalem, 1957).

8   *From the Land of Sheba*, pp. 103–104; new edition, pp. 121–22. For numerous legends on Shabbazi, see Dov Noy, *R. Shalem Shabbazi be-Aggadat ha-'Am Shel Yehude Teman*, pp. 106–31. For the poetry of and bibliography on Shabbazi, see Y. Razaby, "*R. Shalem Shabbazi we-Shirato*" in *Sefunot* 9 (1965), pp. 133–166.

9   *Yalkut Shire Teman*, ed. Yehudah Razaby (Jerusalem, 1968), p. 71.

10   In Hebrew: *Midrash ha-Gadol*, compiled probably in the thirteenth century by David ben Amram Adani.

11   On the travels of Saphir in the East, see his two volume work *Eben Sappir* (Lyck 1866, Mainz, 1874). For two characteristic excerpts from *Eben Sappir* in English translation , see *From the Land of Sheba*, pp. 40–42, 91–93; new edition, pp. 58–60, 109–11. The latter excerpt is especially important; it preserves an ancient tradition of the Yemenite Jews that they came to Yemen "forty two years before the destruction of the First Temple." For a description of the Jewish Quarter, *Qa'al Yahud*, in Sana by an English entomologist, see Hugh Scott, *In the High Yemen* (London, 1942), pp. 134–36.

12   On the sizeable immigration from Yemen in 1881/82 see Y. Razaby, "'Aliyyat Teman le-Or Te'udot Hadashot," *Sinai* 63 (1968), pp. 163–71. Yemenites thought that the Messiah would come in that year on the strength of a numerical interpretation of Song of Songs 7:8: "I say I will climb the *palm tree*." *Be-Tamar* in Hebrew equals 1882.

13   Halévy's reports on his archaelogical mission to Yemen appeared in the following periodicals: *Journal Asiatique* (1872) and *Bulletin de la Société de Géographie de Paris* (1873, 1877). On two popular articles by Halévy in *Revue Israélite* (1873) and *Levanon* XXVI,[45] see S.D. Goitein's Introduction to *Mas'ot Habshush* (Tel Aviv, 1938/39), p. 11.

14   On the composition of that valuable work, see S.D. Goitein's *Preface*, ibid., p. 5.

15   Samuel Javnieli, who emigrated from Russia to the Holy Land in 1905, was sent at his own request by the Zionist organization to Yemen at the end of 1911. On his experience in that land, see his *Massa' le-Teman* (1952). It is estimated that between 1919–1948 almost 16,000 Yemenites emigrated to mandatory Palestine in operation "Magic Carpet" and, between 1949 and 1950, almost 43,000 came to Israel. By 1968 there were only 200 Jews left in Yemen.

16   Isa. 43:6.

17   In *Betrothed* Agnon characterizes the Yemenites as "a nimble, keen-witted tribe." See *Kol Sippurav Shel Shemuel Yosef Agnon* XI (Jerusalem and Tel Aviv, 1952), p. 243. And Goitein cites the case of a blacksmith from Sana who possessed a considerable knowledge of mystic lore and ritual law. See his *A Mediterranean Society* I (Berkeley and Los Angeles, 1967), p. 92.

18   See Imber's long poem "Ha-Temanim" in his *Barkai* (Jerusalem, 1886), pp. 69–72.

19   See Yellin's republished letters from Jerusalem—*Miktavim mi-Yerushalayim* which appeared in *Ha-Meliz* from 1896 to 1904—in *Kitbe David Yellin* I (Jerusalem, 1972), p. 77.

20   Hebrew title of the booklet: *Yehude Teman* (Cologne, 1912?).

21   Hebrew title of the comedy: *Ha-Bahalan*. Reprinted from *Hashkafah*, it appeared in Jerusalem in 1909.

22   Ibid., p. 23.

23   Ibid., p. 29.

24   See notes 11 and 13 to Singer of the Desacralized Land: David Shimoni.

25   The story appeared in Nehamah Puhachevsky's collection of short stories: *Bi-Yehudah ha-Hadashah* (Jaffa, 1910/11).

26   The later stories appeared in a volume entitled *Ba-Kefar u-ba-'Avodah* (Tel Aviv, 1929/30).

27   *Golat Teman* and *Shave Teman*. For excerpts, in English, from *Shave Teman*, see *The Land of Sheba*, pp. 43–46; 104–105; new edition, pp. 61–64; 122–23.

28   In Hebrew: "Kinnoro Shel Yosi" in *Derek Shel 'Afar* (Tel Aviv, 1967), pp. 7–56. For the English translation of the story, see *Argosy* V (Jerusalem, 1957), pp. 7–61.

29   In Hebrew: *Ke-'Esev ha-Sadeh* (Merhavyah, 1960). This is the second edition of the book which first appeared in 1948.

30   Ibid., p. 15.

31   In Hebrew: *Ke-'Ar'ar ba-'Aravah* (Merhavyah, 1957).

32   Eastern Jewry is a popular but inexact term. It includes Jews in Islamic countries, "the so-called Ishmaelite Diaspora." It embraces Jewry of the Iberian peninsula and southern France, Jews of North Africa, the Balkans, Turkey, the Middle East including Persia, Afghanistan, Bukhara, Azerbaijan and even the Caucasus. All these Jewries spoke Judeo-Spanish [Ladino] or Judeo-Arabic or Judeo-Persian. The Ben Zvi Institute, named for the second president of Israel, has fostered studies of remote Jewish communites. For that term see Itzhak Ben-Zvi, *The Exiled and the Redeemed* (Philadelphia, 1961), p. 3.

33   "Lunah" was written in 1914 and shown to Brenner who encouraged Burla to devote his talents to prose and to shun poetry. The story was published after the First World War. See Burla's reminiscences in *Le-Kol ha-Ze'adah* (Ramat Gan, 1965), pp. 171–76.

34   In Hebrew: *Ishto ha-Senuah* (Jerusalem, 1928).

35   In Hebrew: *Naftule Adam* (Jersusalem, 1928/29). The English translation by Joseph Schachter, ed. Murray Roston, appeared in Jerusalem in 1968.

36   In Hebrew: *Nashim* (Tel Aviv, 1958).

37   In Hebrew: *Ba'al be-'Amav* (Tel Aviv, 1961).

38   In Hebrew: *Merannenet* (Tel Aviv, 1930).

39   *In Darkness Striving*, p. 37.

40   In Hebrew: *Bat Zion*, 4 volumes (Tel Aviv, 1930/31).

41   In Hebrew: *'Alilot 'Akabiah* (Tel Aviv, 1968).

42   In Hebrew: *Eleh Masse' Rabbi Yehudah Halevi* (Tel Aviv, 1959). Some protagonists of Burla's stories bear historical names of Sephardic provenance: Lavrat, Abrabanel, Alshek. See the stories "Meir Lavrat," "Sheyarim" and

"Gezar Dino be-Yado" in *Le-Kol ha-Ze'adah,* pp. 68–86; 125–40; 141–52.

43   In Hebrew: *Ba-Ofek* (Tel Aviv, 1946/47).

44   One of his pamphlets, *Mebasser Tov,* sums up his philosophy of nationalism on the very title page of the English translation: *Harbinger of Good Tidings, An Address to the Jewish Nation, by Rabbi Judah Elkali* [sic], *on the Propriety of Organizing an Association to Promote the Regaining of their Fatherland* (London, 1852).

45   See especially *Lunah; Ben Shivte 'Arav* (Tel Aviv, 1925/26) and *Beli Kokab* (Tel Aviv, 1927).

46   Names of the talmudic academies: *Dorshe Zion* and *Tiferet Yerushalayim;* of the Teachers Seminary: *Ezra.*

47   Respective Hebrew titles: "Ha-'Akarah" and "Kofer Nefesh" in *Ha-'Omer* I (1907).

48   *Sippurim 'Ivriyyim me-Hayye 'Aravim,* p. 131.

49   In Hebrew: "Nikmat ha-Avot" in *Sippure Yizhak Shami* (Jerusalem, 1971/72).

50   Quoted in A. Ben Or, *Toledot ha-Sifrut ha-'Ibrit be-Dorenu* II (Tel Aviv, 1955/56), p. 94.

51   See his *Ashab mi-Baghdad* (Tel Aviv, 1970).

52   In Hebrew: *Hitbaharut* (Tel Aviv, 1971/72).

19   Notes to The Totality of Jewry in the Works of Hayyim Hazaz

1   Both effusions of youth were published in *Ha-Shiloah* XXXIV (March, 1918), pp. 274-284 and XXXV (September-October, 1918), p. 249. Respective Hebrew titles: *Ke-Bo ha-Shemesh* and *'Al ha-Mishmar*.

2   On Gnessin, see Eisig Silberschlag, *From Renaissance to Renaissance* I, pp. 223–25.

3   Isa. 8:6.

4   For instance: Dan. 11:16. *Erez ha-Zevi* means Land of the Deer; metaphorically, Land of Beauty.

5   In Hebrew: "Ba-Mishmar." See Schocken's one-volume edition of Tschernichowsky's collected poetry (Jerusalem and Tel Aviv, 1953), pp. 548–50.

6   "Hayyim Hazaz—Freeman of Jerusalem, City of the Future," *The Jerusalem Post* (October 6, 1969).

7   The three stories were first published in *Ha-Tekufah* 21, 22 (Warsaw, 1924) and *Ha-Tekufah* 23 (Warsaw, 1925), ed. Jacob Cahan and F. Lachower. Their respective Hebrew titles: "Mi-Zeh u-mi-Zeh," "Pirke Mahpekah," "Shemuel Frankfurter." The stories fused into the novel *Brazen Gates*. Better translation: *Doors of Brass*. The English translation under the title *Gates of Bronze* appeared in Philadelphia in 1975. For *Daltot Nehoshet*, see *Kol Kitbe Hayyim Hazaz* IV[1,2] (Tel Aviv, 1968).

8   The Hebrew title: *Daltot Nehoshet*. It has been perceptively stated that the element of love is not central to the oeuvre of Hazaz in general or to this novel in particular. But the reasons adduced for this phenomenon are not valid. World revolution and national resurrection—the background and foreground in the fictive works of Hazaz—are not necessarily inimical to the seductions of Eros. On the other hand it is also true that a new and fuller development of the element of love is discernible in the collection of stories which appeared a few months before the death of the author: *Even Sha'ot* (Tel Aviv, 1973). See B.I.

Mikhaly, "*Al Hamishah Sippure Ahavah,*" *Moznayim,* (March, 1974), p. 225. See also Hazaz's posthumous volume *Pa'amon we-Rimmon* (Tel Aviv, 1974).

9 In Hebrew: *Be-Yishuv Shel Ya'ar* (Tel Aviv,1929/30). *Home in the Woods,* Hazaz's stepchild, unfinished in spite of its 427 pages in two volumes, was excluded from the collected edition of his works. Hazaz claimed that the printer's errors left him with a permanent distaste for the book. But there may be deeper reasons for Hazaz's aversion thoug̱h it is difficult to trace them. In an interview with Raphael Bashan, Hazaz reiterated his alienation from his own novel: "This book does not exist. . . . Since its publication I have not read it . . ." See *Ma'ariv* (December 29,1967).

10 In Hebrew: "Dorot ha-Rishonim" in *Kol Kitbe Hayyim Hazaz* VIII, pp. 7–121.

11 *The Jewish Frontier* (January, 1963).

12 In Hebrew: *Rehayim Shevurim, Kol Kitbe Hayyim Hazaz* VIII.

13 "Rahamim," ibid., p. 212.

14 *The Jerusalem Post* (October 6, 1969).

15 In Hebrew:" 'Ashir wa-Rash Nifgashu." The title is taken from Prov. 22:2.

16 The Hebrew title *Ha-Yoshevet ba-Gannim* is part of a verse in Song of Songs 8:13. (Halpern's English translation entitled *Mori Said* appeared in New York in 1956.) In the collected edition: *Kol Kitbe Hayyim Hazaz* VI.

17 Isa. 63:4.

18 Hos. 14:5.

19 Isa. 60:22.

20 The Messiah will come when the world is totally guilty or totally innocent. *Sanhedrin* 98a.

21 *Ha-Yoshevet ba-Gannim,* p. 360. Hazaz made some changes for the version in the collected works. See *Kol Kitbe Hayyim Hazaz* VI, p. 360.

22 Ibid., p. 5.

23 *Kol Kitbe Hayyim Hazaz* VII[1,2,3,4]·Seymour Gitin maintains with youthful exaggeration that Yaish is Hazaz's "greatest work." See his unpublished senior thesis at the Library of Hebrew Union College—Jewish Institute of Religion (Cincinnati, 1962).

24 Ezek. 27:19.

25 Hab. 2:4.

26 In the twelve-volume edition of his collected works Hazaz substituted Hebraisms for some Arabisms. The substitution had been urged by Professor S.D. Goitein after the appearance of *Yaish.* See Jacob Bahat, "Le-'Ikre Shitat ha-Shinuyim be-Yezirat Hayyim Hazaz," *Tarbiz* XXXIX[4] (July, 1970), p. 392, n. 11.

27   *The Jerusalem Post* (October 6, 1969).

28   In Hebrew: *Be-Kolar Ehad, Kol Kitbe Hayyim Hazaz* II.

29   *Ma'ariv* (December 29, 1967).

30   A volume called *Zuzik Nahum Hazaz* with reproductions from his work, with a foreword by Meyer Schapiro, with brief comments by his mother, the poetess Yoheved Bat-Miriam, and by friends, and with excerpts from his letters, was published by *American Fund for Israel Institutions* (New York, 1950).

31   In Hebrew: "Ha-Derashah," *Kol Kitbe Hayyim Hazaz* I, pp. 219–36.

32   "Met Mizvah," *Kol Kitbe Hayyim Hazaz* I, pp. 238–42.

33   *Harat 'Olam,* ibid., p. 138.

34   Ibid., pp. 143–44. Hazaz made considerable changes in this and in the following passages.

35   "Havit 'Akurah," ibid., p. 158.

36   Ibid., pp. 174–75.

37   In Hebrew: *Ofek Natui, Kol Kitbe Hayyim Hazaz* V, pp. 7–134.

38   The quotation is from a speech by Hazaz at the Twenty-third Convention of Hebrew writers in Jerusalem on April 16, 1968. See *Daf* 31, ed. Dov Homsky (Tel Aviv, 1968), p. 7.

39   *The Jewish Frontier* (January, 1963).

40   Four books of Hazaz are fragmentary torsos: *R. Pinhas* which was to deal with Turkish Jewry, *Be-Zillan Shel Malkuyot* which was to deal with immigrant Jews in France, *Haluzim* which was to be his first novel about the Land of Israel and *Elu Hem* on Jesus of Nazareth.

41   In Hebrew: *Be-Kez ha-Yamim, Kol Kitbe Hayyim Hazaz* III, pp. 7–212. The first act of the play first appeared in *Moznayim* (1933); the three subsequent acts in three subsequent issues. The play was adapted for presentation by the National Theater, Habimah, published in 1950. A third version, unpublished, is available in the library of Habimah; it contains changes and deletions in some dialogs, supplementary stage directions, and additional phrases. A fourth edition is available in the collected works of Hazaz. *Kol Kitbe Hayyim Hazaz* (Tel Aviv, 1968). For the new presentation of the play by Habimah in 1972 new changes were made by Hazaz. This new version appeared in a periodical devoted to theatrical arts *(Bamah* 53–54, 1972). In the library of Habimah there is a final and unpublished sixth version, also of 1972. See Hillel Barzel, "Ha-Mahazeh Be-Kez ha-Yamim le-Nosahav," *Moznayim* (March 1974), p. 203.

42   In Hebrew: "Hatan Damim," *Kol Kitbe Hayyim Hazaz* I, pp. 7–43. A deluxe edition of the story with illustrations by Ruth Zorfati was published in Tel Aviv [Year of publication is not indicated].

20   Notes to The Historical Novel

1   *Chronique du Temps de Charles IX* (Paris, 1829).

2   *Nous ne pourons nous representer avec exactitude ce qui n'existe plus.* Anatole France, *Jardin d'Epicure* in *Oeuvres Complètes illustrées* IX (Paris, 1925–1937), p. 407. *Jardin d'Epicure* is the ninth in the twenty-five volume edition of the works of Anatole France.

3   Aristotle, *Poetics* IX.

4   Similarly Butterfield: . . . "the historical novel is a fusion . . . A historical event is 'put to fiction' as a poem is put to music . . . And, just as a composer in choosing a poem set to music, accepts certain limitations, volunteers a certain allegiance . . . so the historical novelist owes a certain loyalty to the history of which he treats." H. Butterfield, *The Historical Novel* (Cambridge, 1924), p. 6.

5   *Waverley Novels* ed. 1829–1833, *Ivanhoe* (XVI), p. XXXIV.

6   On Mapu, see *From Renaissance to Renaissance* I, pp. 136–40. On a fictive narrative about Mapu—in Yiddish—see Eliezer Heiman, *Abraham Mapu—Historishe Derzelung* (Kovno, 1937).

7   In Hebrew: "Kronikah Yeshanah" in Jacob Hurgin, *Be-she-Kevar ha-Yamim* (Tel Aviv, 1968), pp. 94–124.

8   In Hebrew: "Rak Mahatalah," ibid., pp. 125–37.

9   In Hebrew: "Ha-Midyanit," ibid., pp. 5–27.

10   In Hebrew: "Ya'el Eshet Hever Ha-Keni," pp. 28–56.

11   In Hebrew: "Shaul we-ha-Atonot" in the collection of the seven historical stories of Barash under the title *Siah ha-'Ittim-Novelot Historiyyot* (Tel Aviv, no date). Like the immense literary output on Saul in world literature—from the play on the unhappy King by Hans Sachs to the tragedy by André Gide—it is based on 1 Samuel 9-31.

12   In Hebrew *Kivsat ha-Rash* (Merhavyah, 1957). The expression is part of the prophet Nathan's stern rebuke to David: 2 Samuel 12:4.

13   In Hebrew: *Melek Basar we-Dam* (Merhavyah, 1954). English translation by David Patterson.

14   *Siah 'Ittim,* p. 48.

15   In Hebrew: *Divre Yeme Gemini* (Tel Aviv, 1967/68).

16   In Hebrew: *Mul Sha'ar ha-Shamayim.*

17   Ibid., p. 156.

18   In Hebrew: "'Ad ha-Yesod." The title is borrowed from Pss. 137:7.

19   Ibid., p. 81.

20   *Siah 'Ittim,* p. 80.

21   In Hebrew: "Ha-Nishar be-Toledo." English translation: *Argosy* 8 (Jerusalem, 1962), pp. 144–71. The Hebrew original is illustrated by Uri Eliaz, the English translation by Nahum Gutman, the son of Simhah Ben-Zion.

22   Pss. 118:17. The half-verse in Spanish translation in Barash's story: Yo morire, mas vivire.

23   "Last in Toledo", p. 171. My translation differs slightly from the translation in *Argosy.*

24   Judah Leb Gordon also wrote a poem on the first destruction of Jerusalem: "Zidkiyyahu be-Bet ha-Pekudot."

25   In Hebrew: "Be-Pundak Ehad," *Siah 'Ittim,* pp. 107–43.

26   Ecclesiastes 10:1.

27   In Hebrew: "'Azmot R. Shimshon Shapiro" in *Siah 'Ittim,* pp. 157–205.

28   In Hebrew: "Be-Marburg," ibid., pp. 206–11.

29   Salo W. Baron, *A Social and Religious History of the Jews* I, (New York, 1952), p. 4. For a wealth of illustrations from Jewish holidays, Jewish tenets and concepts, ibid., pp. 5–10. The intimate connection between Judaism and history has been noted frequently: "There is no other people whose spirit and evolution are so saturated with Jewish history." Lion Feuchtwanger, "The Jew's Sense of History" in *Jewish Heritage Reader* selected, with introduction by Rabbi Morris Adler and edited by Lily Edelman (New York, 1965), p. 17. Another novelist, Arthur Koestler, declares: "Judaism is a freak of history." See his *Promise and Fulfillment, Palestine 1917–1949* (London, 1949), p. 3.

30   2 Sam. 23:1.

31   The Hebrew title: *Kivsat ha-Rash* (Merhavyah, 1957). The two words appear in 1 Sam. 12:4.

32   Hence the subtitle: *Sippur Uriah ha-Hitti.*

33   Moshe Shamir, *Kivsat ha-Rash,* p. 281.

34   The English translation by David Patterson is a sensitive rendition of the original: *Melek Basar wa-Dam.*

35   Shamir did not have to use the biblical idiom in *Kivsat ha-Rash*: the author of the purported memoirs wrote in Hittite.

36   Deut. 4: 8–9; Josh. 1:7; Pss. 1:2.

37   *Melek Basar wa-Dam*, p. 151–52.

38   In Hebrew: *Milhemet Bene Or*. The title alludes to one of the Dead Sea Scrolls: *Milhemet Bene Or u-Bene Hoshek*.

39   In Hebrew: *Hu Halak b a-Sadot* (Merhavyah, 1947).

40   *Milhemet Bene Or*, p. 169.

41   In Hebrew: *Sanherib b i-Yehudah* (Tel Aviv, 1958).

42   In Hebrew: *Sofer ha-Melek* (Tel Aviv, 1966).

43   In Hebrew: *Mul Herev* (Tel Aviv, 1962).

44   The Hebrew title: *Be-Himmot Mamlakah* (Jerusalem, 1929).

45   In Hebrew: *David u-Batsheva* (Tel Aviv, 1964). It first appeared in the twenties under the title *Yeme David*. But it was refashioned by the author and published first in English translation from a manuscript copy, and from English into Spanish.

46   *David u-Batsheva*, p. 328.

47   Isa. 11:1–3.

48   Ibid., 11:10.

49   Matt. 1:1.

50   See *From Renaissance to Renaissance* I, p. 246. It should be noted that Brenner in *Breakdown and Bereavement* and Phinehas Sadeh in *Life as a Parable* are fascinated by Jesus.

51   In Hebrew: *Ba-Mish'ol ha-Zar* (Tel Aviv, 1937). The English translation by Julian Louis Meltzer was published in 1968 by "Massada Ltd. and Institute for the Translation of Hebrew Literature at the National Council of Culture and Art, attached to the Ministry of Education and Culture, Israel." The title is based on the intertestamental Esdras IV, 7:

> . . . A city is builded, and set upon a broad field, and is full of all good things:
> The entrance thereof is narrow, and is set in a dangerous place to fall, like as if there were a fire on the right hand, and on the left a deep water: And one only path between them both, even between the fire and the water, so small that there could but one man go there at once. If this city now were given unto a man for an inheritance, if he shall never pass the danger set before it, how shall he receive this inheritance?

It should be noted that the Yiddish writer Shalom Asch (1880–1957) created a sensation when his novel *The Nazarene* appeared in English translation. It formed—together with *The Apostle* and *Mary*—the first trilogy on Christianity in Jewish literature.

52   The novel appeared in installments in *Ha-'Olam* between 1927 and 1929; in book form in London in 1928–1929. A detailed comparative study of Brod's *Reubeni* (Munich, 1926) with Kabak's *Molko* might yield interesting results in the treatment of a major theme by two Jewish writers in two different languages. It has been done to a certain extent by Isaiah Rabinowitz *Bizaron* 6 (1948), pp. 287–94 and Werner Weinberg in his comprehensive dissertation on *The Life and Work of Aaron Abraham Kabak* (Hebrew Union College—Jewish Institute of Religion, Cincinnati, Ohio, 1961), pp. 152–54. Interestingly, the phrase "narrow path," Kabak's title for his novel on Jesus, appears in Brod's *Reubeni*, p. 228. *"Welch enger Weg, rechts und links grauenvollste Gefahr . . ."* Brod wrote a novel on Jesus but it appeared after Kabak's death. See Max Brod, *Der Meister* (Gütersloh, 1952).

53   In the unpublished dissertation on the life and letters of Kabak it is stated—and the statement cannot be faulted—that "Kabak's central theme is that of redemption—redemption of the individual and redemption of the nation." See Werner Weinberg, op. cit., p. 1. Kabak felt the need to share his personal reasons for writing *Ba-Mish'ol ha-Zar* with his public. See his published speech in *Musaf le-Davar* (January 13, 1939).

54   Kabak, *The Narrow Path*, p. 80.

55   In Hebrew: *Toledot Mishpahah Ahat* (Tel Aviv, 1942/43—1944/45). For bibliographical details on the work, see Werner Weinberg, op. cit., p. 440. Whether there were to be eight or ten or twelve novels in the series *Toledot Mishpahah Ahat* is an undecided problem. Ibid., p. 525, n. 258. Eight is the number given by Kabak to his brother-in-law Hayyim Tchernowitz in a letter written in 1943, ibid., p. 427.

56   In Hebrew: *Levadah* (Warsaw, 1904).

57   See the massive dissertation by Werner Weinberg referred to in notes 52 and 53.

58   See Eisig Silberschlag, *From Renaissance to Renaissance* I, pp. 319–20. To document his harsh judgment on the lifelessness of the historical novel—with one supposed exception, Shamir's *King of Flesh and Blood*—one critic picked Twersky and Kabak as typical offenders in the genre. Though Kabak is given some good marks for one of his historical novels, *The Narrow Path*, Twersky is summarily condemned as a man whose "dry and pedantic erudition" permeates all his novels. See David Kenaani, *Benam le-Ben Zemanam* (Merhavyah, 1955), pp. 215–19.

59   Ibid., pp. 320–21.

60   In Hebrew: *'Ir Kesumah* (3 vols. Tel Aviv, 1949–51).

61   In Hebrew: *Herev Yeshu'ot* (Tel Aviv, 1966).

62   In Hebrew: *Ben Zefat wi-Yerushalayim* (Jerusalem, 1927).

63   The Churchillian phrase is used in the introductory page.

64 *Herev Yeshu'ot,* p. 412.

65 See *From Renaissance to Renaissance* I, p. 111.

66 Zevi Lieberman, *Nehemiah* (Tel Aviv, 1966), p. 122.

67 Ibid., p. 125.

68 Prov. 31:10.

69 *Sabbath* 132a.

70 1 Sam. 15:29.

21   Notes to Contemporary Israel in Contemporary Fiction and Poetry: Jew and Rural Renascence; Peasant and Poet

1   Zemah played with the idea of another title for the book: *Shanah Ahat.* But Brenner's story of that name induced him to change his title. "And perhaps that's right: Rishonah-first. That means many years will come after the first. . . . " See *Dappe Pinkas,* p. 153.

2   At the Davar Prize Awarding Ceremony for *Shanah Rishonah,* Sadan mentioned Brenner's novel *Breakdown and Bereavement* and *Yesterday, Before Yesterday* which deal with the broken and passive protagonists of the Second Wave of Immigration respectively. "They have not answered the question: how come that these people were such great "doers?" *Shanah Rishonah* answered the question." *Dappe Pinkas,* p. 222.

3   *'Ad Yerushalayim* (Jerusalem, 1968). The title is based on Micah 1:9. The trilogy consists of the following novels: *Be-Reshit ha-Mevukah, Ha-Oniyyot ha-Aharonot, Shammot* (Tel Aviv, 1969). The original title of the first novel was changed at the suggestion of J.H. Brenner to *Be-Reshit ha-Mehumah.* The trilogy was planned as a double trilogy—one on Jerusalem which was finished in 1920, one on the Palestinian territory outside Jerusalem during the First World War. See Dan Miron, "Ha-Trilogiyyah ha-Yerushalmit Shel Aharon Reuveni" in *Yerushalayim* 3–4 (1970) ed. Aven Trainin and Aryeh Lipshitz, p. 195, n. 3.

4   Ibid., p. 161.

5   *'Izzavon* (Tel Aviv, 1929/30).

6   In Hebrew: "'Al Yad ha-Kir" (1916).

7   In Hebrew: *Zerif ha-'Ez* (Jerusalem, 1930). A useful *Bibliography of the kibbutz* has been compiled by Erik Cohen (Giv'at Haviva, 1964).

8   In Hebrew: *Kemo Shayish Yarok* (Tel Aviv, 1967).

9   In Hebrew: *Ke-Or Yahel* in *Sippure Yehudah Yaari* I (Jerusalem, 1969), pp. 3–322.

10   In Hebrew: *Havivim Yissurim.* Ibid., p. 321.

11   Ibid., p. 164.

12   Ibid., p. 198.

13   Respective Hebrew titles: "Darke Ish" and "Ha-Gibbor" in *Sippure Yehudah Yaari* II, pp. 5–64, 65–89.

14   In Hebrew: *Shoresh Ele Mayim, Sippure Yehudah Yaari* III, pp. 3–215.

15   *Sippure Yehudah Yaari* III, p. 15.

16   In Hebrew: *Be-Shiv'ah Derakim* (Jerusalem, 1954).

17   "Le-Hof ha-Kinneret" in *Sippure Yizhak Shenhar* III (Jerusalem, 1960), p. 141. For another translation, see "On Galilean Shores" tr. Israel Schen in *First Fruits,* ed. and intr. James A. Michener, foreword by Chaim Potok (Philadelphia, 1973), p. 79.

18   See the beginning of the story "Ka-'Anavim ba-Midbar" in *Sippure Yizhak Shenhar* III, p. 169.

19   In Hebrew: *Yeme Ziklag* (Tel Aviv, 1958).

20   Respective Hebrew titles: "Be-Terem Yeziah" and "Shayarah Shel Hazot" in S. Yizhar, *Arba'ah Sippurim* (Merhavyah, 1967), pp. 7–39, 139–266. "Be-Terem Yeziah" first appeared in the *Davar Yearbook* (1948/49), "Shayarah Shel Hazot" in 1949/50.

21   S. Yizhar, *Arba'ah Sippurim,* p. 133. For a different translation, see "The Prisoner" tr. V.C. Rycus in *Israeli Stories,* ed. Joel Blocker, intr. Robert Alter (New York, 1966), pp. 168–69.

22   In the original: "Hirbet Hiz'ah," *Arba'ah Sippurim,* pp. 41–111.

23   The locality in the Negev, a city of the tribe of Judah, is mentioned in Joshua and Samuel, Chronicles and Nehemiah. It is frequently associated with David in the Bible.

24   *Yeme Ziklag,* p. 712. That one day, Jewish New Year's Day 5709 (1948) requires almost 170 pages in the novel, pp. 567–734.

25   S. Yizhar, *Yeme Ziklag,* p. 743.

26   Ibid., p. 740.

27   The expression is Kariv's. See S. Yizhar, *Mibhar Maamare Bikkoret 'Al Yezirato,* ed. Hayyim Nagid (Tel Aviv, 1972), p. 40.

28   See especially S. Yizhar, *'Al Hinnuk we-'Al Hinnuk la-'Arakim* (Tel Aviv, 1974).

29   The stories appeared in two volumes: *Be-Raglayim Yehefot* (Jerusalem, 1959) and *Shishshah Sippure Kayiz* (Merhavyah, 1964).

30   See Ehud Ben-Ezer, "Porezim u-Nezurim," *Keshet* X[4] (Summer, 1968) p. 142.

31   Respective Hebrew titles: "Ha-Shavuy," *Arba'ah Sippurim,* pp. 113–38 and "'Al Huddo Shel Kaddur."

32   The name *Mishmar ha-'Emek* = Guard of the Valley [Esdrelon] carries the grim connotation of a military outpost.

33   After the establishment of the State of Israel the name was incorporated into the name of the Army of the Defense of Israel. In Hebrew: *Zeva Haganah le-Yisrael.* In abbreviated acronym: *Zahal.*

34   Respective titles in Hebrew: *Hu Halak bɔ-Sadot* (Merhavyah, 1947) and *Ha-Gevul* (Merhavyah, 1966).

35   In Hebrew: *Ha-Galgal ha-Hamishi* (Merhavyah, 1961).

36   Moshe Shamir, *My Life With Ishmael,* tr. Rose Kirson (London, 1970), p. 4.

37   Ibid., p. 1.

38   Ibid., p. 196.

39   In Hebrew: "Sofo ha-Mar Shel D," *Massa* (December 14 and 21, 1956).

40   *Massa* is the literary supplement of the daily *La-Merhav,* an organ of the leftist Mapam. Founded in 1954, it first appeared as a bi-weekly, then by the end of 1954 as a daily. The supplement *Massa* was originally, between 1951 and 1954, an independent literary organ which published work of younger writers generally sympathetic to left-wing labor policies. Megged was its first editor till 1968 when he was appointed cultural attaché to the Israeli embassy in London. In 1971 he returned to Israel where he became the weekly contributor of a column in the daily *Davar.* See G. Kressel, *Toledot ha-'Ittonut ha-'Ibrit be-Erez Yisrael* (Jerusalem, 1964), pp. 182–83 and the preface to the anthology of Megged's writings in the three decades of his literary career: Aaron Megged, *Hazzot ha-Yom-Mivhar* (Tel Aviv, 1973).

41   In Hebrew: *Ruah Yamim* (Tel Aviv, 1950).

42   In Hebrew: *Hedvah wa-Ani* (Tel Aviv, 1965).

43   The play in two acts *Hannah Szenes* was published in Tel Aviv in 1958.

44   Aaron Megged, *Hedvah wa-Ani,* p. 51.

45   The translation by Minna Givton appeared in *Israel Argosy* 6 (Jerusalem, 1958), pp. 7–25. It was reprinted in *Israeli Stories: A Selection of the Best* [!] *Contemporary Hebrew Writing,* ed. Joel Blocker; intr. Robert Alter (New York, 1962; 1966), pp. 87–106.

46   See Judg. 3:15-39.

47   In Hebrew: *Ha-Hai 'Al ha-Met* (Tel Aviv, 1965). The English translation by Misha Louvish was first published in 1970. The first American edition appeared in New York in 1971 and has been accepted in the Israel Series of the Translations Collections of the United Nations Educational, Scientific and Cultural Organization (UNESCO).

48   The other two sequels to *Ha-Hai 'Al ha-Met: Ha-Hayyim ha-Kezarim*

(Merhavyah, 1972) and *Mahaberot Evyatar* (Merhavyah, 1973). It is mainly the wife who discloses the unsavory side of the hero in Megged's *Living on the Dead*.

49   Aaron Megged, *Ha-Hai 'Al ha-Met*, p. 6. For a different translation, see *Living on the Dead*, p. 4.

50   *Ha-Hai 'Al ha-met*, p. 55.

51   Ibid., p. 229. For a different translation, see *Living on the Dead*, p. 249.

52   In Hebrew: *Ha-Hayyim ha-Kezarim.*

53   In Hebrew: *Mahaberot Evyatar.*

54   Aaron Megged, *Mahaberot Evyatar*² (1974), pp. 126–27.

55   "Shabbat" in *Hazot ha-Yom*, pp. 7–13.

56   "Ish Yehudi," ibid., pp. 350–58. In Hebrew translation by Minna Givton in *Israel Argosy* 6, pp. 171–88.

57   The critic Hillel Barzel argues unconvincingly that "in spite of the decisive difference between the style of the son and the style of the father, the inclination to essentialize complicated phenomena through keen, concentrated observation unites them both. What Steinman does in his thinking . . . Shaham does in the fictive arena. . . ." *Shiv'ah Mesapperim*, ed. Hillel Barzel (Tel Aviv, 1973), p. 227.

58   The title of the book in Hebrew: *Guf Rishon Rabbim* (Tel Aviv, 1968). In a queer English rendition: *The Number is One.*

59   Ibid., p. 10.

60   The story has been translated into English by Minna Givton in *Israel Argosy* 6, pp. 171–88.

61   In Hebrew: *Halok wa-Shov* (Tel Aviv, 1972).

62   Ibid., p. 5.

63   Ibid., p. 229.

64   In Hebrew: "Kol Shabbat Ahare Aruhat Boker." The story was published in *Keshet,* then in the collection of stories entitled *Ha-Geva'ot ha-Ma'ariviyyot* (Ramat Gan, 1970), pp. 25–36.

65   In Hebrew: "Givat ha-'Izzim," *Keshet* 34 (1967).

66   David Maletz, *Ma'agalot* (Tel Aviv, 1945).

67   In Hebrew: *Ha-Sha'ar Na'ul* (Tel Aviv, 1959).

68   In Hebrew: *Piz'e Bagrut* (Tel Aviv, 1965), p. 213. The novel in English *Wounds of Maturity* (New York, 1968), then retitled: *The Brigade*. The novel received the Shlonsky Prize. It won critical acclaim. See the review by Moshe Gil in *Moznayim* (1965), pp. 488–92.

69   *Piz'e Bagrut* p. 213.

70   See especially David Shahar's novel *Yerah ha-Devash we-ha-Zahav* (Tel Aviv, 1958/59), p. 40.

71   See the six stories in *Maggid ha-'Atidot* (Tel Aviv, 1966).

72   The story, translated by Dalya Bilu, and published in *Commentary* 60³ (September, 1975), pp. 47–54, is a section of Shahar's novel in translation: *The Palace of Shattered Vessels*. The published Hebrew version: *Hekal ha-Kelim ha-Shevurim* (Tel Aviv, 1969).

73   *Aforim ka-Sak* (Merhavyah, 1949).

74   *Be-'Arvot ha-Negev* (Tel Aviv, 1949).

75   The Hebrew anagram *Hasambah* stands for *Havurat Sod Muhlat be-Hehlet*.

76   In Hebrew: *Derek Gever* (Tel Aviv, 1953).

77   Yigal Mossinsohn, *Eldorado* (Tel Aviv, 1963), p. 18.

78   Benjamin Tammuz is the author of three collections of stories: *Holot ha-Zahav* (1949/50), *Gan Na'ul* (1957/58), and *Sippur Anton ha-Armeni* (Tel Aviv, 1964); two novels, *Ya'akov* (1971/72) and *Ha-Pardes* (1971/72); a trilogy—*Hayye Elyakum* (1964/65), *Be-Sof Ma'arav* (1966/67), *Elyakum: Sefer ha-Hazayot* (1968/69). An anthology, containing all the stories of *Holot ha-Zahav*, most of the stories of *Gan Na'ul* and *Sippur Anton ha-Armeni* as well as an uncollected story "Pegishah be-Al Abridge," appeared under the title "Angioxil-Terufah Nedirah" (Tel Aviv, 1973).

79   Benjamin Tammuz, *Jacob*, p. 9. Respect him and suspect him: that's the well known popular adage.

80   Ibid., p. 28.

81   Benjamin Tammuz, *Castle in Spain* (London, 1973), tr. Joseph Schachter.

82   In Hebrew: *Ha-Pardes* (Tel Aviv, 1971/72).

83   Ibid., p. 119.

84   *Hagigah* 14b.

85   In Hebrew: *Ha-Sippur 'Al Dodah Shelomzion ha-Gedolah* (Tel Aviv, 1975).

86   Shneour captured the charm of Tel Aviv, a young city, in his poem "Be-Tel-Aviv," *Shirim* I (Dvir, Tel Aviv, 1958), pp. 277–80. And so did Kaniuk in his story "The Parched Earth," well translated by Zeva Shapiro in *Israeli Stories*, pp. 107–33.

87   In Hebrew: *Himmo, Melek Yerushalayim* (Tel Aviv, 1966). It was even translated into French: *Himmo roi de Jerusalem* tr. Erwin Spatz (Paris, 1971). The translator supplied a hasty note on Israeli literature in a postscript. See *"Aperçu sur la littérature israélienne,"* ibid., pp. 171–77.

88   In Hebrew the collection of stories bears the title of the first story: *Ha-*

Yored le-Ma'alah (Jerusalem and Tel Aviv, 1963). As for *The Acrophile,* it was translated into English by Zeva Shapiro and published in New York in 1961.

89   *Ha-Yored le-Ma'alah,* p. 8.

90   Ibid., p. 26.

91   Ibid., p. 43.

92   Yoram Kaniuk, *Adam Resurrected,* tr. Seymour Simckes (New York, 1971).

93   *Adam Resurrected,* pp. 368–69.

94   In a postscript to the book *Kinnrot* (Merhavyah, 1970), the poet indicated that he collected fifty-four poems on "nature and man in the landscape of the Valley of Kinneret." Half of them were written between 1967–1970. See *Kinnrot,* p. 75.

95   Eliyyahu Meitus, *Shiratenu ha-Hadashah* (Tel Aviv, 1938), p. 427.

96   In Hebrew: "Shabbat ba-Kevuzah" in *Ba-Kevuzah* (Tel Aviv, 1938), p. 16; also *Ospe Kayiz* (Tel Aviv, 1966), p. 31; *Kinnrot,* p. 44.

97   *Mi-Midbar Mattanah* (Tel Aviv, 1962); also *Ospe Kayiz,* pp. 153–207.

98   *Ospe Kayiz,* p. 162.

99   *Kinnrot,* p. 13.

100   "*Sadot she-ba-'Emek*" tr. S.J. Kahn in *Israel Argosy* 6, p. 66.

101   Zerubavel Gilead, *'Al ha-'Ayin* (Tel Aviv, 1939), p. 18.

102   Ibid., p. 42.

103   Isaac Ogen, *Be-Hizdakkut* (Tel Aviv, 1935), p. 115.

104   For a sequence of fifteen sonnets—a rarity in Hebrew literature—see Ogen's "Mizmor la-Shavuy" in *Be-Hazrot Yareah* (Jerusalem, 1956), pp. 148–62.

105   In Hebrew: *Shirim El Kezeh Tohelet* (Tel Aviv, 1967).

106   B. Mordecai, *Ze'adim ba-Laylah* (Tel Aviv, 1939), p. 11.

107   Ibid., p. 17.

108   Ibid., p. 10.

109   *Shirat ha-'Eden ha-Avud* (Jerusalem, 1947).

110   In Hebrew: *Ha-Nefilim Hayu ba-Arez* (Tel Aviv, 1964). The phrase is from Genesis 6:4.

111   Ibid., p. 104.

112   The titles: *Ze'adim ba-Laylah; Min ha-Mezar* (Tel Aviv, 1939/40); *Shirat ha-'Eden ha-Avud; Yom ha-Tamid* (Tel Aviv, 1955/56), *Or le-'Et 'Erev* (Tel Aviv, 1960/61), *Ha-Nefilim Hayu ba-Arez.*

113   Benjamin Tene, *Shirim u-Poemot,* pp. 21–22.

114   See the poem "'Amal," ibid., p. 52.

115   See the section "Tarpe Ilanot," ibid., pp. 343–400.

116   In Hebrew: *Massa ba-Galil*, ibid., pp. 43–87.

117   In Hebrew: "Halomi"—a title that resembles the title of Tscherni-chowsky's first published poem: "Ba-Halom." The poem appeared in *Ha-Yom* (January, 1926).

118   Fania Bergstein, *Bazir* (Tel Aviv, 1939) p. 22; *Asif* (Tel Aviv, 1954), p. 31.

119   In Hebrew: *Garin Tamanti (Ha-Kibbuz ha-Meuhad* 1966/67) and *Haruzim Adummim—Sippurim li-Yeladim* (Tel Aviv, 1966).

22   Notes to Jew and Arab

1   In Hebrew: *Erez Ha-Zevi* (Tel Aviv, 1972).

2   Ibid., pp. 35–57, 153–59.

3   Quoted by Y. Harkabi, *Arab Attitudes to Israel*,tr. Misha Louvish (Jerusalem, 1972), p. 2. Harkabi's book is a mine of information for the heights and depths of Arab hatred of Jews in recent times.

4   See Burla's article "Ha-Sifrut ha-'Aravit ha-Hadashah" in *Hatekufah* XVIII (1922/23) pp. 459–73, XIX (1923), pp. 454–63, XXV (1929), pp. 603–10.

5   Shmuel Moreh, "The Arab Literary Revival In Israel," *Ariel* (Spring, 1962), p. 14.

6   Ibid., pp. 15–16.

7   In Hebrew: *Sippurim Palestiniyyim*,ed. and tr. from Arabic into Hebrew by Simon Balas (Tel Aviv, 1970) and *Sippurim 'Arviyyim* selected and tr. Tuvia Shamosh (1973). The quarterly *Keshet* also devoted one of its issues, Number 47 (1973) under the guest editorship of Dr. Sasson Somekh, to Arabic literature.

8   Muhammad Jamil Baihum, "Arabism and Jewry in Syria" in *Arab Nationalism*—an anthology selected and edited, with an introduction by Sylvia G. Haim (Berkeley and Los Angeles, 1964), p. 136.

9   Ibid., p. 146.

10   Ibid., p. 136.

11   Ibid.

12   The quotation is from *The Philosophy of Revolution*, ibid., p. 231. The allusion is to Luigi Pirandello—not Pirandelli—and his play *Six Characters in Search of an Author*. Nasser translated *Sei Personaggi in cerca d'Autore* as *Six Personalities in Search of Actors*. He apparently misunderstood *autore*, "author," and thought it meant "actors."

13   J. Epstein, "Sheelah Na'alamah" in *Ha-Shiloah* XVII (1907), p. 195. The article impressed the contemporary press. See "Po'alim 'Ivriyyim O Po'alim

'Arviyyim", Ha-Shiloah XIX (1908) and an editorial article by Ben-Israel, "Ha-Torah we-ha-Hayyim," in *Ha-Poel Ha-Za'ir* (1908).

14   Ezek. 47:22.

15   Cited by Yaakov Roi, "Yahase Rehovot 'Im Shiknehah ha-'Aravim" in *Ha-Ziyyonut—Meassef le-Toledot ha-Tenu'ah ha-Ziyyonit we-ha-Yishuv ha-Yehudi be-Erez Yisrael* (Tel Aviv, 1970), p. 153.

16   See Ahad Haam's first of two articles "Emet me-Erez Yisrael" in *Kol Kitbe Ahad Haam* (Jerusalem, 1947), p. 24.

17   J.H. Brenner, "Be-Mish'ole ha-Pardesim" in *Sippurim 'Ivriyyim*, p. 48.

18   "Yahase Rehobot 'Im Shiknehah ha-'Aravim," p. 154. In an interesting piece of information we learn that even in the diaspora Arabic was not neglected. Dov Sadan quotes the objectives of an organization called *Haluze Ziyyon* in his native town Brody in Galicia. The protocol for the spring of 1905 states that the members must actively pursue the following studies: " a. Hebrew, b. Arabic, c. Palestinography, d. agronomy, e. socialism, f. political economy, g. hygiene." That Arabic took second place—immediately after Hebrew—among the seven objectives of a Zionist organization in a small town is of more than passing interest. See Dov Sadan, *Alufai u-Meyuda'ai* (Tel Aviv, 1972), p. 43.

19   S. Shalom, *Yoman ba-Galil* (Nuremberg, 1932), p. 9. The diary was also published in S. Shalom, *Sippurim: Yoman ba-Galil; Ha-Ner Lo Kavah* (Tel Aviv, 1967).

20   In Hebrew: "Moker ha-Teenim" in *Sippurim 'Ivriyyim me-Hayye ha-'Aravim*, pp. 23–25.

21   See Isaac Ben-Zvi, *Zikronot u-Reshumot me-ha-Ne'urim 'Ad 1920,* (Jerusalem, 1965/66), pp. 466–69.

22   *Kitbe Yizhak Elazari-Wolkani* [A. Ziyyoni] V (Tel Aviv, 1954), p. 184. The article "Kovshe ha-'Avodah" was published in 1936.

23   For the history of Palestine the defeat of Christian Byzantium at the hands of Mohammedan Arabs in 634–638 is of paramount importance. In 1517 the Turks conquered Palestine, in 1917 the English. The crusades were medieval episodes which had no lasting influence on the country.

24   On the repudiation of the West by Arab intellectuals, see Hisham Sharabi, op. cit. pp. 133–36. The leadership of the so-called Palestine Liberation Movement under Yasir Arafat or Abu Ammar as he is known to his people—*Harakat Tahrir Falastin, FTH* or *Fatah* or *al Fatah* through reversal of the Arabic initials—veers eastward and westward. *Fatah*, "conquest" in English, has an avowed aim—the destruction of Israel—and a propagandistic aim—the establishment of a democratic state on Western models in Palestine for harmonious coexistence of Moslems, Christians, and Jews. Initially an underground guerrilla or *fedayin* force, it now operates openly from bases in Lebanon and Syria. It numbers some 10,000 members who affect a deep nationalism. Its leader Arafat appears invariably in black and white checked headdress—*kuffiyeh*—and proclaims not *jihad* or Holy War against Israel but unho-

ly destruction of Jews in and out of Palestine as the massacres at Maalot and Kiryat Shemonah, Israeli athletes at Munich and innocent guests in Tel Aviv's Savoy Hotel , have amply demonstrated.

25   The poem is easily available in Asher Barash's anthology: *Mibhar ha-Shirah ha-'Ivrit ha-Hadashah*, p. 337, also in *Sippurim 'Ivriyyim me-Hayye ha-'Aravim*, ed. Joseph Arika (Tel Aviv, 1963), p. 7.

26   See *Sippure Yehudah Yaari* (Jerusalem, 1969), pp. 90–104. For an English translation, see Yehuda Yaari, *The Covenant—Ten Stories* (Jerusalem, 1965), pp. 87–97.

27   In Hebrew: "Ben ha-Kelev we-ha-Ro'eh" in *Sippure Yehudah Yaari* II, pp. 173–200; in translation: *The Covenant—Ten Stories*, pp. 132–56.

28   In Hebrew:."We-Zarah ha-Shemesh u-Ba ha-Shemesh"in *Sippure Yehudah Yaari* II, pp. 141–50. The Hebrew title—*We-Zarah ha-Shemesh*, taken from Ecclesiastes 1:5, also served Hemingway who called his first novel *The Sun Also Rises* (New York, 1926).

29   In Hebrew: *Sippurim 'Ivriyyim me-Hayye ha-'Aravim*. See also note 25. The number of selected writers is forty-two, not forty-six as given erroneously in the "Introduction," ibid., p. 9.

30   Ibid., p. 10.

31   See "Ben Shivte 'Arab" in *Kitbe Yehudah Burla* V (Tel Aviv), pp. 197–231.

32   The name of Agnon's novel in Hebrew: *Temol Shilshom;* the name of Zemah's novel in Hebrew: *Shanah Rishonah.*

33   *Tahat ha-Shemesh*, (Merhavyah, 1950), p. 187.

34   In Hebrew: *Be-Kolar Ehad.*

35   See the story "Ha-Matmon" in *Sippurim 'Ivriyyim me-Hayye ha-'Aravim*, p. 306.

36   In Hebrew: *'Al Mazavo Shel ha-Adam* (Tel Aviv, 1967).

37   Phinehas Sadah, *Sefer ha-Shirim*, p. 170.

38   In Hebrew: *Ha-Kerav* (Tel Aviv, 1965/66).

39   See Miriam Schwartz, *Korot Havah Gottlieb* (Tel Aviv, 1967/68).

40   In Hebrew: *Lo La-Gibborim ha-Milhamah* (Tel Aviv, 1971). The title is based on Ecclesiastes 9:11.

41   Meir Wieselthier, "Sealed in a Bottle," *Gilyonot Shirah* 2 (April–May, 1974), ed. Meir Wieselthier (Tel Aviv, 1974), p. 19.

42   See "The White City" in the translation of Aubrey Hodes in *First Fruits*, pp. 136–37.

43   In Hebrew: "Ma'aseh be-'Ez Zayit" in Benjamin Tammuz, *Angioxil, Terufah Nedirah*, pp. 184–88.

44   In Hebrew: "Taharut Sehiyyah," ibid., pp. 189–201.

45   "Pegishah be-Al Abridge" in *Angioxil—Terufah Nedirah*, p. 208.

46   In Hebrew: *Arzot ha-Tan* (Tel Aviv, 1965).

47   Ibid., p. 22.

48   In Hebrew: *Mikael Sheli* (Tel Aviv, 1968). English translation by Nicholas de Lange in collaboration with the author under the title of *My Michael (New York, 1972)*.

49   This is the literal translation of *Makom Aher* (Merhavyah, 1966). The translation of the book by Nicholas de Lange in collaboration with the author bears the title *Elsewhere, Perhaps* (New York, 1973). There is no indication either in a note or in a formal statement that passages, pages and entire chapters of the original have been omitted in translation.

50   *Makom Aher,* p. 55.

51   Ibid., p. 10.

52   Ibid., p. 57.

53   Ibid., p. 59.

54   Ibid., pp. 82–84.

55   Ibid., p. 196.

56   Ibid., p. 213.

57   Ibid., p. 298.

58   Ibid.

59   Ibid., p. 396.

60   In Hebrew: *La-Ga'at ba-Mayim, la-Ga'at ba-Ruah* (Tel Aviv, 1973). The English translation by Nicholas de Lange in collaboration with the author appeared in New York in 1974.

61   Ibid., p. 42.

62   Yehoshua's plays: *Laylah be-May* and *Tippulim Aharonim-Mahazot* (Jerusalem and Tel Aviv, 1974/75).

63   In Hebrew: "Be-Tehillat Kayiz '70" (Jerusalem, Tel Aviv, 1971/72).

64   *Mul ha-Ye 'arot* (Tel Aviv, 1967/68), p. 46. It was first published in *Keshet* 19 (1963). For a different translation by Miriam Arad, see A.B. Yehoshua, "Facing the Forests" in the collection of five stories *Three Days and a Child* (New York, 1970), p. 165.

65   In Hebrew: *Parashat Gabriel Tirosh* (Tel Aviv, 1964). The teacher-student relationship—without political overtones—is also the subject of another novel by Shalev: *Dam wa-Ruah* (Jerusalem—Tel Aviv, 1969/70).

66   Original in *Ma'ariv* (March 11, 1966).

67   Amos Oz, "Crusade," *Commentary* (August, 1971), p. 59.

68   In Hebrew: *Bayit bi-Rehov ha-Mashiah* (Tel Aviv, 1967).

69   Subtitle: *A Compassionate Dialogue Between an Israeli and an Arab* (New York, 1974). Amos Elon is also the author of a controversial book *The Israelis: Founders and Sons* (New York, 1971) and, most recently, *Herzl* (New York, 1975).

70   Ibid., pp. 105–106.

23   Notes to Children's Paradise

1   Every writer on children's literature must be grateful to Menahem Regev who has assembled a useful bibliography of some four hundred annotated items on children's literature in his *Sifrut Yeladim—Mahutah u-Behinotehah* (Jerusalem, 1967). The chronological span of these items ranges from 1902 to 1967. Very useful also is the encyclopedia for children—*'Olam Za'ir—Encyclopedia le-Sifrut Yeladim* (Ramat Gan, 1970), by Uriel Ofek. A cursory article in English can be read with profit—Moshe Hanaami: "Children's Poetry in Hebrew," *Israel Argosy* 8, ed. Isaac Halevy-Levin (Jerusalem, 1962), pp. 66–80 and the translations by various hands; ibid., pp. 81–107.

2   Prov. 13:24.

3   Ibid., 22:6

4   The talmudic observation on favoritism begins with a didactic statement: "A man should never single out one son among his other sons." *Shabbat* 10b.

5   An interesting reason for not promising what cannot be given is adduced by the Talmud: "One should not promise a child to give him something and then not give it to him, because he will thereby teach him lying." *Sukkah* 46b.

6   In the original:
Oifn pripitshok brent a fayerl
Un in shtib is heis.
Un der rebbi lernt di kleyne kinderlech
Dem alef-beys.
The poem was entitled "Alef Beys." Warshawski not only wrote the words; he also composed the melody. Saul Tschernichowsky also wrote an alphabetical poem "Alfa—Beta de—Shaul," *Shirim* (Schocken Edition, Jerusalem and Tel Aviv, 1953), pp. 662–64.

7   On *Comedy of Marriage* see *From Renaissance to Renaissance* I, pp. 10—11.

8   In Hebrew: *Petah Sefat 'Eber li-Yeladim* (Vienna, 1745).

9   Hebrew title: *Bet ha-Sefer* (Vienna, 1802). The name of the first part: *Mesillat ha-Limmud*; the name of the second part: *Limmude ha-Mesharim*.

10 In Hebrew: "Nahnu Yeladim."

11 The name of the play: *He-Haruz we-he-'Azel O Yad Haruzim Ta'ashir* (Breslau, 1817). The alternate title is based on *Proverbs* 10:4. On Samość see *From Renaissance to Renaissance* I, pp. 96–97.

12 Hebrew title: *Nahar me-'Eden* (Breslau, 1836).

13 Hebrew title: *Ma'aseh Robinson* (Breslau, 1824). German title: *Robinson der Jüngere.*

14 Hebrew title: *Meziat Amerikah* (Breslau, 1824). German title: *Columbus oder die Entdeckung von Westindien.*

15 Hebrew title: *Ro'ot Midyan O Yaldut Moshe* (Breslau, 1843).

16 See *From Renaissance to Renaissance* I, pp. 138–40.

17 In Hebrew: *Bet Hanan* (Jerusalem, 1920). It was republished in Warsaw twice under different titles in 1923 and in 1929 respectively: *Ha-Tov we-ha-Ra'* and *Newe Yesharim.* The latter edition was adapted by Jacob Fichmann.

18 See my article "Writer and Educator: Abraham Mapu" in *Philip W. Lown: A Jubilee Volume* (New York, 1967), p. 81.

19 The name stuck; between 1936 and 1939 E. Indelman and S. Rosenhack published in Warsaw a biweekly by the name *'Olami ha-Katan, 'Olami ha-Ketantan* and *'Olami.* In the nineteenth century, in 1892, Yehoshua Hana Rawnitzki founded a publishing house which specialized in children's books and bore the name *'Olam Katon.*

20 On Kipnis, see Yemimah Avidar Tchernowitz, "Ha-Gannan," *Ma'ariv Literary Supplement* (8/29–30), p. 39.

21 In Hebrew literature Abraham Ben-Avigdor must be ranked as the most important entrepreneur in children's literature. His publishing house Tu-shiyyah, founded in 1895, published in the brief period of three years 300 books and booklets for children. The list included Grimm's *Fairy Tales* and a collection of children's songs by Aaron Luboshitzki (1874–1942), a favorite of young and old, especially with his lullaby "Shekav, Heradem, Ben Li Yakir" which vied in popularity with the Yiddish ditty "Oifn Pripitshok."

22 In Yiddish: "Unter di Grininke Baymalah." It was published in a miscellany *Der Yud* in 1901 under the editorship of Bialik's friend and collaborator Yehoshua Hana Rawnitzki.

23 In Hebrew: *Shirim u-Pizmonim li-Yeladim* (Tel Aviv, 1933) and *Wa-Yehi ha-Yom* (Tel Aviv, 1928).

24 In Hebrew: *Alluf Bazlut we-Alluf Shum.* Like *Wa-Yehi ha-Yom* it was rendered into English by H. Danby. See *From Renaissance to Renaissance* I, p. 383, n. 26.

25 Ibid., p. 184.

26 It appeared under the title *He-Halil* (Tel Aviv-Berlin, 1923).

27 Hebrew title: *Shirim le-Yalde Yisrael* (Cracow, 1907).

28 Hebrew title: "Ma'aseh bi-Zeev Ben Zeev." See *He-Halil,* pp. 41–57.

29 On Tschernichowsky's contribution to the literature on children, see my *Saul Tschernichowsky—Poet of Revolt,* pp. 70–72.

30 See his poem "Ha-'Olam bi-Zekuto Shel Mi Kayyam" which was written three and a half years before his death, on March 14, 1940, in *Shirim,* Schocken Edition, p. 661.

31 Hebrew title: *Shire Yeladim* I and II (Warsaw, 1906).

32 See his: "Mi-Shire 'Elem Bahir" in my translation, *From Renaissance to Renaissance* I, p. 210.

33 Hebrew title: *Ahashverosh Melek Tippesh* (Warsaw, 1920) and *Lezane Purim* (Warsaw, 1920) respectively.

34 In Hebrew: *Mi-Mekor Yisrael* (Tel Aviv, 1938-1940).

35 See the *Mibhar me-Ozar ha-Aggadah li-Bene ha-Ne'urim* (Tel Aviv, 1938).

36 Hans Christian Andersen, *Kol Aggadot Andersen,* tr. Aaron Amir (Ramat Gan, 1967).

37 The respective Hebrew titles of these books: *Yonim Levanot* (1942/43) and *Pirhe Bar* (Tel Aviv, 1950/51); enlarged edition (Tel Aviv, 1965).

38 Yehuda Amichai, *Mah she-Karah le-Runny be-New York* (Tel Aviv, 1968). Unpaginated.

39 O. Hillel, *Dodi Simhah* (Tel Aviv, 1964).

40 Moses Feinstein, *'Al Saf ha-Sof* (Jerusalem and Tel Aviv, 1964), pp. 187–205.

41 On the Hebrew anagram *Hasambah,* see chapter 21, note 75.

42 In Hebrew: *Kevar Mutar le-Gallot* (Merhavyah, 1959).

43 In Hebrew: *Zebigelal* (Merhavyah, 1964).

44 In Hebrew: *Shemonah Be-'ikvot Ehad* (Jerusalem, 1971).

24   Notes to Neglected Areas in Hebrew Literature: Drama; Humor; Criticism

1   The papyrus represents "the earliest literary specimen of drama yet known." So Theodor Herzl Gaster, *Thespis—Ritual, Myth, and Drama in the Ancient Near East* (New York, 1950), p. 52.

2   The celebration of the victory over the Egyptians by Miriam and her feminine entourage is a case in point. Choral strophe and antistrophe—as in Greek drama—seem to have dominated the eventful performance. See Exod. 15:20–21.

3   See Ps. 87; possibly Ps. 65.

4   See Ernest Renan, *Le Cantique des Cantiques* in *Oeuvres Complètes* VII (Paris, 1947), ed. Henriette Psichari, pp. 509–25.

5   Ibid., p. 473: *"Le Cantique des Cantiques doit donc être envisagé comme tenant le milieu entre le drame regulier et l'églogue ou la pastorale dialoguée."*

6   Max Brod, *Eine Königin Esther. Drama in einem Vorspiel und 3 Akten* (Leipzig, 1918).

7   J.P. Migne, *Patrologiae Graecae Tomus* LXVI (Paris, 1864), p. 698.

8   See his "Preface" to *Job Expounded*. Theodore Beza, or to give him his French name Théodore de Bèze, authored a tragedy *Abraham Sacrifiant* which was first printed in Geneva in 1550. It was translated into English in 1575 and published in 1577 by Arthur Golding under the title *A Tragedie of Abraham's Sacrifice.*

9   Horace M. Kallen, *The Book of Job as Greek Tragedy* (New York, 1918). In the "Introduction" to Kallen's book, Moore maintains that "it would be a mistake to regard *The Book of Job as a Greek Tragedy* as an ingenious paradox; it is a serious hypothesis . . . "

10   See Kallen's "Preface" in the 1959 edition, p. ix.

11   Karl Fries, *Das philosophische Gespräch von Hiob bis Platon* (Tübingen, 1904), p. 60.

12   Ibid., p. 58: *Das Buch Hiob ist ein philosophischer Dialog* . . .

13   Julian Morgenstern, "The Suffering Servant—A New Solution," *Vetus Testamentum* XI[3] (July, 1961), p. 293.

14   Ibid., XI (October, 1961), p. 407.

15   Ibid., p. 430.

16   Isa. 40–46.

17   Joseph Wieneke, *Ezekielis Judaei poetae Alexandrini fabulae quae inscribitur Exagoge* (Monasterii Westfalorum, 1931), pp. 124–26. For a Hebrew translation, see S. Span, *Shirim we-Sippurim*, pp. 109–24.

18   The phrase is Joseph Wieneke's: *minus elegantes*, ibid., p. 126.

19   *Exagoge*, verses 254–269.

20   *Exod.* 15:27.

21   Emil Schürer, *A History of the Jewish People in the Time of Jesus Christ* III, tr. Sophia Taylor and Rev. Peter Christie (Edinburgh, 1897–98), p. 227.

22   Wieneke, op. cit., p. 119.

23   *'Abodah Zarah* 18b; see also ibid., 42a; see, however, *Ketubot* 5a.

24   *Megillah* 6a.

25   The two other theaters of importance—Ohel and Kameri—were founded in 1926 and 1944 respectively. See Mendel Kohansky, *The Hebrew Theatre*, pp. 100–102, 149–50.

26   *From Renaissance to Renaissance* I, pp. 10–11, 63–66.

27   This assertion can be easily proven by a mere glance at the bibliography of the Hebrew drama. See Abraham Yaari, *Ha-Mahaze ha-'Ivri ha-Mekori we-ha-Meturgam me-Reshito we-'Ad ha-Yom* (Jerusalem, 1956).

28   If there were any doubts on the subject, they were dispelled by the monograph of Gershon Shaked, *Ha-Mahaze ha-'Ivri ha-Histori bi-Tekufat ha-Tehiyyah* (Jerusalem, 1970).

29   A. Ashman, *Mikal Bat Shaul* (Tel Aviv, 1940)

30   In Hebrew *Ha-Homah*. The play, translated by Misha Louvish, is more sophisticated than Zevi Lieberman's novel *Nehemiah*. See *supra*, "The Historical Novel," pp. 240–41.

31   See the play *Sippur Uriah* in *Shotim u-Melakim* (Jerusalem, 1971), pp. 7–57.

32   See the play *Ma'aseh bi-Shete Mizvot*, ibid., pp. 149–83.

33   For the plays of Israel Eliraz: *Sheloshah Mahazot* (Tel Aviv, 1966).

34   In Hebrew: *Yehudah Ish Keriyot* (Jerusalem, 1929/30).

35   *Modern Hebrew Stories*, ed. Ezra Spicehandler (New York, 1971), p. 163.

36 For an English translation of *The Bride and the Butterfly Hunter* by Valerie Arnon, see *Ariel* 36 (Jerusalem, 1974), pp. 4–29.

37 In Hebrew: *Hu Halak be-Sadot* (Merhavyah, 1947) and *Be-'Arvot ha-Negev* (Tel Aviv, 1949) respectively.

38 Dov Sadan, *Polemos we-Shaveh Polemos*, pp. 280-82. It was the excessive love for Jewish holidays—especially Sabbath, Passover, Shabu'ot and Sukkot—which led Sadan to assume their importance for the development of drama. See also his *Galgal Mo'adim* (Tel Aviv, 1964).

39 See "I Gaspiri" ("The Upholsterers") in *The Portable Ring Lardner*, ed. and intr. Gilbert Seldes (New York, 1946). This playlet by the American humorist Ring Lardner had a profound influence on another American master of nonsense and non sequitur, Donald Ogden Stewart.

40 Prov. 27:2.

41 The respective Hebrew names of the treatises: *Masseket Bava Tekhnikah* and *Shas Erez Yisreeli Katan.*

42 *From Renaissance to Renaissance* I, pp. 265–69. Authors of parody who preceded and succeeded Rosenzweig and deserve special mention are Isaac Meir Dick with his *Masseket 'Aniyyut* which castigates social and economic miseries of Lithuanian Jewry a hundred years ago; Abraham Abba Rokovsky, the translator of Disraeli into Hebrew, who poked venomous fun at the world of unethical business in *Masseket Shetarot;* Abraham Shelomoh Melamed who also railed at merchants in *Masseket Soharim* and in the early years of the Red Revolution in Russia, castigated the Bolsheviks in *Masseket Admonim Min Talmud Bolshevi* and published it in Tel Aviv in 1923; Gershon Kiss who wrote a treatise on evasions of prohibition—*Masseket Prohibition*—in the United States when prohibition was the law of the land.

43 In Hebrew: *Masseket Yamim Tovim* (Tel Aviv, 1959).

44 In Hebrew: *Haggadah Shel ha-Bayit ha-Leumi* (Tel Aviv, 1930).

45 Collections of his writings in English translation include *Wise Guy, Solomon*, tr. Yohanan Goldman (New York, 1973), *Look Back Mrs. Lot* (Tel Aviv, 1960), *Noah's Ark, Tourist Class*, tr. Yohanan Goldman (New York, 1962), *The Seasick Whale*, tr. Yohanan Goldman (London, 1965), *So Sorry We Won* (Tel Aviv, 1967). For a bibliography of Kishon's work in English translation: Yohai Goell, *Bibliography of Modern Hebrew Literature in English Translation* (Jerusalem, 1968), p. 70.

46 Ephraim Kishon, *Wise Guy, Solomon* p. 240.

47 Ephraim Kishon, *Ma'arkonim* (Tel Aviv, 1965).

48 Menachem Talmi, *Ke-she-Gever Hayah Gever* (Givatayim-Ramat Gan, 1970).

49 Ibid., p. 164.

50 The Hebrew title of the folklore annual: *Reshumot* (1918–1936). Co-editors: Hayyim Nahman Bialik and Yehoshua Hana Rawnitzki.

51   *Ketavim le-Toledot Hibbat Ziyyon we-Yishuv Erez Yisrael,* 3 vols. (1919–1932).

52   In Hebrew: *Sefer ha-Bedihah we-ha-Hidud,* 3 vols. (Jerusalem, 1939–1945). The anthology first appeared in Frankfurt in 1921/22. The final and third volume in a new and enlarged edition was published in the year of Druyanov's death. A fourth volume was planned—a book on non-Jewish wit under the title *Me-Ozar ha-Bedihah Shel ha-'Ammim.* But death prevented implementation of a labor of love which lasted twenty-six years. See "Introduction," p. 13.

53   In German: *Der Witz und seine Beziehung zum Unbewussten.* It first appeared in 1905.

54   In French: *Le Rire,* first published in 1900.

55   A. Druyanov, *Yalkut Massot,* ed. Y.D. Abramski and Reuben Rabinowitz (Tel Aviv, 1969), p. 114.

56   An interesting example: "Said Rabbi Ilai: By three things may the character of a person be determined: by his cup, by his purse and by his anger; and some say: also by his laughter." The quotation is from *'Erubin* 65. Druyanov also cites popular works such as *Mesillat Yesharim* by Moses Hayyim Luzzatto, Yiddish, Russian, classical, and German authors.

57   Immanuel Olsvanger, *L'Chayim! Jewish Wit and Humor* (New York, 1949). Most of the stories and witticisms were originally published in two Yiddish collections in transliteration: *Rozhinkes mit Mandlen* and *Royte Pomeranzen* (1947).

58   An excellent example: *Pirke Avot* 2:5 in the dissection of Sadan's *Yerid ha-Sha'ashu'im,* pp. 81–88.

59   Respective Hebrew titles: *Ka'arat Zimmukim* (Tel Aviv, 1950), *Ka'arat Egozim* (Tel Aviv, 1953) and *Yerid ha-Sha'ashu'im.* (Ramat Gan, 1964). For Sadan's collected essays on humor, see—*Yerid ha-Sha'ashu'im.* It is not without interest to note that there are a thousand and one items in *Ka'arat Zimmukim* and in *Ka'arat Egozim*—an implicit allusion to their captivating power, not unlike that of *Thousand and One Nights.*

60   Dov Sadan, *Avne Gevul* (Tel Aviv, 1964), p. 84.

61   The title of his autobiography: *Mi-Mehoz ha-Yaldut* (Tel Aviv, 1937/38). This volume was followed by several volumes which concentrated on later stages of the author's life.

62   In Hebrew: *Zelilim.*

63   Zevi Luz, *Meziut we-Adam ba-Sifrut ha-Yisreelit* (Tel Aviv, 1970).

64   Dov Sadan, *Elekah we-Ashuvah* (Tel Aviv, 1971), p. 127.

65   Sadan told a moving story about young immigrants from Soviet Russia who were urged by him to visit the synagogue of the Hasidim of Karlin on *Simhat Torah.* Which they did in khaki and in embarrassment. An old man who

noticed that they did not dare to move beyond the threshold urged them—in Yiddish—to enter: *Kinderlekh, kumt arein, mir seinen oikh Idn* (Come on, kids, we are also Jews.) Ibid., p. 131.

66   Abraham Kariv, *Neratek Et ha-Shalshelet* (Tel Aviv, 1965), p. 146. On Kariv's polemics, see now the third volume of his collected works: *Mi-Shilshom we-'Ad Henah* (Jerusalem, Tel Aviv, Haifa, 1973).

67   Ibid., 65.

68   Ibid., p. 66.

69   Ibid, p. 50.

70   The unassuming and almost forgotten David Aryeh Friedmann (1889-1957) claimed with diffident pride: "As for the true critic—his criticism is his poetry." See his *'Iyyune Shirah* (Tel Aviv, 1964), p. 316.

71   See the author's *Yehidim bi-Reshut ha-Rabbim* (Jerusalem, 1956) and, to a certain extent, the essays which were selected posthumously by the writer's widow Deborah Woislavsky: *Rishonot we-Aharonot* (Jerusalem, 1967).

72   In Hebrew: *'Al ha-Yafeh* (Tel Aviv, 1939).

73   Another book in Hebrew on *The Beautiful*—S.Y. Penueli's *Massah 'Al ha-Yafeh She-bo-Omannut ha-Sifrut* (Tel Aviv, 1964)—is essentially a series of disjointed notes on esthetics with specific references to Hebrew literature.

74   In Hebrew: *Be-Arzot Nod* (Jerusalem, 1924/25).

75   In Hebrew: *Dappe Pinkas* (Jerusalem, 1972).

76   On histories of Hebrew literature, see *From Renaissance to Renaissance* I, pp. VII–IX.

25   Notes to Hebrew Literature as Source of Untapped Values

1   See his excellent paper "The Scientific Study of Values and Contemporary Civilization," *Zygon* 1³ ((September, 1966), p. 233. It was originally read at a meeting of the *American Philosophical Society* on April 26, 1958. Subsequently it was published in the *Proceedings of the American Philosophical Society* CII⁵ (October, 1958) and reprinted in *Zygon*.

2   See his *Philosophical Issues in Adult Education* (Springfield, Illinois, 1963), p. 26.

3   The book was first published in 1905 under the name *Das Wesen des Judentums*. In essence it was a reply to the popular book of Adolph von Harnack: *The Essence of Christianity*.

4   Leo Baeck, *This People Israel: The Meaning of Jewish Existence*, tr. Albert H. Friedlander (New York, 1964), p. xvii. In German it was published in 1955 under the name *Dieses Volk: Jüdische Existenz*. It is the culmination of Baeck's work: reaffirmation of Jewish faith in terms of personal and ethnic experience. Written in the concentration camp of Theresienstadt in the so-called "Protectorate," it marks the fifty-year-long road "from essence to existence, from nineteenth-century optimism to twentieth-century existentialism."

5   Ibid., p. xviii.

6   Louis Jacobs, *Jewish Values* (London, 1960), p. 8.

7   See his "Yahadut wa-Arakehah-Motivim," *Gesher* (December, 1965) pp. 12–15.

8   See his "Hasidut Shel Mistikah wa-Hasidut Shel Emunah" in *Erke ha-Yahadut* (Tel Aviv, 1952), pp. 81–90.

9   See his "Emunot we-De'ot be-Teologiyyah Shel ha-Meah ha-Tesha' 'Esreh," ibid., pp. 91–106.

10   See his "Ha-Mahshabah ha-Leumit ha-Hadashah," ibid., pp. 107–16.

11   See his *Religious Philosophy* (Cambridge, Mass., 1961), p. 271.

12 Many forms of alienation are listed and discussed in an article by Winthrop: alienation from oneself, alienation from the opposite sex, alienation of man from man, alienation of man from society, alienation from work, alienation from nature, alienation from God. See Henry Winthrop, "Alienation and Existentialism in Relation to Literature and Youth," *The Journal of General Education* XVIII[4] (January, 1967), pp. 290–93. Alienated youth is not only the popular subject of radio and television programs; it dominates sometimes entire or almost entire issues of serious periodicals. See the special issue of *School and Society* (April 15, 1967). As a characteristic of Young America alienation has been exhaustively treated by the Yale psychiatrist Kenneth Keniston in his book, *The Uncommitted: Alienated Youth in American Society* (New York, 1965). Far-seeing scholars have begun to project a post-alienation era. See especially Ernest Becker, *Beyond Alienation* (New York, 1967). And Vienna, in its post-Freudian, post-Adlerian era, proclaims a new psychotherapy, logotherapy, for modern futilitarianism. See Viktor E. Frankl, *Man's Search for Meaning* (Boston, 1963), a translation of his book in German: *Ein Psychologe erlebt das Konzentrationslager.*

13 In Hebrew: *Golah we-Nekar* (Tel Aviv, 1929-1932).

14 The concept of alienation flourished in medieval times: man was regarded as a "wayfarer in a strange world." See the excellent study of Gerhart B. Ladner, "Homo Viator: Medieval Ideas on Alienation and Order," *Speculum* XLII[2] (April, 1967), p. 256. Two major texts in the Hebrew Bible furnished the basis for two forms of alienation in the medieval world: Exodus 20:3 and Psalms 39:13: "You shall have no other gods before me" and "For I am a stranger among you, a sojourner, as all my fathers were." Since the words "other gods" in Exodus read *deos alienos* and "a sojourner," *peregrinus* in the Vulgate, alienation was regarded (1) as "a failure to love God," with Satan himself as chief *alienus*, alien; (2) as a pilgrimage on this earth or, as the anonymous author of the *Epistle to Diognetus* expressed the lot of Christians in an early apologetic tract on Christianity: "They dwell on earth, but they are citizens in heaven." Ibid., pp. 235–236.

15 An interesting parallel has been drawn recently: "The relatively low esteem of technology may have been as much reason for the ruin of the [Roman] Empire as an over-emphasis on technology may be an important cause of our decline." See Sir Llewellyn Woodward, "Will Civilization Survive?" in *Journal of Historical Studies* I, no. 1 (Princeton, New Jersey, Autumn, 1967), p. 12.

16 There are even hippie-Hasidim who have a House of Love and Prayer within a half-hour's walk from Haight Ashbury. They combine dance, song, and prayer with hippie practices: occasional drugs, strumming the guitar and "doing their thing." See *The Jerusalem Post* (July 7, 1969), p. 13.

17 Herbert R. Lottman, "A Baedeker of Beatnik Territory," *The New York Times Magazine* (August 7, 1966), p. 53. On Elat as the center of Israeli beatniks, see *Jewish New Year 5727 Picture Supplement of Ha-Aretz*, p. 23.

18 A fourth edition under the original title *Vom Umsturz der Werte* appeared in Bern in 1955.

19   See *Judaism* II[2] (1962), pp. 106–107.

20   On proto-Israelism see E. Silberschlag, *Saul Tschernichowsky: Poet of Revolt*, pp. 36–41.

21   Moshe Shamir, "Renaissance" in the daily *'Al ha-Mishmar*, (April 26, 1957).

22   Pss. 118:26.

23   Name of the academic periodical: *Leshonenu.* Name of the popular series: *Leshonenu la-'Am.*

24   On the historical dictionary of the Hebrew language, planned by the Academy of the Hebrew Language and the Bialik Institute, see the pamphlet *Ha-Millon ha-Histori la-Lashon ha-'Ivrit Shel ha-Akademiyyah la-Lashon ha-'Ivrit* (Jerusalem, 1973).

25   See Dov Sadan, *Ka'arat Egozim*, p. 196.

26   Raphael Bashan, "Reayon ha-Shanah 'Im Abraham Shlonsky," *Ma'ariv* (August 26, 1966), p. 14. The first translation of Pushkin's *magnum opus* by Shlonsky appeared in Tel Aviv in 1937. The new translation is equipped with a formidable commentary of over 100 pages. See *Alexander S. Pushkin*, tr. A. Shlonsky (Jerusalem, 1966), pp. 485–611. Nabokov who, like Shlonsky, is inordinately proud of his translation of *Yevgeni Onegin* into English, has added two volumes of commentary to his translation which appeared in 1964.

27   *Moznayim* (July, 1966), p. 134.

28   In strange aberration *consensus* is invariably spelled *Concensus, Intelligenti* appears as *Intellegenti* and the English word *special* as *spatial.*

29   *Aroma* itself–in conjunction with filter—has become a Hebrew word in a Hebrew advertisement of an American cigarette: *Le-Filter u-le-Aroma En Kamohu.*

30   *Ani Itka* and *Ani Lo Yakol Bil'adehah* are clumsy imports of the English phrases, "I am with you" and "I can't [live] without her." See *Ma'ariv Weekly Supplement* (January 31, 1975), p. 25.

31   In Hebrew: *'Ivrit Shel Shabbat.*

32   In Hebrew: *Ashdodit.* See Neh. 13:24.

BIBLIOGRAPHICAL COMMENT

Though a sequel of *From Renaissance to Renaissance I,* the present volume is largely an independent entity. It concentrates on movements which developed in former Palestine and present-day Israel; it presents writers who were either born or matured in that tiny enclave of the Middle East. While the first volume covered many centuries and many countries, the second volume centers on one country and one century. Geographical and historical widths have been followed—in a pioneering leap of faith—by recovery of contemporaneity in the Promised Land.

The Hebrew texts and periodicals used in the present volume have been indicated in the notes; they also refer to the Hebrew manuscripts of living and dead authors—put at my disposal by the generosity of Dr. M. Nadav, Head of the Department of Manuscripts and Archives at the Jewish National and University Library of Jerusalem and his cooperative staff, and Mr. Dov ben Yaakov, Director of the Bio-Bibliographical Institute *Genazim* in Tel Aviv. A long list of published and unpublished sources, of interpretative critiques and historical elucidations would have added many pages and would have probably increased the cost of the book. The wiser course dictated the reluctant renunciation of a bibliography.

As in the first volume the dot under the *Het, Zade* and *Kof* has been discarded for technical reasons. Again as in the first volume most of the translations of Hebrew texts—poems and prose fragments—have been done by the author.

414

INDEX